GW00689540

The Romantic Poets

Blackwell Guides to Criticism

Editor Michael O'Neill

Blackwell's *Guides to Criticism* series offers students privileged access to and careful guidance through those writings that have most conditioned the historic current of discussion and debate as it now informs contemporary scholarship.

Early historic responses are represented by appropriate excerpts and described in an introductory narrative chapter. Thereafter, materials are represented chronologically in extracts from important books or journal articles according to their continuing critical value and relevance in the classroom. Critical approaches are treated as tools to advance the pursuit of reading and study and each volume seeks to enhance the enjoyment of literature and to widen the reader's critical repertoire.

Published

Roger Dalrymple	*Middle English*
Corinne Saunders	*Chaucer*
Emma Smith	*Shakespeare's Comedies*
Emma Smith	*Shakespeare's Histories*
Emma Smith	*Shakespeare's Tragedies*
Uttara Natarajan	*The Romantic Poets*
Francis O'Gorman	*The Victorian Novel*
Michael Whitworth	*Modernism*

The Romantic Poets

A Guide to Criticism

Edited by Uttara Natarajan

Blackwell
Publishing

Editorial material and organization © 2007 by Blackwell Publishing Ltd

BLACKWELL PUBLISHING
350 Main Street, Malden, MA 02148-5020, USA
9600 Garsington Road, Oxford OX4 2DQ, UK
550 Swanston Street, Carlton, Victoria 3053, Australia

The right of Uttara Natarajan to be identified as the Author of the Editorial Material in this Work has been asserted in accordance with the UK Copyright, Designs, and Patents Act 1988.

First published 2007 by Blackwell Publishing Ltd

1   2007

Library of Congress Cataloging-in-Publication Data

The romantic poets : a guide to criticism / edited by Uttara Natarajan.
        p.   cm. — (Blackwell guides to criticism)
    Includes bibliographical references and index.
    ISBN 978-0-631-22931-5 (alk. paper)
    1. English   poetry—19th   century—History   and   criticism—Handbooks, manuals, etc.   2. English poetry—18th century—History and criticism—Handbooks, manuals, etc.   3. Romanticism—Great Britain—Handbooks, manuals, etc.   I. Natarajan, Uttara.

    PR590.R595 2007
    821′.709145—dc22

                                                                2006034810

A catalogue record for this title is available from the British Library.

Set in 10 on 12.5 pt Caslon
by SNP Best-set Typesetter Ltd, Hong Kong
Printed and bound in Singapore
by C.O.S. Printers Pte Ltd

The publisher's policy is to use permanent paper from mills that operate a sustainable forestry policy, and which has been manufactured from pulp processed using acid-free and elementary chlorine-free practices. Furthermore, the publisher ensures that the text paper and cover board used have met acceptable environmental accreditation standards.

For further information on
Blackwell Publishing, visit our website:
www.blackwellpublishing.com

Contents

2 William Wordsworth (1770–1850)   **63**

3 Samuel Taylor Coleridge (1772–1834)   **117**

Acknowledgements

The editor and publisher gratefully acknowledge the permission granted to reproduce the copyright material in this book:

Northrop Frye, *Fearful Symmetry: A Study of William Blake* (Princeton: Princeton University Press, 1947), pp. 207–18 + notes. © 1947 by Princeton University Press, 1969 revised edition, 1975 renewed PUP. Reprinted by permission of Princeton University Press.

David V. Erdman, *Blake: Prophet against Empire* (Princeton: Princeton University Press, 1954), pp. 226–42. © 1954 by David V. Erdman. Reprinted by permission of the Estate of David V. Erdman.

V. A. De Luca, *Words of Eternity: Blake and the Poetics of the Sublime* (Princeton: Princeton University Press, 1991), pp. 36–52, with excisions. © 1991 by Princeton University Press. Reprinted by permission of Princeton University Press.

William Hazlitt, from 'Mr. Wordsworth' in *The Spirit of the Age* (1825), from *The Fight and Other Writings*, ed. Tom Paulin and David Chandler (London: Penguin, 2000), pp. 305–11.

Geoffrey Hartman, *Wordsworth's Poetry 1787–1814* (New Haven, CT: Yale University Press, 1964), pp. 33–48 + notes. © 1964 by Geoffrey Hartman. Reprinted by permission of the author.

Alan Liu, *Wordsworth: The Sense of History* (Stanford: Stanford University Press, 1989), pp. 23–31, with the notes, pp. 318–20. © 1989 by The Johns Hopkins University Press. Reprinted with permission of The Johns Hopkins University Press.

David Bromwich, *Disowned by Memory: Wordsworth's Poetry of the 1790s* (Chicago: University of Chicago Press, 1998), pp. 1–7 + notes. © 1998 by David Bromwich. Reprinted by permission of the author and The University of Chicago Press.

John Livingston Lowes, *The Road to Xanadu* (Boston: Houghton Mifflin, 1927), pp. 161–4 + notes. Copyright © 1927 by John Livingston Lowes. Copyright © renewed 1955 by John Wilbur Lowes. Reprinted by permission of Houghton Mifflin Company. All rights reserved.

John Beer, *Coleridge the Visionary* (London: Chatto & Windus, 1959), pp. 153–8 + notes. © 1959. Reprinted by permission of The Random House Group Ltd.

Jerome J. McGann, 'The Ancient Mariner: The Meaning of Meanings' from *The Beauty of Inflections: Literary Investigations in Historical Method and Theory* (Oxford: Clarendon, 1985), pp. 150–65. © Jerome J. McGann. Reprinted by permission of the author and Oxford University Press.

Seamus Perry, 'Coda: The Incomprehensible Mariner', *Coleridge and the Uses of Division* (Oxford: Clarendon, 1999), pp. 281–91. © 1999 by Seamus Perry. Reprinted by permission of Oxford University Press.

Joseph Mazzini, 'On Byron and Goethe' from Andrew Rutherford (ed.), *Lord Byron: The Critical Heritage* (London: Routledge, 1995), pp. 332–5. © 1995 by Joseph Mazzini. Reprinted by permission of Taylor & Francis Books UK.

T. S. Eliot, 'Byron' (1937, later reprinted in *On Poetry and Poets*: London: Faber, 1957), pp. 205–6, with excisions. © 1937 by T. S. Eliot. Reprinted by permission of Faber and Faber and Farrar, Straus and Giroux, LLC.

Jerome J. McGann, *Fiery Dust: Byron's Poetic Development* (Chicago: University of Chicago Press, 1968), pp. 3–8, 13–28, with excisions. © 1968 by Jerome J. McGann. Reprinted by permission of the author and The University of Chicago Press.

Jerome Christensen, *Lord Byron's Strength: Romantic Writing and Commercial Society* (Baltimore: Johns Hopkins Press, 1993), pp. 214–15, 234–47 + notes. © 1992 The Johns Hopkins University Press. Reprinted by permission of the Johns Hopkins University Press.

C. E. Pulos, *The Deep Truth: A Study of Shelley's Scepticism* (Lincoln: University of Nebraska Press, 1954), pp. 105–12. Copyright © 1954 by the University of Nebraska Press. Copyright © renewed 1982 by the University of Nebraska Press. Reprinted by permission of the publisher.

Earl Wasserman, *Shelley: A Critical Reading* (Baltimore: Johns Hopkins Press, 1971), pp. 255–61, 270–2. Copyright © 1971 by Earl Wasserman. Reprinted by permission of The Johns Hopkins University Press.

Timothy Clark, 'Alastor', *Embodying Revolution: The Figure of the Poet in Shelley* (Oxford: Clarendon, 1989), pp. 95–109. © 1989 by Timothy Clark. Reprinted by permission of Oxford University Press.

J. G. Lockhart, 'The Cockney School of Poetry', from *The Young Romantics and Critical Opinion 1807–1824*, ed. Theodore Redpath (New York:

St Martins Press, 1973), pp. 467–72. Reprinted by permission of Palgrave Macmillan.

Walter Jackson Bate, *John Keats* (Cambridge, Mass.: The Belknap Press of Harvard University Press, 1963), pp. 236–47. Copyright © 1963 by the President and Fellows of Harvard College. Copyright © renewed 1991 by Walter Jackson Bate. Reprinted by permission of Harvard University Press.

Marjorie Levinson, *Keats's Life of Allegory: The Origins of a Style* (Oxford: Blackwell, 1988), pp. 125–31. © 1988 by Marjorie Levinson. Reprinted by permission of Blackwell Publishing Ltd.

Nicholas Roe, *John Keats and the Culture of Dissent* (Oxford: Clarendon Press, 1997), pp. 253–67. © 1997 by Nicholas Roe. Reprinted by permission of Oxford University Press.

John Barrell, *Poetry, Language, and Politics* (Manchester: Manchester University Press, 1988), pp. 118–23 + notes. © 1988 by John Barrell. Reprinted by permission of the author.

Stuart Curran, 'Romantic Poetry: The I Altered', in *Romanticism and Feminism*, ed. Anne K. Mellor, (Bloomington: Indiana University Press, 1988), pp. 189–95 + notes. © 1988 by Stuart Curran. Reprinted by permission of Indiana University Press.

Every effort has been made to trace copyright holders and to obtain their permission for the use of copyright material. The publisher apologizes for any errors or omissions in the above list and would be grateful if notified of any corrections that should be incorporated in future reprints or editions of this book.

Introduction

The poetry of the six 'major' Romantics has come to constitute, in English literary history, a category of exemplary literary achievement, and the criticism that defines it has been similarly exemplary, stimulating or sustaining the shaping debates of the field of English studies. On both counts, the scholarly discussion of the Romantic poets has by now grown to proportions nearly unmanageable by the first-time student. To that student mainly this volume is addressed. On behalf of the novice, it steers a course, admittedly more precarious than safe, through the sea of critical material in the subject. My method has been to focus in turn on each of the canonical poets, charting a history, in which key critical extracts are embedded, of the poet's reception. By formulating that history in each case as a continuous narrative, I have tried to display the relation between the most recent critical insights and the earliest, in the hope that, exhaustive coverage being impossible, a broad outline of developmental patterns, and of recurrent or dominant topics and trends, might facilitate the student's ongoing negotiation of a body of criticism that continues daily to proliferate and that could otherwise make this book out of date almost before it is published.

Like others in this Blackwell series, the present volume treats an area of literary history where critical attention has been especially concentrated. Thus its purpose is functional and informative rather than polemical. Chiefly, its scope is an established canon of writers, six male Romantic poets (these having generated the greatest mass of critical material over time), of whose works is comprised a canonical genre. The volume does not argue, but presents as a literary-historical given, the poets' inclusion under a single over-arching descriptor. Taking as its remit and title, *The Romantic Poets*, rather than *Romantic Poetry*, it does not explicitly engage the larger theoretical and polemical question, of whether the genre can in fact stand as a unifying category.[1] But by treating the poets separately and without the usual generalizing overview, it attempts to convey a critical history that has progressed only gradually and unevenly from particular poets to the generic and canonical whole. At the same time, the debates about the constituency and ideological implications of the encompassing category recur throughout, in their bearing on the reception of individual poets.

Chronology is the simple ordering principle of each chapter of this volume. The critical extracts[2] are incorporated into the chronological structure of the editorial narrative; the entries in the reading lists appended to each extract are chronologically arranged. Read from top to bottom, each reading list, consisting of these annotated entries, is a kind of developmental narrative in itself, part of the framing editorial narrative of the chapter as a whole. Insofar as chronology loosely coincides with theme, the lists are also thematized, these themes varying from chapter to chapter. Although analogies are perceptible, there is no single template by which individual critical histories are forced into exact analogy with each other.

In putting together what is both a survey and an anthology of criticism, I have sought to avoid, as far as possible, duplicating the work of the very many excellent student 'companions', bibliographical guides and reference works already available. (Manifold versions of the introductory overview I have forgone, for instance, are supplied in these books.) I should mention in particular two bibliographies to which I am especially indebted: *The English Romantic Poets: A Review of Research and Criticism*, ed. Frank Jordan (4th edn., New York: The Modern Language Association of America, 1985) and *Literature of the Romantic Period: A Bibliographical Guide*, ed. Michael O'Neill (Oxford: Clarendon Press, 1998). Instead of the detailed cataloguing, the classification and description of scholarship under multiple thematic and generic heads, undertaken in these works so successfully, but itself daunting to an uninitiated readership, I have, with that readership in mind, painted with a far broader brush, aiming, above all, at simplification and easy reading. In making my selections of criticism, I have preferred studies that give a whole view of an author, over those that focus exclusively on a particular work or works. Similarly, a collection of essays by divers critics tends to figure as a single entry, rather than split into its component chapters. This book is no substitute, then, for the comprehensive taxonomies of existing scholarship contained in the current scholarly bibliographies. By its representative examples and selective reading lists, it shows, instead, the field at a glance.

The most difficult part of my undertaking has been the selection of the critical studies mentioned or quoted in my survey. No one person's view of the critical field coincides with another's, and my omissions (and perhaps some of my inclusions) might justly induce puzzlement or chagrin. My object has been a serviceable list of criticism, in which I have tried to balance the representative, the influential, the accessible, and the up-to-date. Constraints of space alone, however, have precluded the inclusion of many studies with at least one, and some with all, of those characteristics: thus my omissions do not amount to value judgements. Nonetheless, I cannot deny a degree of personal predilection in making my choices. As the Romantics have shown us, all acts of whole-making, of eliciting coherence or pattern by selection and elision, can be called into question; my own, however modest and whatever its uses, is no exception.

Chapter notes

1   For students' reference, the founding debate is between A. O. Lovejoy and René Wellek, the first characterizing Romanticism by its plurality, and arguing therefore, for multiple 'Romanticisms', the second making the counter-claim that an essential and single 'Romanticism' can be identified beyond local difference. See Arthur O. Lovejoy, 'On the Discrimination of Romanticisms', *Publications of the Modern Languages Association of America* 39.2 (June 1924), 229–53 and René Wellek, 'The Concept of Romanticism in Literary Scholarship' (1949), repr. in *Concepts of Criticism* (New Haven: Yale University Press, 1963), 128–98.

2   The critical extracts have all been edited, most of them minimally, some, more extensively. The authors' notes to the extracts have been substantially edited or revised. Where the original note refers to a superseded edition of a poet's primary text, I have substituted the modern standard edition. Notes within square brackets are those that I have added.

1

William Blake (1757–1827)

FROM FIRST RESPONSES TO NORTHROP FRYE

Songs of Innocence and of Experience (1794), in Blake's time, as now, his most accessible poems, drew praise from some of his greatest contemporaries. Coleridge called him 'a man of Genius', exclaiming, in a letter of 6 February 1818, 'verily I am in the very mire of commonplace common-sense compared with Mr Blake, apo- or rather anacalyptic Poet, and Painter!'[1] Wordsworth, according to Crabb Robinson's 'Reminiscences' (1852), declared that 'there is something in the madness of this man which interests me more than the Sanity of Lord Byron & Walter Scott!'[2] But Blake's poetry attracted little public notice in his lifetime. His method of illuminated printing – engraving on copper plates, from which impressions were taken, then coloured and bound by Blake and his wife – made copies scarce and costly.[3] Those who came across them found the prophetic books incomprehensible. The widest circulation of the early lyrics was at second-hand, through a publication of 1806, entitled *A Father's Memoirs of his Child*, by Benjamin Heath Malkin, which contained in its dedication a long notice of Blake, with some of his *Songs*, including 'Holy Thursday' (from *Innocence*) and 'The Tyger'. Malkin's praise of Blake was uniformly dismissed in the contemporary reviews.[4]

Nearly unknown till well into the Victorian period, Blake was propelled into fame by the publication, in 1863, of Alexander Gilchrist's *The Life of William Blake, 'Pictor Ignotus'*, which brought to an end the long neglect described in its opening paragraph:

> From nearly all collections or beauties of 'The English Poets,' catholic to demerit as these are, tender of the expired and expiring reputations, one name has been hitherto perseveringly exiled. Encyclopaedias ignore it. The Biographical Dictionaries furtively pass it on with inaccurate despatch, as having had some connexion with the Arts.[5]

Although Gilchrist sees the poems and designs as 'warp and woof in one texture',[6] it is the poetry that gains most from his treatment. Blake is transformed from a minor to a considerable poet, the belittling tag of 'madness' resolutely dismissed. Gilchrist characterizes Blake both as 'faithful visionary' and 'vehement republican',[7] the two heads under which the greater part of twentieth-century criticism is marshalled.

The Pre-Raphaelites followed in Gilchrist's wake. Swinburne's book-length *William Blake: A Critical Essay* (1868), dedicated to William Michael Rossetti, offered an inclusive survey of the poetry and designs, and the Rossetti brothers, Dante Gabriel and William Michael, contributed to the revised second edition of Gilchrist's *Life* (1880). In 1893, in the 'Preface' to their three-volume *Works of William Blake, Poetic, Symbolic, and Critical*, Edwin J. Ellis and the young William Butler Yeats proclaimed what has since become the thesis of a substantial body of twentieth-century criticism: 'the solidity of . . . [Blake's] myth, and its wonderful coherence'.[8]

With the publication of S. Foster Damon's encyclopaedic *William Blake: His Philosophy and Symbols* (1924), modern-day Blake scholarship was launched. Treating Blake's mysticism as the key to his thought, but dispelling once and for all the 'hints of mysteries and madnesses', Damon attempts, from Blake's symbolism and its literary sources, 'to give a rational explanation of Blake's obvious obscurities, and to provide a firm basis for the understanding of his philosophy'.

> Blake was trying to do what every mystic tries to do. He was trying to rationalize the Divine ('to justify the ways of God to men'), and to apotheosise the Human. He was trying to lay bare the fundamental errors which are the cause of misery. These errors he sought, not in codes of ethic, nor in the construction of society, but in the human soul itself.[9]

Damon's groundbreaking, if overly systematic study, for the first time gave to Blake's last works, especially *Jerusalem*, their present stature. In the following year was published the first complete scholarly edition of Blake's poetry, ed. Geoffrey Keynes.[10] Denis Saurat's *Blake and Modern Thought* was published in 1929, placing Blake at the point of a widespread eighteenth-century shifting of creative power from God to man.

Damon's book remained the beacon of the burgeoning Blake scholarship of nearly the whole of the first half of the twentieth century, until it was eclipsed by the publication, in 1947, of Northrop Frye's *Fearful Symmetry: A Study of William Blake*. In the interim, Blake began increasingly to be linked to the cultural and historical tendencies of his age. But his blinding originality, and his collapse of the boundaries of literature and art, made the notion of an exceptional and isolated genius particularly tenacious: T. S. Eliot's judgement of 1920, 'a certain meanness of culture'; the lack of 'a framework of accepted and traditional ideas', cast a long shadow.[11] Frye's study, towering over Blake criticism till today, catalysed Blake's slow and uneven transition from 'pre-Romantic' to 'Romantic' and the augmenting of the Romantic canon of five poets to six.

Drawing on Damon's reading, especially of Blake's humanism, but rejecting his description of Blake as a 'mystic', Frye contends 'first, that all of Blake's poetry . . . must be taken as a unit' and second, that Blake should 'be placed in his historical and cultural context as a poet who, though original, . . . was neither a freak nor a sport.'[12] Each of the engraved poems 'not only belongs in a unified scheme but is in accord with a permanent structure of ideas.'[13] Although Frye insists that we read in Blake a renewal of Renaissance traditions, rather than an emerging romanticism,[14] his characterization of Blake as a 'visionary' and his eliciting, from the poetry, a humanistic mythology, Christian in bearing, prepare the ground for Blake's inclusion in the defining constructions of romanticism in the mid-twentieth century. Thus Blake is prominently the first of Harold Bloom's 'visionary company' (1961; see below). The implications of Frye's study are canonizing also in a different way. From his critical procedure for Blake, Frye developed his celebrated *Anatomy of Criticism* (1957): 'A theory of criticism whose principles apply to the whole of literature and account for every valid type of critical procedure.'[15]

The most notable of Frye's formulations for Blake, the 'Orc cycle' of tyranny and rebellion, is extracted below.

Extract from Northrop Frye, *Fearful Symmetry: A Study of William Blake* (1947)

Orc, then, is not only Blake's Prometheus but his Adonis, the dying and reviving god of his mythology. Orc represents the return of the dawn and the spring and all the human analogies of their return: the continuous arrival of new life, the renewed sexual and reproductive power which that brings, and the periodic over-throw of social tyranny. He is both a sun-god, the jocund day on the mountain tops,[1] and a god of renewed 'vegetable,' or natural human, life. In religious ritual there may be a distinction between a sun-god and a fertility-god, but there can be none in a properly clarified vision, for both sun and fertility have their cycles of disappearance and renewal, and both are temporal images of fall and apocalypse. Orc dies as the buried seed dies, and rises as it grows; winter nights become long and gloomy, but at the depth of winter the light slowly returns.

Now as the emergent Orc represents a return of life, he represents also a victory over death. Death in Blake is the reduction of the physical body to inert matter such as rock and sand, the 'limit of opacity.' Below this is the chaos that would, if it gained ascendancy, lead us into annihilation or 'Non-Entity.' As it is obviously impossible for nonexistence to exist, it is evident that chaos is kept within bounds. In the Bible this chaos, symbolized by water, is represented by the sea-serpent Leviathan or Rahab. Leviathan is very like the underground monster of many primitive myths who swallows or fights with the sun at night: Job, in cursing the day of his birth, links himself with the children of darkness who hope that some day the sun will be vanquished:

Let them curse it that curse the day, who are ready to raise up Leviathan.[2]

Hence in every sunrise and winter solstice we may see an image of a victory of creative power over something monstrous and sinister, like a dragon.

The orthodox view of the Titanic myth identifies chaos and reviving energy. Thus the false God of *The French Revolution* sees, in a passage we have quoted, the new life emerging in France as the release of the bars of chaos. But chaos and vital energy are opposed principles, and the return of Orc is the defeat of chaos; hence the real monster is Orc's adversary, and Orc himself the monster's conqueror. The myth of the dragon-slayer is a very wide-spread one, a fact which indicates, on Blake's principles, that it belongs to the fundamental pattern of ideas which man is trying to formulate. In all such conflicts the hero represents the progress of vigorous life and civilization, and the dragon stands for darkness, waste, sterility and death. When the dragon is slain, darkness is succeeded by light, the wilderness blossoms as the rose, new life is begotten, and death, the last enemy to be destroyed, is swallowed up in victory.

In most stories of dragon-killers the dragon is laying waste and tyrannizing over a *nation* of which the slayer is the deliverer, and sometimes the eventual king. This latent political aspect of the myth comes out in *The Faerie Queene*, where St. George by killing a dragon liberates the Church of England from the Papal power. The Messiah, too, in the political allegory of the Bible, is to destroy a monster of tyranny. This tyranny is identified with Leviathan by Ezekiel,[3] and is frequently associated in the Bible with the various countries, notably Egypt, Babylon and Rome, who tyrannized over Judea. The Great Whore of the Apocalypse is clearly linked with the latter two. Hence in *America* the dragon is the spirit of English tyranny.

William Blake, *Glad Day* (The Dance of Albion), *c.* 1803–10, engraving. Rosenwald Collection, image © 2006 Board of Trustees, National Gallery of Art, Washington.

The dragon-killing is thus a drama both of the reviving powers of nature and of a freedom from some kind of social oppression. Putting the two things together, we get the principle that such a revolution as is occurring in America is a natural renewal of life in society, and that it therefore does not happen irrationally, but at a definite time, like the dawn and the spring. If this is so, then human history, no less than the natural world, has a cyclic rhythm of decline and revival, and history takes the form of series of cultures or civilizations, each with its own rise, maturity and fall, initiated by a revolution within it and superseded by one without it.

The dragon is rather tentatively developed in *America*, for Orc's real antagonist is the tendency to chaos within the human mind which the dragon represents. That tendency Blake portrays in Urizen, the Old Man, the cloud-gathering Zeus, Jehovah or Odin who in all pantheons is inevitably the 'President of the Immortals,' the Ancient of Days who in Blake's great painting, the frontispiece to *Europe*, crouches over the world marking its limits (Gk. *horizein*)[4] with a compass. Urizen is a sky-god, for the remoteness and mystery of heaven is the first principle of his religion. He is old, but his age implies senility rather than wisdom. He is cruel, for he stands for the barring of nature against the desires and hopes of man. Whereas Orc is 'ruddy,' red being the color of revolution, of blood, of rage and of sexual passion, Urizen is a white terror: his white beard, the freezing snows that cover him and the icicles and hoarfrost that stick on him, suggest the 'colorless all-color of atheism,'[5] the nameless chilling fear of the unknown, that Melville depicts in his albino Leviathan. Urizen's associations are with bleached bones, rocks and deserts; but actually Urizen, being the human belief in the objectivity of nature, is an abstraction, a hazy ghost that is always just going to take definite shape and never quite does.

Blake's source for this image of the contest of Orc and Urizen is doubtless the remarkable poem of Ossian's called *Carric-Thura*, in which Loda, or Odin, is confronted by the young hero Fingal. Loda is an old, cruel and gloomy God, whose 'nostrils pour the blasts of death' and who boasts of his power to kill. He cannot be killed himself, for he is nothing but clouds and air, but he can be struck at and driven away, and as Fingal does this 'the form fell shapeless into the air, like a column of smoke. . . . The spirit of Loda shrieked as, rolled into himself, he rose on the wind.' That 'rolled into himself' reminds us of Blake's 'Spectre' and 'Selfhood.'

As soon as we being to think of the relation of Orc to Urizen, it becomes impossible to maintain them as separate principles. If Orc represents the reviving force of a new cycle, whether of dawn or spring or history, he must grow old and die at the end of that cycle. Urizen must eventually gain the mastery over Orc, but such a Urizen cannot be another power but Orc himself, grown old. The same is true of the dragon: the dragon must be the hero's predecessor and the hero in his turn must become a dragon. But if the dragon *is* death, then when the hero dies he is swallowed by or otherwise absorbed into the dragon. The book of Jonah portrays its hero as swallowed by a leviathan who is death or hell and vomited up again – a humorous image befitting the most humorous book in the Bible. (The medieval paintings showing Jesus walking into the open mouth of a monster when he descends into hell may also be noted, as Blake might have seen one.) But if the dragon is itself the old Orc, then surely is not Orc simply a dragon who has the power to shed his skin from time to time? This is a very abrupt change from our young and heroic dragon-killer, but nevertheless Blake continually associates Orc with the serpent, which is an easy modulation of the dragon symbol. The serpent which appeared on the flags of the revolting Americans would then be an emblem of an infant Orc, and may have been the source of the association.

There are seven major historical cycles in Blake's mythology, the Seven Eyes of God [. . .]. Each runs from a youthful Orc to an aged Urizen, which in terms of social and political symbolism means that it gets less energetic in its cultural efforts and nearer the state of nature as it goes on. Blake's later symbolism deals, not with a sequence of cycles in history, but with the cycle itself as a seven-times-recurring phenomenon of human life. He elaborates three main phases of it. In its first phase, symbolized by the birth and binding of Orc, it produces most of its great works of imaginative power. As it gets older, its religion becomes more abstract, and its social life takes on the characteristics of its growing belief in a mechanical universe. It then declines into a sophisticated rationalism founded on 'common sense,' the insight of mediocrity. In this period cultures produce their Aristotles, their Bacons and Lockes, their empirical science and their metaphysics. This second phase is portrayed under the symbol of Urizen 'exploring his dens,' the Urizenic intelligence gaining the view of the fallen world which is appropriate to it. Eighteenth century rationalism is the seventh of these explorations. The cycle finally dies in a wild cancerous tissue of huge machinery, a blankly materialist philosophy, an inner death of the soul which causes mass wars, and a passive acceptance of the most reckless tyranny. It is in these late periods that new prophets, in whom the spirit of a reviving Orc is stirring, appear to proclaim a new gospel. This last phase is symbolized by the crucifixion of Orc, in the form of a serpent, on the tree of mystery, the binding of human imagination to the vegetable world and the absorption of human life into the order of nature.

The natural world is based largely on the daily return of the sun and the yearly return of vegetable life, and the sun and the tree are therefore the central symbols of the natural cycle. Looked at from the point of view of sense experience, they suggest nothing but a cycle, persisting indefinitely in time. Looked at from an imaginative point of view, their renewal is an image of resurrection into eternity. Hence each of these symbols has two forms, one the form of its eternal life, which appeals to the imagination, the other the form of its death, which appeals to the Selfhood. There is the tree of life man had before the Fall and will have again after it, and there is the tree of morality or death. The latter is Jesus' barren fig-tree, the world-ash Yggdrasil, the tree of mystery and the knowledge of good and evil. The sun of life is, as the Book of Revelation explains, God himself;[6] the sun of death is the scorching furnace to whom Mexicans and Druids offered human sacrifices. Jesus, the seventh Orc of human history, was the true vine and the sun of righteousness, but his empty skin is left hanging on a dead stripped tree, the arms nailed to it horizontally as an image of the spreading rays of the captive sun. Another image of the dead sun is the clawed or hooked cross which Blake evidently associates with the scythed chariots of the 'Druid' Britons.[7] The imaginative status of any nation which has adopted either the rayed sun or the hooked cross for its emblem thus becomes clear.

The crucifixion of Orc as Jesus symbolizes the end of the sixth or Jehovah cycle, and must obviously have happened five times before. The earliest cycles after the fall of Atlantis arose in Africa. Orc, Blake tells us, is bound under 'Mount Atlas' in northwest Africa, where he will remain until the end of time.[8] In the 'Preludium' to *America* Orc is addressed as 'the image of God who dwells in darkness of Africa.' This means among other things that the enslaved negro, the fallen child of the sun, is one of the central symbols of the oppression of fallen man, and the chimney-sweep and 'little black boy' of the *Songs of Innocence* are modulations of this symbol. Here the black skin represents the confined body of fallen man. There is one curious passage in which Blake even speaks of Africa as a giant of the same kind as Albion, and says that he did not wholly fall,[9] which apparently means that the African civilization was equal to, or more probably part of, the Atlantic one. Besides the legends of paradisal Atlantic islands, there are also many allusions in Classical mythology to another prehistoric Golden Age associated with the 'innocent Ethiopians' who are portrayed as dwelling with the gods. Both the *Iliad* and the *Odyssey* open with a reference to a paradisal Ethiopia. The decline of this African culture in Egypt is where recorded history begins. This is presumably why in Plato it is the Egyptians who alone preserve the traditions of Atlantis, and why, in the Old Testament, captivity in Egypt is the first great symbol of the tyranny of the fallen world.

It may be interesting to observe that Blake is not the only poet to associate Ethiopia with the unfallen world from which the fallen world, the 'spiritual Egypt'[10] of the Book of Revelation, has descended. It is in Abyssinia that Coleridge sees himself with the flashing eyes and floating hair of an Orc who has drunk the milk of Paradise. From Abyssinia Rasselas descends to Egypt and finds there a madman who believes that he controls the universe – an excellent image of a bound Orc. If anyone had explained to Johnson what his imagination had produced, his Spectre would have instantly answered, 'Sir, I wrote *Rasselas* to defray the expenses of my mother's funeral'; but Johnson's Spectre did not write *Rasselas*, and knows nothing about it. Swedenborg also gives the Africans a very high place in the spiritual world [. . .][11]

The African civilization comes to a close with the collapse of the third or Elohim cycle, recorded in the story of Adam and Eve, in which the two great symbols of the dying Orc, the cursed serpent and the tree of death, make their appearance. This is described at the end of *The Book of Urizen*. *The Book of Ahania* follows without a break, and describes the growth of new cycles in Asia, the migration to which is reflected in the Biblical account of the Exodus. Then, after a great struggle of Orc and Urizen principles within the Israelites, the former being the pillar of fire that guided them through the night, and the latter the pillar of cloud that befogged them in the day, Urizen, with his moral law and his ten commandments, won out. Orc says in *America*:

> The fiery joy, that Urizen perverted to ten commands,
> What night he led the starry hosts thro' the wide wilderness,
> That stony law I stamp to dust.

The death of this culture was represented by the brazen serpent hung by Moses on a pole, which was accepted by Jesus as a prototype of his own death.[12] In the serpent, the yellow brass and the pole, the symbols of the dead Orc, the dead sun and the dead tree respectively appear.

The hanged serpent is not otherwise directly associated with the crucified Christ, but there is an important connection between them. The serpent of the wilderness was, the Bible tells us, worshiped by the Israelites for centuries.[13] This means that they were worshiping their own death-principle, which in the next cycle would be Antichrist. The dead body of Christ left behind on the cross, his excreted husk, to use Blake's terminology, is the body of Antichrist, 'the mystery of iniquity,' as Paul calls him, because the dead Christ (not the dying Christ, which is Orc) on the tree of mystery is the achieved form of hell's revenge on humanity.

Implicit in the myth of Orc and Urizen is the allegory of the young striking down the old, the most obvious symbol of which is a son's revolt against a father. This form of the myth meets us in the story of Dionysius. But Urizen *is* sterility: he can only destroy children, not beget them, and can no more be the father of the succeeding Orc than Herod could be the father of Jesus. However, in *The Book of Ahania* Blake changes his mind and makes the rebel of the Exodus a son of Urizen, Fuzon, the element of fire (*focus, feu*) in nature (*physis*) which is never quite put out. The use of a son of Urizen in place of Orc in a poem engraved in 1795 indicates that Blake is becoming increasingly aware that by 'Orc' he means something inseparably attached to Urizen.

When the Israelites got from the wilderness into the garden of God which had been promised them, the revolutionary vigor of their revolt against Egypt had collapsed, and all they got was another Egypt from which imagination and desire were excluded as dangerous intruders. This is set forth in the story of the rivalry of Esau and Jacob, in which the red and hairy Esau, the rightful heir, was sent wandering into the desert. The kingdom of Edom remained outside Jacob's priestly theocracy execrated and accursed, and when Isaiah sees the Messiah coming from Edom he is prophesying the destruction of tyranny by the exiled giant of desire.[14] Esau, therefore, is another Biblical Orc. So perhaps is Absalom, the son who rebelled against his father David, David being one of the 'Churches' or subordinate phases of the Jehovah cycle. Absalom's body was pierced with a spear while he was hanging on a tree by his golden hair. Blake often alludes to Orc's flaming hair as an image of the sun, and in *The Book of Ahania* there seems to be a link between Absalom and Fuzon:

His beautiful visage, his tresses
That gave light to the mornings of heaven,
Were smitten with darkness, deform'd
And outstretch'd on the edge of the forest.

The Classical legend of the Golden Fleece doubtless belongs to the same pattern of symbolism. The giant Samson, whose hair was shorn and who went down into the west into the great cities of the Philistines to work at the mill with slaves, is another vision of an Orc cycle, of much larger scope than the others. The mill is Blake's symbol for the late or big-city stage of an historical cycle [. . .]. Then there is the Northern story of Balder, slain by the mistletoe which was sacred to the Druids because it was an emblem of both solar and vegetable cycles at once.[15] And there is Odin's account of himself in the *Hávamál* as hanging on a gallows-tree, 'whose roots no man knoweth' – a tree of mystery – wounded with a spear, and offered as a sacrifice to himself. (The nine nights for which he is there may be compared with the nine nights of *The Four Zoas*.) The fact that Odin is both a hanged god and a hoary tyrant who appears in Ossian as Loda shows again the identity of the dead Orc with the Urizen who kills him.

The spear and arrow in Blake are quasi-phallic symbols of the release of imaginative power; the bow is the tense energy of the human body. The shield, on the other hand, is an image both of the impervious heaven (compare Homer's description of the shield of Achilles) and the carapace of the brooding Selfhood. In *The Book of Ahania* Fuzon's 'pillar of fire' is hurled like a spear and tears open the sterile loins of Urizen; Urizen opposes to this his 'pillar of cloud' in the form of a 'broad Disk' or shield.[16] The fact that Jesus, Odin and Absalom are all pierced with spears is thus linked with the fact that they are sacrifices to themselves, as Odin says, or dead forms of what they were.

If we look at the sequence of cycles as a whole, we see that the center of historical gravity, so to speak, has moved in a counter-clockwise circle from Atlantis to Africa, from Africa to Asia, from Asia to Europe, and from Europe, with the American Revolution, back to Atlantis again. In legend some memory of the first three of these shifts is preserved respectively in the story of Perseus (who journeyed eastward across the African desert with the serpentine head of a female monster or Rahab which turned Ethiopian warriors to stone, and is the prototype of Blake's Tiriel), the Exodus and the Trojan war. The decline of these three civilizations has produced, up to Blake's time, a threefold tyranny symbolized in the Bible by the names of Egypt, Babylon and Rome. The first part of *The Song of Los*, called 'Africa,' sums this up as follows:

> Clouds roll heavy upon the Alps round Rousseau & Voltaire,
> And on the mountains of Lebanon round the deceased Gods
> Of Asia, & on the desarts of Africa round the Fallen Angels
> The Guardian Prince of Albion burns in his nightly tent.

The last line is identical with the first line of *America*.

The seventh Orc cycle, from Jesus to our own time, is described in the very lovely and subtle poem of *Europe*, which outlines its progress from Orc's appearance as Jesus to its decline into a political tyranny based on an inner exhaustion of vitality, eighteen hundred years after Jesus' time, and just as an eighth cycle is opening up in America. But this time something else happens that has never happened before. Orc is not content simply to arise in America and go through the 'same dull round' all over again there: he also explodes in the 'vineyards of red France,' and this is the signal for a world-wide 'strife of blood.' The brilliant revolutionary polemic in *The Song of Los* called 'Asia' postdates *America*, and describes the spreading of the final apocalypse to that continent while the baffled kings of Asia look on in 'bitterness of soul.' The 'Song of Liberty,' a pendant to *The Marriage of Heaven and Hell*, also foresees that the power which has torn down the Bastille will go on to tear down Olympus and rebuild the Atlantic kingdom of the Golden Age.

America was engraved in 1793 and *Europe* in 1794. Within the next few years Blake watched the American and French revolutions gradually subside again into the fallen world. The Americans kept on owning slaves, and the statue of the wrong kind of Reason was set up in Paris. Of the 'improvement of sensual enjoyment' Blake had prophesied there was no sign, and a poet who proclaimed that the loins were the place of the Last Judgment would find little to cheer him in the approach of the nineteenth century, which obviously had no intention of making the loins a part of revealed religion. Voltaire and Rousseau declined in Blake's estimation from fighters in the vanguard of freedom to enemies of light;[17] and in 1804, the year that Napoleon made himself Emperor and Beethoven tore the dedication to him out of the Eroica symphony, Blake was writing:

> I suppose an American would tell me that Washington did all that was done before he was born, as the French now adore Buonaparte and the English our poor George; so the Americans will consider Washington as their god. . . . In the meantime I have the happiness of seeing the Divine countenance in such men as Cowper and Milton more distinctly than in any prince or hero.[18]

The reference to Washington is a little ungracious, considering that Blake had set the Americans the example; it is the last part of the quotation that indicates the direction his thought was taking.

As Blake never abandoned his belief in the potential imminence of an apocalypse, he did not, like Wordsworth or Coleridge, alter the essentially revolutionary pattern of his thinking. But neither could he feel, with Byron or Shelley, any enthusiasm for a political restoration of the Greece and Rome he so much distrusted. The only real change that the decline of revolutionary fortunes made in his thought was in causing him to reject the Orc man as an apocalyptic agent. The only God that exists exists in man, and all religion consists in following the right men. Men of action of the type Blake calls 'heroic villains'[19] are not the right men, and the visionary is on a disastrously wrong course if his vision of the divinity of man leads him to hero-worship of this kind, as Carlyle's did. But the Orc man, the revolutionary leader who is fighting for liberty (Washington is not a very dramatic example of Blake's Orc symbolism; the red-shirted Garibaldi would be much better) does make a real appeal to the imagination. Revolution attracts sympathy more because it is revolution than because of what it proposes to substitute; this is connected with the fact that we indulge the young more than old because they are young and not because they are right. But as Orc stiffens into Urizen, it becomes manifest that the world is so constituted that no cause can triumph within it and still preserve its imaginative integrity. The imagination is mental, and it never has a preponderance of physical force on its side:

> The Whole Creation Groans to be deliever'd; there will always be as many Hypocrites born as Honest Men, & they will always have superior Power in Mortal Things. You cannot have Liberty in this World without what you call Moral Virtue, & you cannot have Moral Virtue without the Slavery of that half of the Human Race who hate what you call Moral Virtue.[20]

We must look elsewhere for the divine in man, for the pure imagination or creative power which does not depend on nature for the source of its energy. Jesus could not have become the Messiah without renouncing heroism, and his role as a young dying god was forced on him by his persecutors.

Orc is a process of birth, death and rebirth in another individual of the same species or form, though sometimes he may take the form of a power of rejuvenation. (There is no doctrine of 'reincarnation' in Blake: that implies a more casual relation between soul and body than he would admit.) In either case Orc is completely bound to the cyclic wheel of life. He cannot represent an entry into a new world, but only the power of renewing an exhausted form in the old one. The sun always gets back safely: its journey is mechanical rather than adventurous, for it is still imprisoned in night, a far greater spiritual night which is the sleep of the human soul, and in which the natural sun that flashes on and off every day is a mechanical device to light up the wall of an underground cave. In the sequence of historical cycles there is, perhaps, as a new dawn begins, a brief flash of an infinitely greater Day, but it is soon lost in the maturing brilliance of the sunrise. No revolution which falls short of a complete apocalypse and transfiguration of the world into Paradise can give us the eternal youth it symbolizes. Wordsworth puts this in terms of its appropriate image:

> Not favoured spots alone, but the whole earth,
> The beauty wore of promise, that which sets
> (As at some moment might not be unfelt
> Among the bowers of paradise itself)
> The budding rose above the rose full blown.[21]

All the achievements, beliefs and hopes of man are parts of gigantic historical movements as closely bound to the natural world, as inevitable in their progress from birth to decay, as the vegetable life which the very word 'culture' is linked with. Men have so far never got what they want, for 'the desire of Man being Infinite, the possession is Infinite & himself Infinite.'[22] The word 'revolution' itself contains a tragic irony: it is itself a part of the revolving of life and death in a circle of pain.

Notes

1   See illustration.
2   Job iii, 8.
3   Ezekiel xxix, 3.
4   F. E. Pierce, 'Etymology as Explanation in Blake', *Philological Quarterly* 10.4 (October 1931), 395–6.
5   Herman Melville, *Moby Dick*, ch. xlii.
6   Revelation xxi, 23.
7   Cf. the reference to the sun as a 'Scythed Chariot of Britain', *Jerusalem*, plate 56.
8   *The Song of Los*, plate 2 ('Africa').
9   *Jerusasalem*, plate 45.
10   Revelation xi, 8.
11   Emmanuel Swedenborg, *True Christian Religion; containing the Universal Theory of the New Church*, sections 835–40.
12   John iii, 14.
13   II Kings xviii, 4.
14   Isaiah lxiii, 1; cf. *The Marriage of Heaven and Hell*, plate 3.
15   The mistletoe is referred to in *Jerusalem*, plate 66.
16   *The Book of Ahania* i, plates 3–6. The image is that of the sun hidden, not by clouds, but by the opaque interposed body of the earth at night.

17   Cf. *The French Revolution*, 1282 with *The Song of Los*, plate 3 ('Africa'). Note that in the former passage the pillar of fire and the pillar of cloud are not yet contrasted. For the loins as the place of the Last Judgement, see *Jerusalem*, plate 30.

18   Letter to William Hayley, May 28th, 1804. See William Blake, *The Complete Writings of William Blake*, ed. Geoffrey Keynes (1957; revised edn., London: Oxford University Press, 1966), 845. [This is a more up-to-date substitute for Keynes's *The Writings of William Blake* (1925), which Frye cites.]

19   Marginalia to Francis Bacon's *Essays* (Blake, *Complete Writings*, 400).

20   *A Vision of the Last Judgement* (Blake, *Complete Writings*, 616).

21   *The Prelude* (1850), Book xi, ll 117–21.

22   *There is No Natural Religion*, second series, vii.

Further reading

Listed below is a selection of the criticism following Frye that addresses Blake's philosophy and myth. The question of unity and coherence – of form, theme and development – is focal. Frye's inclusive view of Blake's work as belonging to a given or fixed system is resisted by alternative views that present it as changing over time, or expose contradiction and inconsistency. Here, and throughout this volume,* indicates a study especially useful as an introduction to the poet's work.

Robert Gleckner, *The Piper and the Bard: A Study of William Blake* (Detroit: Wayne State University Press, 1959). Close reading of *Innocence*, *Experience*, and the works in between, as 'the key elements of an organic and ever-developing "system"' culminating in the prophecies. Its basic conceptions are eternity, fall and return, and a physical world produced from opposite elemental forces (masculine and feminine, inner and outer), with the imagination as the 'summation of . . . the active, masculine series'.

*Harold Bloom, *The Visionary Company: A Reading of English Romantic Poetry* (1961; revised and enlarged edn., Ithaca and London: Cornell University Press, 1971). An 'anthropocentric view is the basis for Blake's apocalyptic humanism.' Fine introduction, prelude to the fully-elaborated argument of *Blake's Apocalypse* (see below). Groups Blake with the five other major Romantic poets.

Hazard Adams, *William Blake: A Reading of the Shorter Poems* (Seattle: University of Washington Press, 1963). Reads in Blake's early lyrics, phases and fragments of the symbolic world of the later poems, describing his 'traditional, archetypal symbolism' by 'the interweaving of three Biblical and Blakean archetypes': the tree, the human body and the city.

Harold Bloom, *Blake's Apocalypse: A Study in Poetic Argument* (Ithaca: Cornell University Press, 1963). Study, in Frye's footsteps, of the body of Blake's poetry, in its chronological order of composition, and with reference to form as well as humanistic content, as showing the development of Blake's cosmic myth of the fall and his prophetic vision of apocalypse and redemption in a fully liberated imagination.

*Jean H. Hagstrum, *William Blake, Poet and Painter: An Introduction to the Illuminated Verse* (Chicago and London: University of Chicago Press, 1964). Treating Blake as an embodiment of the Western tradition by which the verbal and visual arts are united, prescribes 'a method of reading that takes account of all elements of Blake's form – border, design, and word'.

E. D. Hirsch, *Innocence and Experience: An Introduction to Blake* (Chicago and London: University of Chicago Press, 1964). Focusing on *Songs of Innocence and Experience* as spanning 'the whole course of Blake's poetic maturity', usefully challenges the dominant systematizing approach to Blake's poetry. Hirsch contends that Blake's views change radically with time, so that his 'contraries' are temporal rather than dialectical, the stages of a personal spiritual history rather than components of a single unified scheme; thus, any reading of the earlier work in terms of the symbolism of the later must be inadequate.

Kathleen Raine, *Blake and Tradition*, 2 vols. (1969; London: Routledge, 2002). Massive study, finding, in the Neoplatonic tradition, the key to Blake's thought. Some useful, other problematic, identifications of Blake's sources in poetry and art.

Alvin H. Rosenfeld (ed.), *William Blake: Essays for S. Foster Damon* (Providence: Brown University Press, 1969). Miscellany, ranging over literary kinships, designs, philosophy and religion, and poetic form and technique.

Morton D. Paley, *Energy and the Imagination: A Study of the Development of Blake's Thought* (Oxford: Clarendon Press, 1970). Focusing on the two concepts named in its title, studies Blake's thought from the early works through to *Jerusalem* as developing over time, rather than as governed by a fixed teleological 'system'.

S. Curran and J. A. Wittreich (eds.), *Blake's Sublime Allegory: Essays on* The Four Zoas, Milton, Jerusalem (Madison: University of Wisconsin Press, 1973). Range of approaches, with a focus 'on Blake's form of epic-prophecy, on its traditions, its structure, aesthetics, and metaphysics'; 'a related concern' is Blake's relationship with his audience.

David Wagenknecht, *Blake's Night: William Blake and the Idea of Pastoral* (Cambridge, Mass.: Harvard University Press, 1973). 'Interprets the whole of Blake's poetical career in terms of a single, unifying thematic concern or idea: the idea of pastoral.'

Thomas R. Frosch, *The Awakening of Albion: The Renovation of the Body in the Poetry of William Blake* (Ithaca and London: Cornell University Press, 1974). Repudiates transcendence in Blake by emphasizing his concern with the senses and the body. Following the structure of Blake's myth from fall to redemption, studies Albion's resumption of consciousness, showing that for Blake the final transformation of man includes 'a resurrection of his body through a remaking of its sensory organization'.

Anne Mellor, *Blake's Human Form Divine* (Berkeley and Los Angeles, University of California Press, 1974). Disputing Frye's emphasis on consistency, treats the contradiction between Blake's verbal rejection of the human form ('bound or outward circumference') as a Urizenic tyranny and his reliance on form in his visual art; thus, between his philosophical theory and his artistic practice.

J. A. Wittreich, *Angel of Apocalypse: Blake's Idea of Milton* (Madison: University of Wisconsin Press, 1975). From a detailed study of Blake's idea of Milton, exposes as false the dichotomy of tradition and revolution, showing that for Blake the Milton tradition is also a tradition of revolution. Counters Bloom's thesis in *The Anxiety of Influence* (1973) by the argument that the poet, rather than misinterpreting, manifests and clarifies the vision of his precursor.

Susan Fox, *Poetic Form in Blake's* Milton (Princeton: Princeton University Press, 1976). Defines the rhetorical structure of *Milton*, demonstrating its congruency with the poem's system of ideas and so the parity of the formal with the visionary coherence of Blake's prophecies.

W. J. T. Mitchell, *Blake's Composite Art: A Study of the Illuminated Poetry* (Princeton: Princeton University Press, 1978). Persuasive argument for an integrated approach to poetry and designs (cf. Hagstrum, above). Shows that a view of art as composite is fundamental to Blake's aesthetics, which transforms traditional theories of the relation of the 'sister arts' into 'the principles of his own visionary art form'; illustrates, from detailed formal analyses of three illuminated books, the manner in which visual and verbal aspects interact to constitute an organic whole.

Leopold Damrosch, *Symbol and Truth in Blake's Myth* (Princeton: Princeton University Press, 1980). Illuminating study, denying both systematic and developmental coherence in Blake's myth, instead asserting and celebrating its fundamental contradictions and Blake's unsuccessful struggle to resolve them.

Zachary Leader, *Reading Blake's* Songs (London: Routledge & Kegan Paul, 1981). Treats the *Songs*, not in the light of a supposed mythological 'system', but as an independent whole, whose models are the children's books and educational treatises of Blake's time. *Innocence* inculcates a child-like percipience, 'Vision, or the exercise of the Divine Imagination', which is then tested in *Experience*, whose Bard, himself infected by the condition he describes, must be redeemed by our acquired innocent wisdom.

Leslie Tannenbaum, *Biblical Tradition in Blake's Early Prophecies: The Great Code of Art* (Princeton: Princeton University Press, 1982). Important study of the Bible as the 'Great Code' of Blake's art. Traces Blake's biblical heritage, including the exegetic and critical traditions surrounding the Bible, showing its impact on his approach to prophetic form and biblical pictorialism, typology, and history; then examines, in this light, the early prophecies (Lambeth books).

Morton D. Paley, *The Continuing City: William Blake's* Jerusalem (Oxford: Clarendon Press, 1983). '*Jerusalem* presents both the mythic history and the visionary future of mankind, all devolving on the present moment.' Thoroughgoing study of *Jerusalem* as the culmination of Blake's 'drive towards an inclusive myth'; thus, elaborates the final stages of development described in *Energy and Imagination* (see above).

HISTORICAL AND POLITICAL READINGS

Complementing Frye's study, by addressing the large area of historical context deliberately untouched by him, is the other colossus of Blake criticism, David

Erdman's *Blake: Prophet against Empire* (1954). Erdman's superseded two prior historical treatments, both of which, like his, emphasized Blake's radicalism: Jacob Bronowski's *William Blake, 1757–1827: A Man without a Mask* (1944)[16] and Mark Schorer's *William Blake: The Politics of Vision* (1946). In Erdman's comprehensive and copiously detailed reading, the visionary Blake is fundamentally a political poet, in whose work can be traced 'a more or less clearly discernible thread of historical reference.'[17] Erdman offers 'a bold survey of the history of Blake's time as it swirls about and enters into the texture of his emblematic poetry,'[18] arguing that it is not industrialism, but war and peace – the threat of war and the uncertainty of peace – that characterize Blake's perception of his age. Reproduced below is his seminal treatment of what is now a major topic of criticism, Blake's opposition to slavery.

Extract from David Erdman, *Blake: Prophet against Empire* (1954)

The fire, the fire, is falling!

Look up! look up! O citizen of London. enlarge thy countenance; O Jew, leave counting gold! return to thy oil and wine; O African! black African! (go. winged thought widen his forehead.)   *A Song of Liberty*

When Blake came to believe, in the decade after Waterloo, that the revolutions in America and France had been merely bourgeois revolutions, destroying colonial and monarchic restraints only to establish the irresponsible 'right' to buy and sell, he concluded that nearly everything of value in those revolutions had been lost – at least as far as his own countrymen were concerned. When he declared that most Englishmen 'since the French Revolution' had become 'Intermeasurable One by another' like coins in a till and had reduced all values to the experiment of chance, he meant that such Englishmen had absorbed nothing of the real meaning of Republican culture, had not learned that everything that *lives* is holy and without price and that each 'Line or Lineament' is *itself* and is 'Not Intermeasurable with or by and Thing Else.'[1]

Most of his life Blake was more or less confident that the sons and daughters of Albion would learn; would enlarge their views rather than their investments, would 'look up' and open their minds to the visions in the air. For 'counting gold' is not abundant living; and grasping colonies and shedding blood whether in the name of royal dignity or in the name of commerce is not living at all, but killing. When Blake urges the London merchant to turn from banking to the exchange of useful commodities (Biblical 'oil and wine') he is thinking on the one hand of the need to abolish hunger; on the other hand he is thinking of the gold amassed from colonial plunder, traffic in slaves, and open war. The winged thought which must inspire the African slave to revolt must also inspire the British citizen to let 'the British Colonies beneath the woful Princes fade'[2] and to desist from coveting the colonies of France. And it must also inspire the sexes to *love* and let *live* without possessive jealousy.

Blake sees all these matters as interrelated. War grows out of acquisitiveness and jealousy and mischanneled sexual energy, all of which grow out of the intrusion of possessiveness into human relations. 'Number weight & measure' signify 'a year of dearth.'[3] The Rights of Man are not the rights of dealers in human flesh – warriors, slavers, and whoremongers. When Fayette was 'bought & sold' in the service of the royal whore, his and other people's happy morrow was also 'bought & sold.'[4] Purchase and sale only bring the old relationship of tyrant and slave out into the open market.

The economic side of Blake's myth is often expressed in images of fertility and sterility, fire and frost and seasonal growth. The soul of America who sings passionately of 'lovely copulation' is a woman and also a continent longing for fruit in her fertile valleys. To say that she wants to be loved, not raped, is to say, economically, that she wants to be cultivated by free men, not slaves or slave-drivers; for joy, not for profit. The revolutionary energy which appears in history as Orcus pulling tyrants down to the pit appears in husbandry as the plower, sower, and reaper of abundant harvests, symbolized as ὄρχεις [*orcheis*], the root of sexual growth in the womb of the earth. Orc as the spirit of living that transcends the spirit of trading is the divine seed-fire that exceeds the calculations of Urizen, god of commerce. The portrait of Urizen with golden compasses is made in the image of Newton, the mighty spirit of weighing and measuring who thought to reduce the prolific universe to an orrery of farthing balls. When Newton's trump marks the end of weight and measure, the great starry heavens prove to be as light as leaves.

In the symbolic Preludiums of *America* and subsequent poems the rich sexual-agrarian implications of Blake's economics are condensed into a cryptically ritualized myth. But some of the reasoning behind this myth, or more properly the questioning behind it, is available in *Visions of the Daughters of Albion*, 1793, a dramatized treatise on the related questions of moral, economic, and sexual freedom and an indictment of the 'mistaken Demon' whose code separates bodies from souls and reduces women and children, nations and lands, to possessions.

Superficially the *Visions* appears to be a debate on free love with passing allusions to the rights of man, of woman, and of beasts and to the injustices of sexual inhibition and prohibition, of life ruled by 'cold floods of abstraction,' and of Negro and child slavery. Yet love and slavery prove to be the two poles of the poem's axis, and the momentum of its spinning – for it does not progress – is supplied by the oratory of Oothoon, a female slave, free in spirit but physically bound; Bromion, the slave-driver who owns her and has raped her to increase her market value; and Theotormon, her jealous but inhibited lover who fails to recognize her divine humanity. As a lament over the possessiveness of love and the hypocrisy of moral legislators, the poem has been widely explored in the light of Blake's notebook poems on this theme and in the light of Mary Wollstonecraft's *Vindication of the Rights of Woman.* The other pole, equally important in the dynamics of the work, has scarcely been discovered. Yet we can understand the three symbolic persons of the myth, their triangular relationship, and their unresolved debate if we recognize them as, in part, poetic counterparts of the parliamentary and editorial debates of 1789–1793 on a bill for abolition of the British slave trade – the frustrated lover, for example, being analogous to the wavering abolitionist who cannot bring himself openly to condemn slavery although he deplores the *trade.*

Blake, in relating his discussion of freedom to the 'voice of slaves beneath the sun' (*V.D.A.*2:8), was directing the light of the French Revolution upon the most vulnerable flaw in the British constitution, and in doing so he was contributing to the most widely agitated reform movement of the time. The Society for the Abolition of the Slave Trade, formed in 1787, had begun at once to gather evidence, organize town meetings, and enlist the help of artists and writers. Wedgwood produced a cameo of a suppliant Negro, widely used on snuffboxes, bracelets, hairpins. William Cowper wrote a number of street ballads such as *The Negro's Complaint* and *Sweet Meat Has Sour Sauce.* And Blake's *Little Black Boy* coincided with the early phase of this campaign. But the Parliamentary phase began in 1789 and coincided with the revolution in France and the ensuing revolution of slaves in 1791 in French Santo Domingo. It reached its height in 1792–1793, and Wordsworth, returning to England early in 1793 after more than a year in France, was struck by the extent of the English movement: 'little less in verity Than a whole Nation crying with one voice' against 'the Traffickers in Negro blood.'[5] The abolitionists nevertheless were 'baffled.' The bill was defeated in Parliament by the pressure of Antijacobin attacks from Burke and Lord

Abingdon and various slave-agents, of whom Blake's thundering Bromion is a caricature.

This movement 'had diffus'd some truths And more of virtuous feeling through the heart Of the English People,' but its breadth was due partly to the fact that relatively few had any direct stake in the trade. Conservative as well as liberal humanitarians were not unwilling to dissociate British honor and British commerce from 'this most rotten branch of human shame.' Moreover, the slaves themselves made the trade a risky one, both for slave-drivers and for ship owners. Scarcely a year went by without its quota of slave ship mutinies, battles on the African coast, and insurrections in the plantations. Military statesmen complained that merchant seamen died off twice as rapidly in the slave trade as in any other, effecting a loss of manpower for the British navy. And many active abolitionists were merchants who preferred to invest in well-behaved cargoes manufactured in Manchester and Birmingham. It is Blake's view that the movement failed because of an insufficient diffusion of 'truths' and a considerable misapplication of 'virtuous feeling,' to use Wordsworth's terms.

In *Visions of the Daughters of Albion* the true feelings which the Heart must 'know' before there can be human freedom are discussed by Oothoon, Bromion, and Theotormon for the edification of the 'enslav'd' Daughters of Albion – an almost silent audience or chorus, who lament upon their mountains and in their valleys and sigh 'toward America,' and who may be considered the Blakean equivalent of traditional personifications of the trades and industries of Great Britain: in *The Four Zoas* some of them will appear as the textile trades whose 'needlework' is sold throughout the earth. They are of course, in the moral allegory, 'oppressed womanhood,' as Damon points out.[6] They are shown that as long as possessive morality prevails, all daughters remain slaves; and that while the trafficker in Negro blood continues to stamp his signet on human flesh, none of the traffic on the golden Thames is untainted. In short, freedom is indivisible, and Oothoon's is a test case.[7]

2
O African! black African!

Blake's knowledge of the cruelties of slavery came to him doubtless through many sources, but one was directly graphic. In 1791 or earlier Joseph Johnson distributed to Blake and other engravers a sheaf of some eighty sketches of the flora and fauna and conditions of human servitude in the South American colony of Dutch Guiana during some early slave revolts. With more than his usual care Blake engraved at least sixteen plates, including nearly all those which illustrate slave conditions. We know he was working on them during the production of his *Visions of the Daughters of Albion* because he turned in most of the plates in batches dated December 1, 1792, and December 2, 1793. The two-volume work they illustrate was finally published in 1796 as *A Narrative, of a five Years' expedition, against the Revolted Negroes of Surinam, in Guiana, on the Wild Coast of South America; from the year 1772 to 1777*, by Captain J. G. Stedman. We may assume that Blake was familiar with the narrative, available in Johnson's shop – at least with the portions explanatory of the drawings.

Blake's engravings, with a force of expression absent from the others, emphasize the dignity of Negro men and women stoical under cruel torture: the wise, reproachful look of the *Negro hung alive by the Ribs to a Gallows* (pl. 11) who lived three days unmurmuring and upbraided a flogged comrade for crying; the bitter concern in the face of the Negro executioner compelled to break the bones of a crucified rebel; the warm, self-possessed look of his victim, who jested with the crowd and offered to his sentinel 'my hand that was chopped off' to eat with his piece of dry bread: for how was it 'that he, a *white man*, should have no meat to eat along with it?' Though Blake signed most of the plates, he shrank from signing his engraving of this bloody document, *The Execution of 'Breaking on the Rack'* (pl. 71); but the image of the courageous rebel on the cruciform rack bit into his heart, and in the Preludium of *America* he drew Orc in the same posture to represent the spirit of human freedom defiant of tyranny.

For the *finis* page Blake engraved according to Stedman's specifications 'an emblematical picture' of *Europe supported by Africa & America* – three comely nude women tenderly embracing each other, the Negro and the European clasping hands in sisterly equality. Roses bloom auspiciously on the barren ground at their feet. Yet there is a curious difference between this pictured relationship of Europe *supported* by her darker sisters, who wear slave bracelets while she wears a string of pearls, and the 'ardent wish' expressed in Stedman's text, that all peoples 'may henceforth and to all eternity be the props of each other' since 'we only differ in colour, but are certainly all created by the same Hand.' The bracelets and pearls may be said to represent the historical fact; the handclasp, the ardent wish. For one plate Blake had the ironic chore of engraving a 'contented' slave – with Stedman's initials, J.G.S., stamped on his flesh with a silver signet.[8] 'Stampt with my signet,' says Bromion (*V.D.A.*1:21).

In his *Narrative* Stedman demonstrates the dilemma, social and sexual, of the English man of sentiment entangled in the ethical code of property and propriety. A hired soldier in Guiana, Captain Stedman was apologetic about the 'Fate' that caused him to be fighting bands of rebel slaves in a Dutch colony: "'Twas *yours* to fall – but *Mine* to feel the wound,' we learn from the frontispiece, engraved by Bartolozzi: *Stedman with a Rebel Negro prostrate at his feet*. The fortitude of the tortured Negroes and the 'commiseration' of their Negro executioners impressed Stedman and led him to conclude that Europeans were 'the greater barbarians.' Yet he could repeat the myth that these same dignified people were 'perfectly savage' in Africa and would only be harmed by 'sudden emancipation.' His 'ears were stunned with the clang of the whip and the dismal yells'; yet he was reassured by the consideration that the tortures were legal punishment and were not occurring in a *British* colony.[9]

To the torture of female slaves Stedman was particularly sensitive, for he was in love with a beautiful fifteen-year-old slave, Joanna, and in a quandary similar to that of Blake's Theotormon, who loves Oothoon but cannot free her. Stedman managed 'a decent wedding' with Joanna, about which he is shamefaced, and a honeymoon during which they were 'free like the roes in the forest.' But he was unable to purchase her freedom, and when he thought Joanna was to be sold at auction, he fancied he 'saw her tortured, insulted, and bowing under the weight of her chains, calling aloud, but in vain, for my assistance.' Even on their honeymoon, Stedman was harrowed by his inability to prevent the sadistic flagellation of a slave on a neighboring estate. We have Blake's engraving of this *Flagellation of a Female Samboe Slave* (pl. 37). Naked and tied 'by both arms to a tree,' the 'beautiful Samboe girl of about eighteen' had just received two hundred lashes. Stedman's interference only prompted the overseer to order the punishment repeated. 'Thus I had no other remedy but to run to my boat, and leave the detestable monster, like a beast of prey, to enjoy his bloody feast.' The girl's crime had been 'refusing to submit to the loathsome embraces of her detestable executioner.' The captain's own Joanna, to prove the equality of her 'soul' to 'that of an European,' insisted on enduring the condition of slavery until she could purchase freedom with her own labor.[10] Blake's Oothoon invites vultures to prey upon her naked flesh for the same reason. Her lover, Theotormon, is also unable to interfere or to rescue her:

> Why does my Theotormon sit weeping upon the threshold;
> And Oothoon hovers by his side, perswading him in vain
> <div align="right">(<i>V.D.A</i>.2:21–22)</div>

The persons and problems of Stedman's *Narrative* reappear, creatively modified, in the text and illustrations of Blake's *Visions*: the rape and torture of the virgin slave, her pride in the purity and equality of her soul, and the frustrated desire of her lover and husband. Oothoon advertised as pregnant by Bromion is the slave on the auction block whose pregnancy enhances her price; Oothoon chained by an ankle in plate 4 is the *Female Negro Slave, with a Weight chained to her Ancle*[11] – or the similarly chained victim of the infamous Captain Kimber, cited in Parliament in 1792. The cold green wave enveloping the chained Oothoon is symbolic of the drowning of slaves in passage from Africa; the flame-like shape of the wave is symbolic of the liberating fires of rebellion. Her friend beside her hears her call but covers his eyes from seeing what must be done. In another picture Oothoon is fastened back-to-back to Bromion; yet the most prominent chains are on *his* leg, and she has not ceased struggling to be free.[12] Impotent beside these two squats Theotormon, the theology-tormented man,[13] inhibited by a moral code and a white man's God that tell him his love is impure. A caricature of paralyzed will power, he simultaneously clutches himself, buries his face in his arms, and scratches the back of his head. Despite his furtive sympathy ('secret tears') he makes no effective response to

> The voice of slaves beneath the sun, and children bought with money,
> That shiver in religious caves beneath the burning fires
> Of lust, that belch incessant from the summits of the earth[14]

Stedman's anxieties shed light on the moral paralysis of Theotormon; yet we must also be aware of the analogous but more impersonal and political quandary of the Abolition Society, whose trimming announcement in February 1792 that they did not desire 'the Emancipation of the Negroes in the British Colonies' but only sought to end '*the Trade for Slaves*' conflicted with their own humanitarian professions and involved an acceptance of the basic premises of the slavers: that slaves were legitimate commodities and that the rebellion of slaves was legally indefensible.[15] William Wilberforce, the Society's zealous but conservative spokesman in Parliament, became increasingly preoccupied in 1792 with clearing his reputation of the taint of republicanism in an attempt to carry water on both shoulders: to be known as a great friend of the slaves yet as an abhorrer of 'democratical principles.' Also he had obtained a 'Royal Proclamation against Vice and Immorality' and was promoting what became known as the Vice Society, based on the proposition that woman's love is Sin and democracy is Blasphemy.[16] Blake's deliberate emphasis on the delights of 'happy copulation' could be expected to shock such angelic moralists, as if to say: you cannot free any portion of humanity from chains unless you recognize the close connection between the cat-o'-nine-tails and the moral code.[17]

The situation or story of Blake's poem is briefly this. Oothoon, a candid virgin, loves Theotormon and is not afraid to enter the experience of love. She puts a marigold between her breasts and flies over the ocean to take it to her lover; she is willing, that is, to give him the flower of her virginity. But on the way she is seized by Bromion, who rapes her despite her woeful outcries, and advertises her as a pregnant slave (harlot).[18] Her lover responds not by coming to her rescue but by accusing her and Bromion of adultery and secretly bemoaning his fate and hers. Oothoon and Bromion therefore remain 'bound back to back' in the barren relationship of slavery, while Theotormon, failing as a lover, sits 'weeping upon the threshold.' The rest of the poem consists of their three-sided soliloquy. Oothoon argues that she is still pure in that she can still bring her lover flowers of joy, moments of gratified desire; but he cannot act because he accepts Bromion's definition of her as a sinner. She is ready for love, but Theotormon's stasis threatens to turn her love-call into an ironic masochism.

Interpretation of the story on this level is sometimes blurred by failure to distinguish Oothoon's offer of herself to Theotormon from her rape by Bromion. The flower-picking is mistaken for a symbol of the rape,

William Blake, Theotormon and Oothoon, *Visions of the Daughters of Albion*, 1793, plate 9. British Museum, London.

and her later argument is mistaken for defense of an 'affair' with Bromion. But in Blake's plot-source, Macpherson's *Oithona*, where the heroine is similarly raped in her lover's absence, the lover returning does what obviously Theotormon ought to do, consider her still faithful and goes to battle at once in her defense, against great odds.[19] Oothoon's argument is not that she likes Bromion or slavery but that she refuses to accept the status of a fallen woman: only if her lover lets Bromion's name-calling intimidate him will she be 'a whore indeed' (6:18). She is not asking merely for toleration but for love.

The allegorical level, indicated by Oothoon's designation as 'the soft soul of America' (1:3), must not be neglected. Bromion's signet brands not simply a woman but 'Thy soft American plains,' and Bromion is no simple rapist but the slaver whose claim to 'thy north & south' is based on his possession in both North and South America of African slaves: 'Stampt with my signet . . . the swarthy children of the sun' (1:20–21). When the soul of America goes 'seeking flowers to comfort her' she is looking for a further blossoming of the revolutionary spirit (compare the Preludium of *America*), and when she finds a 'bright Marygold' in the 'dewy bed' of 'the vales of Leutha,' she is taking note of the Negro insurrections in Santo Domingo in the Caribbean around which the debate in Parliament raged: 'Bromion rent her with his thunders.'[20] The first risings did not succeed, but the flower or nymph comforts 'Oothoon the mild' both with her own 'glow' and with the observation that the spirit of liberty is irrepressible: 'Another flower shall spring, because the soul of sweet delight Can never pass away.' On this level Theotormon, to whom Oothoon wings over the Atlantic in 'exulting swift delight' expecting him to rejoice at the good news of another rising republic, acts like those English abolitionists who were embarrassed by the thunders of the Antijacobins.

Blake's acquaintance with the abolition debate is evident. The Bromions in Parliament cried that the Africans were 'inured to the hot climate' of the plantations and therefore necessary for 'labour under a vertical sun.' Under Bromion's words Blake draws a picture (see figure) stretching across the page, of a Negro worker smitten into desperate horizontality, wilted like the heat-blasted vegetation among which he has been working with a pickaxe, and barely able to hold his face out of the dirt. The apologists also argued that Negroes understood only 'firmness,' were 'contented and happy' and superstitious, and were now 'habituated to the contemplation' of slavery. Bromion utters the same arguments: that 'the swarthy children of the sun . . . are obedient, they resist not, they obey the scourge: Their daughters worship terrors and obey the violent.'[21]

In Parliament Lord Abingdon accused the 'abettors' of abolition of promoting the new philosophy of leveling: 'Look at the state of the

William Blake, section from Slaves Beneath the Sun, *Visions of the Daughters of Albion*, 1793, plate 5. Fitzwilliam Museum, Cambridge/Bridgeman Art Library, London.

colony of St. Domingo, and see what liberty and equality, see what the rights of man have done there.' They have dried up the rivers of *commerce* and replaced them with 'fountains of human blood.' Moreover the levelers are prophesying that 'all being equal, blacks and whites, French and English [*sic*], wolves and lambs, shall all, 'merry companions every one,' promiscuously pig together; engendering . . . a new species of man as the product of this new philosophy.'

It is this sort of argument that Blake's Oothoon turns right side up again. For, as Abingdon put it, 'what does the abolition of the slave trade mean more or less in effect, than liberty and equality?' Wilberforce joined Burke in a committee for the relief of emigrant royalist priests partly, as he admitted, 'to do away French citizenship' – for the French had misinterpreted his liberalism and named him an honorary French citizen along with Paine and Priestley! Yet this demonstration did not prevent Burke from attacking the Abolition Bill as 'a shred of the accursed web of Jacobinism.' Blake's Theotormon is tangled in the suspicion that his own desires are part of an accursed web.

The argument of Oothoon is triplex, as she herself is. Stedman's emblematical picture treats Europe, Africa, and America as three separate women: Blake makes them into one. He can do this because Oothoon is not a person but a 'soul.' Pictured in chains she is the female slave, but she does not have the black skin and tight ringlets of the Africa of the emblem. Only in the picture of the exhausted worker is the Negro slave directly represented. Allowing for difference in media, Oothoon is the American Indian of the emblem, with the same loose black hair, sad mouth, and angular limbs. See especially the illustration of the title page, where she runs along the trough of a green wave pursued by the mistaken God of slavery.

Yet her skin is not the copper color of the engraved America either, but theoretically 'snowy' white, according to the text. 'I am pure,' she cries 'because the night is gone that clos'd me in its deadly black.'[22] Speaking as America she means that the night of oppressive chivalry is gone with the dawn of freedom. As Africa she means that the time is gone when people's vision was limited to their five senses and they could see only her dark skin and not her inward purity.

Blake had explained this symbolism in his *Little Black Boy*:

> My mother bore me in the southern wild,
> And I am black, but O! my soul is white;
> White as an angel is the English child:
> But I am black as if bereav'd of light.

To avoid a chauvinistic interpretation Blake explained that any skin color is a cloud that cannot obscure the essential brotherhood of man in a fully enlightened society, such as Heaven. 'These black bodies and this sunburnt face,' said the little black boy, are 'but a cloud.' If the Negro is to be free of his black cloud, the little English boy must be likewise free from his 'white cloud,' which is equally opaque. 'When I from black and he from white cloud free,' I will 'be like him and he will then love me.' In the second illustrated page of this Song of Innocence the black boy appears as light-skinned as the English boy – or as Oothoon.[23]

Oothoon's reason for letting the vultures prey upon 'her soft snowy limbs' is to let Theotormon, who is an adult version of the English child, *see* that beneath the skin her 'pure transparent breast' really reflects the same human 'image' as his – that her color is morally that of 'the clear spring, mudded with feet of beasts,' which again 'grows pure & smiles' (2:12–19). As Africa she is urging the London citizen to ignore color differences. As America she is urging British law-makers to rescue her from the muddy feet of the slaver. As a woman enslaved by Marriage Act morality, she is imploring her lover to rise above accusations of adultery.

Beyond arguing her essential purity, she indicates by several analogies that there is something especially beautiful about dark skin and (she suggests both points at once) about pregnancy. Consider the dark skin of worm-ripened fruit, which is 'sweetest'; or the darkness of 'the soul prey'd on by woe'; or

The new wash'd lamb ting'd with the village smoke & the bright swan
By the red earth of our immortal river: I bathe my wings.
And I am white and pure to hover round Theotormons breast.

(3:17–20)

It is the soul rather than the body of the slave that is 'inured,' in being richer in experience. The black boy already loves the English boy and is thus better prepared than he to 'bear the heat' of God's presence.

And still we have not done with the complexity of Blake's symbolism, for in one illustration, on the page of the 'Argument,' Oothoon appears not as an American Indian but as the European woman of the emblem. Or rather in this illustration the Stedman influence is supplanted by that of a French neo-classical painter and engraver, Vien. Here the focus is on the buying and selling of woman's love, and Blake is reversing Vien's picture (based on a Roman original) of a procuress offering 'loves' for sale in a basket: *La Marchande d'Amours*. Oothoon kneels in the same posture as that of the love-merchant, and her hair is knotted at the back of her head in a similar fashion. But whereas Vien's procuress holds one of her cupids by his wings like a captive bird, Oothoon keeps her hands to herself and lightly 'kisses the joy as it flies,' springing not from a basket but from the stem of a marigold.[24]

In the most general sense the soaring joys which Oothoon offers her lover are sparks of Promethean fire or winged thoughts calculated to widen his brow. In her effort to prod him to cross the threshold of indecision – 'I cry arise O Theotormon for the village dog Barks at the breaking day' – Oothoon insists that the revolutionary dawn is at hand and overdue and that the corn is ripe. But this 'citizen of London' does not look up. He is not at all sure 'what is the night or day'; he is nearly deaf to the cries of slaves and blind to visions of a new day: he cannot arise. The springs of rebellion are as obscure to him as those of moral purity. 'Tell me what is a thought,' he pleads, 'and upon what mountains Wave shadows of discontent? and in what houses dwell the wretched' (3:22–4:1). But he fears that the new philosophy may carry his thought to a 'remote land' (America) or may bring 'poison from the desart wilds' rather than 'dews and honey and balm' (4:8–10). And he grows silent when Bromion shakes the cavern with rhetorical questions, just as the Abolitionists were silenced in 1793 by the clamor of Antijacobinism.

Bromion's arguments and those of the apologists of slavery are of the same order: Dare anyone question that subordination must be maintained? Has anyone even in this land of liberty and poverty yet heard of any way to maintain order without the fear of punishment? Are not war and slavery the basis of our Empire? Is not sorrow intended for the poor, joy for the rich? Is not fear of Hell necessary to keep the laborious poor from pursuing 'eternal life'?[25]

On the concluding page we see Oothoon, nevertheless, still daring to cry out – and wrapped in flames of the same bright rose color as the brightest band in the rainbow that arches over her on the title page.

Notes

1   To George Cumberland, Apr. 12, 1827 (Blake, *Complete Writings*, 878). Blake says 'Englishmen are *all*' etc., but excepts himself and his friend.
2   [From a fragment, probably intended for *America*; Blake, *Complete Writings*, 206.]
3   'Proverbs of Hell,' *The Marriage of Heaven and Hell* 7:cf. the motion in Commons Feb. 5, 1790, for 'a return from all cities and market towns of the different weights and measures now in use.'
4   [From a deleted verse in Blake's Notebook; Blake, *Complete Writings*, 186.]
5   *The Prelude* (1805) x.202–227, here and below.
6   [In *William Blake: His Philosophy and Symbols* (1924).]
7   For documentation and illustration of this section and the next, see my 'Blake's Vision of Slavery,' *Journal of the Warburg and Courtauld Institutes*, xv (1952), 242–252.
8   Plate 68; see Stedman's text, I, 206.
9   Ibid., I, 109, 203, 90; II, 298.
10 Ibid., I, 99–106, 208, 312, 319, 325–326; II, 83, 377. Stedman had come back to England without Joanna, but eager to tell the story. Blake, who had caricatured his friend Flaxman as 'Steelyard the Lawgiver,' was forced by his vision of the realities to see a Theotormon in his friend Stedman.
11 Plate 4, engraved by Bartolozzi; cf. the similar weight in *Europe*, pl. 1.
12 *V.D.A.* Plate printed variously as frontispiece or tailpiece – an emblem of the *situation*.
13 The names Oothoon, Theotormon, Bromion, and Leutha have been traced to Ossian's Oithona, Tonthormod, Brumo, and Lutha. (Damon, *Blake*, 329.) But the oo-oo doubling may come from African words in Stedman: apootoo, too-too, ooroocoocoo (snake). A *toremon* is a shiny black bird whose name means 'a tale-bearer, or a spy'; and the rebels 'have an invincible hatred against it.' I, 367–368. If *Theo* is God, an accuser of sin might be considered God's spy, *Theo-toreman*. Unquestionably Theotormon torments and is tormented: see D. J. Sloss and J. P. R. Wallis, *William Blake's Prophetic Writings*, 2 vols. (Oxford: Clarendon Press, 1926). I, 34 n.

In pl. 57, *The Vampire or Spectre of Guiana*, engraved by A. Smith, Dec. 1, 1791, we can see why Blake's Spectre has bat-like wings and is so thirsty 'to devour Los's Human Perfection' (*Jerusalem* 6). A further matter of interest is the information that the eyes of the 'tyger-cat' of South America emit 'flashes like lightning.' Stedman, II, 51.

14   *V.D.A.*2:8–10. Cf. *The Marriage of Heaven and Hell* 18 and Swedenborg's description of the 'hells [which] are everywhere, both under the mountains, hills, and rocks, and under the plains.' Their openings exhale flames which correspond 'to the evils of love of self.' Emmanuel Swedenborg, *A Treatise concerning Heaven and Hell* (1778), paragraphs 584–586. See Blake's comment on par. 588 in Blake, *Complete Writings*, 939.

15   *London Chronicle*, Feb. 2, 1792. Against the explanation that it was simply strategic to concentrate first on abolition of the trade, consider the fact that as soon as the Slave Trade bill was passed, in 1807, the Society dissolved. Slavery itself, and consequently the trade, continued to exist.

16   See Robert I, Wilberforce and Samuel Wilberforce, *The Life of William Wilberforce*, 5 vols. (London: John Murray, 1838) I. 129–38, 342–4, 368–9; W. L. Mathieson, *England in Transition, 1789–1832: A Study of Movement* (London: Longmans, Green, 1920), 70–1.

17   In *V.D.A.*9 (see figure), Theotormon is flaying himself with a three-thonged scourge, while Oothoon runs by unaided.

18   See Stedman, I, 206.

19   Were Oothoon and Theotormon married before the story begins? Critics differ. Bromion's 'Now thou maist marry' suggests they were not; Theotormon's jealousy of 'the adulterate pair' suggests they were. What matters is that the affair was not consummated. Oothoon welcomes the 'experience' that Thel shrank from, but her lover does not.

20   *V.D.A.*7:4–16. In the abolition debates attention was focused on this eruption of 'democratical principles' in the West Indies. The fact that London merchant firms held investments in Santo Domingo in the then large sum of £300,000 'helps to explain why the British government in [1793–1798] sacrificed more than £4,000,000 in an effort to conquer the French colony and maintain or restore Negro slavery. It helps to explain also why Wilberforce's abolitionist program suffered a momentary eclipse.' C. L. Lokke, 'London Merchant Interest in the St. Domingue Plantations of the Émigrés, 1793–1798,' *American Historical Revue*, XLIII (1938), 795–802. Leutha's Vale appears to be Blake's place-name for the French colony, Leutha being the Queen of France. In *Fayette* the Queen is one whose smile spreads pestilence. In *Europe* Leutha is 'the sweet smiling pestilence,' a 'silken Queen' who has 'many daughters' (colonies?), and in a phrase which recalls Paine's remark she is called the 'luring bird of Eden.' In the 'Thiralatha' fragment (Blake, *Complete Writings*, 206) the fading of 'The British Colonies' is compared to the dying of a dream, perhaps of French colonialism, which has left 'obscured traces in the Vale of Leutha.' After the West Indies docks were located in the Isle of Dogs, Blake took to calling it the Isle of Leutha's Dogs. *Jerusalem* 31. Leutha's Vale is 'dewy' perhaps because it lies in the dewy bed of the Caribbean. In Ossian, Lutha is a place-name meaning 'swift stream.' In *Milton* Leutha is a repressive moral force as well as a counterrevolutionary, but I see no support for the suggestion that her name is 'a feminized form of "Luther"' for 'Puritanism.' (Damon, *Blake*, 329).

21   *V.D.A.*1:21–23. See Stedman, 1, 201–6, and Robert Bisset, *A History of the Reign of George 111* (1803–4), new edn., 2 vols. (London, 1816) II, 133.

22   *V.D.A.*2:12, 28–29. Blake usually employed brown inks in printing *V.D.A.* though sometimes he chose pink, purple, or yellow. In contrast, *Europe* and *America* are usually printed in green, blue, or black.

23   Not quite true for all copies. In at least one a slight tint has been given to the black boy in heaven; but the contrast with the solid color of the first page is still pronounced.

24   See illustrations in 'Blake's Vision of Slavery,' cited above in note 7.

25   For a Parliamentary analogue of Bromion's speech (105–110), hear slavery's 'agent for Grenada,' a Mr. Baillie (*Parliamentary History*, Apr. 2, 1793), arguing that the very Empire is based on the right to flog: 'I wish to ask . . . if it is possible to maintain that subordination [in navy and army] that is absolutely necessary . . . without the fear of punishment? . . . Have we never heard of seamen being flogged from ship to ship, or of soldiers dying in the very act of punishment, under the lash . . . exposed in as shameful and ignominious a manner [as slaves]? Have we not also heard, even in this country of boasted liberty, of seamen being kidnapped and carried away . . . without being allowed the comfort of seeing their wives and families? [Nothing extraordinary in the misery of slaves.] I declare there is more wretchedness and poverty in the parish of St. Giles, in which I live, than there is in the whole of the extensive colonies."

Further reading

The sufficiency and stature of Erdman's book is reflected in the paucity of related studies in the years following its publication. But from the 1980s, the line of historicist scholarship over which Erdman presides has continued to develop, through complementary, sometimes competing, historicisms (for the latter, see especially McGann, below). Their common focus is Blake's radicalism, although gaps and discrepancies are increasingly registered.

***A. L. Morton**, *The Everlasting Gospel: A Study in the Sources of William Blake* (London: Lawrence and Wishart, 1958). Inaugurates the discussion of Blake's relationship to antinomianism, the revolutionary religious tradition of the London community of small tradesmen and artisans.

Fred Whitehead, 'William Blake and Radical Tradition' in *Weapons of Criticism: Marxism in America and the Literary Tradition*, ed. N. Rudich (Palo Alto, Calif.: Ramparts Press, 1976), 191–214. Contends that the main structure of Blake's prophecies is the representation of the entire history of European man, dominated by two revolutions: the Urban Revolution which brought about a class society and its concomitant psycho-social divisions, and the Industrial Revolution of Blake's own time which, although reflecting ancient divisions, was to provide the means for resolving them.

David Punter, 'Blake: "Active Evil" and "Passive Good"' in *Romanticism and Ideology: Studies in English Writing 1765–1830*, ed. D. Aers, J. Cook, and D. Punter (London: Routledge & Kegan Paul, 1981), 7–26. Demonstrates the 'social concreteness' of Blake's work by tracing its theme of labour.

Heather Glen, *Vision and Disenchantment: Blake's* Songs *and Wordsworth's* Lyrical Ballads (Cambridge: Cambridge University Press, 1983). Addresses the political implications of Blake's *Songs*. Adopting the genre of eighteenth-century children's verse, Blake defeats, like Wordsworth, the contemporary reader's expectation of a controlling moral viewpoint. But contrary to Wordsworth's pessimism about human possibility, Blake portrays as existing, not utopian, the Innocent mode of relationship, 'which involves the self-realization and the mutuality of all'.

Jackie DiSalvo, *War of Titans: Blake's Critique of Milton and the Politics of Religion* (Pittsburgh, Pa.: University of Pittsburgh Press, 1983). Richly-contextualized Marxist–feminist statement of Blake's egalitarianism, attempting to reconcile Frye's totalizing Blake with Erdman's historicizing one: both celebratory and critical of Milton, Blake undercuts the elitist and patriarchal biases that contradict and qualify Milton's commitment to revolution.

Stewart Crehan, *Blake in Context* (Dublin: Gill and Macmillan, 1984). Polemically Marxist approach to Blake's social, historical and ideological context (taking 'context' especially as class content), so as to counter and critique his 'systematisers and literary source-hunters'.

Michael Ferber, *The Social Vision of William Blake* (Princeton: Princeton University Press, 1985). Fruitful ideological analysis, organized by topic, and celebrating Blake as a 'visionary socialist'; contends also that his social and political vision 'at several points . . . pitches beyond ideology into something more critical, universal, and true.'

****Edward Larrissy**, *William Blake* (Oxford: Blackwell, 1985). Short, accessible treatment of Blake as 'the greatest radical poet in English', emphasizing his radical Protestant background in his divided response to eighteenth-century liberalism and his conse-quent ambivalence about form, an ambivalence that denies the reader the security of authoritative intention, demanding, instead, the labour of interpretation.

Jerome J. McGann, *Towards a Literature of Knowledge* (Oxford: Clarendon Press, 1989). Blake's erasures on plate 3 of *Jerusalem* form the starting point of this argu-ment: for Blake, poetry is rhetorical rather than formal, 'communicative action' rather than representation. Blake's poetry deters us from 'facile interpretive translation'; it engages us in reciprocal transformations, materially exposing its own limits, and the limits of imagination.

Jon Mee, *Dangerous Enthusiasm: William Blake and the Culture of Radicalism in the 1790s* (Oxford: Clarendon Press, 1992). Focusing on Blake's works in the 1790s, turns from Erdman's emphasis on historical representation (content) to the radicalism of Blake's rhetorical practice, presented here as a 'bricolage', or heterogeneous combination, of four discourses: the millenarianism and antinomianism of a popular culture of reli-gious enthusiasm, literary primitivism, mythography, and scriptural criticism.

****E. P. Thompson**, *Witness against the Beast: William Blake and the Moral Law* (Cam-bridge: Cambridge University Press, 1993). Makes focal the Blake who is subtly present throughout *The Making of the English Working Class* (1963). Thompson lucidly expands on the importance to Blake's radicalism of the antinomian tradition of radical dissent, following 'the intellectual routes by which (through Blake) the antinomian tradition came to a conjunction with the Enlightenment and in particular with Jacobin thought, argued with it, and gave rise to the unique Blakean mutation.'

Steve Clark and David Worrall (eds.), *Historicizing Blake* (Basingstoke and London: Macmillan, 1994). Cultural-materialist counter to a perceived predominance of theory. The introduction usefully outlines the main positions of the historicist scholarship of Blake, while individual essays advance the historicizing of Blake 'on all fronts, not merely to see him within the "traditional" radical context, but also by avoiding unnecessary polarizations with mainstream eighteenth-century culture.'

Jackie DiSalvo, G. A. Rosso and Christopher Z. Hobson (eds.), *Blake, Politics, and History* (New York and London: Garland, 1998). Like *Historicizing Blake*, an important historical miscellany: 'seeks to promote a return to the political Blake; to deepen understanding of some of the conversations articulated in Blake's art by introducing new historical material or new interpretations of texts; and to highlight differing perspectives on Blake's politics among historically focused critics.' Includes essays on empire, slavery and gender.

Saree Makdisi, *Romantic Imperialism: Universal Empire and the Culture of Modernity* (Cambridge: Cambridge University Press, 1998). Presents Blake's vision of a Universal Empire – 'a global network of production and exploitation and a political and military system, together forming an indissoluble whole' – whose very unity, because it is a unity of oppressed peoples, can be turned against itself.

Nicholas M. Williams, *Ideology and Utopia in the Poetry of William Blake* (Cambridge: Cambridge University Press, 1998). Reading the major poetry alongside selected 'analogue texts', sets out to heal the divide between 'social' and 'aesthetic' approaches to Blake by showing the 'inter-implication' of ideology and utopia throughout his work. Only a utopian hermeneutic, which 'restores the full meaning of an image in its material context but also carries it to the utopian fulfilment which is its artistic destiny . . . can do justice to both elements of the Blakean text, the corporeal and the intellectual, the social and the apocalyptic, the ideological and the utopian.'

Jason Whittaker, *William Blake and the Myths of Britain* (Basingstoke and London: Macmillan, 1999). Shows in the figure of Albion, important especially to *Milton* and *Jerusalem*, Blake's radicalization of a neglected discourse of eighteenth-century antiquarian interest in British mythology and history.

Christopher Z. Hobson, *Blake and Homosexuality* (Basingstoke: Palgrave, 2000). Reading Blake's poetry – and his republican tradition – in the context of the history of homosexuality in the late eighteenth and early nineteenth centuries, traces, in Blake, a development towards 'a more complex understanding of gender relations in general and homosexuality in particular.'

TO THE PRESENT

Where the politicizing of Blake has extended to sexual politics, his radical standing has been more problematic. David's Aers's chapter, 'Blake: Sex, Society and Ideology' in *Romanticism and Ideology* asserts the radicalism of

Blake's 'understanding of the dialectics of sexual conflict and the internalisation of repressive ideologies by their victims', but also acknowledges the extent to which that understanding remains conditioned by the dominant ideology.[19] Less relenting positions on Blake's sexism have been taken, for instance, by Anne Mellor and Brenda Webster;[20] by contrast, Jackie DiSalvo's persuasive analysis of Blake's engagement with the Miltonic model in *War of Titans* is largely in Blake's favour. A useful brief overview up to the late 1990s, with a range of references, is contained in the introduction to *Blake, Politics, and History*.[21] Subsequently, Mary-Kelly Persyn has argued that 'Blake's treatment of the female, however faulty it may be in the end, speaks his own protest against the late eighteenth century's construction of female identity and possibility';[22] Christopher Hobson's account of Blake and gender, in *Blake and Homosexuality*, is similarly affirming.

Blake's stance on slavery and race, often discussed alongside his view of gender, is equally topical and challenging. In Erdman's reading, *The Visions of the Daughters of Albion* is an allegory or argument endorsing abolition and so attests to Blake's racial and sexual egalitarianism. In stark contrast, Anne Mellor's essay, 'Sex, Violence, and Slavery: Blake and Wollstonecraft' (1995), is typically pugnacious and uncompromising:

> . . . neither the verbal nor the visual representations of sex, violence, and slavery in *Visions of the Daughters of Albion* contests the racist or sexist dimensions of the Enlightenment discourse of Anglo-Africanism Blake inherited. . . . Insofar as the black body can be assimilated into the white body, the black man can enjoy the same 'rights' as the white man. Insofar as the female body gratifies the sexual and psychological desires of the male body, she achieves her freedom.[23]

On the other hand again, Marcus Wood's *Slavery, Empathy, and Pornography* (2002), argues judiciously and persuasively that *The Visions of the Daughters of Albion* and the ninth book of *Vala* consider, with 'a typical Blakean imaginative amplitude', 'the psychological damage which violent abuse within the slave systems exercised over both oppressor and victims';[24] Wood comments too on the implications and ironies of the use of 'The Little Black Boy' as abolition propaganda in the United States in the mid-nineteenth century. An extensive list of related prior criticism is provided in his footnotes. Also on the side of Blake is Saree Makdisi's *William Blake and the Impossible History of the 1790s* (2002), which treats slavery in the context of an argument that Orientalism is 'the key to the radical culture of the 1790s . . . to the culture of romanticism that emerged with it . . . [and] to Blake's divergence from both.'[25] Makdisi's view is challenged in turn in a 2005 article by Edward Larissy, who contends that 'there is some evidence that . . . the emerging discourse of Orientalism is to be found in Blake, too', although, 'At the same time, one should not overstate the case for Blake's acceptance of negative items in Orientalist discourse.'[26]

There remains to be discussed a substantial body of Blake criticism dating from the late 1980s, whose focus is not overridingly social or historical. New developments in critical and linguistic theory stimulated new kinds of attention to the linguistic and formal attributes of Blake's texts, so much so that the historicist approach found it necessary to position itself, at various stages, against the more 'theoretical' views described as dominating the field (see, for instance, the introductions to *Historicizing Blake* and *Blake, Politics, and History*). Today, the historical study of Blake is no longer subordinate to any other kind of critical attitude, and Erdman's enduring relevance is manifest.

If Erdman's study might be presented as complementing Frye's, in turn, to complement recent criticism which (polemically) defines itself as 'historical', I have chosen my third and final extract from a late twentieth-century publication in which Frye's relevance is explicitly reaffirmed. V. A. De Luca's *Words of Eternity: Blake and the Poetics of the Sublime* (1991) describes itself as 'a large-scale unfolding, in an updated critical context, of concerns contained explicitly or implicitly in a few dozen lambent and groundbreaking pages . . . of *Fearful Symmetry*'. Contributing to a range of arguments regarding coherence, discrepancy, and historical context, De Luca treats 'the assumptions and goals of Blake's aesthetic project in the terms of an expansive, idealized subjectivity', yet remains aware that 'the sublime ideology is a historically situated phenomenon like any other.' The following extract sets out his thesis of Blake's ambivalence to the eighteenth-century theorist of the sublime, Edmund Burke.

Extract from V. A. De Luca, *Words of Eternity: Blake and the Poetics of the Sublime* (1991)

Singular and Particular Detail: The Sublime of the Signifier

Blake's best-known remarks on the aesthetics of the sublime are contained in his annotations to the *Discourses* of Sir Joshua Reynolds. Here we observe him engaged in a running argument that focuses on the grand style itself, in which he is forced consciously to stake out positions on the subject in response to alternatives actually posed before him.[1] It is particularly significant, therefore, that Blake's only recorded reference to Edmund Burke and to the *Philosophical Enquiry into . . . the Sublime and Beautiful* should occur in these marginal jottings. These notes often seem to use Reynolds as the occasion for an attack directed specifically against Burke. While we have observed elements in Blake's views that are compatible with a Burkean framework, or at least with a tradition in which Burke's voice is conspicuous, the radical differences between the two writers' ideas of the sublime inevitably demand consideration.

Blake more or less identifies Burke as the baleful shadow behind Reynolds's own aberrations:

> Burke's Treatise on the Sublime & Beautiful is founded on the Opinion of Newton & Locke on this Treatise Reynolds has grounded many of his assertions. in all his Discourses I read Burkes Treatise when very Young at the same time I read Locke on Human Understanding & Bacons Advancement of Learning on Every one of these Books I wrote my Opinions & on looking them over find that my Notes on Reynolds in this Book are exactly Similar. I felt the Same Contempt & Abhorrence then; that I do now. They mock Inspiration and Vision[2]

It is scarcely necessary to dwell here on the obvious revulsion that Blake would feel toward the empiricism, associationism, physiological reductivism, and the psychology of self-interest that underpin Burke's theory of the sublime.[3] These, however, are not Blake's main objects of attack in the Annotations to Reynolds. He is more concerned with the epistemological character of Burke's sublime object itself. Burke's conception of sublime poetry as a form of deliberate indeterminacy seems very much on Blake's mind all along as he reads Reynolds. When Reynolds offers obscurity as 'one source of the sublime,' Burke's famous argument inevitably rises up before us:

> Poetry with all its obscurity, has a more general as well as a more powerful dominion over the passions than the other art [i.e., painting]. And I think there are reasons in nature why the obscure idea, when properly conveyed, should be more affecting than the clear. It is our ignorance of things that causes all our admiration, and chiefly excites our passions. Knowledge and acquaintance make the most striking causes affect but little. It is thus with the vulgar, and all men are as the vulgar in what they do not understand. The ideas of eternity, and infinity, are among the most affecting we have, and yet perhaps there is nothing of which we really understand so little, as of infinity and eternity.

> But let it be considered that hardly any thing can strike the mind with its greatness, which does not make some sort of approach towards infinity; which nothing can do whilst we are able to perceive its bounds; but to see an object distinctly, and to perceive its bounds, is one and the same thing. A clear idea is therefore another name for a little idea.[4]

These remarks are tantalizing because they mingle concepts that would be anathema to Blake with formulations that sound rather like some of his own. Blake would endorse the notion that poetry is a prime locus of the sublime experience. He would agree that 'to see an object distinctly, and to perceive its bounds, is one and the same thing'; indeed the terminology is virtually his own. Moreover, according to a dictum from one of his early tractates, 'The bounded is loathed by its possessor';[5] there is an implied antagonism between the bounded and man's desire for the infinite that consorts comfortably with Burke's view.

A profound gulf, however, separates Burke's notions of infinity from Blake's. As a Lockean empiricist, Burke must insist on our ignorance of infinity and eternity and restrict the understanding only to finite bodies. The infinite, for Burke, is precisely the absence of what we can know. Sublime objects, then, are merely knowable objects that pose as unknowable. They 'make some sort of approach towards infinity' by a process of subtraction, by strategically placed concealments of their bounds. Through the mediation of the indeterminate object, at once accessible and inaccessible, the void of the infinite becomes an implied plenum.[6] An undifferentiated vagueness or generality is therefore useful to Burke's sublime, 'because any difference, whether it be in the disposition, or in the figure, or even in the colour of the parts, is highly prejudicial to the idea of infinity, which every change must check and interrupt, at every alteration commencing a new series.'[7] An alternative mode of sublimity is to crowd the perceptual field excessively, so that it is all broken lines and broken masses: the poetic equivalents are the 'many descriptions in the poets and orators which owe their sublimity to a richness and profusion of images, in which the mind is so dazzled as to make it impossible to attend to that exact coherence and agreement of the allusions.'[8]

Blake will have none of this. The 'bounded' is indeed to be 'loathed' when what is bounded is the understanding itself, conceived by the empiricist as situated in a limited perceptual field of knowable objects circumscribed by a vast unknowable darkness. For Blake, 'some sort of approach towards infinity' from this perimeter is no approach worth speaking of; less than all cannot satisfy man. Taken together, Blake's comments on the sublime in the Reynolds Marginalia make the case for a plainly accessible infinite. They all revolve around the principles of particularity, determinacy, and discrimination – qualities essential for making the forms of the artistic surface distinctly visible to the Intellectual Powers:

> Minute Discrimination is Not Accidental All Sublimity is founded on Minute Discrimination

> Without Minute Neatness of Execution The Sublime cannot Exist! Grandeur of Ideas is founded on Precision of Ideas
>
> Singular & particular Detail is the Foundation of the Sublime
>
> Broken Colours & Broken Lines & Broken Masses are Equally Subversive of the Sublime
>
> Obscurity is Neither the Source of the Sublime nor of any Thing Else[9]

Blake's stress on particularity and distinctness as productive of the sublime may seem, as Weiskel has said, merely 'perverse,' an attempt to overthrow Burke by depriving his key terms of their ordinarily understood meaning.[10] Hence, it is important to note that within the general aesthetic debates of his time, Black speaks from a position of relative strength and within a widely established context. Burke's stance provoked opposition from many quarters, both when the *Philosophical Enquiry* first appeared and several generations thereafter. 'Distinctness of imagery has ever been held productive of the sublime,' insisted one of the reviewers in response to Burke's famous celebration of obscurity.[11] Similarly, in his 'Critical Dissertation on the Poems of Ossian,' Hugh Blair tells us that 'simplicity and conciseness, are never-failing characteristics of the stile of a sublime writer,' and that 'to be concise in description, is one thing; and to be general, is another. No description that rests in generals can possibly be good; it can convey no lively idea; for it is of particulars only that we have a distinct conception.'[12] Bishop Lowth presses much the same point repeatedly: 'the Hebrew poets have accomplished the sublime without losing perspicuity'; their 'imagery is well known, the use of it is common, the signification definite; they are therefore perspicuous, clear, and truly magnificent.' Lowth goes so far as to make perspicuity part of his definition of the sublime: 'that force of composition, whatever it be, which strikes and overpowers the mind, which excites the passions, and which expresses ideas at once with perspicuity and elevation'; and elsewhere he praises a passage in Deuteronomy on the grounds that it 'consists of sentences, pointed, energetic, concise, and splendid; that the sentiments are truly elevated and sublime, the language bright and animated, the expression and phraseology uncommon; while the mind of the poet never continues fixed to any single point, but glances continually from one object to another.'[13] Lowth senses in Hebrew style a kind of scintillating restlessness, a supercharged *pointillisme* ('sentences pointed, energetic, concise') that reminds us of effects rendered by the Blakean wall of words, discussed earlier, as well as of the luminous potential that Blake tells us resides in particular and determinate forms.

The opinions on this topic of Blake's contemporary, the antiquarian and mythographer Richard Payne Knight, are particularly worth pausing over for their relevance to Blake's own views. Knight's *Analytical Inquiry into the Principles of Taste* directs a stream of argument against Burke's *Philosophical Enquiry*:

> The peculiar business of poetry is so to elevate and expand [its objects] that the imagination may conceive *distinct* but not *determinate* ideas of them; and thus have an infinite liberty of still exalting and expanding, without changing or confounding the images impressed upon it. . . . All obscurity is imperfection; and indeed, if obscurity means indistinctness, it is always imperfection. The more distinct a description; and the more clearly the qualities, properties, and energies intended to be signified or expressed, are brought, as it were, before the eyes, the more effect it will have on the imagination and the passions: but then, it should be *distinct* without being *determinate*. In describing for instance, a storm at sea, the rolling, the curling, the foaming, the dashing, and roaring of the waves cannot be too clearly, too precisely expressed: but it should not be told how many yards in a minute they advanced.[14]

In opposing 'distinct' to 'determinate' ideas, Knight appears from a Blakean standpoint to be taking with one hand what he gives with the other, but the example supplied at the end of the passage alleviates this impression. By 'determinate,' Knight appears to mean 'measured' or 'quantifiable' rather than closed or definite. Knight's distinctness is indeed close to Blake's determinacy – and, like Blake, he stresses those elements in the sublime image that give it its *character*, or special form, and eliminates those elements that limit the object to the occasional, the material, or what Blake calls the 'Accidental,' the stuff of 'number, weight, & measure' (*The Marriage of Heaven and Hell* Plate 7, L. 14). For Knight, the mind is not exalted and expanded by confronting a bloated indefiniteness. Rather, it must be pierced by the sharpness of the image, and only then can it expand in an indefinite liberty.

These various formulations – Lowth's splendid and pointed sentences, Blair's 'lively' ideas, or Payne Knight's distinctly clear rolling waves – all pose a sublime based on salience or concentrated force against the Burkean sublime of perceptual deprivation and diffusion. This sublime substitutes intensity for extensiveness – it cuts more sharply and more deeply, vibrates more intensely, and compresses its power more minutely than anything that our ordinary senses provide.[15] This mode subsumes what Morton Paley has called 'the sublime of energy,'[16] and it operates not only in energy's domain of the body but also in the domain of the text, or wherever the multiple and the multifaceted are made altogether manifest in a little moment or a little space. In his

Annotations to Reynolds, Blake provides the most articulate and cogent formulation of this notion of the sublime. When Lowth or Payne Knight call for perspicuity and distinctness in sublime poetry, they do so in part because they think that it will bring the object more sharply into focus; the poet's style is like a pair of new eyeglasses for the myopic imagination. Blake goes beyond such writers in proclaiming the sublimity of determinacy, particularity, and discrimination for their own sake. They are valued not because they make objects more clear, but because they are the 'real' constituents of objects. Indeed, Blake's prescriptions are too rigorous for even the most sharp-edged mimesis of objects to satisfy. Blake calls for a total determinacy, or closure of outline; a total particularity, or representation of all the parts – indeed, all the particles of the image; and a total discrimination or singularity – that is, the separation and differentiation of the image from every other contiguous image. No ordinary perception or ordinary description, however acute, can meet such requirements. In three-dimensional space, objects hide portions of themselves, crowd on one another's outlines, and break their masses, those nearby obscuring those farther away, all distorted by perspective. Nothing in this space can supply the 'lineaments, or forms and features that are capable of being receptacles of intellect.' There are only crowded absences here, not presence.

In his visual art, Blake's stylistic manner of flattening the picture plane and disposing his figures in a 'symmetrical frontality' serves, as W.J.T. Mitchell has pointed out, to minimize these defects of natural seeing. Blake is striving 'to undercut the representational appearance of partricular forms and to endow them with an abstract, stylized existence independent of the natural images with which they are identified.' In essence, as Mitchell's study has effectively shown, 'Blake's visual images move toward the realm of language, operatring as arbitrary signs, emblems, or hieroglyphics.'[17] All lines, pictorial and otherwise, are absorbed into the idea of text, an autonomous structure of writing that is anterior to possible referentiality. The particularity, determinacy, and singularity of language are to be found in its signifers, not in the indefinite plurality and ambiguity of its signifeds. The signifier is finite and, at the same time, 'polyvalent,' or endowed with a surplus of signifying potential in relation to any given signified.[18] 'Not a line is drawn without intention & that most discriminate & particular as Poetry admits not a Letter that is Insignificant so Painting admits not a Grain of Sand or a Blade of Grass Insignificant'.[19] Every line, letter, or grain is 'significant' in the sense that it is impressed with a self-subsistent signifying power, which is its principal glory. Blake's reference to the letter indicates that his interest here is in the forms as signifiers, and not in what they signify

(see the famous crux in *Jerusalem* 3: 'every letter is studied'). The world
of artifacts affords nothing more absolutely and exclusively linear,
minute, determinate, particular, individuated, and differentiated than a
graphic sign or letter. Because it imitates nothing and cannot be represented at all unless all its parts are inscribed completely, the form of a
letter is both perfect and particular, definite and yet open to countless
participations in potential reference. We may speak of the determinate
sublime, then, as a sublime of the signifier, one in which exhilaration
comes from recognition of the creative power of the letter. Behind
the letter resides an unnamed and, to fallen eyes, unseen exactitude,
for which the abstract term 'human intellect' passes as a secular
designation.[20]

Problems remain, however, in this account of Blake's sublime. How
is one to reconcile, after all, the 'indeterminacy' of the sublime moment
with the specification that the sublime image must be 'determinate'?
How indeed does a sublime that requires something 'altogether hidden'
consort with one that banishes obscurity as its source? For all the harsh
attacks on Burke, we may still sense the presence of a Burkean magnetic
field tugging at the needle of Blake's aesthetic compass. Conversely, if
Burke were to scan some knotty, congested passages from Blake's Prophecies, he certainly could not fault them for lack of obscurity or for a
display of 'little ideas.' Even the characters of Blake's script sometimes
fall short of an absolute formal determinacy, so that it is not always easy
for an editor to decide what letter or mark of punctuation in a given
passage is intended. While Blake's poetic and artistic practice is intellectually directed against Burkean assumptions and precepts, it often
betrays a certain fondness for Burkean effects. Compared to Addison,
for example, who finds the Roman Pantheon more sublime than a
Gothic cathedral,[21] Burke and Blake seem to belong to the same camp:
they are unavoidably allied as advocates of a problematic and agonistic
sublime.

It is not in the matter of occasion or of agency that Blake and Burke
differ in their conceptions of the sublime. They both provide a structure
that includes a moment of discontinuity – the episode of 'astonishment'
– and a psychic effect in which the mind becomes self-divided. They
differ in that Blake recognizes the means for a *more thorough* discontinuity and a more radical division of the faculties. Nothing can be more
discontinuous with its surroundings than what is altogether determinate,
particular, and distinct in itself. The more that Blake withholds from
his texts those concessions to referentiality that create the illusion of
representing objects known to our understanding – such as syntactic and
narrative continuity, familiarity of allusion, and the like – the more his

words, letters, and lines take on a distinct intensity of their own, and the more thoroughly they recede from the grasp of the Corporeal Understanding. Yet they do so without any sacrifice to their intrinsic clarity of form. The sublime text must be a clear yet difficult text, its clarity based not on mundane simplicities, but indeed turned severely against them. The element of indeterminacy in the sublime of the text rests not at all with the sublime image itself, but with the expectations of the perceiver, conditioned to encounter signifiers that efface their own presence, the better to operate as servants of referentiality. This is one element of the difficulty involved in the determinate sublime, but obscurity, in the Burkean sense, is not the producer of this difficulty.[22] There is a difference between the obscurity that hides outlines like a formless vapor, demanding difficult and ultimately frustrated labor of attempted penetration, and the burden of a text that imposes on the perceiver the difficulty of apprehending many condensed visions of clarity all at once, none of them hidden; if there is blinding here, it is from an overdeterminate clarity of *presence*.[23] What are present, of course, are the seeds of meaning, not the external meanings themselves. Interpretive labors are still required to fetch these, but if the text is truly efficacious, the sublime event will have occurred before these labors begin. There is difficulty in this event too, perhaps greater than that involved in any of the subsequent labor. This is the struggle with a self that is impatient with discontinuity and paradox, demanding a servitude of language to familiar referentiality. Self-annihilation is the key here, as it is with so much else in Blake. When that is accomplished, paradox becomes visionary freedom and the recalcitrance of the text becomes the autonomy of a respected friend, a companion in the dialectic of desire.

The Poet's Work: His Sublime and His Pathos

'When that is accomplished': it is a tall order. Self-annihilation presumably provides the bridge between 'the Most Sublime Poetry' and the altruism of 'The most sublime act,' which, as Blake states in the Proverbs of Hell, 'is to set another before you' (*The Marriage of Heaven and Hell* plate 7, L. 17). The sublime *experience* must eventuate in a sublime *doing*, or else the interplay of intellect and its self-satisfying desire remains a sterile and narcissistic exercise, quite alien to anything we know of Blake's program. But the subjugation of self and the act of setting another before oneself are problematic processes; to an observer they may as easily provoke a new sublime of terror as provide intimations of altruistic love. Take, for example, Los's famous *agon* with his Spectre in the first chapter of *Jerusalem*:

> Yet ceased he not from labouring at the roarings of his Forge
> With iron & brass Building Golgonooza in great contendings
> Till his Sons & Daughters came forth from the Furnaces
> At the sublime Labours for Los. compelld the invisible Spectre
> To labours mighty, with vast strength
>   *Jerusalem*, plate 10, L. 62–plate 11, L. 1

Los labors here not in order to achieve the sublime experience but because he has already experienced it; he has had access to the Divine Vision and, indeed, keeps it (see *Jerusalem*, plate 95, L. 20). His work is both productive and altruistic, simultaneously paternal and maternal, as Blake suggests by projecting from the word 'Labours' both the products of the womb ('Sons & Daughters') and those of the wage-earning factory artisan. The language of the passage, however, rigorously excludes any overt hint of the loving, the maternal, the soft, the yielding; it is redolent of the hard, muscular, contentious imagery of a masculine world ('roarings,' 'iron & brass,' 'great contendings,' 'compelld,' 'mighty,' 'strength'). If this is a sublime, it is a sublime that meets Burkean prescriptions – or, to use Blake's own words, a Sublime . . . shut out from the Pathos (*Jerusalem*, plate 90, L. 12).

My general point is that Blake often finds it difficult to depict his actors in anything other than a sublime mode that they themselves are ostensibly trying to transcend. This is part of a larger problem attendant upon any production of sublime poetry that has a redemptive purpose: the recalcitrance of corporeal existence in time to which the poet must return after his own moment of astonishment and transformation. Ideally, 'the Poets Work is Done . . . Within a Moment: a Pulsation of the Artery' (*Milton*, plate 29, LL. 1–3), but after that moment has passed, the poet must face the fact that although 'the Work' is done, the necessity of further labor is ongoing and unremitting ('yet ceased he not from labouring'). A posture of heroic endurance is required, which tends to bring with it, in what is supposed to be a labor of love, a disquieting rhetoric of force and compulsion. What goes for poets goes for readers alike; too often, after their own sublime encounter with the Blakean text, in their eagerness to spread the good news they turn into aggressive banner-wavers, relentless explicators, or imperious system builders, as anyone acquainted with the history of Blake criticism can easily attest. The essence of the sublime experience is that it offers *all*, a total gratification of desire to the Intellectual Powers, but the communication of that experience (whether by poets or by readers) too readily operates on a principle of *exclusion*, a casting out of the indulgent, the accommodating, the softer 'feminine' affections.

Blake is thoroughly aware of this disturbing paradox and the shadow it casts on the efficacy of a 'Most Sublime Poetry,' and we may conclude this chapter on his conception of the sublime by examining the ways in which he articulates the problem. We are sometimes told that Blake has no distinct concept of the sublime as a separate category of aesthetic experience, that he uses the term as an indiscriminate epithet of praise, and that he conflates the categories of the sublime and the beautiful at will.[24] Although conflations of this sort do occur at certain points in his work, the fact remains that Blake displays a perfect conversance with the terminology of aesthetic categorization in his day. The categories are listed, for example, with their anatomical seats of origin, in this Proverb of Hell: 'The head Sublime, the heart Pathos, the genitals Beauty, the hands & feet Proportion' (*The Marriage of Heaven and Hell*, plate 10, L. 1). Later in his career he develops a strong preoccupation with these categories, particularly the two chief contraries, the sublime and the pathetic (often subsumed in contemporary accounts by the beautiful). Thus we may infer from some cancelled lines on the frontispiece to *Jerusalem* that he originally intended to make the separation of sublimity from pathos the very argument of his great poetic *summa*. This inference is corroborated by a remarkable account in *A Descriptive Catalogue* of a 'voluminous' work on 'a subject of great sublimity and pathos' (almost certainly *Jerusalem*), which his painting 'The Ancient Britons' was designed to illustrate. It is worth pausing over this account, for it reveals more clearly than anything else in Blake's work a sense of the sublime as a category of limitation or exclusion – not an *all*, but a residue of something prior and greater, for which no aesthetic term is available.

The discussion of the Ancient Britons strangely converts a myth of the origins of history into an allegory of the genesis of aesthetic categories; the myth not only projects 'sublimity and pathos,' it is *about* sublimity and pathos:

> The three general classes of men who are represented by the most Beautiful, the most Strong, and the most Ugly, could not be represented by any historical facts but those of our own country, the Ancient Britons; . . . They were overwhelmed by brutal arms all but a small remnant; Strength, Beauty, and Ugliness escaped the wreck, and remain for ever unsubdued age after age. . . . The Strong man represents the human sublime. The Beautiful man represents the human pathetic, which was in the wars of Eden divided into male and female. The Ugly man represents the human reason. They were originally one man, who was fourfold; he was self-divided, and his real humanity slain on the stems of generation, and the form of the fourth was like the Son of God. How he became divided is a subject of great sublimity and pathos. (*Descriptive Catalogue*)[25]

We are uneasily aware that the 'human sublime' offered to us here is something different from notions of the sublime discussed earlier in this chapter, as deduced from the letter to Butts or the annotations to Reynolds. In those instances, the sublime appears to be a term for an absolute height of value toward which all art must tend; here, it merely connotes one *kind* of aesthetic value among others, existing on a par with other competing values, such as those of the beautiful and the pathetic. In the latter case, the sublime serves as a term of differentiation, just as the terms 'male' and 'female' differentiate subsets of humanity. Some background is useful at this point. Throughout the eighteenth century, ideas of the beautiful and the pathetic tend to separate out from the idea of the sublime.[26] At the same time, as Monk has shown, the pathetic comes increasingly to signify the softer affections aroused by the pitiable and the endearing.[27] Meanwhile, the beautiful tends to lose its ancient conventional association with harmony and proportion, and to acquire feminine sexual connotations. Burke's treatise on the sublime and the beautiful is particularly influential in this latter development. He specifically rejects proportion as the source of beauty and locates it instead in the small, the physically unthreatening, the smooth, and gently curvaceous, all essentially female attributes that, he writes, comprise 'the physical cause of love.' The pathetic and the beautiful thus converge upon a common eroticized femininity. Massive, strong, threatening, rugged, and angular, the sublime is obviously conceived as a contrasting male counterpart.[28] Blake himself shows a post-Burkean understanding of beauty when, in the Proverb from the *Marriage* quoted previously, he specifically divorces proportion from beauty, and locates the latter in the genitals. Likewise, in the account of the Ancient Britons, he accepts the assimilation of pathos and beauty: 'The Beautiful man represents the human pathetic,' and in the fall, this Ancient Briton evolves a female double. Blake substitutes *pathos* for Burke's beauty as the effective contrary term to the sublime ('the human *sublime*,' 'the human *pathetic*'), but he perpetuates the identification of the contraries as masculine and feminine principles.

In his account of the Ancient Britons, Blake categorizes these principles, yet tends to blur the distinctions between them. Among the Ancient Britons there are, after all, no separate females; all three are men. Moreover, some of their attributes tend to slide into one another: the human pathetic is Beautiful, and there is a Beauty 'proper to sublime art' – namely, 'lineaments, or forms and features that are capable of being the receptacles of intellect'.[29] Blake describes his Strong man, the human sublime itself, 'as a receptacle of Wisdom, a sublime energizer; his features and limbs do not spindle out into length, without strength, nor are they too large and unwieldy for his brain and bosom. Strength consists in accumulation of power to the principal seat, and from thence a regular gradation and subordination; strength is compactness, not extent nor bulk'.[30] Strength is, of course, a conventional attribute of the Burkean sublime, but here it is difficult to distinguish from Beauty; if one is a 'receptacle of intellect,' the other is a 'receptacle of Wisdom.' Moreover, the description of Strength, focuses, oddly enough, almost entirely on classical proportion ('regular gradation and subordination') – the traditional criterion for beauty itself, until Burke banished it in favor of a quasi-feminized form. Beauty is thus defined in terms that belong properly to the sublime ('the head Sublime'), and the human sublime is described in terms traditionally proper to beauty. They interpenetrate in a latently erotic union, as compact strength energizes itself within a receptacle of lineaments – lineaments of gratified desire, perhaps.

They interpenetrate, and yet they do not. If the sublime, the beautiful, and the pathetic are one, why establish them as separate personifications in the first place? And why attach these figures to a myth that discovers them to be already diminished forces? For the Strong man, the Beautiful man, and the Ugly man 'were originally one man, who was fourfold; . . . and the form of the fourth was like the Son of God.' If the Strong man is the human sublime, who is this fourth, who, according to the myth, vanished 'In the last Battle of King Arthur [when] only Three Britons escaped'?[31] Indeed, who is the 'one man' whose 'real humanity' was slain? The 'human' of the terms 'human sublime' and 'human pathetic' appears to be something less than 'real humanity,' just as three is an inescapable reduction of four.

Blake would like to have it both ways on this matter. He would like to imagine the three Britons as a small, indefatigable remnant, perpetuating in corporeal time and space the plenary powers of humanity that existed before the fall: 'a small remnant; Strength, Beauty, and Ugliness escaped the wreck, and remain for ever unsubdued, age after age'[32] Thus when he comes to 'say something concerning his ideas of Beauty, Strength and Ugliness,'[33] he presents at least two of these in the interchangeable terms that would have been proper to their ideal status in eternity. The Ugly man, meanwhile, has already taken on the look and actions of lupine or tigerish savagery prominent in the eighteenth-century sublime of terror: 'approaching to the beast in features and form, his forehead small, without frontals; his jaws large; nose high on the ridge, and narrow; . . . The Ugly Man acts from love of carnage, and delight in the savage barbarities of war'.[34] Clearly, there is no perpetuation of a prelapsarian sensibility here. Blake's painting of the ancient Britons thus depicts gradations of fallenness; some residues of the fall have separated farther from the lineaments of intellect and gratified desire than others, but all are separate and diminished to some degree. It is only a matter of time before the Strong man, the human sublime, becomes no more than the brawny, cavern-dwelling '*strong* Urthona' depicted in the early Lambeth books, or the raging, despairing, indefinitely formed Tharmas, 'Parent *power* darkning in the West'. These are mock strengths and mock powers – for the human sublime when it is cut off from pathos, or the love of intellect for form, becomes an elaborate masquerade for despair.

This latter stage of separation is presented in two important passages from *Jerusalem*, briefly cited previously. One of these is from the cancelled inscription on the frontispiece:

> His Sublime & Pathos become Two Rocks fixd in the Earth
> His Reason his Spectrous Power, covers them above
> Jerusalem his Emanation is a Stone laying beneath

Another version of this scene appears late in the poem:

> no more the Masculine mingles
> With the Feminine. but the sublime is shut out from the Pathos
> In howling torment, to build stone walls of separation, compelling
> The Pathos, to weave curtains of hiding secrecy from the torment.

These passages raise the paradoxical idea of a *deprived* sublime, one that is 'shut out' from other forms of sensibility, a sublime that is petrified and, in short, fallen. In the first of these passages, the human reason has advanced to sovereignty over the other faculties. In the second, the 'stone walls of separation' and the curtain of secrecy that the sublime and the pathos place before one another look suspiciously like those thwartings, or barriers, or obscurities that figure so largely in eighteenth-century accounts of the sublime as a mode of deprivation – a view found in its most rationalist form in Burke. A sublime of deprivation becomes automatically a sublime that puts itself in reason's spectrous power, for it requires that we reason the idea of strength or power into being through negative tokens – withdrawals, resistances, incomplete disclosures. But what has really withdrawn is not 'the great' (as Addison called the sublime experience), but rather something so deeply hidden that its absence is unremarked because its appeal is buried (like the Emanation Jerusalem 'laying beneath') or forgotten. The mind's deep quest is for receptacles of intellect, the total gratification of desire in definite, permanent form.

Weiskel has found anxiety at the core of the eighteenth-century fascination with the sublime, 'the anxiety of nothingness, or absence. In its more energetic rendition the sublime is a kind of homeopathic therapy, a cure of uneasiness by means of the stronger, more concentrated – but momentary – anxiety involved in astonishment and terror.'[35] But the unease is never really cured, which is why sublime poems of the period often have to repeat their heightened moments again and again.[36] It is not cured because the true source of the mind's deprivation is concealed from it. The mind is induced into believing that it is deprived from access to 'the great,' and so it dreams up strategies for discovering itself equal or superior to this 'great' – empty strategies from Blake's point of view, for this great does not exist, it is 'not extent nor bulk.' All the while, however, the anxiety, the unease, the stirrings of an unacknowledged desire continue, prompting the mind to ever-renewed feats of grandeur, new 'highs.' The Burkean sublime is despair ('howling torment') that thinks itself to be a plenitude of strength.

The masculinist language of the Burkean sublime is important in this context. When Blake paraphrases the separation of the sublime and the pathos as 'no more the Masuline mingles with the Feminine,' he refers, of course, not to actual men and women. If the masculine mingles no more with the feminine, it is not for lack of physical congress, but rather for lack of something more truly fulfilling. The masculine and feminine principles within the self, which comprise the love dialogue between creative intellect and formal lineaments, have become sundered, so that love is sought in one place and transcendence or the sublime in another, in a masculinist framework divorced from the fulfillment of erotic desire. More accurately, the desires are not quelled, but simply shifted elsewhere. Burke speaks of the softer affections with considerable condescension: 'love approaches much nearer to contempt than is commonly imagined,' and Frances Ferguson has noted Burke's oddly ennervating conception about sexual arousal and the effects of beauty.[37] One reason for this is that the full language of Eros is transferred to another encounter – that with the masculine sublime. Admiration, and then erotic intensity, become attached to strength and bulk. When Burke, describing 'the passion caused by the sublime,' tells us that it 'hurries us on by an irresistible force' and leaves a mind 'entirely filled with its object,'[38] he employs the language of ravishment and reveals the latently homoerotic discourse that underpins much of his aesthetics. In the fall, one forgets what one loves – even though the desire for it remains. To vie in muscular, rocklike strength against the vast rock-face of 'the great' allows one to forget one's loss; it is a transaction that can assimilate desire in a form in which it need not be recognized as such.

As is frequently noted, Blake, too, privileges masculine imagery in his designs and masculine forms of action in his poetry. Even his type of the human Pathetic, is, before an unfortunate postlapsarian division into sexes, a Beautiful *man*. Some recent critics have called attention to homosexual imagery in certain of Blake's designs. Perhaps one purpose of these displays of eroticized male forms in his work is to expose the latent argument of conventional eighteenth-century sublime aesthetics to plain sight.[39] The object of the exposé is not the homoeroticism per se of the Burkean sublime, but rather its structure of subterfuge and displacement. Blake decodes the attraction to male dominance, cloudily concealed in an abstract discourse about 'the great,' by offering clearly delineated, unadorned masculine images of potency and action.

But there is also a more positive impulse at work in Blake's privileging of male form. Strength, struggle, and contest all play a genuine part in the constellation of qualities that he values, because they are all necessary to break down conventional modes of understanding. In the Edenic state, the sublime and the pathetic presumably disappear as separate modes of aesthetic experience and reappear joined in an intellectual form neither male or female. But few readers are already in the Edenic state when they come to Blake, nor would they need the mediation of his art if they were so. The figure of the eroticized male mediates by destabilizing conventional norms of gender polarization, and hence it starts to undo the fall. It thus functions like the Blakean text itself. Blake requires a text that evokes a psychology of response similar to that of the Burkean sublime while presenting an altogether different set of rewards. Hence, he is willing to let a kind of separatist or masculinist aesthetic prevail provisionally in his work, one that defers easy gratification and subjects the reader to various forms of muscular rough treatment – assault on the senses, indecorum, deprivation of the corporeal understanding, unending challenge. The well-delineated muscularity of his masculine images thus serves as a visible epitome of this textual activity.

These images, as images, remain nonetheless a mode of sublimity shut out from the pathos. Yet it is not a sublimity that we can afford to pass unalarmed – as Wordsworth, to Blake's dismay, claimed to do with Jehovah and his shouting angels.[40] The human sublime needs the sublime of greatness and potent terror as a necessary foil, as a first term in a process of educative reading. Let us recall the scene from the cancelled frontispiece of *Jerusalem*, in which a spectrous reason hovers over the two rocks of the sublime and the pathetic, imposed on top of a buried Jerusalem. Once located in the position of the keystone over the arch whereby we enter the poem, the lines plausibly may contain hints to direct our own reading of the poem. We are allowed to see the spectre hovering over the rocky landscape as a rationalist reader might pore over the plates of Blake's sublime allegory. What this reader sees are isolated and ill-defined shapes that he can recognize from the context of eighteenth-century aesthetics – a knottily muscular, surly sublime and an unrefined mass of pathos, a bundle of soft, ineffectual emotions. Both forms emerge murkily from the *Jerusalem* text itself, a stone slab, a plate of scratched metal, a table impressed with a crowd of dead signs. What the spectrous reader does not see is Jerusalem the Emanation, the form of gratified desire, which is a living text.

When Blake cancelled this passage from the frontispiece, so that in all extant copies we enter the gate of the poem wordlessly, he deprived us of these emblematic hints of how to read it. It is one thing to be shown the reasoning spectre reading badly, and quite another to be catapulted directly into the work without posted warnings regarding the spectrous reader in ourselves. This spectrous reader must be conjured up time after time until at last, in our floundering reading of the text, we read *him* and read his sublime (which has been ours until this point) as the vast funerary monument to a displaced erotic desire. Blake forces us to reenact these spectrous readings, to relive these ravishments by 'the great,' or finally to reject them. The arena for these choices and challenges is in that sum of particular signifying acts and forms that we call the poet's style. On the level of style, as well as of idea, there are two sublimes, one darkly mimicking the other – or, rather, in its rough, separately masculine fashion, memorializing the other, namely the lost but potentially recoverable sublime of intellect. Blake treats the Burkean style of the sublime as Los might treat his spectrous brother; it is appropriated, assimilated, hated, and perhaps secretly loved, but ultimately made present as a negation, the better to reveal the outlines of a new, emergent style.

Notes

1   It is always important to keep in mind the degree of serious deliberation involved in Blake's annotations to Reynolds. The annotated British Library copy of Reynolds's *Works* (the first volume of the three-volume second edition of 1798) contains page after page on which Blake's comments are drafted lightly in pencil and then retraced carefully in ink. Blake presumably considered his marginalia an 'official' combat against Reynolds's errors, waged on the very site of their perpetration.

2 William Blake, *The Complete Poetry and Prose of William Blake*, newly revised edition, ed. David V. Erdman, with Commentary by Harold Bloom (Garden City, NY: Anchor Press/Doubleday, 1982), 660.

3 E.g., as the agency of the sublime experience, Burke proposes 'an unnatural tension and certain violent emotions of the nerves,' and he accounts for the delight produced by the sublime as 'a sort of tranquility tinged with terror; which as it belongs to self-preservation is one of the strongest of all the passions'. See Edmund Burke, *A Philosophical Enquiry into the Origin of our Ideas of the Sublime and Beautiful*, ed. J. T. Boulton (London: Routledge and Kegan Paul), 134 and 136. Blake is perhaps indebted directly to Burke for his phrase 'Corporeal Understanding': 'It is probable,' Burke writes, 'that not only the inferior parts of the soul, as the passions are called, but the understanding itself makes use of some fine corporeal instruments in its operation' (ibid., 135).

4 Ibid., 61 and 63.

5 *There is No Natural Religion*: Blake, *Complete Poetry and Prose*, 2.

6 As Weiskel summarizes it, 'the soul is a vacancy, whose extent is discovered as it is filled. Inner space, the infinitude of the Romantic mind, is born as a massive and more or less unconscious emptiness, an absence'. Thomas Weiskel, *The Romantic Sublime: Studies in the Structure and Psychology of Transcendence* (Baltimore: Johns Hopkins University Press, 1976), 15. Ernest Tuveson, 'Space, Deity, and the Natural Sublime' (*Modern Language Quarterly* [March 1951]: 20–38) traces the eighteenth-century tendency to identify the physical preserves of God with outer space itself.

7 *Philosophical Enquiry*, 75.

8 Ibid., 78.

9 Blake, *Complete Poetry and Prose*, 643, 646, 647, 652, 658.

10 *The Romantic Sublime*, 67.

11 See *The Monthly Review* 16 (May 1757): 477n.

12 Hugh Blair, 'A Critical Dissertation on the Poems of Ossian', in *The Poems of Ossian*, trans. James Macpherson, 2 vols. (London: W. Strahan and T. Cadell, 1773). vol. 2, 423 and 385.

13 Robert Lowth, *Lectures on the Sacred Poetry of the Hebrews*, trans. G. Gregory, 2 vols. (London: J. Johnson, 1787), vol. 1, 120, 131, 307, and 325.

14 Richard Payne Knight, *An Analytical Inquiry into the Principles of Taste*, 3d ed. (London: T. Payne and J. White, 1808), 391–2.

15 Cf. Knight on Greek poetry: 'The obscurity of the lyric style of Pindar and the Greek tragedians does not arise from any confusion or indistinctness in the imagery; but from its conciseness and abruptness; and from its being shown to the mind in sudden flashes and corruscations, the connexion between which is often scarcely perceptible' (*Analytical Inquiry*, 401).

16 See Paley, *Energy and the Imagination*, 3–11.

17 Mitchell, *Blake's Composite Art*, 19, 37, and 4.

18 The best discussion of polyvalence or 'polysemy' of signification in Blake is to be found in Hilton, *Literal Imagination*, 10–18.

19 *A Vision of the Last Judgement*: Blake, *Complete Poetry and Prose*, 560.

20   Morris Eaves observes that 'metaphors of precision have very close relatives . . . in teleological metaphors of ultimate truth, of final distinctions, in Christian theology. A universal man – a man who is the universe, such as the figure of Christ who appears at the beginning of Revelation as a conglomerate of divinity-humanity-animal-vegetable-mineral – carries out the Last Judgment with a two-edged sword as his organ of discourse'; see *William Blake's Theory of Art* (Princeton: Princeton University Press, 1982), 20. Speaking more specifically of Blake's small units of language – words – Nelson Hilton says that 'the more deliberately the word is perceived, the more it begins to assert itself – to spell itself out – in all its associations and etymology, its eternal human form. . . . Every word is a parable about linguistic structure as incarnate human imagination' (*Literal Imagination*, 7).

21   Joseph Addison, *Works of Joseph Addison*, 6 vols. (London: T. Cadell and W. Davies, 1811). vol 5, 350ff.

22   See Wittreich, *Angel of Apocalypse*, 188. Wittreich tells us that Blake rejects 'obscurity as opacity,' the obscurity of the Burkean sublime (187). Blake's work demands a complexity of seeing, but this is not the same thing as hindered seeing, which the term 'obscurity' implies. The Corporeal Understanding is hindered not so much by obscurities that the poet imposes as by its own false presuppositions.

23   In 'The Sublime Poem: Pictures and Powers' (*Yale Review* 58 [Winter 1969]: 211), Martin Price, speaking of Blake's occasional pileups of small, sharply visualized details, comments on 'the closeness of attention that all but obliterates the outlines of the natural object in its familiar form, finding in it the effluence of vast powers and rising in wonder to a contemplation of those powers through the object.'

24   See Weiskel, *The Romantic Sublime*, 67.

25   Blake, *Complete Poetry and Prose*, 542–3.

26   For Longinus, the Pathetic 'or the Power of raising passions to a violent and even enthusiastic degree' was an extremely important, though not a necessary, constituent of the sublime (see Dionysus Longinus, *Essay on the Sublime*, trans. William Smith [London: 1756], 17–18). By the first decade of the eighteenth century, John Dennis so fully identifies the sublime with the 'Enthusiastick Passion' that he even takes Longinus to task for suggesting that the sublime can do without it (see *The Grounds of Criticism in Poetry* [London: G. Strahan, 1704], 78). Late in the century, however, the sublime and the pathetic have become quite distinct, as Johnson's comment on the Metaphysical poets serves to indicate: 'Nor was the sublime more within their reach than the pathetick' (Samuel Johnson, *Lives of the English Poets*, ed. G. B. Hill, 3 vols. [Oxford: Clarendon Press, 1905], vol. 1, 20).

27   See Samuel H. Monk, *The Sublime: A Study of Critical Theories in XVIII-Century England* (New York: Modern Language Assocation, 1935), 13 and Paley, *The Continuing City*, 58. Paley provides a good account of Blake's references to the pathetic, particularly with regard to *Jerusalem* (see *The Continuing City*, 58ff.).

28   On female beauty, physical love, and masculine traits, see, respectively, *Philosophical Enquiry*, 115, 151, and 124–5.

29   Blake, *Complete Poetry and Prose*, 544.
30   Ibid., 545.
31   Ibid., 542.
32   Ibid., 542.
33   Ibid., 544.
34   Ibid., 544–5. Dennis is seminal in considering ferocious wild beasts – 'Monsters, Serpents, Lions, Tygers' – as appropriate subjects for arousing 'Enthusiastick Terrour' and, hence, the sublime (*Grounds of Criticism*, 87–8). The sublime, Burke tells us in remarks perhaps not lost on the author of 'The Tyger,' 'comes upon us in the gloomy forest, and in the howling wilderness, in the form of the lion, the tiger, the panther, or rhinoceros.' He adds that 'on account of their unmanageable fierceness, the idea of a wolf is not despicable; it is not excluded from grand descriptions and similitudes' (*Philosophical Enquiry*, 66 and 67). Burke may have in mind the famous and bloodcurdling passage on the ravenous mountain wolves, in James Thomson's 'Winter,' lines 388–413.
35   *The Romantic Sublime*, 18.
36   See, for example, Thomson's unappeasable appetite for introducing catastrophe after catastrophe in *The Seasons*, even in the generally benign contexts of 'Spring' and 'Summer'; on the verbal level, a similar effect is achieved by the jerky, unremittingly exclamatory style of Edward Young's *Night Thoughts*.
37   See Burke, *Philosophical Enquiry*, 67 and Frances Ferguson, 'The Sublime of Edmund Burke, or the Bathos of Experience', *Glyph* 8 (1981), 75–6.
38   *Philosophical Enquiry*, 57.
39   Martin Price has noted that the 'homosexual fantasy' evident in some eighteenth-century Gothic novels ('sublime beauties colored by guilt and ambivalent desire') is connected to 'the summoning up of titanic energies from their caves of suppression' ('The Sublime Poem,' 205). Lately some note has been taken of homoerotic elements in Blake's own work; e.g., Susan Fox, *Poetic Form in Blake's 'Milton'*, 228–9, and W. J. T. Mitchell, 'Style and Iconography in the Illustrations of Blake's Milton,' in *Blake Studies* 6 (Fall 1973): 66–7, raise the question of certain designs in *Milton*; and in her sometimes heavy-handed Freudian study *Blake's Prophetic Psychology* (London: Macmillan Press, 1983), Brenda S. Webster reads these designs as unmistakably homosexual, interpreting them as the poet's quest to acquire the potency of an idealized male muse (261–2). *Milton* is, of course, the work par excellence in which the Poet is overtaken by the 'irresistible' force of the sublime moment.
40   See the famous passage from Wordsworth's 'Prospectus' to *The Excursion*, lines 31–35, and Blake's marginal retort (Blake, *Complete Poetry and Prose*, 666).

Further reading

The impact of modern critical emphases and methods is manifest in the latter sections of the two lists of reading supplied so far, as well as in a growing body of scholarship not readily locatable on either of those lists. A sample of such scholarship is provided below. The entries towards the end of the list represent the new technological developments that have begun to define Blake studies in the present: both a new attention to the material process of Blake's production – Blake's technology of print-making – and the electronic Blake archive, made possible by modern digital technology.

Nelson Hilton, *Literal Imagination: Blake's Vision of Words* (Berkeley: University of California Press, 1983). Counters the preoccupation with Blake's symbolism by arguing the 'polysemous' and 'multidimensional' aspect of his words, which demand attention to their 'sound, etymology, graphic shape, contemporary applications, and varied associations'; thus, emphasizes verbal play and the reader's participation in the building of signification.

Dan Miller, Mark Bracher and Donald Ault (eds.) *Critical Paths: Blake and the Argument of Method* (Durham and London: Duke University Press, 1987). 'Some of the contributors take up the issue of method itself; others consider how Blake studies can proceed in a world of conflicting and competing methods; others investigate and perform those methods that are transforming the field.'

David Fuller, *Blake's Heroic Argument* (London: Croom Helm, 1988). Treating form as well as historical and intellectual context, shows that the argument of Blake's poetry is a 'substantially developing and changing one', tracing, with close reference to particular works, his evolving ideas of politics, religion and sexuality. Concludes with a discussion of contemporary theory and critical practice.

Robert Essick, *William Blake and the Language of Adam* (Oxford: Clarendon Press, 1989). Relating Blake's linguistics to theories of language current in his time, finds in him a 'view of language with transactional events instead of difference as its essence', and so aligns Blake with Heidegger against Derrida in the historical debate between phenomenological and structuralist approaches.

Peter Otto, *Constructive Vision and Visionary Deconstruction: Los, Eternity, and the Productions of Time in the Later Poetry of William Blake* (Oxford: Clarendon Press, 1991). Subtle analysis, demonstrating parallelism and divergence between Blake and Derrida. Corrects the dominant focus (led by Frye) on Blake's construction of a self-sufficient world-forming imagination in the argument that this imagination is only a portion of a prophetic imagination that tries to open up the closed world of the self to others. Existence or reality is not a function of the self's perception; rather, perception is located in a reality (ontology) of relationships that exceeds the self-constituted world. Blake's prophecy is the attempt to show this reality; his deconstruction, the exposure of the limits of the self-constituted world, and his vision, the figuring forth of its transformation.

Steven Vine, *Blake's Poetry: Spectral Visions* (Basingstoke and London: Macmillan, 1993). Arguing that the traditional idealist readings overlook the trauma and struggle of poetic creation in Blake, focuses on his 'Spectre' as the shadowy ironic opposite of vision or imagination, so as to examine 'the creative possibilities and falls which empower and erode Blake's account of poetic vision in his prophetic books.'

Joseph Viscomi, *Blake and the Idea of the Book* (Princeton: Princeton University Press, 1993). Authoritative study, insisting that criticism take direct account of Blake's technique: 'by placing Blake's modes of production in their historical, technical, and aesthetic context . . . makes possible new readings of Blake's poetry and assists in revealing how profoundly Blake's theories of art and imagination are grounded in practice.'

***Peter Ackroyd**, *Blake* (1995; 2nd edn., London: Minerva, 1996). Engaging, informed modern biography.

Steve Clark and David Worral (eds.), *Blake in the Nineties* (Basingstoke and London: Macmillan, 1999). Assesses Blake's work in the 1790s in the context of the critical debates of the 1990s, 'drawing on three main traditions of Blake criticism . . . editorial, hermeneutic and historical'. Includes essays informed by the new emphasis on the materiality of Blake's printmaking.

Tim Fulford (ed.), *Romanticism and Millenarianism* (Basingstoke: Palgrave, 2002). Blake is the 'shifting, elusive center' of this collection of essays on writers and artists of the Romantic era 'united by a common tendency to use figurations of the millennium to interrogate and transform the worlds in which they lived and moved.' Three essays, by G. E. Bentley, Martin Butlin, and (jointly) Joseph Viscomi, Robert Essick and Morris Eaves, focus specifically on Blake, addressing literary and material representation.

Kevin Hutchings, *Imagining Nature: Blake's Environmental Poetics* (Montreal and Kingston: McGill-Queen's University Press, 2002). Eco-critical or 'Green Romanticist' reading of Blake, showing a 'distinctively Blakean view of the relationship between humanity and nature . . . that productively challenges the traditional Western notion that humans should exercise a hierarchical and narrowly anthropocentric "dominion" over the entire non-human portion of creation.'

David Wagenknecht (ed.), *The Once and Future Blake*, special issue of *Studies in Romanticism* 41.2 (Summer 2002). Essays focusing on reproduction, materiality and representation in the context of the major new developments in Blake studies: the exploration and effect of Blake's techniques as a printmaker and the electronic Blake archive.

***Morris Eaves** (ed.), *The Cambridge Companion to William Blake* (Cambridge: Cambridge University Press, 2003). Indispensable up-to-date collection of essays by top scholars, seeking 'to respond to the difficulties [of reading Blake] with a variety of critical and historical explanations from several perspectives'. The essays in Part I variously address topics such as poetic form, printmaking, politics, religion, Romanticism; Part II consists of discrete readings of different parts of Blake's corpus.

Morton D. Paley, *The Traveller in the Evening: The Last Works of William Blake* (Oxford: Oxford University Press, 2003). Dating Blake's last works from his gaining of financial stability in 1818 to his death in 1827, shows here an increasing affinity to Gnosticism, as well as other attitudes and combinations of (often contradictory) beliefs, which although not entirely new, constitute an autonomous context or frame for each work, independent of, or inconsistent with, the larger symbolic structure of the works to *Jerusalem*.

Nick Rawlinson, *William Blake's Comic Vision* (Basingstoke: Palgrave Macmillan, 2003). Discusses Blake as a comic writer, whose use of comedy belongs to a tradition of Christian humanism. The comic, being both subversive and constructive, is the key to Blake's vision, offering him a model for creative reading, and providing a thematic unity to his work.

Julia M. Wright, *Blake, Nationalism, and the Politics of Alienation* (Athens, Ohio: University of Ohio Press, 2004). Shows, despite Blake's concern with individual liberty, his awareness of the inseparability of the individual and the communal (where 'communal' refers especially to national community), with discourse, especially print, mediating between the two.

Matthew J. A. Green, *Visionary Materialism in the Early Works of William Blake: The Intersection of Enthusiasm and Empiricism* (Basingstoke: Palgrave Macmillan, 2005). Presents, in Blake's writings from 1788 to 1795, a hybrid of philosophical empiricism and religious enthusiasm, and so locates his world-view – his tenets of being and knowledge – at the conjunction of the material and the spiritual.

Jeremy Tambling, *Blake's Night Thoughts* (Basingstoke: Palgrave Macmillan, 2005). By means of a close reading of the poetry, examines Blake's preoccupation with night and its implications in terms of gender, identity and madness.

Useful editions

The standard edition is *The Complete Poetry and Prose of William Blake*, ed. David Erdman. Of comparable standing are *The Complete Writings of William Blake*, ed. Geoffrey Keynes and *William Blake's Writings*, ed. G. E. Bentley, 2 vols. (Oxford: Clarendon Press, 1978). A useful edition for students is *William Blake: The Complete Poems*, ed. W. H. Stevenson (1971; rev. edn., London: Longman, 1989).

Reference material

G. E. Bentley, *Blake Records* (London and New Haven: Yale University Press, 2003). This is an updated edition of Bentley's *Blake Records* (1969) and *Blake Records Supplement* (1988), collating all known documentary records relating to Blake's life.

Morris Eaves, Robert N. Essick and Joseph Viscomi (eds.), *The William Blake Archive* (http://www.blakearchive.org). The most important new resource for students and scholars, this is a free site on the World Wide Web, enabling searches of reproductions and texts, catalogues, scholarly tools and other archival material.

Chapter notes

1　S. T. Coleridge, *The Collected Letters of Samuel Taylor Coleridge*, ed. E. L. Griggs, 6 vols. (Oxford: Clarendon Press, 1956–71), IV. 834.

2　G. E. Bentley (ed.), *Blake Records* (Oxford: Clarendon Press, 1969), 536.

3　Only three works were conventionally printed: *Poetical Sketches* (1783), *The French Revolution* (1791), and the *Descriptive Catalogue* (1809) of his exhibition.

4　See G. E. Bentley (ed.), *William Blake: The Critical Heritage* (London and Boston: Routledge & Kegan Paul, 1975), 44–6.

5　Alexander Gilchrist, *Life of William Blake, 'Pictor Ignotus'* (London and Cambridge: Macmillan, 1863), 1.

6　Ibid., 70.

7　Ibid., 68, 93.

8　E. J. Ellis and W. B. Yeats, *The Works of William Blake: Poetic, Symbolic, and Critical* (London: Bernard Quaritch, 1893), viii.

9　S. Foster Damon, *William Blake: His Philosophy and Symbols* (London: Constable, 1924), ix.

10　*The Writings of William Blake*, ed. Geoffrey Keynes, 3 vols. (London: Nonesuch, 1925).

11　T. S. Eliot, 'William Blake' (1920), repr. in *Selected Essays* (3rd enlarged. edn., London: Faber, 1951), 321, 322.

12　Northrop Frye, *Fearful Symmetry: A Study of William Blake* (Princeton: Princeton University Press, 1947), 5.

13　Ibid., 14.

14　Ibid., 167–8.

15　Northrop Frye, *Anatomy of Criticism: Four Essays* (Princeton: Princeton University Press, 1957), 14.

16　Revised and republished as *William Blake and the Age of Revolution* (London: Routledge & Kegan Paul, 1972).

17　David Erdman, *Blake: Prophet against Empire; A Poet's Interpretation of the History of his Own Times* (1954; 3rd rev. edn., Princeton: Princeton University Press, 1977), xiv–xv.

18　Ibid., xv.

19　David Aers, 'Blake: Sex, Society and Ideology' in *Romanticism and Ideology*, 27–43.

20　Anne K. Mellor, 'Blake's Portrayal of Women' in *Blake: An Illustrated Quarterly* 16 (Winter 1982–3), 148–55; Brenda S. Webster, 'Blake, Women, and Sexuality' in *Critical Paths: Blake and the Argument of Method*, ed. D. Miller, M. Bracher and D. Ault (Durham and London: Duke University Press, 1987), 204–24.

21　*Blake, Politics, and History*, xxix–xxx.

22　Mary-Kelly Persyn, '"No Human form but Sexual": Sensibility, Chastity, and Sacrifice in Blake's *Jerusalem*', *European Romantic Review* 10.1 (Winter 1999), 54.

23　Anne Mellor, 'Sex, Violence, and Slavery: Blake and Wollstonecraft', *Huntington Library Quarterly* 58.3–4 (1995), 368.

24 Marcus Wood, *Slavery, Empathy, and Pornography* (Oxford: Oxford University Press, 2002), 183, 186.

25 Saree Makdisi, *William Blake and the Impossible History of the 1790s* (Chicago and London: University of Chicago Press, 2002), 4.

26 Edward Larrissy, 'Blake's Orient', *Romanticism* 11.1 (2005), 3, 11.

2

William Wordsworth (1770–1850)

THE CONTEMPORARY RECEPTION

Lyrical Ballads (1798) and more especially the 'Preface' that Wordsworth wrote to the 1800 edition, brought him to his contemporaries' notice as an experimenter and a poet with a 'system'. Thereafter, his fame, or notoriety, was assured. By 1820, the *Blackwood's* reviewer was exclaiming, 'we doubt, whether the writings of Spencer, or of Dryden, or even of Milton himself, be at this instant truly familiar to a larger portion of the Reading Public of England than those of Wordsworth.'[1] The principles of the *Lyrical Ballads* 'Preface' continued to be associated with Wordsworth's practice in the poetry that followed. Debating his principles became integral to judging his poetry, and the major participants in that debate contributed vitally to the development of Romantic poetics and its impact upon public taste.

Wordsworth's reputation reached its lowest ebb with the publication of his *Poems in Two Volumes* (1807), which brought on him widespread charges of infantilism and puerility, although they contained what later became his most frequently anthologized poems, including the Ode 'There was a time' (popularly known as the Intimations Ode or the Immortality Ode), 'The Solitary Reaper', and 'I wandered lonely as a cloud'. Chief among his detractors was Francis Jeffrey with whom the label 'Lake School' originated, and who, over two decades, continued to attack Wordsworth in the *Edinburgh Review* as a genius perverted and a desecrator of tradition, his review of *The Excursion* opening, famously, 'This will never do.'[2] Elsewhere, however, Wordsworth's standing recovered. Lamb's 1814 review of *The Excursion* in the *Quarterly* constructs the high Romantic Wordsworth familiar to us today: the poet of nature, the original genius, and successor to Milton.[3] The *Blackwood's* reviewer, probably John Wilson, a one-time follower of the Lake School, dismisses Jeffrey's criticisms in a succession of encomiums from 1818 to 1822, lauding

Wordsworth as a philosopher-poet and declaring that 'never was the alliance between church and state so philosophically illustrated as by this prevailing poet.'[4] A more qualified admiration is expressed in the *British Critic* in a series of reviews of 1815–21 by an anonymous reviewer (now identified as Coleridge's nephew, John Taylor Coleridge) who, warmly praising Wordsworth's achievement, still judges him to have 'failed', in sacrificing to his system his poetry's intelligibility to the general reader.[5]

Outside of the reviews, an extensive if equivocal defence of Wordsworth may be found in Coleridge's *Biographia Literaria* (see especially chapters 4, 14, 17–22). Keats's tag 'wordsworthian or egotistical sublime' has become a critical commonplace.[6] But the most memorable contemporary assessment is surely Hazlitt's, who, in a richly nuanced portrait in *The Spirit of the Age* (1825), brilliantly captures the multiple paradoxes of a poetry that is at once egalitarian and exclusive, humane and egotistical, sublime and farcical.

Extract from William Hazlitt, 'Mr. Wordsworth', in *The Spirit of the Age* (1825)

Mr Wordsworth's genius is a pure emanation of the Spirit of the Age. Had he lived in any other period of the world, he would never have been heard of. As it is, he has some difficulty to contend with the hebetude of his intellect, and the meanness of his subject. With him 'lowliness is young ambition's ladder':[1] but he finds it a toil to climb in this way the steep of Fame. His homely Muse can hardly raise her wing from the ground, nor spread her hidden glories to the sun. He has 'no figures nor no fantasies, which busy *passion* draws in the brains of men':[2] neither the gorgeous machinery of mythologic lore, nor the splendid colours of poetic diction. His style is vernacular: he delivers household truths. He sees nothing loftier than human hopes; nothing deeper than the human heart. This he probes, this he tampers with, this he poises, with all its incalculable weight of thought and feeling, in his hands; and at the same time calms the throbbing pulses of his own heart, by keeping his eye ever fixed on the face of nature. If he can make the life-blood flow from the wounded breast, this is the living colouring with which he paints his verse: if he can assuage the pain or close up the wound with the balm of solitary musing, or the healing powers of plants and herbs and 'skyey influences',[3] this is the sole triumph of his art. He takes the simplest elements of nature and of the human mind, the mere abstract conditions inseparable from our being, and tries to compound a new system of poetry from them; and has perhaps succeeded as well as any one could. '*Nihil humani a me alienum puto*'[4] – is the motto of his works. He thinks nothing low or indifferent of which this can be affirmed: every thing that professes to be more than this, that is not an absolute essence of truth and feeling, he holds to be vitiated, false, and spurious. In a word, his poetry is founded on setting up an opposition (and pushing it to the utmost length) between the natural and the artificial; between the spirit of humanity, and the spirit of fashion and of the world!

It is one of the innovations of the time. It partakes of, and is carried along with, the revolutionary movement of our age: the political changes of the day were the model on which he formed and conducted his poetical experiments. His Muse (it cannot be denied, and without this we cannot explain its character at all) is a levelling one. It proceeds on a principle of equality, and strives to reduce all things to the same standard. It is distinguished by a proud humility. It relies upon its own resources, and disdains external show and relief. It takes the commonest events and objects, as a test to prove that nature is always interesting from its inherent truth and beauty, without any of the ornaments of dress or pomp of circumstances to set it off. Hence the unaccountable mixture of seeming simplicity and real abstruseness in the *Lyrical Ballads*. Fools have laughed at, wise men scarcely understand them. He takes a subject or a story merely as pegs or loops to hang thought and feeling on; the incidents are trifling, in proportion to his contempt for imposing appearances; the reflections are profound, according to the gravity and the aspiring pretensions of his mind.

His popular, inartificial style gets rid (at a blow) of all the trappings of verse, of all the high places of poetry: 'the cloud-capt towers, the solemn temples, the gorgeous palaces', are swept to the ground, and 'like the baseless fabric of a vision, leave not a wreck behind'.[5] All the traditions of learning, all the superstitions of age, are obliterated and effaced. We begin *de novo*, on a *tabula rasa* of poetry.[6] The purple pall, the nodding plume of tragedy are exploded as mere pantomime and trick, to return to the simplicity of truth and nature. Kings, queens, priests, nobles, the altar and the throne, the distinctions of rank, birth, wealth, power, 'the judge's robe, the marshall's truncheon, the ceremony that to great ones' longs',[7] are not to be found here. The author tramples on the pride of art with greater pride. The Ode and Epode, the Strophe and the Antistrophe, he laughs to scorn. The harp of Homer, the trump of Pindar and of Alcæus are still. The decencies of costume, the decorations of vanity are stripped off without mercy as barbarous, idle, and Gothic. The jewels in the crisped hair,[8] the diadem on the polished brow are thought meretricious, theatrical, vulgar; and nothing contents his fastidious taste beyond a simple garland of flowers. Neither does he avail himself of the advantages which nature or accident holds out to him. He chooses to have his subject a foil to his invention, to owe nothing but to himself. He gathers manna in the wilderness, he strikes the barren rock for the gushing moisture. He elevates the mean by the strength of his own aspirations; he clothes the naked with beauty and grandeur from the store of his own recollections. No cypress-grove loads his verse with perfumes: but his imagination lends 'a sense of joy

> To the bare trees and mountains bare,
> And grass in the green field.'[9]

No storm, no shipwreck startles us by its horrors: but the rainbow lifts its head in the cloud, and the breeze sighs through the withered fern. No sad vicissitude of fate,[10] no overwhelming catastrophe in nature deforms his page: but the dew-drop glitters on the bending flower, the tear collects in the glistening eye.

> 'Beneath the hills, along the flowery vales,
> The generations are prepared; the pangs,
> The internal pangs are ready; the dread strife
> Of poor humanity's afflicted will,
> Struggling in vain with ruthless destiny.'[11]

As the lark ascends from its low bed on fluttering wing, and salutes the morning skies; so Mr Wordsworth's unpretending Muse, in russet guise, scales the summits of reflection, while it makes the round earth its footstool,[12] and its home!

Possibly a good deal of this may be regarded as the effect of disappointed views and an inverted ambition. Prevented by native pride and indolence from climbing the ascent of learning or greatness, taught by political opinions to say to the vain pomp and glory of the world, 'I hate ye',[13] seeing the path of classical and artificial poetry blocked up by the cumbrous ornaments of style and turgid *common-places*, so that nothing more could be achieved in that direction but by the most ridiculous bombast or the tamest servility; he has turned back partly from the bias of his mind, partly perhaps from a judicious policy – has struck into the sequestered vale of humble life, sought out the Muse among sheep-cotes and hamlets and the peasant's mountain-haunts, has discarded all the tinsel pageantry of verse, and endeavoured (not in vain) to aggrandize the trivial and add the charm of novelty to the familiar. No one has shown the same imagination in raising trifles into importance: no one has displayed the same pathos in treating of the simplest feelings of the heart. Reserved, yet haughty, having no unruly or violent passions, (or those passions having been early suppressed), Mr Wordsworth has passed his life in solitary musing, or in daily converse with the face of nature. He exemplifies in an eminent degree the power of *association*; for his poetry has no other source or character. He has dwelt among pastoral scenes, till each object has become connected with a thousand feelings, a link in the chain of thought, a fibre of his own heart. Every one is by habit and familiarity strongly attached to the place of his birth, or to objects that recall the most pleasing and eventful circumstances of his life. But to the author of the *Lyrical Ballads*, nature is a kind of home; and he may be said to take a personal interest in the universe. There is no image so insignificant that it has not in some mood or other found the way into his heart: no sound that does not awaken the memory of other years.

'To him the meanest flower that blows can give
Thoughts that do often lie too deep for tears.'[14]

The daisy looks up to him with sparkling eye as an old acquaintance: the cuckoo haunts him with sounds of early youth not to be expressed: a linnet's nest startles him with boyish delight: an old withered thorn is weighed down with a heap of recollections: a grey cloak, seen on some wild moor, torn by the wind, or drenched in the rain, afterwards becomes an object of imagination to him: even the lichens on the rock have a life and being in his thoughts.[15] He has described all these objects in a way and with an intensity of feeling that no one else had done before him, and has given a new view or aspect of nature. He is in this sense the most original poet now living, and the one whose writings could the least be spared: for they have no substitute elsewhere. The vulgar do not read them, the learned, who see all things through books, do not understand them, the great despise, the fashionable may ridicule them: but the author has created himself an interest in the heart of the retired and lonely student of nature, which can never die. Persons of this class will still continue to feel what he has felt: he has expressed what they might in vain wish to express, except with glistening eye and faltering tongue! There is a lofty philosophic tone, a thoughtful humanity, infused into his pastoral vein. Remote from the passions and events of the great world, he has communicated interest and dignity to the primal movements of the heart of man, and ingrafted his own conscious reflections on the casual thoughts of hinds and shepherds. Nursed amidst the grandeur of mountain scenery, he has stooped to have a nearer view of the daisy under his feet, or plucked a branch of white-thorn from the spray: but in describing it, his mind seems imbued with the majesty and solemnity of the objects around him – the tall rock lifts its head in the erectness of his spirit; the cataract roars in the sound of his verse; and in its dim and mysterious meaning, the mists seem to gather in the hollows of Helvellyn, and the forked Skiddaw hovers in the distance. There is little mention of mountainous scenery in Mr Wordsworth's poetry; but by internal evidence one might be almost sure that it was written in a mountainous country, from its bareness, its simplicity, its loftiness and its depth!

His later philosophic productions have a somewhat different character. They are a departure from, a dereliction of his first principles. They are classical and courtly. They are polished in style, without being gaudy; dignified in subject, without affectation. They seem to have been composed not in a cottage at Grasmere, but among the half-inspired groves and stately recollections of Cole-Orton.[16] We might allude in particular, for examples of what we mean, to the lines on a Picture by Claude Lorraine, and to the exquisite poem, entitled *Laodamia*. The last of these breathes the pure spirit of the finest fragments of antiquity – the sweetness, the gravity, the strength, the beauty and the languor of death –

'Calm contemplation and majestic pains.'[17]

Its glossy brilliancy arises from the perfection of the finishing, like that of careful sculpture, not from gaudy colouring – the texture of the thoughts has the smoothness and solidity of marble. It is a poem that might be read aloud in Elysium, and the spirits of departed heroes and sages would gather round to listen to it! Mr Wordsworth's philosophic poetry, with a less glowing aspect and less tumult in the veins than Lord Byron's on similar occasions, bends a calmer and keener eye on mortality; the impression, if less vivid, is more pleasing and permanent; and we confess it (perhaps it is a want of taste and proper feeling) that there are lines and poems of our author's that we think of ten times for once that we recur to any of Lord Byron's. Or if there are any of the latter's writings, that we can dwell upon in the same way, that is, as lasting and heart-felt sentiments, it is when laying aside his usual pomp and pretension, he descends with Mr Wordsworth to the common ground of a disinterested humanity. It may be considered as characteristic of our poet's writings, that they either make no impression on the mind at all, seem mere *nonsense-verses*, or that they leave a mark behind them that never wears out. They either

'Fall blunted from the indurated breast' –[18]

without any perceptible result, or they absorb it like a passion. To one class of readers he appears sublime, to another (and we fear the largest) ridiculous. He has probably realized Milton's wish, – 'and fit audience found, though few':[19] but we suspect he is not reconciled to the alternative. There are delightful passages in the EXCURSION, both of natural description and of inspired reflection (passages of the latter kind that in the sound of the thoughts and of the swelling language resemble heavenly symphonies, mournful *requiems* over the grave of human hopes); but we must add, in justice and in sincerity, that we think it impossible that this work should ever become popular, even in the same degree as the *Lyrical Ballads*. It affects a system without having any intelligible clue to one; and instead of unfolding a principle in various and striking lights, repeats the same conclusions till they become flat and insipid. Mr Wordsworth's mind is obtuse, except as it is the organ and the receptacle of accumulated feelings: it is not analytic, but synthetic; it is reflecting, rather than theoretical. The EXCURSION, we believe, fell still-born from the press.[20] There was something abortive, and clumsy, and ill-judged in the attempt. It was long and laboured. The personages, for the most part, were low, the fare rustic: the plan raised expectations which were not fulfilled, and the effect was like being ushered into a stately hall and invited to sit down to a splendid banquet in the company of clowns, and with nothing but successive courses of apple-dumplings served up.

Notes

[Hazlitt's allusions, referenced below, draw Wordsworth into a richly suggestive conglomeration of intertexts.

1 *Julius Caesar*, II. i. 22.
2 Cf. ibid., II. i. 231–2.
3 *Measure for Measure*, III. i. 9.
4 'I think nothing human foreign to me'. Terence, *Heautontimorumenos*, I. i. 77.
5 Cf. *The Tempest*, IV. i. 151–6.
6 'anew', 'blank page'. The allusion is to Locke's description of the human mind in *An Essay Concerning Human Understanding*.
7 Cf. *Measure for Measure*, II. ii. 59–61.
8 Cf. William Collins, 'The Manners: An Ode', 55.
9 Wordsworth, 'Lines written as a Small Distance from my House', 6–8.
10 Edward Young, *Night Thoughts*, vi. 108.

11   Wordsworth, *The Excursion*, vi. 568–72.
12   Cf. Isaiah 66: 1.
13   Cf. *Henry VIII*, III. ii. 365.
14   Cf. Wordsworth, 'Intimations Ode', 205–6.
15   This sentence alludes broadly to a number of Wordsworth's poems, including 'To the Daisy', 'To the Cuckoo', 'The Thorn' and 'Alice Fell'.
16   The residence of Wordsworth's friend, Sir George Beaumont.
17   Cf. Wordsworth, 'Laodamia', 72.
18   Cf. Oliver Goldsmith, *The Traveller*, 232.
19   Cf. *Paradise Lost*, vii. 31. 20.
20   Cf. Pope, 'Epilogue to the Satires', ii. 126.]

Further reading

See also Hazlitt's review of *The Excursion*, in three essays in *The Examiner* (Aug. 21 1814, 541–2; Aug. 28 1814, 555–8; Oct. 2 1814, 636–8), later included in *The Round Table* (1817); Keats's 'wordsworthian or egotistical sublime' is paraphrased from these essays. (For the *Round Table* essays, see *The Complete Works of William Hazlitt*, ed. P. P. Howe, 21 vols. [London and Toronto: J. M. Dent, 1930–4], IV. 111–20 and 120–3.) An extensive collection of contemporary reviews can be found in Donald Reiman (ed.) *The Romantics Reviewed, Part A: The Lake Poets*. A useful smaller selection is contained in John O. Hayden, *Romantic Bards and British Reviewers* (Lincoln and London: University of Nebraska Press, 1971). Another valuable compilation of contemporary reviews and criticism is Robert Woof (ed.), *The Critical Heritage: William Wordsworth*. I: *1793–1820* (London and New York: Routledge, 2001).

ARNOLD TO HARTMAN: FROM 'NATURE' TO 'VISION'

To his Victorian admirers, Wordsworth was pre-eminently the poet of nature, his poetry characterized by its sincerity and lack of artifice. Focal to the key Victorian appraisals is the question foregrounded by Coleridge, of the philosophical content of Wordsworth's poetry in its bearing on the merits of his work. *The Prelude* was published in 1850, adding to *The Excursion* a new weight of exposition, and Wordsworth's 'philosophy' was also especially known from the Immortality Ode. To some Victorians, his poetry expressed a doctrine of natural religion,[7] to others, notably Leslie Stephen, he offered a systematic and more secular 'ethics'.[8] But the most powerful arguments for Wordsworth in the Victorian period are those that assert a poetic value not augmented, but diminished by 'system'. In the 'Preface' to his *Poems of Wordsworth* (1879), Matthew Arnold dismisses the judgement that predicates poetic value on philosophy in Wordsworth, declaring that what is flattest and most uninspired in his poetry is its didactic or expository part. Celebrating Wordsworth's 'poetical performance' as being 'after that of Shakespeare and Milton, . . . the most considerable in our language from the Elizabethan age to the present time', Arnold argues that Wordsworth's best poetry does not moralize, but is profoundly moral, inasmuch as it is a 'criticism of life'.[9] Poetry is moral where it offers an insight into life itself; Wordsworth's insight is of nature as a universal source of joy:

> Wordsworth's poetry is great because of the extraordinary power with which Wordsworth feels the joy offered to us in nature, the joy offered to us in the simple primary affections and duties, and because of the extraordinary power with which, in case after case, he shows us this joy, and renders it so as to make us share it.
>
> The source of joy from which he thus draws is the truest and most unfailing source of joy accessible to man. It is also accessible universally.[10]

Critical to Arnold's construction of Wordsworth is his emphasis on selection, and his subordination of *The Excursion* and *The Prelude* to Wordsworth's shorter poems. Less, to Arnold, is more; to edit is not to diminish but enhance Wordsworth's corpus. Arnold's notion of a pure or essential Wordsworth is manifest too, in his praise, mirroring Wordsworth's own nostalgia for beginnings, of the early poetry. 'Wordsworth composed verses during a space of some sixty years; and it is no exaggeration to say that within one single decade of those years, between 1798 and 1808, almost all his really first-rate work was produced.'[11] That 'Great Decade' has had an enduring influence on Wordsworth scholarship; it is confirmed in de Selincourt's seminal publication in 1926 of the 1805 *Prelude* and in our continuing to prize that early poem over *The Excursion* and *The Prelude* of 1850.

Arnold's pronouncement on Wordsworth is the landmark of the Victorian phase of the critical reception, yet it is most valuable, perhaps, as a statement of Arnold's poetics. Walter Pater's account of Wordsworth as a poet of nature and consciousness in an 1874 essay 'On Wordsworth' in the *Fortnightly Review*, subsequently reproduced in *Appreciations* (1889), is the closer and more perceptive reading, anticipating not only many of the cardinal points of the Arnold essay, but also, in its emphasis on 'contemplation', the 'visionary' Wordsworth of later criticism. Wordsworth's poetry is politically contextualized in Émile Legouis' *The Early Life of William Wordsworth, 1770–1798* (1897), which also attests to the growing centrality of *The Prelude* in Wordsworth studies.

The diversity of topic and focus in the Victorian responses to Wordsworth cannot be adequately generalized, nor were those responses uniformly laudatory. But by the end of the century, the canonization of Wordsworth was well under way, in the Victorian anthology, in the founding of the Wordsworth Society (1880), and in the monumental editions of William Knight (1882–9) and Edward Dowden (1892–3).

In the twentieth century, Wordsworth gains a significant new dimension in A. C. Bradley's *Oxford Lectures on Poetry* (1909). Bradley complicates the poet of nature dear to the Victorians by recognizing in Wordsworth a quality which he variously terms 'mystic', 'visionary' or 'sublime', and which, more importantly, he attributes to the perception (or epistemology) theorized by Kant and his followers in Germany.

> His poetry is immensely interesting as an imaginative expression of the same mind which, in his day, produced in Germany great philosophies. His poetic experience, his intuitions, his single thoughts, even his large views, correspond in a striking way, sometimes in a startling way, with ideas methodically developed by Kant, Schelling, Hegel, Schopenhauer. . . .
>
> And we may observe at once that in this there is always traceable a certain hostility to 'sense'. . . . The regular action of the senses on their customary material produces, in his view, a 'tyranny' over the soul.[12]

Bradley's insight, locating Wordsworth's 'philosophy', not simply in the expository passages deplored by Arnold, but in a type of perception fundamental to his poetry, reappears in the formative criticism of the present day.

Other developments of the first half of the twentieth century include George McLean Harper's two-volume *William Wordsworth: His Life, Works, and Influence* (1916), which publishes for the first time Wordsworth's liaison with Annette Vallon, presenting to the twentieth century a sexualized poet unknown to the Victorians. Clarifying chronology and revision, the textual studies of Ernest de Selincourt and Helen Darbishire constitute a major critical breakthrough.[13]

In 1953, the correspondence noted by Bradley, between Wordsworth's poetic experience and the theories of the German idealists, is reaffirmed in M. H. Abrams's *The Mirror and the Lamp: Romantic Theory and the Critical Tradition*, which, characterizing Romantic poetics by its shift from a mimetic to an expressive theory of art, makes Wordsworth a key figure in that transition. Subsequently, Bradley is explicitly acknowledged as a precursor in what is arguably the single most celebrated work of Wordsworth criticism of the twentieth century, Geoffrey Hartman's *Wordsworth's Poetry 1787–1814* (1964).

Hartman's thesis is of a radical opposition between nature and imagination in Wordsworth's thought, the resolution of which emerges in his poetry as a notion that Hartman calls the *via naturaliter negativa*: nature itself teaches the mind to be free of nature. Extracted below is his synopsis of his argument, with his landmark analysis of the Simplon Pass episode in Book VI of *The Prelude*.

Extract from Geoffrey Hartman, *Wordsworth's Poetry 1787–1814* (1964)

The Via Naturaliter Negativa

Many readers have felt that Wordsworth's poetry honors and even worships nature. In this they have the support of Blake, a man so sensitive to any trace of 'Natural Religion' that he is said to have blamed some verses of Wordsworth's for a bowel complaint which almost killed him.[1] Scholarship, luckily, tempers the affections, and the majority of readers have emphasized the poet's progression from nature worship or even pantheism to a highly qualified form of natural religion, with increasing awareness of the 'ennobling interchange' between mind and nature and a late yielding of primacy to the activity of the mind or the idealizing power of imagination. A very small group, finally, has pointed to the deeply paradoxical character of Wordsworth's dealings with nature and suggested that what he calls imagination may be *intrinsically* opposed to nature.[2] This last and rarest position seems to me closest to the truth, yet I do not feel it conflicts totally with more traditional readings stressing the poet's adherence to nature. It can be shown, via several important episodes of *The Prelude*, that Wordsworth thought nature itself led him beyond nature; and, since this movement of transcendence, related to what mystics have called the negative way, is inherent in life and achieved without violent or ascetic discipline, one can think of it as the progress of a soul which is *naturaliter negativa*.

1

The Prelude opens with a success immediately followed by a failure. Released from the 'vast city' and anticipating a new freedom, the poet pours out a rush of fifty lines: 'poetic numbers came / Spontaneously to clothe in priestly robe / A renovated spirit' (I.51–53).[3] Here is the consecration, the promise of poetry as a sacrament, a gift efficacious beyond the moment. Why should a chance inspiration assume such significance?

The reason is that Wordsworth was not used to make 'A present joy the matter of a song'; yet here, apparently, is evidence that he may soon become self-creative, or need no more than a 'gentle breeze' (the untraditional muse of the epic's opening) to produce a tempest of poetry. 'Matins and vespers of harmonious verse!' is the hope held out to him, and having punctually performed matins the poet is content to slacken, to be gradually calmed by the clear autumn afternoon.

He meditates beneath a tree on a great poetic work soon to be begun. The sun sets, and city smoke is 'ruralised' by distance. He starts to continue his journey, but now it is clearly time for vespers:

> It was a splendid evening, and my soul
> Once more made trial of her strength, nor lacked
> Aeolian visitations. (I.94–96)

An outside splendor challenges the creative mind. Is the poet strong enough to answer it spontaneously, as if he needed only a suggestion, the first chord?

>   but the harp
> Was soon defrauded, and the banded host
> Of harmony dispersed in straggling sounds,
> And lastly utter silence! 'Be it so;
> Why think of any thing but present good?' (I.96–100)

Wordsworth once again sees present good, like present joy, strangely opposed to the quickening of verse. The poetic outburst which he had considered a religious thing ('punctual service high . . . holy services') is now disdained as profane and *servile*:

> So, like a home-bound labourer I pursued
> My way beneath the mellowing sun, that shed
> Mild influence; nor left in me one wish
> Again to bend the Sabbath of that time
> To a servile yoke. (I.101–05)

His reversal of mood is surprisingly complete. One who, at the impassioned outset of his reflections, had been so sure of the freely creative, autonomous nature of his poetic soul that famous passages on the emancipated spirit – from *Paradise Lost* and Exodus[4] – swell the current of his verse, while he thinks to possess total freedom of choice,

>   now free,
> Free as a bird to settle where I will (I.8–9)

that same person now writes of himself, with a slight echo of Gray's *Elegy*:

> So, like a home-bound labourer I pursued
> My way.

The meaning of the reversal is not immediately clear. It does not deject the poet; it endows him, on the contrary, with a Chaucerian kind of cheer and leisure:

> What need of many words?
> A pleasant loitering journey, through three days
> Continued, brought me to my hermitage.
> I spare to tell of what ensued, the life
> In common things – the endless store of things. (I.105–09)

The form of the reversal is that of a return to nature, at least to its rhythm. For the moment no haste remains, no tempest, no impatience of spirit. It is the mood of the hawthorn shade, of a portion of Wordsworth's Cambridge days, when he laughed with Chaucer and heard him, while birds sang, tell tales of love (III.278–81).

In the exultant first lines of *The Prelude*, Wordsworth had foreseen the spirit's power to become self-creative. Though fostered by nature it eventually outgrows its dependence, sings and storms at will (I.33–38). The poet's anticipation of autonomy is probably less a matter of pride than of necessity: he will steal the initiative from nature so as to freely serve or sustain the natural world should its hold on the affections slacken. His poetic power, though admittedly in nature's gift, must perpetuate, like consecration, vital if transitory feelings. Without poetry the supreme moment is nothing.

> Dear Liberty! Yet what would it avail
> But for a gift that consecrates the joy? (I.31–32)

But he is taught that the desire for immediate consecrations is a wrong form of worship. The world demands a devotion less external and willful, a wise passiveness which the creative will may profane. The tempest 'vexing its own creation' is replaced by a 'mellowing sun, that shed / Mild influence.' Nature keeps the initiative. The mind at its most free is still part of a deep mood of weathers.

Wordsworth's failure to consecrate, through verse, the splendid evening is only the last event in this reversal. It begins with the poet placing (so to say) the cart before the horse, Poetry before Nature: 'To the open fields I told / A prophecy: poetic numbers came . . .' (I.50 ff.). He never, of course, forgets the double agency of inward and outward which informs every act of poetry. So his heart's frost is said to be broken by both outer and inner winds (I.38 ff.).[5] Such reciprocity is at the heart of all his poems. Yet he continually anticipates a movement of transcendence: Nature proposes but the Poet disposes. Just as the breeze engendered in the mind a self-quickening tempest, so poetry, the voice from that tempest, re-echoing in the mind whence it came, seems to increase there its perfection (I.55 ff.). The origin of the whole moves farther from its starting point in the external world. A *personal* agent replaces that of nature: 'I paced on . . . down I sate . . . slackening my thoughts by choice' (I.60 ff.). There is a world of difference between this subtle bravado and the ascendancy of *impersonal* constructions in the final episode: 'Be it so; / Why think of any thing but . . . What need of many words? . . . I pursued / My way . . . A pleasant loitering journey . . . brought me to my hermitage.'

This change, admittedly, is almost too fine for common language. Syntax becomes a major device but not a consistent one. In the 1850 text, while the poet muses in the green, shady place, certain neoclassical patterns, such as the noble passive combined with synecdoche, create an atmosphere in which personal and impersonal, active and passive, blend strongly:

> Many were the thoughts
> Encouraged and dismissed, till choice was made
> Of a known Vale, whither my feet should turn. (I.70–72)

Devices still more subtle come into play. In the passage immediately preceding, Wordsworth describes the quiet autumn afternoon:

> a day
> With silver clouds, and sunshine on the grass,
> And in the sheltered and the sheltering grove
> A perfect stillness. (I.67–70)

'Sheltered and sheltering' – typical Wordsworthian verbosity? The redundance, however, does suggest that whatever is happening here happens in more than one place; compare 'silver clouds, and sunshine on the grass.' The locus doubles, redoubles: that two-fold agency which seems to center on the poet is active all around to the same incremental effect. The grove, sheltered, shelters in turn, and makes 'A perfect stillness.' The poet, in a sense, is only a single focus to something universally active. He muses on this intensifying stillness, and within him rises a picture, gazing on which with *growing* love 'a higher power / Than Fancy' enters to affirm his musings. The reciprocal and incremental movement, mentioned explicitly in I.31 ff., occurs this time quite unself-consciously, clearly within the setting and through the general influences of Nature.

No wonder, then, that the city, which the poet still strove to shake off in the first lines, appears now not only distant but also 'ruralised,' taking on the colors of nature, as inclosed by it as the poet's own thought. The last act of the reversal is the episode of the splendid sunset. Wordsworth not only cannot, he *need* not steal the initiative from nature. Her locus is universal, not individual; she acts by expedients deeper than will or thought. Wordsworth's failure intensifies his sense of a principle of generosity in nature. That initial cry of faith, 'I cannot miss my way' (I.18), becomes true, but not because of his own power. The song loses its way.

Wordsworth's first experience is symptomatic of his creative difficul-ties. One impulse vexes the creative spirit into self-dependence, the other exhibits nature as that spirit's highest object. The poet is driven at the same time from and toward the external world. No sooner has he begun to enjoy his Chaucerian leisure than restiveness breaks in. The 'pilgrim,' despite 'the life / In common things – the endless store of things,' cannot rest content with his hermitage's sabbath. Higher hopes, 'airy phantasies,' clamor for life (I.144 ff.). The poet's account of his creative difficulties (I.146–269) documents in full his vacillation between a natural and a more than natural theme, between a Romantic tale and one of 'natural heroes,' or 'a tale from my own heart' and 'some philo-sophic song' – but he adds, swinging back to the more humble, 'Of Truth that cherishes our daily life.' Is this indeterminacy the end at which nature aims, this curious and never fully clarified restlessness the ultimate confession of his poetry?

It would be hard, in that case, to think of *The Prelude* as describing the 'growth of a poet's mind'; for what the first part of Book I records is, primarily, Wordsworth's failure to be a visionary or epic poet in the tradition of Spenser and Milton. No poem of epic length or ambition ever started like his. The epic poet begins confidently by stating his subject, boasts a little about the valor of his attempt, and calls on the Muse to help him. Yet Wordsworth's confident opening is deceptive. He starts indeed with a rush of verses which are in fact a kind of self-quotation, because his subject is poetry or the mind which has separated from nature and here celebrates its coming-of-age by generously return-ing to it. After this one moment of confidence, all is problematic. The song loses its way, the proud opening is followed by an experience of aphasia, and Wordsworth begins the story of the growth of his mind to prove, at least to himself, that nature had intended him to be a poet. Was it for this, he asks, for this timidity or indecision, that nature spent all her care (I.269 ff.)? Did not nature, by a process of both accommodation and weaning, foster the spirit's autonomy from childhood on? Yet when the spirit tries to seize the initiative, to quicken of itself like Ezekiel's chariot, either nature humbles it or Wordsworth humbles himself before her. 'Thus my days,' says Wordsworth sadly, 'are past / In contradiction; with no skill to part / Vague longing, haply bred by want of power, / From paramount impulse not to be withstood, / A timorous capacity from prudence, / From circumspection, infinite delay' (I.237–42).

Wordsworth never achieved his philosophic song. *Prelude* and *Excursion* are no more than 'ante-chapels' to the 'gothic church' of his unfinished work. An unresolved opposition between Imagination and Nature prevents him from becoming a visionary poet. It is a paradox, though not an unfruitful one, that he should scrupulously record nature's workmanship, which prepares the soul for its independence from sense-experience, yet refrain to use that independence out of respect of nature. His greatest verse *still takes its origin* in the memory of given experiences to which he is often pedantically faithful. He adheres, apparently against nature, to natural fact.

2

There are many who feel that Wordsworth could have been as great a poet as Milton but for this return to nature, this shrinking from visionary subjects. Is Wordsworth afraid of his own imagination? Now we have, in *The Prelude*, an exceptional incident in which the poet comes, as it were, face to face with his imagination. This incident has many points in common with the opening event of *The Prelude*; it also, for example, tells the story of a failure of the mind vis-à-vis the external world. I refer to the poet's crossing of the Alps, in which his adventurous spirit is again rebuffed by nature, though by its strong absence rather than presence. His mind, desperately and unself-knowingly in search of a nature adequate to deep childhood impressions, finds instead *itself*, and has to acknowledge that nature is no longer its proper subject or home. Despite this recognition, Wordsworth continues to bend back the energy of his mind and of his poem to nature, but not before we have learned the secret behind his fidelity.

Having finished his third year of studies at Cambridge, Wordsworth goes on a walking tour of France and Switzerland. It is the summer of 1790, the French Revolution has achieved its greatest success and acts as a subtle, though, in the following books, increasingly human background to his concern with nature. Setting out to cross the Alps by way of the Simplon Pass, he and a friend are separated from their companions and try to ascend by themselves. After climbing some time and not overtaking anyone, they meet a peasant who tells them they must return to their starting point and follow a stream down instead of further ascending, i.e. they had already, and without knowing it, crossed the Alps. Disappointed, 'For still we had hopes that pointed to the clouds,' they start downward beset by a 'melancholy slackening,' which, however, is soon dislodged (VI.557–91, 616 ff.).

This naive event stands, however, within a larger, interdependent series of happenings: an unexpected revelation comes almost immediately (624–40), and the sequence is preceded by a parallel disappointment with the natural world followed by a compensatory vision (523 ff.). In addition to this pattern of blankness and revelation, of the soulless image and the sudden renewed immediacy of nature, we find a strange instance of the past flowing into the present. Wordsworth, after telling the story of his disappointment, is suddenly, in the very moment of composition, overpowered by a feeling of glory to which he gives expression in rapturous, almost self-obscuring lines (VI.592 ff.). Not until the moment of composition, some fourteen years after the event, does the real reason behind his upward climb and subsequent melancholy slackening strike home; and it strikes so hard that he gives to the power in him, revealed by the extinction of the immediate external motive (his desire to cross the Alps) and by the abyss of intervening years, the explicit name Imagination:

> Imagination – here the Power so called
> Through sad incompetence of human speech,
> That awful Power rose from the mind's abyss
> Like an unfathered vapour that enwraps,
> At once, some lonely traveller. I was lost;
> Halted without an effort to break through;
> But to my conscious soul I now can say –
> 'I recognise thy glory.' (VI.592–99)

Thus Wordsworth's failure vis-à-vis nature (or its failure vis-à-vis him) is doubly redeemed. After descending, and passing through a gloomy strait (621 ff.), he encounters a magnificent view. And crossing, one might say, the gloomy gulf of time, his disappointment becomes retrospectively a prophetic instance of that blindness to the external world which is the tragic, pervasive, and necessary condition of the mature poet. His failure of 1790 taught him gently what now (1804) literally *blinds* him: *the independence of imagination from nature.*

I cannot miss my way, the poet exults in the opening verses of *The Prelude.* And he cannot, as long as he respects the guidance of nature, which leads him along a gradual via negativa to make his soul more than 'a mere pensioner / On outward forms' (VI.737 f.). It is not easy, however, to 'follow Nature.' The path, in fact, becomes so circuitous that a poet follows least when he thinks he follows most. For he must cross a strait where the external image is lost yet suddenly revived with more than original immediacy. Thus a gentle breeze, in the first book, calls forth a tempest of verse, but a splendid evening wanes into silence. A magnificent hope, in the sixth book, dies for lack of sensuous food, but fourteen years later the simple memory of failure calls up that hope in a magnificent tempest of verse. When the external stimulus is too clearly present the poet falls mute and corroborates Blake's strongest objection: 'Natural Objects always did and now do weaken, deaden, and obliterate Imagination in Me.'[6] The poet is forced to discover the autonomy of his imagination, its independence from present joy, from strong outward stimuli – but this discovery, which means a passing of the initiative from nature to imagination, is brought on gradually, mercifully.

Wordsworth does not sustain the encounter with Imagination. His direct cry is broken off, replaced by an impersonal construction – 'here the Power.' It is not Imagination but his 'conscious soul' he addresses directly in the lines that follow. What, in any case, is the soul to do with its extreme recognition? It has glimpsed the height of its freedom. At the end of his apostrophe to Imagination, Wordsworth repeats the idea that the soul is halted by its discovery, as a traveler by a sudden bank of mist. But the simile this time suggests not only a divorce from but also (proleptically) a return to nature on the part of the soul,

> Strong in herself and in beatitude
> That hides her, like the mighty flood of Nile
> Poured from his fount of Abyssinian clouds
> To fertilise the whole Egyptian plain. (VI.613–16)

3

It follows that nature, for Wordsworth, is not an 'object' but a presence and a power; a motion and a spirit; not something to be worshiped and consumed, but always a guide leading beyond itself. This guidance starts in earliest childhood. The boy of *Prelude* I is fostered alike by beauty and by fear. Through beauty, nature often makes the boy feel at home, for, as in the Great Ode, his soul is alien to this world. But through fear, nature reminds the boy from where he came, and prepares him, having lost heaven, also to lose nature. The boy of *Prelude* I, who does not yet know he must suffer this loss as well, is warned by nature itself of the solitude to come.

I have suggested elsewhere how the fine skating scene of the first book (425–63), though painted for its own sake, to capture the animal spirits of children spurred by a clear and frosty night, moves from vivid images of immediate life to an absolute calm which foreshadows a deeper and more hidden life.[7] The Negative Way is a gradual one, and the child is weaned by a premonitory game of hide-and-seek in which nature changes its shape from familiar to unfamiliar, or even fails the child. There is a great fear, either in Wordsworth or in nature, of traumatic breaks: *Natura non facit saltus* [Nature does not make jumps].

If the child is led by nature to a more deeply meditated understanding of nature, the mature singer who composes *The Prelude* begins with that understanding or even beyond it – with the spontaneously creative spirit. Wordsworth plunges into *medias res*, where the *res* is Poetry, or Nature only insofar as it has guided him to a height whence he must find his own way. But Book VI, with which we are immediately concerned, records what is chronologically an intermediate period, in which the first term is neither Nature no Poetry. It is Imagination in embryo: the mind muted yet also strengthened by the external world's opacities. Though imagination is with Wordsworth on the journey of 1790, nature seems particularly elusive. He goes out to a nature which seems to hide as in the crossing of the Alps.

The first part of this episode is told to illustrate a curious melancholy related to the 'presence' of imagination and the 'absence' of nature. Like the young Apollo in Keats' *Hyperion*, Wordsworth is strangely dissatisfied with the riches before him, and compelled to seek some other region:

> Where is power?
> Whose hand, whose essence, what divinity
> Makes this alarum in the elements,

> While I here idle listen on the shores
> In fearless yet in aching ignorance?[8]

To this soft or 'luxurious' sadness, a more masculine kind is added, which results from a 'stern mood' or 'underthirst of vigor'; and it is in order to throw light on this further melancholy that Wordsworth tells the incident of his crossing the Alps.

The stern mood to which Wordsworth refers can only be his premonition of spiritual autonomy, of an independence from sense-experience foreshadowed by nature since earliest childhood. It is the 'underground' form of imagination, and *Prelude* II.315 ff. describes it as 'an obscure sense / Of possible sublimity,' for which the soul, remembering *how* it felt in exalted moments, but no longer *what* it felt, continually strives to find a new content. The element of obscurity, related to nature's self-concealment, is necessary to the soul's capacity for growth, for it vexes the latter toward self-dependence. Childhood pastures become viewless; the soul cannot easily find the source from which it used to drink the visionary power; and while dim memories of a passionate commerce with external things drive it more than ever to the world, this world makes itself more than ever inscrutable.[9] The travelers' separation from their guides, then that of the road from the stream (VI.568), and finally their trouble with the peasant's words that have to be 'translated,' express subtly the soul's desire for a *beyond*. Yet only when poet, brook, and road are once again 'fellow-travellers' (VI.622), and Wordsworth holds to Nature, does that reveal – a Proteus in the grasp of the hero – its prophecy.

This prophecy was originally the second part of the adventure, the delayed vision which compensates for his disappointment (the 'Characters of the great Apocalypse,' VI.617–40). In its original sequence, therefore, the episode has only two parts: the first term or moment of natural immediacy is omitted, and we go straight to the second term, the inscrutability of an external image, which leads via the gloomy strait to its renewal. Yet, as if this pattern demanded a substitute third term, Wordsworth's tribute to 'Imagination' severs the original temporal sequence, and forestalls nature's renewal of the bodily eye with ecstatic praise of the inner eye.

The apocalypse of the gloomy strait loses by this the character of a *terminal* experience. Nature is again surpassed, for the poet's imagination is called forth, at the time of writing, by the barely scrutable, not by the splendid emotion; by the disappointment, not the fulfillment. This (momentary) displacement of emphasis is the more effective in that the style of VI.617 ff., and the very characters of the apocalypse, suggest that the hiding places of power cannot be localized in nature.[10] Though the apostrophe to Imagination – the special insight that comes to Wordsworth in 1804 – is a real peripety, reversing a meaning already established, it is not unprepared. But it takes the poet many years to realize that nature's 'end' is to lead to something 'without end,' to teach the travelers to transcend nature.

The three parts of this episode, therefore, can help us understand the mind's growth toward independence of immediate external stimuli. The measure of that independence is Imagination, and carries with it a precarious self-consciousness. We see that the mind must pass through a stage where it experiences Imagination as a power separate from Nature, that the poet must come to think and feel as if by his own choice, or from the structure of his mind.[11]

VI-a (557–91) shows the young poet still dependent on the immediacy of the external world. Imagination frustrates that dependence secretly, yet its blindness toward nature is accompanied by a blindness toward itself. It is only a 'mute Influence of the soul, / An Element of nature's inner self' (1805, VIII.512–13).

VI-b (592–616) gives an example of thought or feeling that came from the poet's mind without immediate external excitement. There remains, of course, the memory of VI-a (the disappointment), but this is an internal feeling, not an external image. The poet recognizes at last that the power he has looked for in the outside world is really within and frustrating his search. A shock of recognition then feeds the very blindness toward the external world which helped to produce that shock.

In VI-c (617–40) the landscape is again an immediate external object of experience. The mind cannot separate in it what it desires to know and what it actually knows. It is a moment of revelation, in which the poet sees not as in a glass, darkly, but face to face. VI-c clarifies, therefore, certain details of VI-a and *seems* to actualize figurative details of VI-b.* The matter-of-fact interplay of quick and lingering movement, of up-and-down perplexities in the ascent (VI.567 ff.), reappears in larger letters; while the interchanges of light and darkness, of cloud and cloudlessness, of rising like a vapor from the abyss and pouring like a flood from heaven have entered the landscape bodily. The gloomy strait also participates in this actualization. It is revealed as the secret middle term which leads from the barely scrutable presence of nature to its resurrected image. The travelers who move freely with or against the terrain, hurrying upward, pacing downward, perplexed at crossings, are now led narrowly by the pass as if it were their rediscovered guide.

---

* VI-c was composed before VI-b, so that while the transference of images goes structurally from VI-b to VI-c, *chronologically* the order is reversed.

4

The Prelude, as history of a poet's mind, foresees the time when the 'Characters of the great Apocalypse' will be intuited without the medium of nature. The time approaches even as the poet writes, and occasionally cuts across his narrative, the imagination rising up, as in Book VI, 'Before the eye and progress of my Song' (version of 1805). This phrase, at once conventional and exact, suggests that imagination waylaid the poet on his mental journey. The 'eye' of his song, trained on a temporal sequence with the vision in the strait as its final term, is suddenly obscured. He is momentarily forced to deny nature that magnificence it had shown in the gloomy strait, and to attribute the glory to imagination, whose interposition in the very moment of writing proves it to be a power more independent than nature of time and place, and so a better type 'Of first, and last, and midst, and without end' (VI.640).

We know that VI-b records something that happened during composition, and which enters the poem as a new biographical event. Wordsworth has just described his disappointment (VI-a) and turns in anticipation to nature's compensatory finale (VI-c). He is about to respect the original temporal sequence, 'the eye and progress' of his song. But as he looks forward, in the moment of composition, from blankness toward revelation, a new insight cuts him off from the latter. The original disappointment is seen not as a test, or as a prelude to magnificence, but as a revelation in itself. It suddenly reveals a power – imagination – that could not be satisfied by anything in nature, however sublime. The song's progress comes to a halt because the poet is led beyond nature. Unless he can respect the natural (which includes the temporal) order, his song, at least as narrative, must cease. Here Imagination, not Nature (as in I.96 ff.), defeats Poetry.

This conclusion may be verified by comparing the versions of 1805 and 1850. The latter replaces 'Before the eye and progress of my Song' with a more direct metaphorical transposition. Imagination is said to rise from the mind's abyss 'Like an unfathered vapour that enwraps, / At once, some lonely traveller.' The (literal) traveler of 1790 becomes the (mental) traveler at the moment of composition. And though one Shakespearean doublet has disappeared,* another implicitly takes its place: does not imagination rise from 'the dark backward and abysm of time' (*The Tempest*, I.2.50)? The result, in any case, is a disorientation

---

* De Selincourt, *William Wordsworth, The Prelude* (1959), p. 559, calls 'Before the eye and progress of my Song' a Shakespearean doublet, which is right except that the text he refers us to should be *Much Ado about Nothing*, IV.1.238, rather than *King John*, II.1.224.

of time added to that of way; an apocalyptic moment in which past and future overtake the present; and the poet, cut off from nature by imagination, is, in an absolute sense, lonely.

The last stage in the poet's 'progress' has been reached. The travelers of VI-a had already left behind their native land, the public rejoicing of France, rivers, hills, and spires; they have separated from their guides, and finally from the unbridged mountain stream. Now, in 1804, imagination separates the poet from all else: human companionship, the immediate scene, the remembered scene. The end of the via negativa is near. There is no more 'eye and progress'; the invisible progress of VI-a (Wordsworth crossing the Alps unknowingly) has revealed itself as a progress independent of visible ends, or engendered by the desire for an 'invisible world' – the substance of things hoped for, the evidence of things not seen. Wordsworth descants on the Pauline definition of faith:

> in such strength
> Of usurpation, when the light of sense
> Goes out, but with a flash that has revealed
> The invisible world, doth greatness make abode,
> There harbours; whether we be young or old,
> Our destiny, our being's heart and home,
> Is with infinitude, and only there;
> With hope it is, hope that can never die,
> Effort, and expectation, and desire,
> And something evermore about to be. (VI.599–608)

Any further possibility of progress for the poet would be that of song itself, of poetry on longer subordinate to the mimetic function, the experience faithfully traced to this height. The poet is a traveler insofar as he must respect nature's past guidance and retrace his route. He did come, after all, to an important instance of bodily vision. The way is the song. But the song often strives to become the way. And when this happens, when the song seems to capture the initiative, in such supreme moments of poetry as VI-b or even VI-c, the way is lost. Nature in VI-c shows 'Winds thwarting winds, bewildered and forlorn,' as if they too had lost their way. The apocalypse in the gloomy strait depicts a self-thwarting march and counter-march of elements, a divine mockery of the concept of the Single Way.

But in VI-c, nature still stands over and against the poet; he is still the observer, the eighteenth-century gentleman admiring a new manifestation of the sublime, even if the lo! or mark! is suppressed. He moves

haltingly but he moves; and the style of the passage emphasizes conti-
nuities. Yet with the imagination athwart there is no movement, no
looking before and after. The song itself must be the way, though that
of a blinded man, who admits, 'I was lost.' Imagination, as it shrouds
the poet's eye, also shrouds the eye of his song, whose tenor is nature
guiding and fostering the power of song.

It is not, therefore, till 1804 that Wordsworth discovers the identity
of his hidden guide. VI-c was probably composed in 1799, and it implies
that Wordsworth, at that time, still thought nature his guide. But now
he sees that it was imagination moving him by means of nature, just as
Beatrice guided Dante by means of Virgil. It is not nature as such but
nature indistinguishably blended with imagination that compels the poet
along his Negative Way. Yet, if VI-b prophesies against the world of
sense-experience, Wordsworth's affection and point of view remain
unchanged. Though his discovery shakes the foundation of his poem,
he returns after a cloudburst of verses to the pedestrian attitude of 1790,
when the external world and not imagination seemed to be his guide
('Our journey we renewed, / Led by the stream,' etc.).[12] Moreover, with
the exception of VI-b, imagination does not move the poet directly, but
always through the agency of nature. The childhood 'Visitings of imaginative power' depicted in Books I and XII also appeared in the guise or
disguise of nature. Wordsworth's journey as a poet can only continue
with eyes, but the imagination experienced as a power distinct from
nature opens his eyes by putting them out. Wordsworth, therefore, does
not adhere to nature because of natural fact, but despite it and because
of human and poetic fact. Imagination is indeed an *awe-full* power.

Notes

1   See *Blake, Coleridge, Wordsworth, Lamb, etc., Being Selections from the Remains of
    Henry Grabb Robinson*, ed. E. J. Morley (Manchester: Manchester Univ. Press,
    1922), 5 and 15.
2   See the Critical Bibliography (*Wordsworth's Poetry*, 349–51).
3   Throughout this book, quotations from *The Prelude* (unless otherwise stated) are
    from the 1850 text as printed by De Selincourt and Darbishire in *William Word-
    sworth, The Prelude* (Oxford: Clarendon Press, 1959), short-titled *Prelude*.
4   Emancipated – but through exile. For the allusions to *Paradise Lost* and Exodus,
    see *Prelude* I.14 and 16–18.
5   Cf. M. H. Abrams, 'The Correspondent Breeze: A Romantic Metaphor,' in
    English Romantic Poets, ed. Abrams (Galaxy paperback, New York: Oxford Univ.
    Press, 1960), pp. 37–54.

6   Marginalia to Volume I of Wordsworth's *Poems* of 1815. I may venture the opinion that Wordsworth, at the beginning of *The Prelude*, goes back to nature not to increase his chances of sensation but rather to emancipate his mind from immediate external excitements, the 'gross and violent stimulants' (1800 Preface to *Lyrical Ballads*) of the city he leaves behind him.

7   Geoffrey Hartman, *The Unmediated Vision: An Interpretation of Wordsworth, Hopkins, Rilke and Valery* (New Haven: Yale Univ. Press, 1954), pp. 17–20.

8   *Hyperion* III.103–7.

9   Cf. the Intimations Ode; also *Prelude* I.597 ff.

10   Of the four sentences which comprise lines 617–40, the first three alternate the themes of eager and of restrained movement ('melancholy slackening . . . Downwards we hurried fast . . . at a slow pace'); and the fourth sentence, without explicit transition, commencing in mid-verse (line 624), rises very gradually and firmly into a development of sixteen lines. These depend on a single verb, an unemphatic 'were,' held back till the beginning of line 636; the verb thus acts as a pivot that introduces, without shock or simply as the other side of the coin, the falling and interpretative movement. This structure, combined with a skillful interchange throughout of asyndetic and conjunctive phrases, always avoids the sentiment of abrupt illumination for that of a majestic swell fed by innumerable sustaining events, and thereby strengthens our feeling that the vision, though climactic, is neither terminal nor discontinuous.

11   Cf. Preface (1802) to *Lyrical Ballads*: '[The poet] has acquired a greater readiness and power in expressing . . . especially those thoughts and feelings which, by his own choice, or from the structure of his own mind, arise in him without immediate external excitement.'

12   The 'return to nature' is anticipated by the last lines of VI-b (lines 613–16).

Further reading

What follows is a representative selection of the criticism which, elucidating imagination, consciousness and selfhood in Wordsworth's poetry, asserts or assumes his humanism, on philosophical or thematic grounds.

John Jones, *The Egotistical Sublime: A History of Wordsworth's Imagination* (London: Chatto & Windus, 1954). Registers in Wordsworth's poetry of the 'Great Decade' a dual sense of the sufficiency of the individual mind and the relational significance of the external world, charting, in the decline of this notion of 'attachment-in-solitude' in the later poetry, the transition from a secular to a Christian imagination.

David Ferry, *The Limits of Mortality: An Essay on Wordsworth's Major Poems* (Middletown: Wesleyan University Press, 1959). Wordsworth's major poetry transforms its subjects, locatable in time and place, into symbols of man's relations with the eternal; this commitment to a metaphysical, eternal nature implies a hostility to physical or actual nature.

John F. Danby, *The Simple Wordsworth: Studies in the Poems 1797–1807* (London: Routledge & Kegan Paul, 1960). De-emphasizes 'nature' in Wordsworth by presenting the simplicity of the published poems of 1797–1807 as the product of a sophisticated moral and social consciousness that aligns Wordsworth with a Renaissance tradition, of poetry entailing public responsibility.

*Harold Bloom, *The Visionary Company: A Reading of English Romantic Poetry* (1961; revised and enlarged edn., Ithaca and London: Cornell University Press, 1971). Characterizes Wordsworth's great poetry, in the context of a survey of the Romantic imagination, by a heroic and naturalistic humanism that celebrates 'the possibilities inherent in our condition, here and now.'

Christopher Salvesen, *The Landscape of Memory: A Study of Wordsworth's Poetry* (London: Edwin Arnold, 1965). Focuses on memory rather than imagination as key to Wordsworth's poetry and the ground of his originality.

Melvin Rader, *Wordsworth: A Philosophical Approach* (Oxford: Clarendon Press, 1967). Usefully presents the idealistic and transcendentalist strain in Wordsworth's thinking in relation to a range of philosophical contexts, emphasizing, at the same time, his freedom from formal philosophical commitments.

Jonathan Wordsworth, *The Music of Humanity* (London: Nelson, 1969). Strong affirmation of Wordsworth's sympathy and humanitarianism, by means of a close analysis of the original drafts of the early poetry.

*M. H. Abrams, *Natural Supernaturalism: Tradition and Revolution in Romantic Literature* (New York and London: W. W. Norton, 1971). Presents Wordsworth as the exemplar of a Romantic movement in literature and philosophy taking place across England and Germany, characterized by its secularizing of key religious (especially Biblical) paradigms and concepts.

S. M. Parrish, *The Art of the* Lyrical Ballads (Cambridge, Mass.: Harvard University Press, 1971). Demonstrates Wordsworth's commitment to and practice of conscious artistry in *Lyrical Ballads*, emphasizing, in so doing, his partnership with and differences from Coleridge, and reasserting his originality on the grounds of his experiments with the ballad form.

Harold Bloom, *The Anxiety of Influence: A Theory of Poetry* (New York: Oxford University Press, 1973). Wordsworth's relationship to Milton is made part of the seminal formulation, drawing upon Freud and Nietzsche, of the 'anxiety of influence', that is, the antagonistic relation of poets to their precursors, generating poetic texts that are misreadings of precursor texts. (The topic of Wordsworth and Milton is treated in greater detail in Bloom's *Poetry and Repression: Revisionism from Blake to Stevens* [New Haven and London: Yale University Press, 1976].)

Paul Sheats, *The Making of Wordsworth's Poetry, 1785–1798* (Cambridge, Mass.: Harvard University Press, 1973). Examines Wordsworth's early poetic development, and especially the conceptions of mind and nature that become the major themes of his maturer work, through a close analysis of his textual practice in the poetry to 1798.

Mary Jacobus, *Tradition and Experiment in Wordsworth's* Lyrical Ballads *(1798)* (Oxford: Clarendon Press, 1976). Describes as simultaneous and inseparable, experimentalism and the renewal of tradition in *Lyrical Ballads*, the work that is critical to

Wordsworth's self-definition and the development (partly under Coleridge's influence) of his literary identity as a poet of the human heart.

Frances Ferguson, *Wordsworth: Language as Counter-Spirit* (New Haven and London: Yale University Press, 1977). Treats language as 'an explicit subject of speculation' for Wordsworth. The argument that the complex relationships between language and consciousness in Wordsworth's poetry call into question the existence of a unitary self anticipates subsequent critical developments.

John Beer, *Wordsworth and the Human Heart* (London: Macmillan, 1978). The importance attached by Wordsworth to the human heart – to understanding which both Coleridge and Dorothy Wordsworth are integral – is the key to his sense of humanity; his commitment to the culture of the heart persists in and mitigates the egotism and conservatism of his declining years.

James H. Averill, *Wordsworth and the Poetry of Human Suffering* (Ithaca and London: Cornell University Press, 1980). In his early poetry through to *Lyrical Ballads* and *The Prelude*, Wordsworth manifests an interest in and response to suffering inherited from the eighteenth-century traditions of sensibility and sentimentalism, intensified and reworked in his own poems of human life.

D. D. Devlin, *Wordsworth and the Poetry of Epitaphs* (London and Basingstoke: Macmillan, 1980). Elicits, from Wordsworth's *Essays upon Epitaphs*, the reconcilement of opposites as the aim of poetry; the exemplary mode of that reconcilement is the epitaph, which is also the figure for Wordsworth's own finest writing.

Thomas McFarland, *Romanticism and the Forms of Ruin: Wordsworth, Coleridge, and Modalities of Fragmentation* (Princeton: Princeton University Press, 1981). Contains an important account of the mutual influence ('symbiosis') of Wordsworth and Coleridge, contextualized within a study of the 'diasparactive' emphasis – the dominance of forms of incompleteness, fragmentation and ruin – in Romanticism, complementary to its impulse to unity, or need for 'reticulation'.

Jonathan Wordsworth, *William Wordsworth: The Borders of Vision* (Oxford: Clarendon Press, 1982). Paying close attention to chronology, and centring on the years of *Prelude* composition (1798–1805), reads, in the concern with borderers and border conditions in Wordsworth's poetry of this period, an aspirational, idealistic and millenarian tendency.

Don H. Bialostosky, *Making Tales: The Poetics of Wordsworth's Narrative Experiments* (Chicago and London: University of Chicago Press, 1984). Argues that the enjoyment of *Lyrical Ballads* calls for a truer understanding of the poetic system upon which it is based, which is a poetics of speech, fundamentally separate and distinct from the Aristotelian poetics of imitated actions.

Kenneth R. Johnston, *Wordsworth and* The Recluse (New Haven and London: Yale University Press, 1984). Studies *The Recluse* as an extant (rather than non-existent) Romantic epic, sharing the fragmentary and peculiarly Romantic condition produced by the unresolved tension between its artistic motivations and its social intentions, but integral nonetheless to understanding the relation of self to nature and to society in Wordsworth's poetry.

Lucy Newlyn, *Coleridge, Wordsworth, and the Language of Allusion* (Oxford: Clarendon, Press, 1986). Tracks, through the changing pattern of mutual allusion in

Wordsworth's and Coleridge's early poetry, the emerging disparities between their constructions of imagination and selfhood.

HISTORICIZING WORDSWORTH

Hartman describes himself as reconciling the two poles of Wordsworth criticism, 'nature' and 'consciousness' (corresponding to the dualism that Hazlitt has already noted, of 'natural description' and 'inspired reflection', in Wordsworth's poetry), but his own work has produced, or made manifest, another polarity, also anticipated in Hazlitt's essay. Hazlitt registers both the historical context of the poetry ('It partakes of, and is carried along with, the revolutionary movement of our age') and its visionary, ahistorical tendency ('Remote from the passions and events of the great world, he has communicated interest and dignity to the primal movements of the heart of man, and ingrafted his own conscious reflections on the casual thoughts of hinds and shepherds'). That second tendency finds its exemplary response in Hartman's book, in which the debates about 'nature' and, first 'philosophy', then 'consciousness', culminate. Hartman's approach is deliberately (and influentially) psychological rather than historical. The parallel critical approach, emphasizing the historical context of Wordsworth's poetry has persisted from Hazlitt, through Émile Legouis, to the historical readings of the modern day. Marilyn Butler's popular and widely-used *Romantics, Rebels and Reactionaries* (1981) asserts the importance of 'studying Romantic literature against its historical background', emphasizing 'Wordsworth's representativeness' in that study.[14] More polemically, breaking away from a traditional line of historical criticism, which reads in the poetry the *expression* of specific historical and political contexts, the 'new' historicist criticism finds in the poetry a *repression* of those contexts. Significantly, the arguments about Wordsworth's 'denial' of history gain ground from the key accounts of the 'visionary' Wordsworth, which recognize in his transforming imagination something inimical to actual, physical nature or, as in Ferry, to the here-and-now. In articulating a counter to such accounts, the new historicist critic refuses the linear or causal assumption implicit in providing a historical context for what Marjorie Levinson calls 'manifest theme'.[15] Instead, Wordsworth's engagement with history is elicited by a deploying of historical knowledge, not of what is manifest, but of what is displaced or erased in his poetry. Because of the sheer plurality of the unspoken, the new historicist criticism is, at its best, a heady combination of creative interpretation and scrupulously researched historical background.

The *tour de force* of the new historicist criticism of Wordsworth is Alan Liu's *Wordsworth: The Sense of History* (1989). Just as Hartman sought to reconcile 'nature' and 'consciousness', so too, in his turn, Liu argues that 'the

parting of the sea . . . between the representations of history and the apocalyptic and visionary imagination championed by Hartman is too severe. . . . strong
denials of history are also the deepest realizations of history: apocalyptic
Imagination is the very threshold, the "sublime" of the "representations of
reality as historical process." "[16] The following extract, one of Liu's revisions of
Hartman's reading of the Simplon Pass episode, captures the flair of his
approach. Wordsworth's denial of history is figured as the spectre of Napoleon,
the Imagination's 'uncanny double' which it attempts, by mimicking, to
eradicate.

Extract from Alan Liu, *Wordsworth: The Sense of History* (1989)

Imagination and Napoleon

But Book 6 cannot be read wholly on its own. Let me now open the
aperture completely to view Simplon Pass in the overall context of *The
Prelude* and 1804, when Book 6 and much of the rest of the poem were
composed. In this context, it becomes important to stare fixedly into,
and *through*, the mirror of the Imagination. In the construction of the
total *Prelude* in 1804, I believe, Wordsworth inserted background
reminders of historicity in the Imagination passage as avenues toward a
realization that 'the mind' must finally enroll (literally enlist, as Wordsworth did in the Grasmere Volunteers in 1803[1] in a collective system
authorized from some source 'elsewhere' than the self: in the grounded
or demystified Nile that is history.[2] Specifically, Book 6 and the Imagination passage look forward to the direct concern of the Revolution
books (Books 9 and 10) with a deluge of history. Wordsworth probably
began composing much of Books 9 and 10 soon after finishing 6 in late
April 1804 (with additional work in October to December of that year);[3]
and there is the possibility that all three books dealing with France were
composed in a single manuscript.[4] In the movement of the total poem,
the denial (and de-Nile) of history in 6b really warns that the nature and
self thus far imagined are antediluvian. Wordsworth is about to go on
to open the floodgates in order to let in a ferocious tributary of his Nile:
the river of 'shapeless eagerness,' as we will later see, that rushes us into
explicit history at the opening of Book 9.

What preoccupies Imagination in 1804 such that it at once prevents
and presages history? MS. WW of *The Prelude*, we know, shows that

Wordsworth originally inserted what is now 8.711–27 – the first part of the simile of the cave – between 6a and 6b.[5] Imagination, I suggest, is as hollow as this cave. The more we look into it, the more we submit to an interior, self-motivated reality bodying forth (in the language of the simile) 'Shapes and Forms and Tendencies to Shape.' Specifically, Imagination cavitates nature to show the protruding bones of the historical world of 1804. In 6b, Imagination sees in nature not just its own reflection but that of a firmly *historical* genius of imagination – of the Imaginer who, in a manner of speaking, wrote the book on crossing the Alps. I believe that if we look into 6b, we will see through the self and mind in the foreground, through even the nature in the middle ground, to a frightening skeleton in the background. Whatever else it is, Imagination is the haunt of Napoleon, the great Bone of the time (a standard play on words in the early 1800's; see below). More precisely, if Imagination reflects upon nature as a mirror, the mirror is of magistrates and shows Imagination to itself as a canny double for uncanny Napoleon. Imagination at once mimics and effaces Napoleon in an effort, anticipatory of Books 9–10 and after, to purge tyranny by *containing* tyranny within itself.[6]

We need to be careful here with degrees of certainty. An adequate reading of Wordsworth's texts in their historical context, I will suggest, requires not so much positivistic method as a deflected or denied positivism able to discriminate absence. For the moment, however, we can reach our goal simply by positing a ladder of increasing certainty. No single piece of evidence in the following presentation leads absolutely to the conclusion that Napoleon stands in the background of 6b, but the sum, I believe, has plausibility; and such plausibility in the specific thesis will be sufficient to carry the general argument that 6b is decisively engaged with history. I highlight the most telling specifics in italics, but I also include supplementary suggestions based on circumstances and sometimes wordplay that might appear farfetched in normal times. After reading in the literature and art of British reactions to Napoleon in the years of war fever – including the standard plays on the skeletal nature of 'Bone-apart' and the fabulous apocalyptic interpretations of Bonaparte's name as the Number of the Beast[7] – I believe that no accident possible to be interpreted should be omitted in detailing an imagination of Napoleon. In any case, the plausibility I aim for does not rest finally on one-to-one correspondence between history and the Imagination passage, but on the alliance between text and context considered as wholes.

18 Brumaire. In 1799 Napoleon returned unexpectedly to France from his Egyptian campaign, reached Paris on October 16 with massive popular support, and took control of the Directory in the coup d'état of 18 Brumaire (actually 18–19 Brumaire; November 9–10).[8] *The Annual Register* (years 1758–92, 1794–96, 1800, 1802–11, and 1814–20 were in Wordsworth's Rydal Mount library);[9] banners the world's astonishment at this advent as if from nowhere, choosing a style of language – 'in defiance of reason . . . not any one . . . could have imagined' – that we will need to consider later:

> Whether we contemplate the great affairs of nations in a political or military point of view, the return of Buonaparte to France . . . is the grand and leading event in the history of 1800. . . . Who could have believed that a simple sub-lieutenant of artillery, a stranger to France, by name and by birth, was destined to govern this great empire, and to give the law, in a manner, to all the continent, in defiance of reason? . . . There is not any one in the world who could have imagined the possibility of an event so extraordinary.[10]

'Brumaire' is the month of mists in the vividly imagined Revolutionary calendar, and Napoleon's takeover climaxed in his famously violent personal appearance before the hostile Council of Five Hundred at Saint-Cloud (spoken of simply as 'Cloud' in the early Revolution because of antisacral doctrine).[11] In the world's eye, we might say, Napoleon burst upon the scene as a kind of 'vapour,' or cloud, an upstart and illegitimate spirit.

In 6b Wordsworth begins with a coup d'état of Imagination retracing something like the spirit of 18 Brumaire: an 'unfather'd vapour' starts up in defiance of all expectation, comes with 'Power' upon a poet who, like France in 1799, was 'Halted, without a struggle to break through,' and changes the regime with such 'strength/Of usurpation' that the astonished poet, like France before Napoleon's renewed spectacles of state,* must say, 'I recognise thy glory.' Such recognition of glory – the great instance of bright obscurity – merely makes official what the poet had unconsciously, in an analogy to French popular support for Napoleon, depended upon all along.

Anchoring the reading of Imagination as coup d'état is Wordsworth's strong use of the figure 'usurpation,' a use prepared for in the chronicle of Mont Blanc. Usurpation in Book 6 is a figure backed up by allusion to *Macbeth*, the poem's preferred exemplar of the usurper.[12] Just after describing the descent through Gondo Gorge, Wordsworth describes 'innocent Sleep' lying 'melancholy among weary bones' (6.579–80; *Macbeth* II.ii.33). In one sense, the allusion points ahead in the poem,

---

* Beginning with the pageantry of Napoleon's symbolic move to the Tuileries on February 19, 1800 (Sydenham, *First French Republic*, 235).

and backward in time, to Book 10 and the night in 1792 when the poet heard a voice in the Paris hotel quoting the regicide Macbeth: 'Sleep no more' (10.77; *Macbeth* II.ii.32). Since Book 10 moves on immediately to the confrontation between Robespierre and Louvet, we can guess that Wordsworth's Macbeth, in the context of 1792, figures Robespierre (who in 10.461–62 is also represented as an offspring of Lear). But in another sense, the allusion to *Macbeth* in Book 6 with its addition of the image of bones points to Old Boney: *in the context of the years immediately preceding 1804, 'usurper' cannot refer to anyone other than Napoleon.*

After 18 Brumaire, 'usurper' was applied to Bonaparte in English parliamentary speeches, pamphlets, and newspapers with the consistency of a technical term and irrespective of party affiliation or sympathy with French republicanism. Whether he was thought merely to epitomize republicanism or to break with it, the premise was that Napoleon was a usurper. Use of the epithet peaked first in 1799–1800 after 18 Brumaire and Napoleon's subsequent offer of peace to George III, which the Government chose to perceive as an insult because Napoleon took the stance of equal. The *Times* of London, for example, named Bonaparte 'usurper' immediately after his coup.[13] In his forceful speech of February 3, 1800, Pitt then referred repeatedly to Napoleon as 'usurper' and his government as a 'usurpation'.[14] Similarly, Sheridan spoke of Bonaparte in 1800 as 'this ferocious usurper'.[15] Use of the epithet then peaked a second time in 1803–4 upon the resumption of hostilities after the Peace of Amiens, when *The Annual Register*, for example, labeled Bonaparte 'the Corsican usurper' and the *Times* similarly issued a virtual litany of 'usurpers,' 'audacious usurpers,' and 'Corisican Usurpers.'[16] Perhaps the best way to suggest the possible impact upon Wordsworth of the usurpation epithet in these years is to read Coleridge in the *Morning Post*. In 1800, Coleridge characterized Bonaparte, his regime, or various French decrees in such barbed phrases as 'this insolence in the usurper' and a 'low Harlequinade of Usurpation.' On March 11, 1800, Coleridge's rhetoric drives the point home: Napoleon's rise is a usurpation, he says repeatedly, and 'In his usurpation, Bonaparte stabbed his honesty in the vitals'.[17]

Marengo and Aboukir. Completing the coup is the 'battle' of Imagination. *A Swiss mountain pass in 1804 was first and foremost a military site:* the avenue of the 'modern Hannibal,' as Coleridge later described Napoleon's forces.[18] It is even more suggestive that 6b inscribes within the literal setting of the Swiss Alps the figure of the Nile, and so folds into Simplon Pass the two most crucial scenes of battle in the Napoleonic wars prior to Trafalgar in 1805: Switzerland (together with northern Italy) and Egypt. The Alpine region, Wordsworth's model of political independence, was the ground of Napoleon's most brilliant successes, and the mouth of the Nile that of his only major defeat to date. The lamination of the two is interpretive: if 6b begins with coup d'état, such illegality becomes progressively transformed until, by the end, Wordsworth has purged tyranny from Imagination in the flow of the Nile.

To begin with, 6b may be read as the conflation of the several Alpine campaigns: 'Halted, without a struggle to break through,' the poet is in the position of French troops awaiting the imagination of Napoleon to lead them through the pass. To some extent, Imagination's progress of blockage followed by rapid breakthrough may reflect the 1796 Italian campaign that first made Napoleon famous. Blocked by the numerically superior Austrians and Piedmontese at the Maritime Alps just to the south of Switzerland, Napoleon gestured toward Genoa, stabbed past the Alps to divide and defeat the enemy armies, and created out of Italy the Cisalpine, Cispadane, and Transpadane republics – a creation accompanied by the first of his wholesale 'spoliations,' as *The Annual Register* terms them, of treasuries and art.[19] To a larger extent, Imagination's progress may reflect France's repeated occupation of Switzerland. Wordsworth later said that this conquest was the culminating factor in his turn of sympathy against France, but linking his various statements on the matter to a specific historical action has proved problematic. J. C. Maxwell argues persuasively that the interventions of 1798 and 1802 – the former not directly led by Napoleon – are equally likely (or unlikely) to have provoked Wordsworth's turn.[20] It seems that Wordsworth conflated the two invasions in hindsight and attached them both to Bonaparte. The 1798 occupation of Switzerland by French armies (while Napoleon prepared for Egypt) and the consequent declaration of the Helvetic Republic were also accompanied by vast 'spoliations' of treasuries.[21] The 1802 action occurred during an insurrection against the French-instituted Helvetic Republic when Napoleon, despite promises to the contrary, intervened both by sending troops under General Ney and by transmitting a manifesto that *The Annual Register* says 'will ever be memorable for its despotic arrogance'.[22] One of Napoleon's special interests in both the 1798 and 1802 occupations, we may note, was to secure the Valais canton and so the link between Paris and Italy through the Simplon Pass.[23]

To the largest extent, however, Imagination's progress in 6b reflects Napoleon's most astonishing stroke to date: his 1800 passage through the Swiss Alps leading to the Battle of Marengo. Newly become First Consul, Napoleon set off in May as de facto head of the Italian campaign to take the Austrian army from the rear. *Like Wordsworth, Napoleon arrived at Geneva, followed the northern shore of the lake eastward to the*

Rhone River, and then turned southward toward Chamonix. Here he diverged, but only slightly, from Wordsworth's 1790 route. While part of his army crossed at Mount Cenis, Little St. Bernard, and Mount St. Gotthard, and a demibrigade of approximately 1000 men was sent to demonstrate as loudly as possible that the crossing would be at Simplon, Napoleon himself accompanied the main army through Great St. Bernard Pass (about 50 miles southwest of Simplon). In an action comparable to Hannibal's crossing by elephant, he broke down his artillery and sledded it through the snow-blocked defile. *This was the first blockage to be overcome in a march widely reported as a series of halts followed by breakthroughs.* The next blockage occurred at Fort Bard, which seemed to impede a narrow defile just past Great St. Bernard. 'There was no alternative,' *The Annual Register* admires; 'the fort must either be taken or another passage sought. Each had its difficulties, but Buonaparte's genius surmounted them'.[24] After some skirmishing, Napoleon raised a cannon on top of a nearby church and battered the fort into surrender.[25] The final, decisive instance of halt followed by breakthrough was the Battle of Marengo itself, which Napoleon turned from defeat into victory. Posted in the rear of the Austrians, Napoleon's inferior forces began retreating under heavy Austrian artillery fire at the village of Marengo. Only with the arrival of Corps Commander Desaix's division from the south could Napoleon mount a charge, supported by all his artillery and cavalry, that broke the Austrian forces.

In the context of 1804, then, any imagination of an Alpine pass would remember the military 'genius' of Bonaparte. It seems natural that Wordsworth's halt 'without a struggle to break through' at the beginning of 6b should lead to the 'banners militant' toward the close. The martial air of 6b, indeed, fairly trumpets itself. If we read in the spirit of the banners, Wordsworth's 'visitings/Of Awful promise, when the light of sense / Goes out in flashes that have shewn to us / The invisible world' hint the violence of artillery. Even Wordsworth's great rallying speech has a military ring:

> Our destiny, our nature, and our home
> Is with infinitude, and only there;
> With hope it is, hope that can never die,
> Effort, and expectation, and desire,
> And something evermore about to be.

Whatever else it is, this speech – in its very cadence – is a double of Napoleon's widely publicized rallying speeches to his armies. After the 1796 breakthrough in the Maritime Alps, for example, *The Annual Register* quotes Bonaparte addressing his troops:

You have precipitated yourselves, like a torrent, from the heights of the Appennines. You have routed and dispersed all who have opposed your progress. . . . Yes, soldiers, you have done much; but does there remain nothing more to be done? Though we have known how to vanquish, we have not known how to profit of our victories. . . . Let us depart! we have yet forced marches to make, enemies to subdue, laurels to gather, injuries to revenge.[26]*

But the parade of banners militant, of course, does not conclude the martial review of 6b. Wordsworth continues:

The mind beneath such banners militant
Thinks not of spoils or trophies, nor of aught
That may attest its prowess, blest in thoughts
That are their own perfection and reward.

Here, even amid the military anthem, his act of purging Napoleon begins. *Wordsworth's stress in 1804 that the Imagination is its own reward, and so eschews spoils and trophies, should be seen to reject precisely Napoleon's famed spoliations.* His homage to the overflowing Nile – which enriches, rather than, like the 'torrent' of Napoleon's armies, robs – then speaks the final 'no' to tyranny. Even as French forces occupied Switzerland in 1798, Bonaparte was preparing to sail for Egypt in an effort to disrupt British commerce with the Far East. Despite great successes on land, victory was robbed from him by Nelson, who destroyed the French fleet at Aboukir on the mouth of the Nile and so left Bonaparte's forces suddenly stranded in Egypt. More important than the actual British victory was the fact that Napoleon's myth of invincibility was for the first time broken. Aboukir was a moral victory, the prophecy of British triumph even in the years of greatest French conquest. Layering the Nile into the Alps, Wordsworth predicts the 'Character of the Happy Warrior.'**

The Spirit of Imagination. In sum, Wordsworth in 6b makes a preliminary trial of the method by which history can be cleansed of tyranny

* Coleridge's comments in the *Morning Post* for January 1, 1800, on a similar speech of Napoleon's could almost be taken to describe Wordsworth's 'egotistical sublime' as well: 'Through all these proclamations the fierce confidence, and proud self-involution of a military despot, intoxicated with vanity, start out most obtrusively'. (Coleridge, *Essays on His Times*, I. 63)

** Writing in the *Morning Post* for March 11, 1800, Coleridge similarly 'grounded' the Nile by reference to Napoleon: 'the Chief Consulate . . . pretends to no sacredness; it is no Nile, made mysterious by the undiscoverableness of its fountainhead; it exists, because it is suitable to existing circumstances; and when circumstances render it unnecessary, it is destructible without a convulsion' (Coleridge, *Essays on His Times*, I. 209).

so that only the shining 'genius' figured by Napoleon – and shared by the poet – will reign. Here we reach the most telling point of correspondence between Wordsworth's Imagination and Napoleon – that of pure spirit. While general British reaction to Bonaparte fluctuated from uncertainty before his usurpation in 1800 to enthusiasm during the Peace of Amiens in 1802 and finally to renewed hostility, *one species of reaction was constant, if officially inadmissible: admiration of the 'genius,' 'sublimity,' and 'imagination' represented by Napoleon.* Bonaparte, as Scott would later call him in his biography, was the 'master-spirit' of the age.[27] *The Annual Register*, for example, consistently admired Napoleon's gifts of mind until its first notes of distrust in the 1802 volume (published in 1803). In its character sketch of 1800, for instance, it discovers Napoleon's youthful 'spark of genius,' and then marvels at his mature genius: Bonaparte possesses 'a firm and undaunted spirit, and a genius penetrating, sublime, and inventive,' and 'his letters, his speeches, his actions, all proclaimed a sublimity of courage, imagination, and design, beyond the limits of vulgar conception'.[28] Hazlitt would later take the same approach in his biography, apostrophizing the Battle of Marengo as 'the most poetical of his battles,' a battle as 'romantic and incredible' as if 'Ariosto, if a magician had planned a campaign'.[29] And Scott's biography will announce Napoleon's imagination in these terms:

> No man ever possessed in a greater degree than Buonaparte, the power of calculation and combination necessary for directing such decisive manoeuvres. It constituted indeed his secret – as it was for some time called – and that secret consisted in an imagination fertile in expedients which would never have occurred to others.[30]

In his superb rendering of the Battle of Marengo, Scott then makes it sound as if Bonaparte in Great St. Bernard Pass were indeed Wordsworth confronting nature in Simplon Pass:

> [He proceeded] to the little village called St. Pierre, at which point there ended every thing resembling a practicable road. An immense and apparently inaccessible mountain, reared its head among general desolation and eternal frost; while precipices, glaciers, ravines, and a boundless extent of faithless snows, which the slightest concussion of the air converts into avalanches capable of burying armies in their descent, appeared to forbid access to all living things but the chamois, and his scarce less wild pursuer. Yet foot by foot, and man by man, did the French soldiers proceed to ascend this formidable barrier, which Nature had erected in vain to limit human ambition . . . in places of unusual difficulty, the drums beat a charge, as if to encourage the soldiers to encounter the opposition of Nature herself.[31]

Recall the diversionary force that Napoleon sent to demonstrate in Simplon Pass. If my presentation has even the barest plausibility, it will appear that Wordsworthian nature is precisely such an imaginary antagonist against which the self battles in feint, in a ploy to divert attention from the real battle to be joined between *history* and self. Whatever the outcome of the skirmish (called dialectic) between nature and self, history, the real antagonist, is thus momentarily denied so that when it debouches at last, it will be recognized with shock by the feinting mind as the greatest power of the Wordsworthian defile. As envisioned in the framework of the total *Prelude* – where the books of unnatural history then come at the point of climax rather than, as in *Paradise Lost*, of denouement – denial is the threshold of Wordsworth's most truly shocking act of Imagination: the sense of history. The true apocalypse will come when history crosses the zone of nature to occupy the self directly, when the sense of history and Imagination thus become one, and nature, the mediating figure, is no more.

Notes

1   See Mary Moorman, *William Wordsworth: A Biography*, 2 vols. (Oxford: Clarendon Press, 1957–65), I. 602–3.

2   Barbara Gates studies Wordsworth's use of rivers as images of history in 'Wordsworth and the Course of History', *Research Studies* 44 (1976), 199–207. Partly under the guidance of R. G. Collingwood in *The Idea of History* (1946; repr. Oxford: Oxford University Press, 1977), she also speaks of the historical imagination in 'The Prelude and the Development of Wordsworth's Historical Imagination', *Etudes Anglaises* 30 (1977), 169–78, but her approach is to make historical imagination a secondary faculty, in addition to 'apocalyptic imagination.'

3   See Jonathan Wordsworth, M. H. Abrams, and Stephen Gill (eds.), *'The Prelude': 1799, 1805, 1850: Authoritative Texts, Context and Reception, Recent Critical Essays* (New York: Norton: 1979), 518–19; Mark L. Reed, *Wordsworth: The Chronology of the Middle Years, 1800–1815* (Cambridge, Mass.: Harvard University Press, 1975), 650–3.

4   Wordsworth et al., *'The Prelude'*, 519.

5   Ibid., 216n.

6   Turner's *Snowstorm: Hannibal and His Army Crossing the Alps*, exhibited in 1812, provides an analogue of the combined mimesis and effacement of Napoleon I indicate here. Napoleon is nowhere to be seen in Turner's celebrated landscape of human diminishment – no more so than Hannibal himself. But as Lynn R. Matteson shows, such invisibility is not simple absence. Relevant are Turner's earlier sketches on the Hannibal theme and the link between *Hannibal and His*

Army Crossing the Alps and ancient British, as well as contemporary French, history (made more pointed, perhaps, by Turner's private viewing of David's *Napoleon at the St. Bernard Pass* in Paris in 1802, coupled with general British interest in the 1809 uprising against Napoleon in the Tyrolean Alps; see Lynn R. Matteson, 'The Poetics and Politics of Alpine Passage: Turner's *Snowstorm: Hannibal and His Army Crossing the Alps*', *Arts Bulletin* 62 (1980), 385–98, especially 393–6. These factors allow us to posit – i.e., to hypothesize and further confirm or dis-prove – the absence of Napoleon with a precision we usually reserve for positive fact. The absence of the Emperor known as the contemporary Hannibal may be firm enough, indeed, to shape the very landscape: imperial absence is the vortex, or revolution, that is Turner's totalitarian vision of nature. With assured relevance, then, we see in *Hannibal and His Army Crossing the Alps* the fact that the man who would cross nature – in more than one sense – is definitively *not* there. He has been crossed out.

7   See, for example, John Ashton, *English Caricature and Satire on Napoleon I* (1888; repr. New York: B. Blom, 1968), 5–11 and *passim*.

8   Contemporary accounts of Napoleon and the Napoleonic years will be cited when used; I have also benefited from modern accounts, the two most helpful for my purposes being M. J. Sydenham, *The First French Republic, 1792–1804* (London: Batsford, 1974) and David Chandler, *The Campaigns of Napoleon* (New York: Macmillan, 1966).

9   Chester L. Shaver and Alice C. Shaver, *Wordsworth's Library: A Catalogue* (New York: Garland, 1979), 9.

10   *Annual Register* (1800), 66.

11   See Jean Robiquet, *Daily Life in the French Revolution*, trans. J. Kirkup (London: Weidenfield and Nicolson, 1964), 62.

12   Since publishing an early version of this chapter in 1984, I have discovered Mary Jacobus's excellent 1983 essay, '"That Great Stage Where Senators Perform": *Macbeth* and the Politics of Romantic Theater', *Studies in Romanticism* 22 (fall 1983), 353–87. In arguing the 'dangerous theatricality of the imagination,' Jacobus anticipates many of the points I make in the following discussion about Wordsworth's use of Macbeth, including the linkage between Macbeth and the concept of usurpation (p. 356) and between Macbeth and Robespierre (p. 363).

13   *Times*, November 18, 20, 22, 1799.

14   William Pitt, *The War Speeches of William Pitt the Younger*, ed. R. Coupland (Oxford: Clarendon Press, 1915), 273, 276, 278.

15   F. J. Maccunn, *The Contemporary English View of Napoleon* (London: Bell, 1914), 21.

16   *Annual Register* (1802), 224. The 1802 volume of the *Annual Register* appeared in 1803. For the usage of 'usurper' and 'usurpation' in the *Times* in 1804, see the issues of Apr. 16 and 20; May 30; June 2; Nov. 19. (The Nov. 19 issue brands Napoleon a 'usurper' five times within the space of a single column.)

17   Samuel Taylor Coleridge, *Essays on His Times in 'The Morning Post' and 'The Courier'*, 3 vols. (Vol. 3 of the *Collected Works of Samuel Taylor Coleridge*, Bollingen

series no. 75), ed. David Erdman (Princeton, NJ: Princeton University Press, 1978), I. 63, 91, 207–11.

18 Coleridge, *Essays on His Times*, II. 138.

19 *Annual Register* (1796), 96.

20 [In 'Wordsworth and the Subjugation of Switzerland', *Modern Language Review* 65 (1970), 16–18.]

21 *Annual Register* (1798), 36.

22 *Annual Register* (1802), 233.

23 R. R. Palmer, *The World of the French Revolution* (New York: Harper & Row, 1972), 171; Alan Palmer, *An Encylopaedia of Napoleon's Europe* (New York: St. Martin's Press, 1984), 148.

24 *Annual Register* (1800), 191.

25 According to the *Annual Register* (1800), 192. But D. Chandler notes that the Fort, though essentially bypassed, held out until June (Chandler, *Campaigns of Napoleon* 280).

26 *Annual Register* (1796), 91.

27 Sir Walter Scott, *The Life of Napoleon Buonaparte, Emperor of the French, with a Preliminary View of the French Revolution*, Vol. I (Exeter: J. & B. Williams, 1843), 216.

28 *Annual Register* (1800), 11.

29 William Hazlitt, *The Life of Napoleon Buonaparte*, vol II (Philadelphia: J. B. Lippincott, 1875), 177.

30 Scott, *Life of Napoleon Buonaparte*, 216.

31 Ibid., 336–7.

Further reading

Listed below are readings of Wordsworth in his historical context. The demarcation between this and the preceding list is not clear-cut; chronology plays a part in the demarcation, and the overlap is considerable. Broadly, however, the emphasis here is political rather than philosophical. Two strands are present throughout in this body of criticism, one emphasizing Wordsworth's radicalism, the other, his conservatism. A further refinement of this distinction emerges in the 1980s, when the 'traditional' begins to be distinguished from the 'new' historicism.

F. M. Todd, *Politics and the Poet: A Study of Wordsworth* (London: Methuen, 1957). Traces Wordsworth's political conservatism to his experience of English and French politics between 1790 and 1830, and to the inherently conservative view of human life in his poetry, even the poetry of his radical period.

*****E. P. Thompson**, 'Disenchantment or Default? A Lay Sermon' in *Power and Consciousness*, ed. C. C. O'Brien and W. D. Vanech (London: University of London Press and New York: New York University Press, 1969). Denies the disengagement of Wordsworth's poetry from his politics, by reading in his creativity, a 'Jacobinism-in-recoil', with equal emphasis on both parts of the phrase, that is, a tension between a 'boundless' radical aspiration and 'a peculiarly harsh and unregenerate reality'.

Carl Woodring, *Politics in English Romantic Poetry* (Cambridge, Mass.: Harvard University Press, 1970). Examines the effects of Wordsworth's changing political beliefs on his poetry, to illustrate the thesis that politics is 'a generative force and argumentative presence in the romantic movement in England', and that the discrepancies between political liberalism and romantic idealism result in a dilemma of political belief for the major romantic writers.

David Erdman, 'Wordsworth as Heartsworth; or, Was Regicide the Prophetic Ground of those "Moral Questions?"', in *The Evidence of the Imagination: Studies of Interactions between Life and Art in English Romantic Literature*, ed. D. H. Reiman, M. C. Jaye and B. T. Bennett (New York: New York University Press, 1978), 12–41. Argues that *The Borderers* is 'a play about the events of 1792–1793 in France', dramatizing arguments about regicide (the execution of Louis XVI), and warning that killing in the guise of revolutionary action is both cause and effect of the poisoning of the human heart.

Heather Glen, *Vision and Disenchantment: Blake's* Songs *and Wordsworth's* Lyrical Ballads (Cambridge: Cambridge University Press, 1983). Insightful comparison, arguing that the originality of the two works is not their 'simplicity', which follows an existing fashion in late eighteenth-century verse, but rather the defeat of the eighteenth-century reader's expectation of a controlling authorial moral viewpoint. Glen contributes to the burgeoning discussion of the political bearing of Wordsworth's poetry by finding in his vision, by contrast with Blake's, a pessimism about human possibility that is inimical to political praxis.

*__Jerome J. McGann__, *The Romantic Ideology: A Critical Investigation* (Chicago and London: University of Chicago Press, 1983). This seminal work, especially powerful in the pronouncedly moral note that it sounds, argues that the record of consciousness in Wordsworth's poetry annihilates history, and in so doing illustrates the (ideologically conservative) tendency of Romantic poems 'to occlude and disguise their own involvement in a certain nexus of historical relations'.

James K. Chandler, *Wordsworth's Second Nature: A Study of the Poetry and Politics* (Chicago and London: University of Chicago Press, 1984). By 1798, and hence in his major work, Wordsworth's is a politically conservative ideology, deriving from Burke and appealing, not to nature, but the 'second nature' constituted by custom, tradition and habit; accommodating this ideology takes the form of 'disguise, distortion, and dislocation' in the poetry.

David Erdman, *Commerce des Lumières: John Oswald and the British in Paris, 1790–1793* (Columbia, Miss.: University of Missouri Press, 1986). Influential study of the Jacobin John Oswald, that sheds light on 'the involvement of British intellectuals [including Wordsworth] in revolutionary thought and action' in France in the early 1790s.

*__Paul Hamilton__, *Wordsworth* (Brighton: Harvester Press, 1986). Recognizes the inseparability of epistemological and political concerns in Wordsworth's poetry, finding, in his poetic radicalism, a form of political conservatism implicit in it from the very start.

***Marjorie Levinson**, *Wordsworth's Great Period Poems: Four Essays* (Cambridge: Cambridge University Press, 1986). Particularly useful for its lucid introduction and positioning of the new historicist approach, illustrated in relation to four key poems, 'Tintern Abbey', 'Michael', the 'Intimations' Ode and 'Peele Castle'.

John Turner, *Wordsworth: Play and Politics. A Study of Wordsworth's Poetry 1787–1800* (Basingstoke and London: Macmillan, 1986). Reasserts the political radicalism of Wordsworth's early humanitarian poetry.

David Simpson, *Wordsworth's Historical Imagination: The Poetry of Displacement* (New York and London: Methuen, 1987). Sets out to replace the unitary Wordsworthian self with the 'radical incoherence' of an imagination that is 'historical' in its social and political engagement, but for which that engagement takes the form of alienation, negation and displacement.

K. R. Johnston and G. W. Ruoff (eds.), *The Age of William Wordsworth: Critical Essays on the Romantic Tradition* (New Brunswick and London: Rutgers University Press, 1987). Usefully accessible essays by major scholars, directed towards the informed general reader. The perspective here is historical and the focus threefold: Wordsworth's cultural and political context, his artistic practice and his heritage.

John Barrell, *Poetry, Language and Politics* (Manchester: Manchester University Press, 1988). Influential manifesto for the cultural materialist as against the humanistic, universalist approach to literary texts, arguing that the refusal of the historically specific contexts for the production and reception of texts is also a refusal of the political. The chapter, 'The Uses of Dorothy: "The Language of Sense" in "Tintern Abbey"', describes the class and gender discrimination implicit in the language of meditation or reflection (distinct from the language of natural description) in 'Tintern Abbey'.

Nicholas Roe, *Wordsworth and Coleridge: The Radical Years* (Oxford: Clarendon Press, 1988). Establishes (*vide* Thompson) the continuity of the political and the literary in Wordsworth, by a detailed historical and biographical study of his early radicalism – his hopes of the French Revolution and of Godwinian philosophy – from which draws the power of a poetry conceived of as restitution for revolutionary disappointment.

***Stephen Gill**, *William Wordsworth: A Life* (Oxford: Clarendon Press, 1989). Standard and best biography, thoroughly informed by the insights of twentieth-century scholarship and engaging closely with the discrepancies between Wordsworth's self-representation and the historical and biographical context; valuable too, in the space it accords to Wordsworth's later years and the growth of his importance in the national culture.

William H. Galperin, *Revision and Authority in Wordsworth: The Interpretation of a Career* (Philadelphia: University of Pennsylvania Press, 1989). Argues that present-day revisionist approaches to the visionary and humanistic poet of the Great Decade are anticipated and superseded by Wordsworth's own later poetry which contests the humanistic authority – the authority of the individual self – of the earlier work.

John Williams, *Wordsworth: Romantic Poetry and Revolution Politics* (Manchester and New York: Manchester University Press, 1989). Disputes the unqualified categorization of Wordsworth's 'conservatism' in the aftermath of the French Revolution by identifying in his writing to 1808 a persistent political aspiration.

K. Hanley and R. Selden (eds.), *Revolution and English Romanticism: Politics and Rhetoric* (Hemel Hempstead: Harvester Wheatsheaf, 1990). Three essays (by Jonathan Wordsworth, Kenneth Johnston and Anne Janowitz) focus on Wordsworth, participating in the ongoing debate about the form of his political and 'revolutionary' engagement.

Thomas Pfau, *Wordsworth's Profession: Form, Class, and the Logic of Early Romantic Cultural Production* (Stanford: Stanford University Press, 1997). Treats Wordsworth in the light of an emerging class-consciousness in the late eighteenth century, showing how his 'poetry is connected with . . . the narrative of a rising middle class'.

Kenneth R. Johnston, *The Hidden Wordsworth: Poet, Lover, Rebel, Spy* (New York and London: W. W. Norton, 1998). Lively reconstruction of the poet's youth, adducing a wealth of historical and biographical material to support the eliciting of a youthful radicalism, references to which are encoded and suppressed within the poetic text. This book demands attention nearly as much by its size as by the sensationalism of the claims listed in its title (the second edition of 2000 is more restrained).

TO THE PRESENT

Two other strands of Wordsworth criticism should be mentioned separately, as reflecting present-day social and political concerns.

Notable among a significant body of gender-based studies is the third section of Mary Jacobus's *Romanticism, Writing, and Sexual Difference* (1989), which considers, with reference to *The Prelude,* 'the role of gender in Romantic self-representation and Romantic pedagogy.'[17] In a chapter entitled 'Writing the Self/Self Writing: William Wordsworth's *Prelude*/Dorothy Wordsworth's *Journals*' in *Romanticism and Gender* (1993), Anne Mellor describes the self constructed by Wordsworth in *The Prelude* as a 'specifically *masculine* self', by contrast with the relational and physically embodied self represented in Dorothy Wordsworth's *Journals.*[18]

Of more recent existence is the field of Romantic 'ecological' criticism to which Wordsworth is central. In *Romantic Ecology: Wordsworth and the Environmental Tradition* (1991), Jonathan Bate rediscovers the Victorian 'poet of nature', negated both in Hartman and Bloom's readings of the 'visionary' poet, and in the ideological readings inaugurated by McGann. Bate's claim is Wordsworth's centrality to a 'tradition of environmental consciousness' that is immediately germane to the most pressing political (ecological) issues of the present day.[19] The topic of Wordsworth and ecology is treated prior to Bate by Donald Hayden and Karl Kroeber,[20] and in his later work, *Ecological Literary Criticism: Romantic Imagining and the Biology of the Mind* (New York:

Columbia University Press, 1994), which discusses Wordsworth along with other major Romantic figures, Kroeber explicitly aligns himself with Bate.

Fittingly, the last of my extracts is taken from a study of the first decade of Wordsworth's career, and so returns us nearly to the vantage-point of his earliest reviewers, to whom the 'Preface' to *Lyrical Ballads* is key and *The Prelude* unknown. David Bromwich's *Disowned by Memory: Wordsworth's Poetry of the 1790s* (1998) offers valuable new readings of particular, sometimes neglected, poems, including 'The Old Cumberland Beggar', 'The Idiot Boy' and 'Nutting'. For its detailed explications of particular works, readers should refer to the book itself. What I have extracted below is the overview – something of a manifesto – provided in its introduction. Bromwich's response to 'the culture-based criticism of the past several years' is that 'a man wrote the poems'; his aim is restitution and reclamation.

Extract from David Bromwich, *Disowned by Memory: Wordsworth's Poetry of the 1790s* (1998)

Wordsworth turned to poetry after the revolution to remind himself that he was still a human being. It was a curious solution, to a difficulty many would not have felt. The whole interest of his predicament is that he did feel it. Yet Wordsworth is now so established an eminence – his name so firmly fixed with readers as a moralist of self-trust emanating from complete self-security – that it may seem perverse to imagine him as a criminal seeking expiation. Still, that is the picture we get from *The Borderers* and, at a longer distance, from 'Tintern Abbey.' The community he wants to defend has as its center and motive for being a social anomaly like the old Cumberland beggar. And his characteristic heroes and heroines of the nineties – the shiftless brutal itinerant vendor who has abandoned 'a dozen wedded wives'; the deserted half-mad woman who wails for the two-year-old child she may have drowned; the mother who leaves behind a friend on her sickbed to search for her lost idiot boy; the miserable returning sailor who robs and kills a traveler in sight of his own house – draw upon Wordsworth the reproach of being an aberrant and maybe a dangerous writer. The present book has been written from the belief that on that primitive point of information his earliest reviewers were right. The celebration of necessity in 'Tintern Abbey,' of a force that 'rolls through all things' and is 'in the mind of man,' and the poem's interest in passing from seclusion to 'thoughts of more deep seclusion,' do not belong to a different life from that of the convicts, drifters, deserted wives and mad mothers with whom the poet was accused of indulging in unclean sympathies. He is one of them.

We have honored him for uninteresting virtues; but the fault is not entirely his. Art of a certain dignity risks being fancied in the minds of spectators as a monumental thing. Wordsworth was a disagreeable man and an interesting poet, but a man wrote the poems and it seems worth keeping him in view, as disagreeably as possible. There are people his poetry will never touch. They should confess that they find him opaque, as he often found himself, but not put down the effect to a design of stupefying commonness. We bring our own moralism to poetry, a dingy certitude that presents an encumbrance of its own. Wordsworth's hope of sustaining a life of imagination, which he had the nerve to connect with the survival of human nature, is original, whether or not we share his fear that human nature can be lost. He made as new a beginning as any poet after Milton, but it was self-questioning that drove him to poetry, and he is telling the truth about himself in the memory-fragment of 1799 when he says that he has written to disclose a buried life,

> feeling, as I fear,
> The weakness of a human love for days
> Disowned by memory.

He does not pretend to know the meaning of those days.

Yet he knows that the life he tells of belonged to childhood, to 'the radiance which was once so bright,' and also to later days he spent in France,

> standing on the top of golden hours,
> And human nature seeming born again.

These different times are never far apart in his view, and it dawns on us gradually that what Wordsworth cannot say about the revolution he will often consent to say about his childhood, and what he cannot say of childhood he will say of the revolution. His deepest fear is that his ambition to change the world may succeed for himself at a price to nature – a theft, a betrayal, a scar on the landscape, even if it appears on no one's map but his. What, then, could be the appeal of *common life* – that life of familiar persons and places which he always seems to defend – to a poet so gifted with peculiar energy? Common life doubtless held for him the promise of a counter-tendency. It gave a depth and the weight of a past to a mind heated by imaginings of the future.

In portraying his childhood and young manhood, Wordsworth frequently lets us see him as a listener. The Boy of Winander pausing as 'mimic hootings' pass between himself and the owls, and the republican radical stopping on the road in France to notice the hunger-bitten girl his friend has pointed out with the words ''Tis against *that* / That we are fighting,' are recognizably the same person caught in the same gesture. He hears a call to which others are oblivious. When he is drawn to a scene of risk, he is apt to look on himself as a hidden cause of the risk. The dream of book 5 of *The Prelude* is instructive here. The Arab 'of the Bedouin tribes' who shows the dreamer the stone and the shell is a man with practical needs like Sancho Panza, but the dreamer regards him as a figure of romance like Don Quixote. The stone and shell accordingly turn into mystical relics; and the poet, listening to the shell alone, hears

> A loud prophetic blast of harmony;
> An Ode, in passion uttered, which foretold
> Destruction to the children of the earth
> By deluge, now at hand.

They flee the place together, the poet somehow more slowly, keeping closer to the flood; and the poet, looking back to follow the Arab's gaze, perceives

> over half the wilderness diffused
> A bed of glittering light.

At the sight, says Wordsworth, the man's countenance grew disturbed. Or was it the sight of the poet that disturbed him? In this dream, Wordsworth contrives to place himself between the agency of destruction and the man who fears its power; he is half guardian, half accomplice: a character that, when you think of it, fits him in much of his poetry of the nineties. A wanderer, and, when he stands still, an unsettling presence, he does not believe that he will be a blessing to others.

I have tried to hold this image of Wordsworth steadily enough to explain his doubtful opinion of himself and his desire to attach himself to the world. He does not sentimentalize or soften down his craving for excitement. He knows that the memory of terror, at a sufficient distance, may enforce his feeling of attachment as vividly as love. Thus he comes to Paris in 1792, soon after the September massacres, regretting that the catastrophe is 'Divided from me by one little month,' but he finds the sensations of the killings still so close that he can see them and touch, while the rest of what passed is 'conjured up / From tragic fictions or true history, / Remembrances and dim admonishments.' The admonishments were perhaps the warnings of friends to stay out of trouble; and, perhaps, compunctions about the trouble into which he had cast others. And yet, with no reason for lingering there, Wordsworth wants to feel that the world supports his placement on the scene; and speaking as a traveler of his motives for stopping, he says that his sense of excitement justified itself: 'I felt most deeply in what world I was.' Whatever was in this premonition of the later Terror for those who suffered – and he does not gloss over the sufferings – Wordsworth felt intoxicated as well as chastened, and he tells us so.

The idea that Wordsworth was never an actor in such scenes, but a contemplative observer, we owe above all to Coleridge.[1] His was an original but a normalizing view of the poetry, keen on making it exemplary for the central range of human experience. This view may seem inescapable now, because it guided Wordsworth himself starting in the early 1800s. Coleridge wanted to believe for reasons of his own, and he persuaded Wordsworth also to believe, that a young poet's gradual development toward self-consciousness was his major theme, and that its truth for morals was gratitude to nature for having made him what he was. With that description of the poet's work came the burden of a special project, of which Wordsworth was the destined executor – a theodicy, both metaphysical and historical in scope, whose leading evidences would come from the receptive and infinitely associable mind of the poet. Little will be found in these pages on this theme of consciousness, though I believe that Wordsworth had a mind and that it thought. But his friend's ambitions were mismatched to his own talents. When you have disposed of the philosophy of *The Prelude*, you have not disposed of Wordsworth but only of a notion someone once had of him, which he unfortunately came to share. The long poem he withheld for most of his life is a record of accidents, to which the author hoped to give coherence. The accidents interest me and I have called on them wherever they seemed to solicit entry into the story of his poetry of the nineties.

Wordsworth published his first two books, *An Evening Walk* and *Descriptive Sketches*, to prove to his family, friends, and guardians that his time at Cambridge had not been wasted. But it was the time in France that had shown him what he was, and in what world he was; this could not be divulged in any poetry he knew of, or yet could write. He was well advised to try the subject in drama first; there, at least, he had a working model in Schiller. Political concealment was not his aim, and in May 1794 one finds him writing to his friend William Mathews, in negotiations to start a political magazine, that 'I am of that odious class of men called democrats, and of that class I shall for ever continue.' He declares in a subsequent letter – in the mood of one who would fairly advertise what he is, before asking another to collaborate with him – 'I disapprove of monarchical and aristocratical governments, however modified. Hereditary distinctions and privileged orders of every species I think must necessarily counteract the progress of human improvement: hence it follows that I am not amongst the admirers of the British constitution.'[2] This is as much as to announce himself a despiser of the established system of property. It is not clear to me when, if ever, he parted from this prejudice completely; but among the early poems, *Michael* and 'Hart-Leap Well' may be taken to define subtly different points of view regarding the link between property and human feeling. The tacit consolation of *Michael* is the freedom that remains to the hero after his son is gone, and that freedom is associated with his return to a loved and familiar place, which he knows as an extension of himself. A poem more overt in its moral, 'Hart-Leap Well' suggests that any exhilaration drawn from 'sorrow of the meanest thing that feels' is wicked, however it may be associated with monuments of distinguished ownership. The modest inheritance of an upright man like Michael touches the poet as the estate of the aristocrat Sir Walter does not; but it is doubtful a modern reader can know the feelings of disgust with which Wordsworth revolved in his mind the idea of a 'pleasure-house.' Every *making* of property must be a celebration of vanity. This was perhaps the one form of invention of which he disapproved in principle. To inherit passively is as much the right thing to do with property as it is the wrong thing to do with feelings.

Yet he recognizes the irresistibility of the human instinct for appropriation; for he can trace it in himself. In 'Nutting' his tearing the branches from the tree, to let the sky look in, is done to yield a picturesque enclosure, a 'view' composed for him alone. Yet he closes the poem with a desire that the beauty of the place be known to all, and possessed by no one. The figure who stands as Wordsworth's most intuitive test of feeling, the old Cumberland beggar, has no property and no place to call his own; the persons who are brought into relation by his presence must, in order to care for him, suspend all ordinary categories of status and rooted feeling. This suspense, coming under various names, often in proximity to an idea of admonishment from unknown regions, is the truth that Wordsworth was put into the world to show. What is suspended is the rational conception of a person, a plan of life, a social context with intelligible meanings and obligations. They are brought up short, turned back upon themselves, in the presence of something simply and radically human. Wordsworth believed we are humanized by a process in which thoughts become habitual. But a feeling or sympathy makes itself memorable in its first moment – always a moment of shock when it comes from an unexpected source. This explains the far from customary interest that his poetry takes in the very old and the very young.

We should not forget the pertinence of his theme to the experiments of living that Wordsworth entered into in the nineties. The raising of the child of Basil Montagu was a brave undertaking, an act of sustained deliberate and active sympathy that he shared with his sister at Race-down and Alfoxden. It was a proof of his solidarity in friendship, but also a practical test of the communism of moral sentiments he came to credit when in France. In his portrait, in *The Prelude*, of 'a race of real children,'

> Fierce, moody, patient, venturous, modest, shy;
> Mad at their sports like withered leaves in winds,

he generalizes the experience of his own childhood and the younger Basil's. Education on Wordsworth's terms must assure that this spontaneity of impulse is not crushed; if it has an end, it is only to pre-serve, as far as possible, what was there in its beginnings. The task of nourishing a principle of hope implies a further link between the early years of childhood and the earliest period of the French Revolution. Through the sonnets of August 1802 and the *Prelude* of 1805 and the *Convention of Cintra* of 1809, Wordsworth will continue to see himself as one who 'in these times of fear, / This melancholy waste of hopes o'erthrown' still refuses to adopt a duty that would confine itself to a familiar neighborhood.[3] Conventional morality seems to him a lower morality, and the experience of liberty a promise of happiness from some wider source. Right through the last book of *The Excursion*, he will go on saying so; whether one considers a child of a modest or a large inheritance,

> whatever fate the noon of life
> Reserves for either, sure it is that both
> Have been permitted to enjoy the dawn.
> (IX.281–83)

The wish for liberty will have been the same for all.

Wordsworth held to no single prescriptive doctrine, but if a name is wanted for the principle that compelled his thinking, I suggest that we call it a sense of radical humanity. I do not know if the phrase has been used before. The idea need not be universalist, for the life in question is not a composite image drawn by a citizen of the world. Neither is it particularist in the modern anthropological and identitarian sense. Wordsworth's particulars are natural and what he meant by nature is merely everything that culture is not. If you read literature for reasons of culture, Wordsworth will be a dead letter to you, and to describe his work as selfish will seem a fair way of proving that his difficulty has no point. That has been the direction of the culture-based criticism of the past several years. The view, widely held in the previous generation, that literary history wrote the poems was displaced for a brief interim by the theory that 'a mobile army of metaphors, metonyms, and anthropo-morphisms' wrote the poems, and once the tonic inhumanism of the theory had become conventional it was understandable for a rising school of moral detectives to assert that property wrote the poems. My view that a man wrote them – which cannot claim novelty, either – presupposes an account of the first twenty-five years of his life.

Notes

1   Among the ranked 'excellencies' of Wordsworth in *Biographia Literaria* chap. 22: 'Fifth: a meditative pathos, a union of deep and subtle thought with sensibility; a sympathy with man as man; the sympathy indeed of a contemplator, rather than a fellow-sufferer or co-mate (*spectator, haud particeps*)'; see *Biographia Literaria*, Everyman ed. (London: Dent, 1956), 270.

2   *The Letters of William and Dorothy Wordsworth: The Early Years 1787–1805*, ed. Ernest de Selincourt, 2nd edn. rev. by Chester L. Shaver (Oxford: Clarendon Press, 1967), 119, 123–24.

3   My sense of Wordsworth's fidelity to a democratic idealism (though in defensive and specialized forms) a full decade after Napoleon's attack on the Swiss republic cooled his enthusiasm for France, has not been shared by many recent commentators. An exception was E. P. Thompson; see 'Disenchantment or Default?' and 'Wordsworth's Crisis' in his posthumous collection of essays, *The Romantics* (New York: New Press, 1997).

Further reading

Return or redress, of one kind or another, is the tendency in the following works, including the eclectic collections that emphasize plurality, published in the wake of the new historicist critiques of Wordsworth.

Geoffrey H. Hartman, *The Unremarkable Wordsworth* (London: Methuen, 1987). Collection of essays spanning nearly a quarter-century since his celebrated study, reasserting the claim for his 'phenomenological' method, which he uses to reiterate (although acknowledging the fading of the descriptor 'Romantic') Wordsworth's philosophical importance and the originality and radicalism of a poetry characteristically sober and undramatic.

Paul Magnuson, *Coleridge and Wordsworth: A Lyrical Dialogue* (Princeton: Princeton University Press, 1988). Argues for a 'dialogic reading' of the 'Coleridge-Wordsworth canon as a single work', each poem in which is a fragment that takes its significance from the context of the whole.

Alan Bewell, *Wordsworth and the Enlightenment: Nature, Man, and Society in the Experimental Poetry* (New Haven and London: Yale University Press, 1989). Valuable analysis of Wordsworth's moral philosophy, establishing the extent to which Enlightenment anthropology offered him a model for the general history of imagination that was his life's project and experiment.

George H. Gilpin (ed.), *Critical Essays on William Wordsworth* (Boston: G. K. Hall, 1990). Fine representative collection of the development and range of late twentieth-century approaches to the poet and his major writings. The introductory context is the history of critical opinion, and the emphasis is plurality.

K. R. Johnston, G. Chaitin, K. Hanson and H. Marks (eds.), *Romantic Revolutions: Criticism and Theory* (Bloomington and Indianapolis: Indiana University Press, 1990). Wordsworth is the focus of this impressive selection of 'current critical and theoretical work in English and American Romantic literature', which brings together established and newer scholars so as to participate in the ongoing process of dialogue and debate.

Robin Jarvis, *Wordsworth, Milton, and the Theory of Poetic Relations* (Basingstoke and London: Macmillan, 1991). New directions in Freud, Bloom, and intertextuality, in a fresh examination of the relations between *The Prelude* and *Paradise Lost*. At once theoretically engaged and faithful to the text, Jarvis attempts to circumvent the established polarity of 'theory' and 'text' in literary studies.

R. Brinkley and K. Hanley (eds.), *Romantic Revision* (Cambridge: Cambridge University Press, 1992). Editorial insights into creative process; close textual criticism in five essays by different scholars paying particular attention to Wordsworth's revisions.

Thomas McFarland, *William Wordsworth: Intensity and Achievement* (Oxford: Clarendon Press, 1992). Essays on diverse topics; the unifying and polemical subtext is a feisty reassertion of 'presence' against what McFarland calls the 'clamour of absence' in new historicism, denounced as inadequate to the greatness of Wordsworth's poetry.

Nicholas Roe, *The Politics of Nature: Wordsworth and Some Contemporaries* (1992; 2nd edn., Basingstoke: Palgrave, 2002). Argues, against the thesis of the Romantic 'displacement' of history by nature, the inseparability of politics, nature and the imagination in the 1790s. Roe descries the coercive tendency of new historicism, seeking instead 'to integrate the strengths of "traditional" literary and historical scholarship with newer approaches to texts and contexts.'

Lucy Newlyn, Paradise Lost *and the Romantic Reader* (Oxford: Clarendon Press, 1993). Demonstrates (and in so doing debates Bloom's model of influence) the inter-relatedness of specific textual allusions and the larger cultural reception of Milton, who is shown to be central both to the self-definition of individual Romantic writers, Wordsworth among them, and to the 'macrocosmic evolution of what is called "Romanticism"'.

Zachary Leader, *Revision and Romantic Authorship* (Oxford: Clarendon Press, 1996). The emphasis upon Wordsworth's 'original' compositions by modern editors amounts to an unexamined absorption of the Romantic championing of 'primary process', which ignores Wordsworth's own revisionary practices, overriding his intentions and denying the continuity of personality on which he himself insisted.

Richard E. Matlak, *The Poetry of Relationship: The Wordsworths and Coleridge, 1797–1800* (London: Macmillan, 1997). Study of the biographical and literary relations between the Wordsworths and Coleridge. Matlak examines psychological as well as intertextual relations, and incorporates Dorothy Wordsworth into the subject treated by McFarland, Newlyn and Magnuson.

Simon Jarvis, 'Wordsworth and Idolatry', *Studies in Romanticism* 38.1 (Spring 1999), 3–27. Persuasively challenges the ideological critique of Wordsworth by describing in his poetry an understanding of 'the subterranean connections between idolatry and idol-breaking' that refuses the absolutes of both idealism and materialism.

J. Douglas Kneale, *Romantic Aversions: Aftermaths of Classicism in Wordsworth and Coleridge* (Liverpool: Liverpool University Press, 1999). Focusing on genre and rhetoric, argues in Wordsworth (and Coleridge) 'a textual attitude towards classicism and neoclassicism that at once incorporates repetition and difference, occupation and aversion, in a mutually assured contestation.'

Richard W. Clancey, *Wordsworth's Classical Undersong: Education, Rhetoric and Poetic Truth* (Basingstoke and London: Macmillan, 2000). Arguing (cf. Kneale) that the 'operative presence and normative value of the classics are a constant in Wordsworth, especially perceived in his overarching prophetic intention', locates the origins of that intention – humanity's realization of its potential for poetic vision – in Wordsworth's classical training at Hawkshead school.

Keith Hanley, *Wordsworth: A Poet's History* (Basingstoke: Palgrave, 2001). Combining psychoanalytic and Marxist methods with detailed textual readings, continues the uncovering of the 'secret histories', both personal and political, that produced the literary and linguistic, hence social and cultural, effects of Wordsworth's poetry.

J. Robert Barth, *Romanticism and Transcendence: Wordsworth, Coleridge, and the Religious Imagination* (Columbia and London: University of Missouri Press, 2003). In the context of its overall contention, that Wordsworth's and Coleridge's emphasis on the individual's imagination implies Christian belief, focuses, in a series of chapters, on *The Prelude*, defending the 1850 revisions.

*Stephen Gill (ed.), *The Cambridge Companion to Wordsworth* (Cambridge: Cambridge University Press, 2003). First-class essays by major critics, covering a range of topics, including poetic craft, nature, philosophy, history, politics, gender and reception.

Richard Gravil, *Wordsworth's Bardic Vocation, 1787–1842* (Basingstoke: Palgrave Macmillan, 2003). Starting with Wordsworth's interest in bardic and druidic lore, finds, in his poetry, the manifestation of 'a self-consciously bardic vocation', a sense of himself as belonging to a line of British bards, and thus as a national poet.

Kurt Fosso, *Buried Communities: Wordsworth and the Bonds of Mourning* (Albany, N.Y.: State University of New York Press, 2004). Presents Wordsworth's exploration of the socially cohesive effects of mourning, in his imagining of community in the poetry of 1785–1814, relating this imagining to the political turbulence of the time.

Useful editions

The five-volume *Poetical Works* ed. Ernest de Selincourt and Helen Darbishire is still used as a standard edition. Gill's *William Wordsworth* in *The Oxford Authors* series (Oxford and New York: Oxford University Press, 1984) offers a broad selection of carefully edited texts, with notes. The best edition of *The Prelude* for students is *The Prelude 1799, 1805, 1850*, ed. J. Wordsworth, M. H. Abrams and S. Gill. The Cornell Wordsworth Series (1975–) is an indispensable scholarly resource, perpetuating Wordsworth's emphasis on origins in its efforts to present the earliest versions of his work.

Reference material

Mark L. Reed, *Wordsworth: The Chronology of the Early Years, 1770–1799* and *Wordsworth: The Chronology of the Middle Years, 1800–1815* (Cambridge, Mass.: Harvard University Press, 1967, 1975). Painstaking collation of the details of Wordsworth's day-to-day life.

W. J. B. Owen and J. W. Smyser (eds.), *The Prose Works of William Wordsworth* (Oxford: Clarendon Press, 1974). Useful edition of Wordsworth's prose.

N. S. Bauer, *William Wordsworth: A Reference Guide to British Criticism, 1793–1899* (Boston, Mass.: G. K. Hall, 1978). Most useful in its comprehensive listing of the Victorian writings on Wordsworth, annotated and arranged chronologically.

Duncan Wu, *Wordsworth's Reading 1770–1799* and *Wordsworth's Reading 1800–1815* (Cambridge: Cambridge University Press, 1993, 1998). Valuable catalogues of Wordsworth's reading in the early years of composition and in the period of his best poetry.

Chapter notes

1 ?John Wilson, review of Wordsworth's *River Duddon: a series of Sonnets: Vaudracour and Julia: and other Poems* (1820), in *Blackwood's Edinburgh Magazine* vii (May 1820), 207. Reproduced in Donald Reiman (ed.) *The Romantics Reviewed,*

Part A: The Lake Poets, 2 vols. (New York and London: Garland, 1972), I. 101.

2   See Francis Jeffrey, reviews of Southey's *Thalaba* (incorporating an attack on the *Lyrical Ballads* and 'Preface'), of Wordsworth's *Poems in Two Volumes* (1807), of *The Excursion* (1814), of *The White Doe of Rylstone* (1815) and of *Memorials of a Tour on the Continent* (1822), in *Edinburgh Review* i (Oct. 1802), especially 65–72; xi (Oct. 1807), 214–31; xxiv (Nov. 1814), 1–30; xxv (Oct. 1815), 355–63; xxxvii (Nov. 1822), 449–56 (*Romantics Reviewed, Part A*, II. 416–20, 429–38, 439–53, 454–8, 496–500).

3   Charles Lamb, review (revised by William Gifford) of *The Excursion* in *Quarterly Review* xii (Oct. 1814), 100–1 (*Romantics Reviewed, Part A*, II. 826–31). Lamb's original text, superior by far to the heavily revised version, can be found in *The Works of Charles and Mary Lamb*, ed. E. V. Lucas, 7 vols. (London: Methuen 1903–5), I. 160–72.

4   See ?John Wilson's reviews of *The White Doe of Rylstone*, of *Peter Bell* (1819), of *The Waggoner* (1819), of *River Duddon*, of *Ecclesiastical Sketches* (1820) and *Memorials of a Tour*, in *Blackwood's Edinburgh Magazine* iii (July 1818), 369–81; v (May 1819), 130–6; v (June 1819), 332–4; vii (May 1820), 206–13; xii (Aug. 1822), 175–91 (*Romantics Reviewed, Part A*, I. 78–90, 90–6, 97–9, 100–7, 108–24). This last review, from which my quotation is taken (185–6; *Romantics Reviewed, Part A*, I. 118–19) is also significant in its recognition of the impact of Wordsworth's poetics on the poetic practice of his age. The radical implications of the 'Preface' to *Lyrical Ballads* (made manifest in Hazlitt's *Spirit of the Age* essay) are unexamined both by the reviewer for the conservative *Blackwood's*, who defends Wordsworth, and the liberal editor of the *Edinburgh*, who traduces him.

5   See reviews of *The Excursion*, of the *Thanksgiving Ode* (1816), of *Peter Bell*, of *The Waggoner*, of *River Duddon*, in *British Critic*, 2nd series, iii (May 1815), 449–67; vi (Sept. 1816), 313–15; xi (June 1819), 584–603; xii (Nov. 1819), 464–79; xv (Feb. 1821), 113–35 (*Romantics Reviewed, Part A*, I. 138–47, 148–9, 165–75, 175–83, 184–95).

6   To Woodhouse, 27 October 1818, in John Keats, *The Letters of John Keats: 1814–1821*, ed. H. E. Rollins, 2 vols. (Cambridge, Mass.: Harvard University Press, 1958), I. 287.

7   See especially Stopford A. Brooke, *Theology in the English Poets* (London: King, 1874), 93–286.

8   Leslie Stephen, 'Wordsworth's Ethics', *Cornhill Magazine* 34 (August 1876), 206–26, expanded in *Hours in a Library*, 3rd series (London: Smith, Elder & Co.: 1879), 178–229.

9   Matthew Arnold, 'Wordsworth' in *The Complete Prose Works of Matthew Arnold*, ed. R. H. Super, 10 vols. (Ann Arbor, Michigan: University of Michigan Press, 1960–77), IX. 40, 46.

10   Ibid., IX. 51.

11   Ibid., IX. 42.

12   A. C. Bradley, 'Wordsworth' in *Oxford Lectures on Poetry*, 2nd edn. (London: Macmillan, 1909), 129–30.

13   From which was produced the new, and for many years, standard edition, *The Poetical Works of William Wordsworth, edited from the Manuscripts, with Textual and Critical Notes*, ed. E. de Selincourt and H. Darbishire, 5 vols. (Oxford: Clarendon Press, 1940–9).

14   Marilyn Butler, *Romantics, Rebels and Reactionaries: English Literature and its Background 1760–1830* (Oxford: Oxford University Press, 1981), 9, 57.

15   Marjorie Levinson, *Wordsworth's Great Period Poems: Four Essays* (Cambridge: Cambridge University Press, 1986), 1.

16   Alan Liu, *Wordsworth: The Sense of History* (Stanford, Calif.: Stanford University Press, 1989), 32.

17   Mary Jacobus, *Romanticism, Writing, and Sexual Difference: Essays on* The Prelude (Oxford: Clarendon Press, 1989), vii. Elsewhere in the same work (69–93), Jacobus treats the topic of Wordsworth and slavery, identifying 'the entire *Prelude* as a site of historical repression'. Wordsworth's negotiation of 'the hermeneutic relation between colonizer and colonized' is treated by Alison Hickey in 'Dark Characters, Native Grounds: Wordsworth's Imagination of Imperialism' in *Romanticism, Race, and Imperial Culture, 1780–1834*, ed. A. Richardson and S. Hofkosh (Bloomington and Indianapolis: Indiana University Press, 1996), 283–310.

18   Anne Mellor, 'Writing the Self/Self Writing: William Wordsworth's *Prelude/* Dorothy Wordsworth's *Journals*' in *Romanticism and Gender* (New York and London: Routledge, 1993), 144–69.

19   Jonathan Bate, *Romantic Ecology: Wordsworth and the Environmental Tradition* (London and New York: Routledge, 1991), 9.

20   Donald Hayden, 'William Wordsworth: Early Ecologist', in *Studies in Relevance: Romantic and Victorian Writers in 1972*, ed. T. M. Harwell (Salzburg: University of Salzburg, 1973), 36–52; Karl Kroeber, '"Home at Grasmere": Ecological Holiness' (1974), repr. in *Critical Essays on William Wordsworth*, ed. G. H. Gilpin (Boston: G. K. Hall, 1990), 179–96.

3

Samuel Taylor Coleridge (1772–1834)

In 1798, on its first appearance in *Lyrical Ballads*, Robert Southey, later himself derided as a member of the 'Lake School', damned the 'Rime of the Ancient Mariner' as 'a Dutch attempt at German sublimity'.[1] Other reviewers of Coleridge, whether pronouncing his genius and sublimity, or his extravagance and lack of taste, were usually equally vehement, if less pithy. On the whole, praise and censure of Coleridge's poetry were very nearly balanced until 1816, when, with the publication of the *Christabel* volume (containing, with 'Christabel', 'Kubla Khan' and 'The Pains of Sleep'), the consensus turned against him. Coleridge was charged with the faults of the Lake School – childishness, vulgarity and affectation – and his tendency to mysticism and obscurity widely deplored.[2]

The most enduring of the contemporary characterizations of Coleridge has come in time to epitomize the 'Romanticism' to which he has been made increasingly central: incompletion. Conder's simile for 'Christabel' captures what is now acknowledged as paradigmatically 'Romantic', its fragmentary form: 'It may be compared to a mutilated statue, the beauty of which can only be appreciated by those who have knowledge or imagination sufficient to complete the idea of the whole composition.'[3] That completion is not actual but imaginary for Coleridge is implicit also in the deferral or postponement of achievement recognized as typical of him. Hazlitt puts it bluntly in the *Edinburgh*: 'He is always promising great things, in short, and performs nothing.'[4]

An important defence, attributed to John Gibson Lockhart, appears in *Blackwood's Edinburgh Magazine* in October 1819. Markedly departing from *Blackwood's* earlier antagonism, and especially praising 'The Ancient Mariner' and 'Christabel', Lockhart becomes an early proponent of the notion of a small but superlative canon.

... he has created a few poems, which are, though short, in conception so original, and in execution so exquisite, that they cannot fail to render the name of Coleridge co-extensive with the language in which he has written, and to associate it for ever in the minds of all feeling and intelligent men, with those of the few chosen spirits that have touched in so many ages of the world the purest and most delicious chords of lyrical enchantment.[5]

Other memorable contemporary portraits and references include Lamb's 'Comberbatch, matchless in his depredations!',[6] Keats's antithesis to 'negative capability',[7] and the lost leader celebrated in Hazlitt's 'My First Acquaintance with Poets'. In a letter of 1819, Keats describes a walk in which 'in . . . two Miles he broached a thousand things', and Hazlitt captures the same quality on a larger scale in 'Mr. Coleridge' in *The Spirit of the Age*, mimicking, in a single stupendous sentence, part felicitation, part parody, the compendious, digressive, and perpetually changeable mind of his subject.[8] De Quincey's anecdotes of Coleridge, in a series of articles in *Tait's Edinburgh Magazine* (1834–5), later reprinted in his *Literary Reminiscences* (1854), contain the first serious allegations of plagiarism.

In the Victorian period, Coleridge's prose – his religious and political philosophy – bulks larger than his poetry and poetics. In companion essays on Bentham (1838) and Coleridge (1840), John Stuart Mill famously presents Coleridge, with Bentham, as one of 'the two great seminal minds of England in their age',[9] arguing his impact as the primary English representative of the 'Conservative philosophy' derived from the Germans, and praising his theories of the Church and the Constitution. Religious thinkers, such as F. D. Maurice and John Henry Newman, also emphasize Coleridge's importance as a Christian philosopher.[10] Less sympathetically, the disjunction of poetry and prose is perpetuated in the contentions that Coleridge's philosophy represents his degeneration as a poet: implicit here is a moral censure, informed by the fact of Coleridge's opium addiction. Carlyle's chapter on Coleridge in his *Life of John Sterling* (1851) maintains that Coleridge's 'ray of heavenly inspiration' was expended in 'vague daydreams, hollow compromises, in opium, in theosophic metaphysics.'[11] Walter Pater, again, to whom Coleridge's sensibility is German and 'romantic', finds that his vocation was 'in the world of the imagination, the theory and practice of poetry,' but his 'struggle . . . to "apprehend the absolute," . . . was . . . an effort of sickly thought' that 'limited the operation of his unique poetic gift'.[12] Such a perception persists into the twentieth century, for instance, in T. S. Eliot's description of Coleridge: 'the disastrous effect of long dissipation and stupefaction of his powers in transcendental metaphysics . . . bringing him to a state of lethargy.'[13] In E. K. Chambers' biography, similarly, illness coincides with metaphysics, and Coleridge 'is conscious of the conflict within himself between the call to speculation and the call to poetry.'[14]

But forcefully countering the Victorian legacy, where notice of the philosophy, favourable or unfavourable, marginalizes or diminishes the poet, is a landmark publication of 1927, John Livingston Lowes' *The Road to Xanadu*. Assuming a canon of three poems, of which he focuses on two, the 'Ancient Mariner' and 'Kubla Khan' ('Christabel' is outside the scope of his study), Lowes locates, in the intricate maze of Coleridge's reading, the creative origins of his poetry. In Lowes' study, Coleridge's materials, generated by a spontaneous process of association, are shaped into poetic form by a powerful, working imagination that persuasively challenges nineteenth-century stereotypes. Lowes' tracking of sources, to produce a myriad associated contexts for the poetry, despite a now unfashionable floridity of style, is still the principle of some of the most influential modern-day scholarship. A sample follows.

Extract from J. L. Lowes, *The Road to Xanadu* (1927)

With the splendidly imaginative gloss: 'No twilight within the courts of the Sun,' Coleridge commented on an even more superb stanza:

> The Sun's rim dips; the stars rush out:
> At one stride comes the dark;
> With far-heard whisper, o'er the sea,
> Off shot the spectre-bark.[1]

Did there once lie, beneath that entire and perfect crysolite, 'shattered fragments of memory' which 'flashed images,' and coalesced?

In April, 1797, Southey wrote his brother Tom: 'Have you ever met with Mary Wollstonscroft's [*sic*] letters from Sweden and Norway? She has made me in love with a cold climate, and frost and snow, with a northern moonlight.'[2] In Coleridge's Note Book, scrawled in pencil between 'Mrs. Estlin's Story of the Maniac who walked round and round,' and the entry about the sun painting rainbows on the vast waves at the Cape, stands the following: 'Epistle to Mrs. Wolstoncraft urging her to Religion. Read her travels.'[3] Whether Coleridge carried out his pious purpose with reference to the future mother of Mary Shelley, I do not know. He afterwards thought Godwin 'in heart and manner . . . all the better for having been [her] husband,' and, 'thinking' (as he says) 'of Mary Wollstonecraft,' he was oppressed one day he dined there after her death, by 'the cadaverous silence of Godwin's children [which] is . . . quite catacombish';[4] so I suppose his interest in her soul was friendly. His interest in her travels – whether friendly too, or sheer omnivorousness, or both – bore fruit in something more definite than falling in love with a cold climate and a northern moonlight. For he read, in the *Letters written during a Short Residence in Sweden, Norway, and Denmark*, this sentence: 'Getting amongst the rocks and islands as the moon rose, and *the stars darted forward* out of the clear expanse, I forgot that the night stole on.'[5] And one of those 'vivid spectra,' which were incessantly leaving their imprint on his memory, flashed as he read.

The absence of twilight in the tropics he knew from his keen and long-standing interest in the West Indies and the Nile, and the ocular impressions from his reading seem to have carried scraps of phrases with them into their subliminal half-way house. 'In the afternoons, *the sun is no sooner dipped*, than a sensible change in the air . . . is immediately felt.'[6] That is Long, from a page devoted to the crepuscular phenomena of the West Indies, which so took Bryan Edwards's[7] fancy that, after the happy practice of the travel-books, he appropriated part of it intact. 'I regret the want of twilight here,' says the author of a gossipy little volume on the West Indies, printed in 1790, 'for *the dark comes on very suddenly, a few minutes after the sun is beneath the horizon*.'[8] 'In these Parts,' Rochefort writes in his *History of the Carriby-Islands*, 'there is in a manner *no Crepusculum or Twilight*.'[9] And Bruce, in a context of unusual interest to Coleridge, agrees for the regions of the Nile: 'In countries such as . . . Hanno was then sailing by . . . there is *no twilight*.'[10] And later in Bruce's great narrative Coleridge would read: 'The twilight . . . is very short, almost imperceptible. . . . As soon as the sun falls below the horizon, night comes on, and all the stars appear.'[11]

There was, moreover, a strange, crack-brained book, with flashes of imaginative splendour playing through its incoherence, written by a young barrister, himself a native of Antigua, whom Coleridge knew in his Bristol days. It is *The Hurricane: A Theosophical and Western Eclogue*, 'grounded,' the Preface tells us, 'on a THEOSOPHICAL view of the relation between AMERICA and EUROPE, but concatenated . . . with the two old Quarters of the Globe,' and its copious Notes are as mad as a hatter.[12] It was, however, a noble mind that was here o'erthrown, and both Wordsworth and Southey have paid tribute to its powers.[13] Coleridge, Cottle tells us, 'once objected to the metre of some of Gilbert's lines,' and Gilbert's Advertisement is an answer to these strictures.[14] There is evidence elsewhere, as we shall see, that snatches from *The Hurricane*, the scene of which is laid in the West Indies, stuck in Coleridge's memory, and two lines are pertinent here:

> *No* lingering *twilight* in the proud-robed WEST
> Shews indecision in the Paths of Day![15]

This, then, is roughly what we have in the travel books: 'the sun is no sooner *dipped*'; 'the stars *darted forward*'; '*the dark comes on very suddenly*'; 'there is *no twilight.*' And Coleridge wrote:

> The Sun's rim *dips*; the stars *rush out:*
> *At one stride comes the dark –*

with the gloss: '*No twilight* within the courts of the Sun.'

There, it would seem, are both the shattered fragments of memory, and the surpassing form with which the 'inward creatrix' fitted them. I am not, indeed, so rash as to assert categorically that the identical phrases which I have quoted, and only those, were the star-dust of the stanza. Some, if not all, without doubt had stamped impressions on a brain which 'had the impression of individual images very strong,'[16] and on a memory of extraordinary tenacity. Coleridge had read *The Hurricane* not only with a friend's, but with a critic's eye. How effectively Bruce had seeded the crannies of his memory we shall later have to see. Mrs. Wollstonecraft, as the Note Book shows, would certainly fall neither by the wayside, nor on stony ground. Long's three volumes were among the standard works on the West Indies, and Coleridge's ardent interest in the islands dates as far back as the halcyon days of the Greek Ode at Cambridge. About the *Short Journey to the West Indies* one cannot feel so sure [. . .] But whether facts and phrases reached him from these books or from others, the point of capital significance is this. The magnificent conception of the fall of the tropical night is once more the result of a fusing flash of imaginative energy through chaos – that very 'chaos of elements and shattered fragments of memory' of which Coleridge himself was so keenly cognizant. Every shattered fragment has been new-minted – sharp, and clear, and salient as the sun that stood above the mast, or the emerald ice. 'The sun's *rim*[17] dips. . . . *At one stride comes the dark.*' Reread, for a fresh commentary on the intensely visualizing quality of Coleridge's imagination, the phrases from the books: '*The sun* was no sooner dipped'; 'The dark comes on *very suddenly.*' Yet that vivid concreteness must yield first place to something else – to a synthesis of disparate elements which even for Coleridge is remarkable.

For the large, general impression of a sudden shift from day to night diffused through the various accounts which he had read, all at once gathers and concentrates into a downward leap of night like that of lightning, while on the instant,

> With far-heard whisper o'er the sea,
> Off shot the spectre-bark.

I doubt whether even Dante has surpassed, for sheer trenchancy and compression, the art with which Coleridge has made, through the agency of his scraps of recollection, the sense of an appalling swiftness palpable. And the unification of a clutter of details from Norway, the West Indies, and the Nile into one breathless instant between sky and sea epitomizes once again the ways of that shaping spirit of imagination which is our theme.

Notes

1   'The Rime of the Ancient Mariner', 199–202. The first two lines are printed for the first time in *Sibylline Leaves*, 1817.
2   Robert Southey, *The Life and Correspondence of Robert Southey*, ed. by his son, the Rev. Charles Cuthbert Southey, 6 vols. (London: Longman, Brown, Green & Longmans, 1849–50), I. 311.
3   *The Notebooks of Samuel Taylor Coleridge*, ed. K. Coburn, 5 vols. (London: Routledge, 2002), I, n. 261.
4   *The Collected Letters of Samuel Taylor Coleridge*, ed. E. L. Griggs, 6 vols. (Oxford: Clarendon Press, 1956–71), I. 553.
5   Mary Wollstonecraft, *Letters Written during a Short Residence in Sweden, Norway, and Denmark* (London: J. Johnson, 1796), 178.
6   Edward Long, *A History of Jamaica*, 3 vols. (London: T. Lowndes, 1774), I. 371.
7   Bryan Edwards, *The History, Civil and Commercial, of the British Colonies in the West Indies*, 2 vols. (London, 1793).
8   *A Short Journey in the West Indies, in which are Interspersed Curious Anecdotes and Characters*, 2 vols. (London: John Murray, 1790), I. 36.
9   Cesar de Rochefort, *The History of the Caribby-Islands, Rendred into English by John Davies of Kidwelly* (London: Dring and Starkey, 1666), 3.
10 James Bruce, *Travels to Discover the Source of the Nile, in the Years 1768, 1769, 1770, 1771, 1772, and 1773*, 5 vols. (Edinburgh: Ruthven, 1790), II. 565. Moreover, Bruce's very next sentence describes the instantaneous *vanishing* of the stars: 'The stars, in their full brightness, are in possession of the whole heavens, when in an instant, the sum appears without a harbinger, and they all disappear together.' And that is coupled, on the same page, with the startling swiftness of the fall of night: 'But no sooner does the sun set, than a cold night instantly succeeds a burning day.'
11 Ibid., III. 353.

[12   William Gilbert, *The Hurricane: A Theosophical and Western Eclogue, to which is subjoined A Solitary Effusion in a Summer's Evening* (Bristol: R. Edwards, 1796).]

13   Joseph Cottle, *Early Recollections; Chiefly Relating to the late Samuel Taylor Coleridge, during his Long Residence in Bristol,* 2 vols. (London: Longman, Rees, 1837), I. 66–8.

14   Ibid., II. 333–4.

15   Gilbert, *The Hurricane,* p. 16.

16   Samuel Taylor Coleridge, *Table Talk Recorded by Henry Nelson Coleridge (and John Taylor Coleridge),* (Vol. 14 of the *Collected Works of Samuel Taylor Coleridge,* Bollingen series no. 75), ed. Carl Woodring, 2 vols. (Princeton: Princeton University Press, 1990), I. 75.

17   Coleridge was recalling his own lines in *Osorio,* Act III, 246–7: 'A rim of the sun yet lies upon the sea – /And now 'tis gone!'

Further reading

The following represent three milestones in the early canonization of Coleridge, establishing, in addition to the 'mystery' or 'supernatural' poems, the central canonical texts: the 'conversation' poems and *Biographia Literaria*.

*J. Shawcross, 'Introduction', in S. T. Coleridge, *Biographia Literaria,* edited, with his aesthetical essays, by J. Shawcross, 2 vols. (Oxford: Oxford University Press, 1907), xi–lxxxix. Lucid introduction to the transcendental philosophy of *Biographia,* tracing its development from Coleridge's earlier poetry and prose, and judiciously assessing its relation to German romanticism, especially the extent and importance of Coleridge's debt to Kant.

George McLean Harper, 'Coleridge's Conversation Poems', in *Spirit of Delight* (London: Ernest Benn, 1928), 3–27. Designates, and argues for the serious study of, Coleridge's 'conversation' poems.

I. A. Richards, *Coleridge on Imagination* (1934; London: Routledge, 2001). Influential analysis of Coleridge's theory of poetry as 'the utterances of an extreme Idealist', asserting its continuing relevance to our ongoing exploration of 'the modes of language as working modes of the mind'.

IDEALIZING COLERIDGE

The canonization of Coleridge in the early decades of the twentieth century is primarily on the basis of the *annus mirabilis* poetry, 1797–8; of his prose, only *Biographia Literaria* gains a comparable canonical status. By bringing to bear on the great poems unpublished notebook entries, Lowes elicits a continuity of published poetry and private prose. As criticism expands to a more unified view of Coleridge's works, concomitant with the developing study of the poetry are the mammoth projects in the unpublished prose. The first volume of the *Collected Letters*, ed. Earl Leslie Griggs, is published in 1956, and the first volume, in two parts, of Kathleen Coburn's monumental edition of the *Notebooks*, in 1957. At the same time, the construction of a philosopher–poet supersedes an earlier critical tendency to compartmentalize poetry and philosophy. Amplifying the lesser poet of the Victorian readings, Lowes still stands away from the 'metaphysical lucubrations' that ensue upon Coleridge's 'loss' of poetic power; to Lowes, Coleridge's imagination shapes spontaneously generated materials on a purely aesthetic principle: 'out of chaos the imagination frames a thing of beauty.'[15] In direct opposition, Robert Penn Warren's symbolic reading of 'The Ancient Mariner' (1946) presents the poem's consistency 'with Coleridge's basic theological and philosophical views', making it a 'symbol' in the Coleridgean sense, participating in, as well as rendering, the imagination's 'sacramental vision' of the 'One Life' of the universe.[16]

Explicating symbol and myth in Coleridge's poetry, John Beer's *Coleridge the Visionary* contributes significantly, in 1959, to a major new trend, of studies of a 'visionary' romanticism, with the poet at the centre of a secularized Judaeo-Christian world-view. Examining the particular characteristics of Coleridge's romanticism, Beer finds at its heart a visionary optimism, culminating in the *annus mirabilis* and fading in the later years, 'that the true poet is, within his finite limitations, a type of God the Creator.'[17] A brief extract, on 'The Ancient Mariner', follows.

Extract from John Beer, *Coleridge the Visionary* (1959)

[. . .] we may turn to an examination of the events of the poem in their due order. The opening presents few difficulties [. . .]. The ship sets sail cheerfully enough, and if we pause to consider the first impression, it is of a company of men living according to custom and tradition. Observing the taboos of their lore, they proceed happily on their way, and, even when they sail into thick snow and ice, a combination of the helmsman's skill with fortunate circumstances keeps them from harm.

The mariners have been happily described as 'hommes moyens sensuels',[1] in fact: they are this and more. They live in what appears to them to be a pleasant, well-ordered universe, unaware that the calm is no more than the precarious equilibrium between apparent mighty forces.

The mention of snow and mist is the first point at which an observant reader might be aware of deeper elements in the poem than at first appear, for these are symbols which have appeared elsewhere in

Coleridge's writings. In *Religious Musings*, for example, he describes how the 'dayspring of Love' rises glorious in his soul,

> As the great Sun, when he his influence
> Sheds on the frost-bound waters . . .[2]

In *Biographia Literaria*, likewise, he describes the 'alleviation that results from "*opening out* our griefs:" which are thus presented in distinguishable forms instead of the mist, through which whatever is shapeless becomes magnified and (literally) *enormous*'.[3] Mist is used again and again by Coleridge to symbolize a state where ignorance and slavery to the passions results in a distorted picture of the world, or (where the mist is veiling the sun) of God.

Ice and snow, on the other hand, seem to have an ambivalent position in Coleridge's symbolism. They can stand for the coldness of the unawakened heart – but they are also attractive, by reason of their brightness and purity. This ambivalence may well be intended to represent the state of the mariners, who, if they lack insight and awareness of any world beyond that of their immediate senses, display an elementary goodness in their fellowship and their active kindness to the albatross.

The shooting of the albatross brings this state of affairs to an end; and I have already suggested that the Mariner's action combines detachment from his fellows with moral ignorance. In connection with the latter characteristic, it is interesting to discover that, some years after writing the poem, Coleridge saw a hawk being shot at from the ship on which he was travelling and wrote in his notebook a reduced but recognizable version of the idea: 'Poor Hawk! O Strange Lust of Murder in Man! – It is not cruelty/it is mere non-feeling from non-thinking.'[4]

As the ice and snow disappear, it becomes clear that in spite of causing danger and discomfort, they have been acting as a protection for the ship and its crew. The Mariner's companions hail their departure, but soon find themselves in far worse plight, exposed to the merciless, untempered heat of the sun's rays. There is a parallel to this image in a snippet of verse by Coleridge entitled, significantly, *Napoleon*:

> The Sun with gentle beams his rage disguises,
> And like aspiring Tyrants, temporises –
> Never to be endured but when he falls or rises.[5]

The heat of the sun is, as we have seen, an essential element in the speculations of Jacob Boehme. Boehme's insistence on the benevolence of God led him to the doctrine that if God at times seemed angry, this was no more than an appearance, engendered by the diseased imagination of fallen man. Cut off from the light of God, he could experience only the heat of his presence: and any exposure to his full glory would therefore be felt as nothing less than exposure to unendurable fire.

Heat and thirst are one element in the mariners' torment; solitude and endless monotony are the other. And just as the one torture is due to the fact that the sun is untempered, so the other is due to the fact that time is unmodified. A passage in *Biographia Literaria* helps to bring out the full significance of this.

> It sometimes happens that we are punished for our faults by incidents, in the causation of which these faults had no share: and this I have always felt the severest punishment. . . . For there is always a consolatory feeling that accompanies the sense of a proportion between antecedents and consequents. The sense of Before and After becomes both intelligible and intellectual when, and *only* when, we contemplate the succession in the relations of Cause and Effect, which, like the two poles of the magnet manifest the being and unity of the one power by relative opposites, and give, as it were, a substratum of permanence, of identity, and therefore of reality, to the shadowy flux of Time. . . . Hence . . . the Mystics have joined in representing the state of the reprobate spirits as a dreadful dream in which there is no sense of reality, not even of the pangs they are enduring – an eternity without time, and as it were below it – God present without manifestation of his presence.[6]

According to some vague reminiscences by De Quincey, Coleridge had, before writing *The Ancient Mariner*, meditated a poem 'on delirium, confounding its own dream-scenery with external things, and connected with the imagery of high latitudes'.[7] It seems likely that some such plan was forming in his mind when he wrote, on a page of the Gutch notebook,[8]

> in that eternal & delirious misery –
>   wrathfires –
>   inward desolations –
>   an horror of great darkness
>   great things that on the ocean
>   counterfeit infinity –

Fallen humanity cannot bear the revelation of infinity: and the Ancient Mariner, by breaking through the veils of convention and custom with which mankind normally defends itself from the unbearable supernatural, has brought upon himself the curse of Cain. According to Boehme, Cain was regarded by his parents, Adam and Eve, as the son who would fulfil the prophecy, and vanquish the serpent, but he, in his pride as a man and a hunter, and knowing only the use of violence, destroyed not the serpent but his brother Abel.[9] Thus the serpent came to 'bruise the heel' of mankind.

This legend seems to have its place in the poem, along with a good deal more of the serpent lore and daemonology that has been examined above. We have already suggested that Coleridge was familiar with the Egyptian symbol of the Sun, the Serpent and the Wings, especially in its use as an emblem of the Trinity and the divine creativity. The sun proceeds into eternal generation in the serpent, which is in its turn exalted and winged, to soar back to the sun. We know from Coleridge's many references elsewhere that he was fond of using the image of God as the sun, already a cliché of the emblem-writers and other symbolists. In a note from the *Aids to Reflection*, cited earlier, he puts forward the theory that the serpent, in Egyptian temple-language, represented the wisdom of the flesh. And it is reasonable to suppose that he was conversant, also, with the ambivalence of the serpent in Egyptian lore, where the daemonic could represent either the serpent alone (the cacodaemon Typhon), or Cneph the winged, good daemon.

We can learn more about Cneph from Maurice's *History of Hindostan*, which Coleridge read with some attention. Maurice, in discussing the rise of mythology, follows tradition in making Japhet founder and guardian of the Greek nation, and also sees him as prototype of Neptune. The connecting figure between these two is, for him, Canopus, the Egyptian god of mariners, whom he describes as follows:

> Canopus is a bright star of the first magnitude in the stern of the ship Argo, which we shall presently see was no other than the ark of Noah, turned into a constellation; and Cneph, or Canupha, (for that is the Coptic and Arabian primitive) by which the Egyptians meant the guardian genius, who with his expanded wings hovered over the waters, was therefore the proper pilot of that vessel.[10]

If we accept this final link in the chain of evidence, the albatross can be identified with the guardian daemon even more closely than before. In terms of the Egyptian hierogram, the Mariner, in killing the albatross, destroys the connection between the sun and the serpent. In consequence, the two become separate, and equally alien to man. The serpent, representative of flesh, becomes loathsome and corrupt, while the sun, now that the true inward vision is lost, is apprehended only as heat or wrath. Or, in psychological terms, the Mariner is trapped between the fearful wrath of his conscience, which is all that remains of his Reason, and his consequent loathing of the flesh. Caught in this vicious circle, he is truly in Hell.

> For the sky and the sea, and the sea and the sky
> Lay like a load on my weary eye,
> And the dead were at my feet.[11]

Further evidence that the 'slimy things' of the poem are intentional symbols of corruption may be found in *The Destiny of Nations*, where they are used in this sense, while Love is imaged as a winged spirit, or a breeze:

> . . . Love rose glittering, and his gorgeous wings
> Over the abyss fluttered with such glad noise,
> As what time after long and pestful calms,
> With slimy shapes and miscreated life
> Poisoning the vast Pacific, the fresh breeze
> Wakens the merchant-sail uprising.[12]

If this explanation of the symbolism of the early poem is accepted, it becomes clear that in the killing of the albatross and its result, Coleridge has given us an image of the fall of mankind. This image differs in one important respect, artistically speaking, from normal representations. The Fall, as conventionally described, is from a static state of bliss to a dynamic state of evil. In Coleridge's developed thinking, however, it is a separation from 'the suspending Magnet, the Golden Chain from the Staple Ring fastened to the Footstool of the Throne'.[13] In other words, he evidently accepts the idea of the Great Chain of Being, which, logically pursued, makes the state of virtue dynamic and reduces man after the fall to a static condition of monotony and privation. Any redemptive force in such a condition must therefore have a dynamic quality, if it is to help re-establish the cycle of divine creativity.

Notes

1 ['average sensual men'].
2 'Religious Musings', 416–9.
3 S. T. Coleridge, *Biographia Literaria or Biographical Sketches of my Literary Life and Opinions* (Vol. 7 of the *Collected Works of Samuel Taylor Coleridge*, Bollingen series no. 75), ed. W. J. Bate and J. Engell, 2 vols. (Princeton: Princeton University Press, 1983), II. 235.
4 Coleridge, *Notebooks* II, n. 2090.

5   See S. T. Coleridge, *The Complete Poetical Words of Samuel Taylor Coleridge*, ed. E. H. Coleridge, 2 vols. (Oxford: Clarendon Press, 1912), II. 1010. Coleridge's authorship is likely, but not certain.

6   Coleridge, *Biographia Literaria* II. 234.

7   *The Collected Writings of Thomas De Quincey*, ed. D. Masson, 14 vols. (Edinburgh: A. & C. Black, 1889), II. 145.

8   Coleridge, *Notebooks* I, n. 273.

9   Jacob Boehme, *The Three Principles of the Divine Essence* in *The Works of Jacob Behmen, the Teutonic Theosopher . . . with Figures, Illustrating his Principles, left by the Reverend William Law, M.A.*, 4 vols. (London: Richardson, 1764–81), I. ii. 204.

10   Thomas Maurice, *The History of Hindostan*, 2 vols. (London: Bulmer, 1795–8), I. 241; cf. I. 67.

11   242–4. Coleridge was fond of speculating on the theme of Hell as a state of mind, a projection of the imagination diseased by sin.

12   'The Destiny of Nations', 276–81.

13   Coleridge, *Notebooks* V, n. 5813.

Further reading

The following list is of representative constructions of the poet-thinker. To indicate a development increasingly informed by key theoretical debates, regarding, for instance, Coleridge's stature as a thinker and critic, his philosophy of language, and the origins and extent of his idealism, I have included the bare minimum of prose studies; space precludes a larger selection.

M. H. Abrams, *The Mirror and the Lamp: Romantic Theory and Critical Tradition* (London: Oxford University Press, 1953). Consonant with his age, Coleridge makes the poet's mind the focus of aesthetic reference, but where to Wordsworth nature is the highest criterion of poetic value, to Coleridge it is the imaginative synthesis of antithetic qualities. Coleridge's aesthetics of organism, describing the process of imagination by metaphors of organic growth, refutes the antithesis of nature and art that underlies Wordsworth's theory.

*****Humphrey House**, *Coleridge: The Clark Lectures 1951–2* (London: Rupert Hart-Davis, 1953). Still useful introduction, arguing for the integration of poetry, philosophy and biography, and resisting the isolating of Coleridge's 'great' poetry. Influential especially in the importance it accords to the conversation poems.

Elisabeth Schneider, *Coleridge, Opium and* Kubla Khan (Chicago: University of Chicago Press, 1953). Landmark study, disputing Coleridge's account of the poem's spontaneous, opium-induced composition in 1797 (Schneider attributes a late date), and locating its origin 'in the contemporary network of pseudo-oriental writing', thus raising questions about 'Coleridge's life and character, his critical theories, and development as a poet.'

René Wellek, 'Coleridge' in *A History of Modern Criticism: 1750–1950*, vol. ii: *The Romantic Age* (1955; repr. London: Jonathan Cape, 1966). Denies the originality of Coleridge's critical theory, described here as derivative especially of Kant and Schelling, but credits Coleridge, nonetheless, with a unified vision in which philosophy is continuous with aesthetics and critical theory.

*Harold Bloom, *The Visionary Company: A Reading of English Romantic Poetry* (1961; revised and enlarged edn., Ithaca and London: Cornell University Press, 1971). Charts, through readings of individual poems in chronological succession, the complex and evolving relation of man, Nature and God in Coleridge's thought, leading, through a growing distrust of imagination, to the abdication of nature as muse.

James Boulger, *Coleridge as Religious Thinker* (New Haven: Yale University Press, 1961). Shows Coleridge's idealism to be conditioned by his search for a revitalized Christian orthodoxy, leading eventually to an intellectual acceptance of Christian dogma, which, although finally at the expense of the emotional force of his 'great' poetry, makes his religious musings 'a monument of poetic expression in the prose medium.'

H. W. Piper, *The Active Universe: Pantheism and the Concept of Imagination in the English Romantic Poets* (London: Athlone Press, 1962). Studies Romantic pantheism (including its radical, and, in Coleridge's case, Unitarian contexts) in the development of the Romantic theory of imagination as a response to the living qualities of natural objects or 'active universe'.

Edward Bostetter, *The Romantic Ventriloquists: Wordsworth, Coleridge, Keats, Shelley, Byron* (1963; rev. edn. Seattle and London: University of Washington Press, 1975). Challenges the optimism and largeness of Romantic idealization by showing, from unfinished Romantic poems, including 'Kubla Khan' and 'Christabel', the disjunction between the poet's affirmations of an ideal and his awareness or knowledge of the reality.

Max F. Schulz, *The Poetic Voices of Coleridge: A Study of his Desire for Spontaneity and Passion for Order* (Detroit, Mich.: Wayne State University Press, 1963). Combining the values of spontaneity and form, Coleridge develops poetry in the form of different 'voices', carefully wrought to suggest the immediacy of felt experience, and reflecting his ruling tenet, of the reconciliation of nature and art.

George Watson, *Coleridge the Poet* (London: Routledge & Kegan Paul, 1966). Explicates the formal achievement of Coleridge's poetry, so as to refute the notions of failure and incompletion characterizing Coleridge and the Romantics more generally.

*Walter Jackson Bate, *Coleridge* (New York: Macmillan, 1968). Short, accessible, critical biography, linking Coleridge's writings with his life and personality.

Thomas McFarland, *Coleridge and the Pantheist Tradition* (Oxford: Clarendon Press, 1969). Asserting the interdependence of Coleridge's philosophy, poetry and theology, McFarland presents, in the context of Romanticism's thrust to unify, the 'reticulation' in Coleridge's thought, defending by it Coleridge's plagiarism, and finding in his inability wholly to accept or reject (Spinozistic) pantheism, the central truth of his philosophical activity and the ground of his integrity.

G. N. G. Orsini, *Coleridge and German Idealism: A Study in the History of Philosophy with Unpublished Materials from Coleridge's Manuscripts* (Carbondale and Edwardsville: Southern Illinois University Press, 1969). Essential scholarly study of Coleridge's Kantianism, deliberately resisting critical totalizing by keeping philosophy discrete from poetry and religion.

Stephen Prickett, *Coleridge and Wordsworth: The Poetry of Growth* (Cambridge: Cambridge University Press, 1970). Examines, as part of the same 'romanticism', the 'fruitful tension of ideas' between Coleridge and Wordsworth, producing the revolution in thinking contained in their model of the imagination as a perceptual relationship between man and nature.

M. H. Abrams, *Natural Supernaturalism: Tradition and Revolution in Romantic Literature* (New York and London: W. W. Norton, 1971). Linking Coleridge to Blake, presents Coleridge's 'view of man's fall as division and isolation and of redemption as a reconciliation,' referring, in illustration, to 'The Ancient Mariner' and 'Dejection: an Ode'. (The theological, especially Judaeo-Christian, legacy in Coleridge's poetry is treated also in two essays, 'Structure and Style in the Greater Romantic Lyric' [1965] and 'Coleridge's "A Light in Sound": Science, Metascience, and the Poetic Imagination' [1972], reprinted in M. H. Abrams, *The Correspondent Breeze: Essays on English Romanticism*, with a foreword by Jack Stillinger [New York and London: W. W. Norton, 1984], 76–108, 158–91.)

Owen Barfield, *What Coleridge Thought* (London: Oxford University Press, 1971). Valuable in its eschewing of comparisons and source-hunting, to present Coleridge's philosophy as a coherent and integral body of thought; explicates 'primary' and 'secondary' imagination and also 'fancy' and 'imagination'.

Geoffrey H. Hartman (ed.), *New Perspectives on Coleridge and Wordsworth* (New York and London: Columbia University Press, 1972). Contains important essays on poetic representation (Fletcher, Cooke) and influence (McFarland, Bloom).

Molly Lefebure, *Samuel Taylor Coleridge: A Bondage of Opium* (London: Gollancz, 1974). Biographical study, explaining Coleridge's problems, of incompletion, plagiarism, and imaginative failure, by his opium addiction, and asserting his heroism in his struggle to overcome his habit.

Paul Magnuson, *Coleridge's Nightmare Poetry* (Charlottesville: University of Virginia Press, 1974). Finds, in Coleridge's poetic language and imagery, the expressions of the state of a mind in its ultimately futile (hence nightmare) quest to create and know, through poetry, an ideal unitary self: an individuality grounded and defined within an ultimate reality.

Reeve Parker, *Coleridge's Meditative Art* (Ithaca and London: Cornell University Press, 1975). Emphasizing both conscious artistry and intellectual content, shows, in the conversation poems, Coleridge's interest in, and mastery of, the 'cultivated art of meditation'.

J. Robert Barth, S. J., *The Symbolic Imagination: Coleridge and the Romantic Tradition.* (1977; 2nd edn., New York: Fordham University Press, 2001). Discusses the centrality to Coleridge's thought of symbol as sacrament, and symbol-making as an act of faith. The conceiving of poetry as symbolic utterance, between literal and metaphorical, repudiates pure subjectivism, not only for Coleridge, but also for the Romantics more generally.

John Beer, *Coleridge's Poetic Intelligence* (London and Basingstoke: Macmillan, 1977). Presents Coleridge's exploration (up to 1805) of human intelligence and organic nature so as to establish a correspondence between natural processes and the human psyche's transforming power over the apparent fixities of the universe.

Laurence S. Lockridge, *Coleridge the Moralist* (Ithaca and London: Cornell University Press, 1977). Constructs Coleridge's moral thought from his life, theories and poetry, analyzing the paradoxes of the moral struggle 'to develop and preserve the integrity of the conscious, feeling, imagining self'.

Kathleen Coburn, *Experience into Thought: Perspectives in the Coleridge Notebooks* (Toronto and London: University of Toronto Press, 1979). Three lectures, the third especially concerned with showing that 'the poet and the philosopher were one and the same man.'

Edward Kessler, *Coleridge's Metaphors of Being* (Princeton, N. J.: Princeton University Press, 1979). Persuasive defence of the late poetry, arguing that for Coleridge, the end of the poetic process is not the poem as artefact, but a new awareness of being; thus, he eventually discards conventional metaphor or natural representation (which locates the poet in the physical world) for symbol and paradox in the form of the fragment (which can point towards the wholeness of '*ultimate Being*').

James Engell, *The Creative Imagination: Enlightenment to Romanticism* (Cambridge, Mass.: Harvard University Press, 1981). Pursuing the idea of the imagination in diverse fields, Coleridge invariably uses modes and categories already established by eighteenth-century thinkers; yet, retaining, in all the diversity of its application, his sense of the creative imagination as a single fundamental principle of nature and mind, he draws connecting lines between different thinkers, in which consist his originality and centrality.

Thomas McFarland, *Romanticism and the Forms of Ruin: Wordsworth, Coleridge, and Modalities of Fragmentation* (Princeton: Princeton University Press, 1981). Emphasizes, within a thesis of the 'diasparactive' emphasis in Romanticism – the dominance of forms of incompleteness, fragmentation and ruin, complementary to its impulse to unity, or need for 'reticulation' – the mutual influence ('symbiosis') of Wordsworth and Coleridge, and the interpenetration of philosophy and poetry in Coleridge's thought.

K. M. Wheeler, *The Creative Mind in Coleridge's Poetry* (London: Heinemann, 1981). Presents, from Coleridge's poetry, his philosophic theory of the creative mind, illustrated both in composition and in perception or reading. Coleridge's 'demand for reader participation breaks down the boundary of art and reality, the reader as subject and the object as text and sets up the poem as a unity of opposites in the state of process and becoming'.

Raimonda Modiano, *Coleridge and the Concept of Nature* (London and Basingstoke: Macmillan, 1985). Explains Coleridge's varied responses to nature in the different stages of his career, from naturalistic zeal to a later withdrawal from nature, by a combination of personal and intellectual developments, including his relationships with Wordsworth and Sara Hutchinson and the impact of German transcendentalism.

James McKusick, *Coleridge's Philosophy of Language* (New Haven and London: Yale University Press, 1986). Linking Coleridge's linguistic theories with seventeenth- and eighteenth-century developments in the philosophy of language, shows that his 'quest for a criterion of linguistic "naturalness" is a persistent element in his poetical, critical, and philosophical endeavours'.

Lucy Newlyn, *Coleridge, Wordsworth, and the Language of Allusion* (Oxford: Clarendon, Press, 1986). Insightful intertextual study, eliciting from the changing pattern of the mutual allusions in their poetry, the developing disparity between Coleridge's and Wordsworth's constructions of selfhood and imagination.

Ian Wylie, *Young Coleridge and the Philosophers of Nature* (Oxford: Clarendon Press, 1989). Reasserts, against the tendency to overlook the empiricist influence on Coleridge's thought, the importance to his early (including best) poetry of his study of natural philosophy, especially Newton, in the 1790s.

DECONSTRUCTING COLERIDGE

A chronological marker might be used to divide the criticism just listed, neatly, almost at the bicentenary of Coleridge's birth in 1972. Fittingly associated with the bicentenary is the Bollingen edition of the *Collected Works*, an ongoing feat of scholarly achievement under the general editorship of Kathleen Coburn that has continued, from its inception a few years prior to the bicentenary, materially to shape Coleridge criticism thereafter. In a quite different way, the bicentenary is also marked by Norman Fruman's controversial publication, *Coleridge: The Damaged Archangel* (1971). Taking up the charges of plagiarism intermittently levelled against Coleridge from De Quincey onwards, Fruman, with something of the censoriousness of Coleridge's Victorian detractors, seeks to silence the apologists for Coleridge's unacknowledged borrowings by expos- ing those borrowings in their all their blatancy and extent as the hallmarks of a brilliant but neurotic, hence flawed, personality. The tracking of sources, manifested in the meticulous annotations of the *Collected Works*, is also Fru- man's activity, which thus disputes the canonizing thrust of the collection.

If the criticism that takes the romantic affirmation in good faith constructs a unitary, because sincere, poetic self, a self whose language and belief are one, the assertion of the poet's bad faith fractures that self, dividing its language (expression) from its belief, knowledge or experience. Fruman's findings, of the 'lifelong conflicts among Coleridge's various selves',[18] sustain the disjunc- tion argued by Bostetter, between affirmation and experience or awareness in Coleridge's writing, and, like Bostetter's, not only call into question the poet's ability to sustain his (romantic) ideal but also, in so doing, problematize the ideal itself. In another more theoretical context, the registering of discrepancy or disunity – see, as well as Bostetter and Fruman, Schneider and Magnuson, above – belongs to a critical awareness of the gaps between the romantic self and its fictions, fundamental to the radical de-mystification called for in Paul de Man's seminal critique of the romantic, and Coleridgean, 'symbol' (1969).[19]

Two major studies of 1980, undertaken in de Man's wake, skilfully negotiate scepticism and belief. Tilottama Rajan's *Dark Interpreter: The Discourse of Romanticism* contests the 'organicist' or idealistic criticism which insistently resolves contradictions and paradox into a unity, yet Rajan's own deconstructive reading, of the Romantic ambiguity regarding the transforming power of art, neither simplifies nor dismisses Romantic idealism, but rather argues the co-existence (dialectic) of idealism and irony in Romantic poetry, including Coleridge's. Anne Mellor's 'romantic ironist' shares the doubleness of Rajan's: although lacking the certainties of the secularized Judaeo-Christian vision posited by Abrams and his followers, 'he is as much a romantic as an ironist', thus, 'he deconstructs his own texts in the expectation that such deconstruction is a way of keeping in contact with a greater creative power.' But Coleridge, to Mellor, is distinguished from the 'authentic romantic ironist' by his inability wholeheartedly to embrace 'a vision of the universe as dynamic becoming'. He affirms an 'irrational and amoral world of "pure imagination" and at the same time guiltily rejects this world as blasphemous and evil.'[20]

Sometimes fusing, in its most recent mutations, with the deconstructionist attitude in Coleridge criticism, is an existing older strand, which challenges the sufficiency of the thinker–poet by emphasizing the political content and implications of his work. The association of Coleridge's poetry with his renouncing of political radicalism is suggested early on by Hazlitt in *The Spirit of the Age* (1825): 'Mr. Coleridge sounded a retreat . . . by the help of casuistry, and a musical voice.'[21] Subsequent political, usually Marxist, criticism has continued to fashion a largely conservative Coleridge, although the emphasis on his early radicalism has informed more than one major study. From the 1980s onwards, there emerge a number of influential and explicitly polemical critiques, concerned to expose not only the political content of the poet's work, but also the perpetuation of his ideology in critical reception and interpretation.

In a powerful essay, entitled 'The Ancient Mariner: The Meaning of Meanings', first published in 1981 and later republished in *The Beauty of Inflections* (1985), Jerome McGann argues that any interpretation, insofar as it attempts to determine content or meaning in Coleridge's text, is already always under the dominion of a hermeneutic model initiated by Coleridge and implicated in the 'Romantic ideology', that 'historical phenomenon of European culture, generated to save the "traditional concepts, schemes, and values" of the

Christian heritage.'[22] McGann's essay, which builds upon and extends Elinor Shaffer's findings regarding Coleridge's use of the textual principles and methods of the 'Higher Criticism' of the bible,[23] refers specifically to the composition and critical history of the 'Ancient Mariner', but its general thesis, of the subjugation of interpretation to the Romantic ideology, is that proposed in his *Romantic Ideology* (1983). The core of McGann's argument is extracted below.

Extract from J. J. McGann, 'The Ancient Mariner: The Meaning of Meanings' in *The Beauty of Inflections* (1985)

The 'Rime' and the Critical Tradition

As far as the 'Rime' is concerned, we have to note the special importance of certain aspects of this body of thinking. I refer specifically to the idea, which Coleridge explicitly endorsed, that the biblical narratives were originally bardic (oral) poetry which gradually evolved into a cycle of communal literary materials. Embedded in primitive and legendary saga, the Scriptures grew by accretion and interpolation over an extended period of time. They do not represent a 'true' narrative of certain fixed original events; rather, they are a collection of poetic materials which represent the changing form of 'witness' or testament of faith created by a religious community in the course of its history.[1] The function of the Higher Criticism, as a method, was to reveal the various 'layers' of this poetic work by distinguishing the Bible's different religious/poetic styles, or forms of expression, from the earliest and most primitive to the latest and most sophisticated.

This general approach toward historically transmitted texts produced two specific theories which bear particularly on the 'Rime'. Geddes' 'Fragment Hypothesis' argued that the Pentateuch 'was put together by an editor out of a collection of independent and often conflicting fragments'.[2] Coleridge accepted this interpretation but modified it by arguing that the conflation of the disparate fragments was a communal process rather than a unique event.

The second theory, put forth by Wolf in his *Prolegomena ad Homerum* (1795), argued that the *Iliad* was a redaction of different lays which had been passed down through a bardic tradition. Wolf's ballad theory of the epic partly drew its inspiration from the scholarship developed in the writings of the ballad revival. The argument in Percy's influential

'Essay on the Ancient Minstrels of England', which introduced his *Reliques*, is paradigmatic. According to Percy, England's ancient poetic tradition from the pagan skalds to the old Christian minstrels was a continuous one; and although 'the Poet and the Minstrel early with us became two persons', 'the ancient minstrels' preserved in their ballad and song traditions a profound continuity with the old pagan skalds. Indeed, the common practice of the ancient minstrels – in contrast to the new, developing line of leisured poets – was not to compose new works but to adapt and extend the older ones which descended through the tradition from primitive pagan times.[3]

The foregoing is the ideological framework for the following remarkable passage. The quotation is Coleridge's marginal gloss in his copy of Eichhorn's *Einleitung in das alte Testament* and is itself a theory, or explanation, of the meaning of glosses and textual interpolation. Commenting on Genesis 36:31, Coleridge writes: 'Buy why *not* consider this as a gloss introduced by the Editors of the Pentateuch, or Preparers of the Copy that was to be layed up in the Temple of Solomon? The authenticity of the Books would be no more compromised by such glosses, than that of the Book before me by this marginal Note of mine'.[4] Coleridge means that, given a coherent cultural tradition, the text which exhibits marks of its historical passage (in the form of later interpolations, glosses, and other textual additions and 'impurities') retains its ideological coherence despite the process of apparent fragmentation. Such a text is, in truth, a Book of Revelation by itself, an apocalypse of its evolved and interconnected poetic/religious coherences.

When Coleridge applies these critical views to non-Scriptural texts, as he does in 'The Destiny of Nations', his idea is that the pagan bards of Greenland initiated a body of poetic material whose traditions culminated in the Christian revelation. Ancient 'superstition', in these poetic repositories, will eventually 'Seat Reason on her throne' through the processive movement of spiritual history. The textual history of primary epic and ballad materials exhibits in a concrete way the process of continuous spiritual revelation.

The 'Rime' is presented as just this sort of text, and its own bibliographical history illustrates *in fact* what Coleridge fictively represents his poem to be *in imagination*. The special significance of the gloss, as far as the 'Rime' is concerned, lies in its (imagined) historical relation to the ancient ballad which Coleridge has represented through his poem. By the time Coleridge has 'evolved' his 1817 text, we are able to distinguish four clear layers of development: (*a*) an original mariner's tale; (*b*) the ballad narrative of that story; (*c*) the editorial gloss added when the ballad was, we are to suppose, first printed; and (*d*) Coleridge's own point of view on his invented materials. This last represents Coleridge's special religious/symbolic theory of interpretation founded upon his own understanding of the Higher Critical analytic.

From Coleridge's viewpoint the 'Rime' is a poem which illustrates a special theory of the historical interpretation of texts. In its earliest state (1798), the theory is not easy to deduce, though it is certainly in operation; when the glosses are added, however, Coleridge has extrapolated fully, and thereby made explicit, his religious theory of interpretation which has its roots in the Higher Critical tradition.

Like all literary ballads, the 'Rime' is a *tour de force*, for Coleridge built it according to theories of the ballad (and of other historically transmitted works) which he had studied and which he expected his readers to know and to recognize. Certain stylistic facts about the poem demonstrate – on the authority of Percy – that the text has material which 'dates back' to the early days of the ancient minstrels.[5] On the other hand, other stylistic aspects of the text, including the gloss, show that its 'date' is relatively late, certainly after Columbus, but perhaps before Magellan's voyage to the Pacific. In general, Coleridge means us to understand that the ballad narrative dates from the sixteenth century, that the gloss is a late seventeenth-century addition, and, of course, that Coleridge, at the turn of the nineteenth century, has provided yet another (and controlling) perspective upon the poetic material. Indeed, Coleridge certainly intended his more perspicuous readers – that is, those read in the theory and practice of the new historical criticism – to see that the 'Rime' was an imaginative presentation of a work comprising textual layers of the most primitive, even pre-Christian, sort. No one schooled in the new German textual criticism could fail to 'see' that the opening portions of part 6 represented a textual survival of the most ancient kind of pagan lore.

Coleridge's final (Broad Church) grasp of the 'Rime' demonstrates his great theme of the One Life.[6] Like the Bible, the *Iliad*, and all great imaginative works possessed and transmitted by different cultures, the 'Rime' is Coleridge's imitation of a culturally redacted literary work. The special function of the poem was to illustrate a significant continuity of meaning between cultural phenomena that seemed as diverse as pagan superstitions, Catholic theology, Aristotelian science, and contemporary philological theory, to name only a few of the work's ostentatiously present materials. The 'Rime', in its 1798 or its 1817 form, reconciles many opposite and discordant qualities.

A well-known passage from *The Table Talk* sets out the structural and thematic foundation of the 'Rime' in its most general philosophic formulation:

My system, if I may venture to give it so fine a name, is the only attempt I know, ever made to reduce all knowledges into harmony. It opposes no other system, but shows what was true in each; and how that which was true in the particular, in each of them became error, *because* it was only half the truth. I have endeavoured to unite the insulated fragments of truth, and therewith to frame a perfect mirror. I show to each system that I fully understand and rightfully appreciate what that system means; but then I lift up that system to a higher point of view, from which I enable it to see its former position, where it was, indeed, but under another light and with different relation; so that the fragment of truth is not only acknowledged, but explained. Thus the old astronomers discovered and maintained much that was true; but, because they were placed on a false ground, and looked from a wrong point of view, they never did, they never could, discover the truth – that is, the whole truth. As soon as they left the earth, their false centre, and took their stand in the sun, immediately they saw the whole system in its true light, and their former station remaining, but remaining as a part of the prospect.[7]

The 'Rime' is structured around three fundamental ideologies: pagan superstition and philosophy, Catholic legend and theology, and Broad Church Protestantism. As noted, the poem's formal layering reflects this material. The pre-Coleridgean 'fragments of truth' represent 'a wrong point of view' on the material of human experience. The 'events' treated in the poem actually represent interpretations of events carried out in terms of certain fragmentary 'systems' of human thought, and the purpose of the poem is to 'lift [these systems] to a higher point of view' whence they will be open to a critical, self-conscious, but sympathetic valuation. This 'higher point of view', which *The Table Talk* passage represents as a final (divine) one, is Coleridge's own 'system' where 'the whole truth' adumbrated by the (historically relative) fragments of truth is discovered. *What* that whole truth constitutes is (*a*) that there is a whole truth which justifies and is the ground of all the fragments of the truth; and (*b*) that this whole truth is in a perpetual process of becoming – indeed, that its being is *the process of its being*.

Coleridge's system, then, is justified in the continuous and developing history of human thought. In terms of the 'Rime', Coleridge's ideological commitment to a preconditioned ground of processive truth sanctions in its readers a diversity of interpretations based upon their particular lights. Because 'the whole truth', recognized or not, subsumes a *priori* all the interpretations, readers are encouraged to formulate their particular expressions of the truth. Coleridge's much-discussed symbolic method in the poem is nothing more (or less) than his rhetorical machinery for producing such interpretive results. In Coleridge's terms, the symbolically grounded interpretations are acts of witness rather than definitions, human events which dramatically testify to the desire to know and continuously create the truth that has always set men free.

In this context, when Haven shows the congruence between nineteenth- and twentieth-century interpretations of the 'Rime', we are able to extrapolate the significance of his research. The basic continuum of thought comprising the poem's many interpretations testifies to the power of Coleridge's own poetic project. Although a few critics have attempted to resist the tradition outlined by Haven – I will return to them in a moment – the vast majority follow the model set forth in Coleridge's own comprehensive hermeneutic system established through the poem itself. The interpretive tradition licensed by the 'Rime' corresponds to the network of ideological institutions (the Clerisy) which Coleridge's ideas helped to create. Before Coleridge, the Church for centuries had been the principal ideological state apparatus, but *On the Constitution of Church and State*, among other works, marks the change which Coleridge was promoting. With him we witness the retreat of the Church and the emergence of the educational system, the academy, as Western society's principal ideological institution. As John Colmer recently remarked, in referring to educators in today's secular world, 'We are the clerisy'.[8] To measure the influence of Coleridge's programme one need but recall the dominant ideologues in Anglo-American culture during the past one hundred and fifty years: from Coleridge, through Arnold, Emerson, Leavis, and Eliot, to Trilling, Abrams, and the contemporary apologists for English and American Romantic thought.

The complex cultural problems related to the hegemony of this tradition appear again, in miniature form, when we approach Coleridge's great literary ballad. The history of the poem's criticism reveals, for example, that readers have not found it easy to escape the power of Coleridge's hermeneutics. From Babbitt to Empson and Pirie, a few critics have struggled against the dominant tradition of readers. Their characteristic method is to attack either the Romantic-symbolical readings – ridiculed by Empson and Pirie, for example – or Coleridge himself and the entire project ('spilt religion') which generated such readings. Sometimes, as in Empson's case, a distinction is drawn between the 'early', 'secular' Coleridge – author of the 1798 'Rime' – and the late, Christian dodderer – author of the 1817 revisionist piece. This antithetical tradition is important chiefly because it corroborates, from a hostile position, the basic ideological uniformity which underlies the dominant symbolic tradition initiated by Coleridge.

The problem with such antithetical readings is that they are at war with the differentials they themselves emphasize and corroborate. Babbitt and Empson are married, by antithesis and anxiety, to the positions they are attacking. The rules for such relationships, which have been laid down in the theoretical works initiated by Harold Bloom's *The Anxiety of Influence*, produce what can well be called 'the fate of reading'. What this means – I merely state the basic problem in another form – is that a historical process begins to appear as a fatal one; specifically, the act of literary criticism comes to seem so repetitional that drastic evasive measures begin to be taken. Babbitt's and Empson's violence succeeds to the play of differences in post-structuralism because acts which make a difference, in the mind as well as in the world, begin to seem difficult if not impossible to achieve. When traditional human activities seem as unimportant as academic criticism has grown to seem in this period of our culture – when it appears to make no difference what, if any, literary criticism you read or write – movements begin (deconstructionism in this period, aestheticism and naturalism at the end of the nineteenth century) which throw into relief the crisis line of an ideological tradition.

In terms of the critical history of the 'Rime', antithetical critics like Babbitt and Empson seem to violate the past of its treasures, while the traditional line seems to have exhausted its future and left us with nothing to follow. At such moments a historical analysis becomes a cultural imperative, for it is through such an analysis that we can recover what the past has sent to us and redefine the future of our own work. Such a method demands that differences be sharpened and clarified historically. The resources made available through the 'Rime' and its critical history will not be recovered until we begin to specify clearly the ideological gulf which separates us from them both. A poem like the 'Rime' dramatizes a salvation story, but it is not the old story of our salvation *in* Christ; rather, it is the new story of our salvation *of* Christ. Coleridge would have us believe that the latter story is the latest expression of the former and hence that the former retains its cultural truth. To the critical view of a contemporary materialist and historical consciousness, however, the advanced Christian machinery of the 'Rime' represents a view of the world only qualitatively less alien to ourselves than the ideology which supports the *Iliad* or the writings of Confucius. These works, we must come to see, transcend their particular cultural circumstances not because they contain unchanging human truths but rather because their *particular* truthfulness has been so thoroughly – so materially – specified.

Like the *Iliad* or *Paradise Lost* or any great historical product, the 'Rime' is a work of transhistorical rather than so-called universal significance. This verbal distinction is important because it calls attention to a real one. Like the *Divine Comedy* or any other poem, the 'Rime' is not valued or used always or everywhere or by everyone in the same way or for the same reasons. Poetical and artistic works have chequered critical histories which testify to their discontinuous power and employment. The study of a work's critical history is imperative precisely for that reason: the analysis reveals to us, in yet another form, the special historical life which a work has been living in the dialectic of its processive career. Historical analysis uncovers, therefore, a paradox of thought which yet contains a fundamental human truth: that the universal or transhistorical significance of an ideological product is a function of the specific limits of place and circumstance which are inscribed, and therefore 'immortalized', in those works we call poems which are created and re-created over time. The importance of great art is that it has always made a difference.

Anyone who has taught ancient or culturally removed literature has experienced the difficulty of transmitting historically alienated material. Nor does it help much to assume or pretend that what Bacon says in 'Of Education', what Sophocles dramatizes in the *Oedipus*, or what the Jahwist has presented in his Genesis can be appreciated or even understood by an uneducated student or reader. Of course, the problem can be solved if the teacher avoids it altogether and asks the student to deal with the work in its present context only, that is, to supply it with a 'reading'. Alien works may be, as we say, 'interpreted'. But we must understand that such exercises, carried out in relative historical ignorance, are not *critical* operations. Rather, they are vehicles for recapitulating and objectifying the reader's particular ideological commitments.[9] To 'read' in this way is to confront Ahab's doubloon, to read self-reflexively. The danger in such a method is that it will not be able to provide the reader with a social differential that can illuminate the limits of that immediate interpretation. The importance of ancient or culturally removed works lies precisely in this fact: that they themselves, as culturally alienated products, confront present readers with ideological differentials that help to define the limits and special functions of those current ideological practices. Great works continue to have something to say because what they have to say is so peculiarly and specifically their own that we, who are different, can learn from them.

Though the 'Rime' is not nearly so removed from the present as the *Oedipus*, we must not allow its alienation to escape us. The force of a line like 'It is an ancient mariner' comes from one's sense that an ancient minstrel did not write it but that Coleridge did. This is an awareness which was, and was meant to be, available to audiences from the poem's first appearance. But with the passage of time other perspectives become both possible and necessary. *We* see, for example, that the minstrel represented to us here is *not* the figure known to Child or Gummere but the one specifically available to a reader and admirer of Percy. To see this fact, even in so small an event as that line, is to be able to read the line *in* its own terms but without being made *subject* to those terms. We willingly suspend our disbelief only when disbelief, or critical distance, is the ground of our response. Such critical scepticism (it is not an attitude but a method) is especially important for a work like the 'Rime', since the poem itself seeks to break down a sense of ultimate discontinuity through the structure of its artistic illusions. Criticism must penetrate those illusions and specify what is involved in the particular uses to which they have been put. The meaning of the 'Rime' emerges through the study of the history of its illusions.

The 'Rime' and the Meaning of Symbol

In his introduction to the *History of the Russian Revolution*, Trotsky defends himself against the charge that he is a biased reporter by attacking the concept of 'objective history'. No historian's presentation can ever be free of tendentious and ideological elements, Trotsky argues. His position is not, however, subjectively relativistic. On the contrary, one judges the adequacy of a historian's work by its value as an explanation of the phenomena, by its congruence and comprehensiveness in relation to the objective circumstances. But the explanation must be constructed, Trotsky says, from an ideological vantage of some sort, and in his own case Trotsky argues that he is both more objectively correct in his vantage and analysis and more subjectively honest and clear about his methods. Trotsky, that is to say, makes every effort not to disguise his ideological position behind a specious appeal to objectivity but instead builds and objectifies his bias into the very structure of the analysis and keeps the reader aware of it all the time. Trotsky does this because, in his view, the ideology is a crucial part of the analysis, as much a part of his historical subject as it is the basis of his historical method.

Trotsky's ideology corresponds to what Coleridge called 'first principles', except that the former is a structure of scientific thought and the latter a theological, or what Coleridge termed a metaphysical, system. The general argument in the *The Statesman's Manual* – that the Bible is the most reliable guide for secular statecraft – is based upon a view wholly analogous to Trotsky's: that history, whether lived or narrated, is not a sequence of atomized movements or facts but a structured phenomenon, the praxis of a living and related set of commitments. For Coleridge, the crucial importance of a work like the Bible lies in its continuous historical existence. Because it must be read through the mediation of its transmitters, that is, through the Church, readers cannot receive its words except through acts of faith or, as we should say, through tendentious interpretations, acts of conscious commitment to the received materials. The Bible comes to us bearing with it the history of its criticism; it is a writing which also contains its own readings and which generates the cumulative history of its own further retransmissions and reinterpretations.

As already seen, Coleridge's views on the Bible were merely paradigmatic of his views on all literary texts. A committed Christian, he necessarily saw the Bible as the world's central literary event; but, like his contemporaries, he understood very well that other non-Christian cultures had their equivalent of the Western Bible. Indeed, as Coleridge argued in 'The Destiny of Nations', the West's central pre-Christian documents, for example, the saga literature of the skaldic bards, were important scriptual events not merely in themselves but in relation to the general development of mankind's religious cultures. German biblical critics were revealing the non- and pre-Judaic stands in the Scriptures, and the new philologists of primitive and classical texts were at work on similar projects.

The 'Rime', as readers have known all along, is an imitation or literary ballad modelled on works like those contained in Percy's *Reliques*, or on translations of Gottfried Bürger's imitation ballads. What has not been so clear is Coleridge's ideological motive in producing the 'Rime'. The context of his religious and critical thought shows quite clearly, I believe, that the poem is, as it were, an English national Scripture; that is to say, the poem imitates a redacted literary text which comprises various material extending from early pre-Christian periods through a succession of later epochs of Christian culture, and the ultimate locus of these transmissions is England. We must also understand, however, that for Coleridge each redaction specifies and calls attention to the series of distinct epochal (that is, ideological) interpretations through which the poetic material has been evolving.

By re-presenting not merely a text but an evidently *mediated* text, Coleridge provided both a spur and a model for later readers, who have been encouraged to elucidate for themselves and their own special needs the meaning and significance of the poem's symbolic statements. Ultimately, however, although Coleridge's project aimed to generate an unlimited number of readings, it was equally committed, by its own hermeneutic ideology, to a certain sort of reading. These are the interpretations which Haven has synthesized for us. Coleridge's theory of symbolism is a Western and a Judeo-Christian theory, and the hermeneutics of the 'Rime' has always been governed by this general frame of reference and set of, what Coleridge called, 'facts':

> Christianity is especially differenced from all other religions by being *grounded* on *facts* which all men alike have the means of ascertaining, the same means, with equal facility, and which no man can ascertain for another. Each person must be herein querist and respondent to himself; Am I sick, and therefore need a physician? – Am I in spiritual slavery, and therefore need a ransomer? – Have I given a pledge, which must be redeemed, and which I cannot redeem by my own resources?[10]

Such facts are, of course, what we call ideology. The important thing to see, however, is that Coleridge knew perfectly well that these facts were 'interpreted facts', faith-determined and faith-constitutive. To read the 'Rime' in such a 'redemptive' frame is, as Coleridge maintained (and as we must agree), to reduplicate its determinative, a *priori* ideology. In this way does the 'Rime' assume into itself its own critical tradition.

Through works like the 'Rime' Coleridge successfully sustained his theistic and Christian views about nature and human history in the institutions of Western education. Hence the literary criticism of the 'Rime' has never been, in the proper sense, *critical* of the poem but has merely recapitulated, in new and various ways, and not always very consciouly, what Coleridge himself had polemically maintained. To a *critical* view, however, what Coleridge re-presents in the 'Rime' is a historically and culturally limited set of ideas. Readers have not always found it easy to see this fact when they interpret the poem's 'symbols' because they characteristically regard their interpretations as something which *they bring to* the pre-existent 'text'. The 'Rime' is one thing, and its interpretations are something else, separated by time, place, and person. But Coleridge's own poem, as well as his involvement in the German critical tradition, ought to remind us that an act of interpretation may be assumed a *priori* in the materials to be interpreted. In the case of a poem like the 'Rime', hermeneutics is criticism's grand illusion.

A properly critical view of the 'Rime' can only begin with the recognition that what needs criticism and interpretation is not simply the work's set of symbolic paraphernalia (albatross, mariner, spectre-bark, water snakes, rain, sun, moon, etc.); these are 'in' the poem and therefore the objects of our analysis, but they are only in the poem *as symbols*. That is to say, they enter the reader's horizon as objects-bearing-meaning, as already significant (or pre-interpreted) phenomena. A critical analysis of the poem's poetic materials, therefore, cannot be carried out by erecting a thematic elucidation of albatross, sun, moon, water, and so on but only by erecting an analysis of the *meaningful* albatross, the *significant* sun, moon, stars, water. The materials dealt with by the 'Rime' are not – indeed, never were – mere 'secular' or 'natural' facts; they are predesigned and pre-interpreted phenomena. We may, indeed must, read the poem's symbols, but what we must critically elucidate are the meanings of the symbols. Readers of the 'Rime' generate its meanings; critics set out and explain the meaning of its meanings.

The albatross, for example, is an interpreted phenomenon *ab initio*: the bird is part of the mariner's superstitious preconceptions. So too the mariner himself: by virtue of his association with the Wandering Jew, for example, he has been incorporated by the poem into a special structure of signification. In each case the reader is reading the meaning not of the bird or mariner in isolation but of bird and mariner as they represent or locate certain superstitious (and, ultimately, religious) forms of thought. Similarly, the terms 'Bridegroom' and 'Wedding-Guest' are delivered to and through the Western, nineteenth- and twentieth-century readers in terms of their Christian frame of reference. These are not words from an innocent, 'natural' language, as it were, but from a particular symbolic and religious context of discourse.

In general, what Coleridge does in his poem is to present us, via an imitation ballad, with a wide variety of culturally and historically mediated material; and he arranges this material, formally, according to philological rules which governed the constitution and transmission of ancient texts and which were just then being formulated in the circles of the Higher Critics. This formal procedure empowers Coleridge to produce a wide variety of poetic effects. It enables him, for example, to achieve the wit of lines like 'We were the first that ever burst/Into that silent sea (lines 105–6), where the contemporary reader encounters an 'explanation' for how the Pacific Ocean (*Mare Pacificum*) may originally have received its name (see also line 110). More significantly, the Higher Critical model gave Coleridge a structure in which various materials apparently alien to each other could be reconciled and harmonized. Different sorts of superstitious phenomena are held in a significant relation with various Christian ideologies. We are enabled to 'interpret', for example, the originally pagan Polar Spirit in terms of a redemptive Christian scheme because the philological model tells us that the two are historically related via the operation of processes of textual transmission and interpolation. One important function of Coleridge's Polar Spirit, therefore, is to remind us that such superstitious phenomena retain their power of signification in history even after their ideology has ceased to play a dominant role in the institutions of a culture; that they retain this power by virtue of their incorporation by later ideological systems; and, finally that they are available to such incorporation precisely because they are, originally, *interpreted* rather than merely natural phenomena.

Creating this sort of poem required Coleridge to imitate a transmitted ballad. He had to establish a text which displayed several textual 'layers', as we have already seen, and the poem's lexicon is the ultimate carrier of this set of textual layers. The 'Rime' cannot work if it does not contain words which the reader will associate with diverse historical periods. Attention has always been drawn to the archaic diction of the ballad, but equally important is the modern diction. 'Bassoon' and 'lighthouse' are seventeenth-century words, and their appearance in the text indicates (fictively, of course) 'late interpolated passages'. In general, the archaic diction is only significant in its relation to the more modern dictions; the poetic system that holds them together is using both as the formal foundation for its work of symbology.

Coleridge takes it for granted that an 'Enlightened' mind of his or a later period will not believe that the spectre-bark ever had a concrete and objective existence or that the creatures called Death and Life-in-Death ever did what the poem reports or ever existed in the ordinary sense. The Enlightened mind will recognize such phenomena to be mental projections of the mariner's delirium; indeed, he will see all the fabulous events in this way, that is, as phenomena mediated either by the mariner, or by the balladeer(s), or by some still later editor or scribe, like the writer of the gloss. All of these are pre-Enlightenment minds. But to Coleridge's (post- and anti-Enlightenment) mind, this Enlightened view is itself a limited one. The Enlightenment (Higher Critical) attitude sees (*a*) that all phenomena are mind-mediated and (*b*) that these mediations are culturally and historically determined. What it does not see, in Coleridge's view, is that the entire system (or history) of the mediations is organized a *priori* and that the history of the mediations is an evolving process whereby the original (God-instituted and redemptive) system is raised up into human consciousness by the processive acts of human consciousness itself.

This Coleridgean view of the poem is what has licensed its traditions of symbolic interpretation. But this view must itself finally be laid aside as a determinative one. Coleridge's appeal to historical process and his insistence that symbolic interpretation (the meaning of symbols) is a function of specific cultural and historical factors ultimately overtake his own poetic ideology. For his is a sacramental and Christian view of symbols in which history itself is revealed as a sacramental Christian symbol. The 'Rime' imitates or re-presents a process of textual evolution,

and the symbolic meaning of that process – which is the poem's dominant symbolic event – is that the process *has* a symbolic value and
meaning, that is, a religious, a Christian, and ultimately a redemptive
meaning. In this we can see very clearly the living operation of processive
historical events. At the outset of the nineteenth century and in reaction
to the revolutionary intellectual developments of the Enlightenment,
Christian ideas find a new birth of freedom, not in the *fact* of Christ's
resurrection, which is the traditional Pauline view, but in the symbol of
the resurrection, in its *meaning*.

Notes

1 See Shaffer, *'Kubla Khan' and the Fall of Jerusalem*, 75–9.
2 See ibid., 78.
3 See Thomas Percy, *Reliques of Ancient English Poetry*, ed. J. V. Prichard, 2 vols.
   (London: Bell, 1905), xxiii–xxvi and nn.
4 Coleridge quoted in Shaffer, 79.
5 See the discussion in Percy, pp. xlii–xliii, of the diction of the ancient minstrels
   (e.g. the accentuation of words like Coleridge's 'countree', 1. 407).
6 See Charles Sanders, *Coleridge and the Broad Church Movement* (Durham, NC:
   Duke Univ. Press, 1942), and Boulger, *Coleridge as Religious Thinker*.
7 Coleridge, *Table Talk*, I. 248–9.
8 John Colmer, *Coleridge: Critic of Society* (Oxford: Clarendon Press, 1959), 32.
9 This result lies in the nature of hermeneutics itself, at least as presently understood. See, for example, Heinrich Ott's 'Hermeneutics and Personhood', where
   he states the basic principle of this interpretive method: 'In my first knowledge
   of the subject matter I already know implicitly all that which I later learned in
   addition' (from *Interpretation: The Poetry of Meaning*, ed. S. R. Hopper and D. L.
   Miller [New York: Harcourt Brace, 1967], 17).
10 Coleridge, *Lay Sermons* (Vol. 6 of the *Collected Works of Samuel Taylor Coleridge*,
   Bollingen Series no. 75), ed. R. J. White (Princeton: Princeton Univ. Press, 1972),
   55.

Further reading

The works listed below variously address the elision of the political (including sexual
politics) in Coleridge criticism.

*Carl Woodring, *Politics in the Poetry of Coleridge* (Madison: University of Wisconsin
   Press, 1961). Attending to topical allusions and the political context of genre, presents a largely conservative Coleridge in its study of 'the variety of ways by which he
   put political ideas, feelings, and dilemmas to work in his poems.'

William Empson, 'The Ancient Mariner' (1964), repr. in *Argufying: Essays on Literature and Culture*, ed. J. Haffenden (London: Hogarth Press, 1988), 297–319. Provocatively un-Christian reading of the poem as a psychological study of superstition produced by 'neurotic' (unaccountable or unidentifiable) guilt, here associated with European maritime expansion.

Kelvin Everest, *Coleridge's Secret Ministry: The Context of the Conversation Poems 1795–1798* (Sussex: Harvester; New York: Barnes & Noble, 1979). Resisting the over-emphasis on Romantic internalization by insisting on social and historical context, Everest argues that Coleridge's conversation poems of the 1790s, with their ideal of a domestic community in nature, are a compensatory response to his alienation from English society as a radical in this period, explaining both his efforts towards a philosophy of unity and his anxiety to establish a sympathetic audience.

David Aers, Jonathan Cook and David Punter, 'Coleridge: Individual, Community and Social Agency' in *Romanticism and Ideology: Studies in English Writing 1765–1830*, ed. D. Aers, J. Cook and D. Punter (London: Routledge & Kegan Paul, 1981), 82–102. Argues that Coleridge's texts offer 'powerfully evasive abstractions' in place of concrete social and political analysis, and suggests that this is 'close to a paradigm of the romantic predicament and strategy'.

Marilyn Butler, 'The Rise of the Man of Letters: Coleridge' in *Romantics, Rebels and Reactionaries: English Literature and its Background 1760–1830* (Oxford: Oxford University Press, 1981), 69–93. Within a larger thesis, of Coleridge's construction of himself as a new literary type and of a literary strategy (including the use of an elitist language) directed by his search for an ideal social community, presents his shift (and its loyalist implication) from a public to a private focus in the poems of 1797–8, as a response to the fragmentation of the English radical movement in the mid-1790s.

Paul Hamilton, *Coleridge's Poetics* (Oxford: Blackwell, 1983). Coleridge's philosophical standpoint is inseparable from his thinking about language, at the heart of which is the linguistic ideal of desynonymy, exemplified in poetry. Such an ideal, affording us a sense of our own potential for progress, has radical implications, deliberately obscured in the transcendentalist (elitist) language of *Biographia*.

Jerome McGann, *The Romantic Ideology: A Critical Investigation* (Chicago and London: University of Chicago Press, 1983). Preliminary comment on Coleridge's use of biblical criticism in the sustenance of the ideology of a 'clerisy'; today, the 'culture-guardians' centred in the academies.

Karen Swann, '"Christabel": The Wandering Mother and the Enigma of Form', *Studies in Romanticism* 23.4 (Winter 1984), 533–53. Dramatizing hysteria and provoking it in its audience, 'Christabel' both exploits and exposes the links between gender and genre in the culture of its time.

Marjorie Levinson, *The Romantic Fragment Poem: A Critique of a Form* (Chapel Hill and London: University of North Carolina Press, 1986). Readings of 'Christabel' and 'Kubla Khan' within a more general argument: the Romantic fragment poem invites a unity of poet and reader in a reception that proceeds beyond the text to a teleological construct, the 'poem'. Criticism, as it replaces the work's fractures and conflicts with an ideal consistency, constitutes such a reception, remaining subject to the orthodoxy of 'High Romanticism' where it should submit it to a radical interrogation.

Nigel Leask, *The Politics of Imagination in Coleridge's Critical Thought* (Basingstoke and London: Macmillan, 1988). Cultural materialist study of the historical and ideological formation of Coleridge's 'Imagination', as 'a seminal moment in the liberal idealization of the imagination' and in 'its institutionalization and removal from the social and political domain'. Leask argues that notwithstanding Coleridge's later conservatism, the poetry of 1797–1805 promotes 'the civic values of an egalitarian commonwealth, and [is] not the product of conservative reaction to the failure of French and English radicalism.'

Nicholas Roe, *Wordsworth and Coleridge: The Radical Years* (Oxford: Clarendon Press, 1988). Where for Wordsworth, revolutionary disappointment is compensated by poetic power, for Coleridge, it results in breakdown and creative paralysis. Roe usefully details the divergences in the nature, course and conceptualization of the two writers' otherwise compatible early radicalism, including the inseparability of Coleridge's radicalism from his religious principles in this period.

Julie Ellison, *Delicate Subjects: Romanticism, Gender, and the Ethics of Understanding* (Ithaca and London: Cornell University Press, 1990). The romantic subject's association of the feminine stereotype with the receptivity of understanding makes gender the site of interpretive ethics, thus calling for a feminist perspective on Coleridge's political apostasy and poetical decline.

Camille Paglia, 'The Daemon as Lesbian Vampire: Coleridge' in *Sexual Personae: Art and Decadence from Nefertiti to Emily Dickinson* (1990; London and New Haven: Yale University Press, 2001). Confronting, with other of Coleridge's poems, the 'daemonism of nature', 'Christabel' is 'a pornographic parable of western sex and power' in Paglia's lively account of the 'pagan' undercurrents in western culture.

Tim Fulford, *Coleridge's Figurative Language* (Basingstoke and London: Macmillan, 1991). Treats the connections of language, self and society in Coleridge's understanding of figurative language, its conditioning by his authorial and political conflicts, and its ongoing relevance today; counters the oversimplified view of Coleridge's 'elitism'.

Patrick Keane, *Coleridge's Submerged Politics: The Ancient Mariner and Robinson Crusoe* (Columbia and London: University of Missouri Press, 1994). Two-part study: the first, focusing on Coleridge's silence regarding slave-trading in his marginalia on Defoe's *Robinson Crusoe*, re-examines his position on slavery and the slave-trade; the second treats the dungeon-grate image of 'The Ancient Mariner' as a political intrusion in an apparently apolitical poem, which, contextualized within the political upheavals of 1797–8, contests or complicates the moral argument of the poem and its prose gloss.

Tim Fulford, *Romanticism and Masculinity: Gender, Politics and Poetics in the Writings of Burke, Coleridge, Cobbett, Wordsworth, De Quincey, and Hazlitt* (Basingstoke and London: Macmillan, 1999). Coleridge's response to Burkean aesthetics and politics is central to Fulford's study of Romanticism's interrogation of masculinity in poetry, aesthetics and political criticism.

TO THE PRESENT

My last extract is from a study that eschews the two poles of Coleridge criticism – unity (or coherence) and division (including bad faith) in its subject – by contending that 'Coleridge's thought is best understood, not as the solution to a *problem*, but as the experience and exploration of a *muddle*.' In *Coleridge and the Uses of Division* (1999), Seamus Perry describes in Coleridge an abiding and genuine irresolution of the opposite values of unity and division, not as a problem or flaw, but, as he puts it, 'a kind of vindication'.[24] Reprinted below is his 'Coda', on 'The Ancient Mariner'.

Extract from Seamus Perry, *Coleridge and the Uses of Division* (1999)

Coda: The Incomprehensible Mariner

> As a young man I snatched at any chance to hear wisdom drop from Mr T. S. Eliot, and he once remarked that the test of a true poet is that he writes about experiences before they have happened to him.
>
> William Empson[1]

I have left 'The Ancient Mariner' for a last word, not because I think it in any way peripheral, but because so many Coleridgean elements meet in the poem that it seemed misleading to reserve it for any one chapter. Haven rightly calls it 'the central document in Coleridge':[2] Coleridge returned to it compulsively, more so than to any other work, which implies a deep and nagging relevance; and any interpretation of his thought must try and decide what its implications are for the poem. Leslie Stephen once said, lightly but profoundly, that 'The germ of all Coleridge's utterances may be found – by a little ingenuity – in the "Ancient Mariner"':[3] on the voyage to Malta, Coleridge himself came to think of the poem as a prophetic self-portrait; and since I have been urging upon the reader the doubled theme of unity-and-division as fundamental, I should now try and persuade him that that predicament lurks at the heart of the great poem too. Of course, the idiom is utterly different from the inspired waywardness of the notebooks and the abstraction of the later metaphysical prose, but I think the kinds of philosophical drama I have been describing, a mind torn between the end of unity and the experience of differentness, can be traced backwards to this early and surprising masterpiece – and so too can the informing indecision of Coleridgean division, hesitating between the relative virtues (and demerits) of oneness and multiplicity. It is a work poised between a blessed vision of unity and the catastrophe of chaos – but also, to experience the same division but the other way up, between a cribbed nightmare of centripetal monomania and a redemptive resort to the free existence of other things.

I suppose the standard reading to be some kind of One Life allegory, which very obviously puts foremost the virtue of unity – indeed its divinity. The Mariner, in killing the albatross, commits 'a crime against the one Life . . . possible only to a man who had not seen the unity of all life in the world';[4] and he is punished for it: a 'sordid solitary thing', ignorant of '[t]he moral world's cohesion', he experiences a nightmarish 'Anarchy of Spirits', vividly realising the theological hypotheses that Coleridge had speculated about in 'Religious Musings' (149, 145, 146). It is the most scarifying picture Coleridge ever drew of the unhappy spirit craving atonement. In the depths of his darkness, the Mariner is appalled by the horrific plenitude of his rotting universe: 'And a million, million slimy things/Lived on; and so did I' (238–9). But this suffering proves salutary, a *via negativa* leading the Mariner to bless those same snakes, creatures even more off-putting than Charles's creeking rook, so a particularly testing case; but the Mariner passes the test, finally recognising the interdependent fraternity of all creation. The poem, that is, is about the redemption of other things – their transformation, indeed, from 'slimy things' to 'happy living things'. Many distinguished critics interpret the poem along these lines: Abrams, say, who sees the Mariner learning a 'lesson of community'[5]; or Peter Kitson, who sees the Mariner led 'to reintegrate himself with the One Life'.[6] (Another version of this reading sees the poem as an eco-parable.) Such readings make a strongly intuitive sense, which I hardly dispute; certainly, something very like that was the gist of the poem which Wordsworth suggested in the first place: 'some crime was to be committed which would bring upon the Old Navigator, as Coleridge afterwards delighted to call him, the spectral persecution, as a consequence of that crime and his own wanderings'.[7] But the poem Coleridge wrote obscures so consequentially clear a logic of retribution: when you come to puzzle things through, it is surprisingly hard to make several of the more outstanding details fit.

Some of the problems are carried over from the theology, and concern the mysteries of individuality and optimism: how is it possible for the Mariner to commit an evil act, one worthy of avenging, if this is a universe of benevolent determinism? The theological context of the One Life confuses any ambitions to treat sin, requital, and repentance: '*Guilt* is out of the Question,' as we have heard him tell Thelwall[8]. Instead, individual acts participate without exception in 'the Divine Providence that regulates into one vast harmony all the events of time, however calamitous some of them may appear to mortals'[9]: the poem can be felt warily revolving about the puzzle of evil. The theology dissolves the autonomous agency of the individual into a greater whole, and, as though in keeping with that principle, Coleridge contrives to make the Mariner seem somehow non-volitional while killing the albatross, as he is at the second of the poem's two apparent turning-points, the blessing of the snakes.[10] Wordsworth's extraordinary note to the poem in the 1800 *Lyrical Ballads* complained that the Mariner did not act but was 'continually acted upon', which is hardly fair (see Empson, 38); but it does pin-point the strange inactivity marking the cruces of the allegory: the bird is shot before we know it, with any description of intent or motive or decision quite elided; and the snakes are blessed 'unaware', the action recognised for what it was only in retrospect (81–2, 285). (You wonder if the note isn't drawn from Coleridge's own self-deploring talk.)

Even if the possibility of personal guilt were somehow granted, as some sort of poetic fiction, other problems remain: pre-eminently, the wrong people are punished. Stephen's dry summary remains unanswerable: 'the moral, which would apparently be that people who sympathise with a man who shoots an albatross will die in prolonged torture of thirst, is open to obvious objections'.[11] In several other crucial regards, the attempt to find in the poem a redemptive allegory finds itself oddly frustrated. After the 'crime', for instance, the weather sends very conflicting signals about God's feelings; it soon improves, leading the crew (who are evidently disposed to scrutinise nature for such signs) to congratulate the Mariner on killing 'the bird / That brought the fog and mist' (99–100), and hardly unreasonably. Then again, after the obscurely redemptive moment with the snakes, when his 'kind saint took pity' (286), the Mariner is still forced to endure the horror of the 'ghastly crew' (340), which doesn't seem a massive improvement. Indeed, the whole notion of the water-snakes episode as the pivotal event in the Mariner's spiritual journey, which seems so certain when you think about the idea of the poem, feels much less self-evident when you return to the real thing: it happens far too early in the work for it to be the expected climax. A student of mine remarked that the poem consistently surprises on rereading by being, throughout, fuller of horrors than you remembered; and while the summarising moral (610–17) expresses a sentiment evidently close to the optimistic emotions of Coleridge's religion, most readers must feel its inadequacy, and even its bathos. Burney's remark that the poem is a cock-and-bull story, like *Shandy*, makes a good point in an unkind way[12] – as perhaps does Coleridge's famous (alleged) remark to Barbauld about it having 'too much moral',[13] if the sense is of a moral unearned. It is as though the poem is made to contain the sort of event that puts an optimistic religious philosophy under the most severe strain: after such traumatic terror, it seems somewhat lacking to end with advice not to 'pull poor pussy's tail' (Empson, 78). Anyway, it is a very moot point how much atonement the Mariner actually receives: the note in the margin soothingly announces that the curse is finally expiated, but it doesn't feel that way, least of all to the Mariner himself, who experiences periodic torture ever after; and his redemption is evidently incomplete enough for the pilot's boy to think he's the devil (568–9) and for the Wedding Guest seriously to entertain the idea that he's walking-dead (224–31). The misfitting nature of this supposedly One Life cosmos is most emphatically implied by the dice-throwing episode, a decisive moment of apparently sheer randomness: God doesn't play dice, as Einstein is supposed to have said.

Given such intractables, a rival reading has arisen, stressing not the deep, benevolent unity proposed by the poem, but, on the contrary, its stark, inconsolable chaos. Unity and diversity would then feature in the poem not in the form of a unifying vision that redeems an experience of disorder, but as a futile, superstitious dream of salvation perpetually thwarted by an unyielding meaninglessness. The Mariner is awakened into a consciousness of his isolated condition, his shooting of the bird an act of tragic individuation: 'With my cross-bow / I shot the ALBATROSS' (81–2). Not an exemplification of Unitarian theology, but its absurdist counter-vision, the poem in this reading is a ghastly parody of the sunlit world of 'This Lime-Tree Bower': more like a modernist text; indeed the expression of those fears that the unifying theology came to salve.[14] But this engaging account has its complications too. For a start, the Mariner himself doesn't subscribe to such a view; nor is such a reading supported by the running gloss in the margin (added in the 1817 edition). The notes seem secure in describing a meaningful and unified spiritual narrative, from shooting the pious bird of good omen, to the albatross's vengeance, to the spell beginning to break, to the curse finally expiated; and this might reasonably seem the spelling-out of a moral always intended, 'added to assist the bewildered readers of the first published version'.[15] For example, the Mariner tells us that the ship hails the bird 'As if it had been a Christian soul', and the marginal note takes over the suggestion eagerly, soon referring confidently to 'the pious bird of good omen' (65; note to 79); and when the Mariner attributes the blessing of sleep to the intervention of the Virgin, the editorial commentary obediently confirms that his relief is thanks to 'the grace of the holy Mother' (294; note to 297).

But then how much authority are we to give the editorial commentary? The style is self-consciously literary and antiquated: not Coleridge's usual prose, anyway; and McGann usefully suggests that the marginal notes are the words not of *Coleridge* exactly, but of an imaginary antiquarian of the seventeenth or eighteenth century, editor of the medieval ballad.[16] And how shrewd an editor is he? He looks wildly off the mark at points, in his desire to be upbeat about the end of the terrors he's annotating ('The curse is finally expiated'); he is frequently gratuitously expansive, spilling out of the margins and across the page between the stanzas, sometimes beautifully (note to 263), but sometimes comically (the note to 422 is winningly bluff): all of which might seem designed to insinuate his possible unreliability. The editorial voice, that is to say, is 'placed', to use a Leavisite expression.

Once the ideas of interpretation and fallibility are abroad, the poem changes its colours dramatically, because we realise that our only source of evidence for any conclusion about the nature of the poem's universe is the Mariner himself. The predominant world of the poem is that uncertain *intermundium* between objective and subjective which Coleridge found so compellingly occupied by ghosts and spectres; and if a dramatised fallibility characterises the editorial commentary, then might it not be an attribute of the Mariner too, who also speaks in a way obviously distant from the poet's own voice. What I am worrying at here is the odd fact that the Mariner's language is the language of a firm (if bewildered) medieval Catholic: he believes in spirits and angels, offers thanks to Mary Queen and his kind saint, and takes for granted 'the ordinary Catholic practices of confession, absolution and church-going'[17]. One of the few theological positions that we can confidently declare Coleridge to have consistently shunned was Catholicism: his anti-Catholicism is often vehement[18]; and that makes it very remarkable that both his great narrative poems should have been written in a deliberately crafted Catholic voice. ('Jesu, Maria, shield her well!', the almost parodically fallible narrator of 'Christabel' exclaims.) The Catholic Mariner, perhaps, has had the experience but missed the meaning, trapped within his education's spiritual paradigms of sin, guilt, repentance, and atonement ('"O shrieve me, shrieve me, holy man!"'), and sure of the purgatorial virtues of suffering – none of which can be made properly to fit the unforgiving details of what happened. His narrative strays abundantly around the inclusive interpretation that he attempts to impose on it, too full of inexplicable, continuing sufferings.

That persistent attempt to make sense of his story reintroduces an idea of unity to the poem, but in a tragically subjective way: pathologically, as an aspect of the needy spirit, badgering the disparities of experience for the consolation of a coherent, resolving meaning. Wordsworth's note complained that the poem was insufficiently dramatised, the Mariner never saying very much about being a mariner; but it is hard to see how passing remarks about knots or trade winds would have improved the poem, and anyway the point is precisely that the Mariner is regarding his experiences not as an episode in his nautical career but as the turning point of his spiritual life. In this light, the poem looks very thoroughly dramatised indeed, in an almost Jamesian way, something like *Turn of the Screw*. Or, you might say, in a Wordsworthian way: it begins to look much more of a dramatic monologue or monodrama, like Wordsworth's contemporaneous 'The Thorn', which was narrated by a superstitious seafarer with a disturbingly over-creative brain (as Wordsworth's note helpfully explained). Coleridge is rather less convinced in his seafarer's poem than Wordsworth is in *his* that there is a psychological explanation to account for things adequately; but both poems could still be engaged in the same sort of work – not expressing a theological vision, but fulfilling the task prominently announced in the 'Preface' to *Lyrical Ballads*, exploring 'the manner in which we associate ideas in a state of excitement'[19]. Excitement in this case is less the heat of the moment, than a protracted obsession, for he has told the story ten thousand times already, Coleridge said:[20] if the plan of the poem was indeed as much Wordsworth's contribution as he told Isabella Fenwick, then Coleridge's greatest move was to put the whole story back a step from the reader. For, like *Heart of Darkness*, the poem is not about a disastrous voyage, but about an old tar, years later, *retelling the story* of a disastrous voyage; the background presence throughout of voices coming from a world elsewhere is an understated but important part of the total effect (the Wedding Guest interrupts at 79–80, 224–9, 345). And like Marlow's, the Mariner's working-up of his story proves more than polishing an anecdote: it is an attempt repeatedly to make sense, to convince himself of his shaky grasp of the telling events. That sounds impossibly pat for so tormented a poem (although a kind of habitual mundanity is not wrong: as Empson says, 'telling the whole story has become his routine': Empson, 36); but the genius of the piece lies precisely in its showing how passionate and driven may be the desire to gather one's experience into an intelligible thesis. The Mariner demonstrates that 'the meanest of men has his Theory: and to think at all is to theorize'[21]; but the instinct in his case takes a monomaniacal form, unifying as a form of dementia – 'that state of madness which is not frenzy or delirium, but which models all things to the one reigning idea'[22], like mad Lear. This is one important way in which we 'associate ideas in a state of excitement': it is the sort of ruinous psychological phenomenon about which a Wedding Guest might well become wiser and sadder.

We are returned, then, to the Coleridgean ground which I first scouted in Chapter I: 'Facts – stubborn facts! – none of your Theory'[23]. It is a widely known 'fact' that the poem is about what happens to the Mariner *because* he shot the albatross: certainly, that is the Mariner's theory. But the crucial role of the bird, which is so obvious, seems, on a second look, to have only the most precarious claim to metaphysical significance: strong evidence turns out, on closer viewing, to be less strong. Disembodied voices firmly identify the Mariner as a man who must serve penance for having 'laid full low / The harmless Albatross'; but the Mariner himself allows that these voices come to him 'ere my living life returned' and are 'in my soul discerned' (400–1, 395–6), which allows very pointedly for their purely subjective existence, as in a guilt-stricken hallucination. It is the superstitious and erratic crew who initially decide that killing the bird caused all the trouble, an attribution which understandably lodges deep in the Mariner's fevered mind, as a Cain-like crime would ('wash away / The Albatross's blood': 512–13) – and lodges deeply too in the editor (much more so than, say, the sacrifice of the biscuit worms, 67). The centrality of the albatross has consolidated itself into certain truth with every attempt the Mariner makes to locate the singular catastrophe of his story, some crucial event which will unify the whole bewildering sequence of events into a meaningful narrative. The Mariner returns to it compulsively, at the end of most of the sections, as to an *idée fixe*, his narrative 'expressive of that deranged state, in which . . . the sufferer's attention is abruptly drawn off by every trifle, and in the same instant plucked back again by the one despotic thought'[24]. (Reaching for a simile to describe the souls flying to heaven and hell, for example, one suggests itself irresistibly – 'every soul, it passed me by, / Like the whizz of my cross-bow!': 222–3.) Analogously, when he dwells wonderingly upon the supposedly restoring moment with the water-snakes, it is as though seeking to convince himself that it *must* be there that significance lies (because that is what the interpretation requires), although the evidence can't really be said to look very promising:

> A spring of love gushed from my heart,
> And I blessed them unaware:
> Sure my kind saint took pity on me,
> And I blessed them unaware.
>
> (284–7)

'Sure' is needy enough to imply anything but sureness; and what does it mean to bless something *unaware*: the feeling is of a kind of enduring desperation, as though of someone forced to burden the moment with a necessary significance (for this is when the bird fell off) which was quite hidden at the time, and hardly confirmed in the aftermath.

But if it is too simple to see the poem as a parable, green or otherwise, a work cogently exemplifying a thesis, then it is quite as wrong to think of it as an absurdist masterpiece, which treats only with dismissive irony the attempts of the Mariner to bring things to a kind of order, the desperate workings of a false consciousness deforming the world in its neurotic 'Co-caption, or *Together-taking*'.[25] The poem is altogether a fuller embodiment of Coleridgean division; and while challenging the coherence of the Mariner's emotive and obsessional thesis with counter-evidence of the most disturbing kind, yet Coleridge still evidently regards with the keenest sympathy his character's repeated attempts to intuit within his experience a 'unity (Beginning, Middle, and End)'.[26] In its exhibition of the powerful need for unified significance, and yet the exhibition too of that need's frustration, we meet our old Coleridgean impasse, raised to Gothic heights. Coleridge himself described the poem as 'incomprehensible',[27] which is not just customary self-deprecation. Comprehension is more than getting the right end of the stick: it is a seizing or catching together (as in *comprehendo*), and is charged in its Coleridgean life with the unitary passion lying behind the Reason's impulse for 'the comprehension of all as one'.[28] If the poem's incomprehensibility is so especially striking, it is because it includes within itself so remarkably powerful a sense of the '*at-one-ment*'[29] that comprehension might bring – but also so strong a warning of how imprisoning the wrong kind of unifying would be. The Mariner's continuing, futile attempts to rationalise his experience into meaning might indeed be a type of parable, then, not of theological order, but of the human need to discern order at all, and of the pathos of that need. The Mariner's ostentatious religious difference from his author might imply less his intrinsic wrongness, and more that such an impulse is a deep human instinct, independent of its theological environment, at work even in minds (as Coleridge would see it) dominated by the grossest superstition. The Mariner's totalising interpretation, eagerly expanded upon by the well-meant obtuseness of the fictive editor, repeatedly discovers itself to be inadequate as it re-encounters again and again in memory the events it is meant to comprehend: the Mariner is, you might say, a reluctant diversitarian. He seeks desperately to gather all under 'the one despotic thought'; but his story exceeds his narration: his 'illustrations swallow up [his] thesis'.[30] And it is not only the Mariner and his obedient editor who cling so tenaciously to their comprehensive master-narrative in the teeth of the ill-fitting particulars: so do many of the critics. This means that criticism of the poem often rehearses its own version of the predicament which the poem describes, a wavering confrontation between visions of completed unity ('a circular journey':[31] and uncontrollable diversity ('the unwelcome recognition of our interpretive helplessness').[32] When, in an exemplary encounter, House reproves Warren for 'forcing' elements of the poem into congruence with his theory, and 'minimising differences',[33] he replays a Coleridgean discrimination ('the arbitrary bringing together of things that lie remote & forming them into a Unity'[34]).

Meanwhile, the poem abides the muddle of its critics by encompassing it, in its fully Coleridgean, divisive life: even in this poem full of the fear of incoherence, diversity also makes its positive claim heard. Most of the thesis-defying details in 'The Ancient Mariner' are scarily at odds, which implies the darkening horror that accompanies the obstruction of oneness; but we know from the logic of Coleridgean division that the absence of encompassing unity is only inconsistently deplored, and that sometimes diversity is the occasional source of realist delight; and here too, though I agree in a muted way, the poem anticipates the great career, instinctively exploring the disputed claims of realist diversitarianism and egocentric unity that are articulated (as we know) throughout Coleridge's life. Southey's insult, that the poem makes 'a Dutch attempt at German sublimity',[35] may be taken as a mean-spirited expression of the tension at stake, one between diversitarian attention to minute particulars and the unifying ambitions of the gathering consciousness. (Again, I wonder if he didn't gather the idea from Coleridge's conversation, so ringing an example of opposites meeting does it seem.) Southey means to be unkind, but his crack anticipates the division between realism and idealism that Coleridge's philosophy of mind would worry over so intently and that his literary mythology would later apotheosise into Shakespeare and Milton: a universe of little things, such as 'Dutch' realism describes, is not always contemptible; and even in the darkness of 'The Ancient Mariner' some of the incomprehensible details are not fearsomely bewildering so much as happily free. They are loose ends – in the sense that they are ends in themselves; odd particulars, they resist the duty of expressing the Mariner's 'interior meaning',[36] residing instead in the uncompromised, digressive plenitude of themselves, 'some thing *out of* him'.[37] Momentarily released from the Mariner's monomania, the poem is refreshed by a world elsewhere, living 'by feeding abroad'[38] a world that sometimes sidles into the poetry, as we have seen happen elsewhere in Coleridge, through the passing opportunity of a simile:

> . . . yet still the sails made on
> A pleasant noise till noon,
> A noise like of a hidden brook
> In the leafy month of June,
> That to the sleeping woods all night
> Singeth a quiet tune.
>
> (367–72)

Or, in its sudden brilliant mundanity, the prosaic surprise of 'The silly buckets on the deck' (297), a phrase conjuring up, in John Beer's astute phrase, 'a whole world of relief.'[39] That world, plain and simple ('silly'), innocent of any especially symbolical duties, is at once a world which brings relief, and one which places in relief the persecutory claustrophobia of the poem's mental space. It is the common plural world where we and the Wedding Guest live, an ordinary world of other things, which offers its own tentative kinds of consolation, and for which Coleridge's resilient sensibility retained an instinctive and complicating diversitarian love.

Notes

1   William Empson, *Essays on Renaissance Literature, Volume One: Donne and the New Philosophy* (Cambridge: Cambridge University Press, 1993; repr. 1995), 127.

2   Richard Haven, *Patterns of Consciousness: An Essay on Coleridge* (Amherst: University of Massachusetts, 1967), 18.

3   Leslie Stephen, *Hours in a Library*, rev. edn., 3 vols. (London: Smith Elder, 1909), 335.

4   Beer, *Coleridge the Visionary*, 209.

5   Abrams, *Natural Supernaturalism*, 274.

6   Peter Kitson, 'Coleridge, the French Revolution, and the Ancient Mariner: A Reassessment', *Coleridge Bulletin*, ns 7 (Spring 1997), 30–48, at 46.

7   Jared Curtis (ed.), *The Fenwick Notes of William Wordsworth* (London: Bristol Classical Press, 1933), 2.

8   Coleridge, *Letters* I. 213.

9   'Argument' to 'Ode to the Departing Year', Coleridge, *Poetical Works*, ed. E. H. Coleridge, I. 160.

10   'Why the Mariner blesses the snakes is of course as much a mystery as why he shot the Albatross': Empson, 43.

11   Stephen, *Hours in a Library*, 335.

12   J. R. ed J. Jackson (ed.), *Coleridge: The Critical Heritage*, 56.

13   Coleridge, *Table Talk*, I. 272–3.

14   Most influentially argued by Edward E. Bostetter, 'The Nightmare World of *The Ancient Mariner*'; in Kathleen Coburn (ed.), *Coleridge: A Collection of Critical Essays* (Englewood Cliffs, NJ; Prentice-Hall, 1967), 65–77.

15   Abrams, *Natural Supernaturalism*, 272.

16   McGann, *The Beauty of Inflections*, 141–2. McGann refers to Huntington Brown, 'The Gloss of the Ancient Mariner', *Modern Language Quarterly*, 6 (1945), 319–24.

17   House, *Coleridge*, 89

18   Coleridge, *Notebooks* II, n. 2324.

19   Wordsworth, *The Prose Works of William Wordsworth*, ed. W. J. B. Owen and J. W. Smyser, 3 vols. (Oxford: Clarendon Press, 1974), I. 123–5.

20   Coleridge, *Table Talk* I. 274.

21   Samuel Taylor Coleridge, *The Friend* (Vol. 4 of the *Collected Works of Samuel Taylor Coleridge*, Bollingen series no. 75), ed. B. E. Rooke, 2 vols. (Princeton: Princeton University Press, 1969), I. 189.

22   Samuel Taylor Coleridge, *Lecture 1808–1819 On Literature* (Vol. 5 of the *Collected Works of Samuel Taylor Coleridge*, Bollingen series no. 75), ed. R. A. Foakes, 2 vols. (Princeton: Princeton University Press, 1987), I. 380.

23   Coleridge, *Notebooks* III, n. 3737.

24   Coleridge, *Biographia Literaria* II. 150.

25   Coleridge, *Notebooks* II, n. 4268.

26   Coleridge, *Letters* IV. 574.

27   Coleridge, *Biographia Literaria* I. 28.

28   Coleridge, *Lay Sermons*, 60.

29   Ibid., 55.

30   *Notebooks* II, n. 2372.

31   Abrams, *Natural Supernaturalism*, 272

32   Susan Eilenberg, *Strange Power of Speech: Wordsworth, Coleridge, and Literary Possession* (New York: Oxford Univ. Press 1992), 32.

33   House, *Coleridge*, 110.

34   Crabb Robinson, *Blake, Coleridge*, 31–2.

35   *Coleridge: The Critical Heritage*, 53.

36   Coleridge, *Letters* II. 866.

37   Coleridge, *Notebooks* II, n. 2672. An instinctive sense that the poem's elements have a kind of barely restrained life within the would-be inclusive authority of the allegory animates the ingenious cartoon version of the poem by Hunt Emerson: Hunt Emerson and Samuel Taylor Coleridge, *The Rime of the Ancient Mariner* (London: Knockabout Comics, 1989).

38   Coleridge, *Notebooks* III, n. 3420.

39   Beer, *Coleridge the Visionary*, 212.

Further reading

The following is a sample of some of the more eclectic developments in Coleridge criticism from the 1980s to the present. Once again, the prioritizing of the poetry criticism has entailed the omission of important recent discussions of the prose.

Jean-Pierre Mileur, *Vision and Revision: Coleridge's Art of Immanence* (Berkeley: University of California Press, 1982). Deconstructionist approach: tracing the 'immanent Coleridge who comes into being in the dialogue of text with text', shows, in the canonical poems, the contradiction between that immanence and Coleridge's identity or creative will, and, in *Biographia*, the working out, to which the Bible is instrumental, of the contradiction.

Richard Gravil, Lucy Newlyn and Nicholas Roe (eds.), *Coleridge's Imagination: Essays in Memory of Pete Laver* (Cambridge: Cambridge University Press, 1985). Range of approaches and contexts, both historical and theoretical, in diverse essays by established scholars revisiting individual poems and key topics, including nature and pastoral, primary and secondary imagination, and the Coleridge–Wordsworth relation.

Paul Magnuson, *Coleridge and Wordsworth: A Lyrical Dialogue* (Princeton: Princeton University Press, 1988). Argues for a 'dialogic reading' of the 'Coleridge–Wordsworth canon as a single work', each poem in which is a fragment that takes its significance from the context of the whole.

Richard Holmes, *Coleridge: Early Visions* (London: Hodder & Stoughton, 1989). Coleridge's life to the age of 31. Reasserts and reinstates a canonical, visionary Coleridge; emphases include the importance of the conversation poems to *The Prelude* and to our notion of 'Romanticism'.

Tim Fulford and Morton D. Paley (eds.), *Coleridge's Visionary Languages: Essays in Honour of J. B. Beer* (Cambridge: D. S. Brewer, 1993). Valuable new readings of the writings and their contexts, taking 'visionary' (from Beer) as 'transformative process', and treating Coleridge's transformation, in his discourses, of the variety of materials available to him in his time and place.

Lucy Newlyn, Paradise Lost *and the Romantic Reader* (Oxford: Clarendon Press, 1993). Includes, in an examination of the interconnectedness of textual allusions and the cultural reception of Milton in the Romantic period, the politics of Coleridge's allusions to Milton and his rewriting of the Fall in 'The Ancient Mariner'.

Jack Stillinger, *Coleridge and Textual Instability: The Multiple Versions of the Major Poems* (New York and Oxford: Oxford University Press, 1994). Argues against the concept of a single authoritative text for each of Coleridge's major poems, instead making the case for recognizing multiple authoritative versions.

Anthony Harding, *The Reception of Myth in English Romanticism* (Columbia and London: University of Missouri Press, 1995). Reads, in 'The Ancient Mariner', Coleridge's response to and rejection of mythography, and in 'Christabel', his reinterpretation of the temptation myth in Genesis.

Rosemary Ashton, *The Life of Samuel Taylor Coleridge: A Critical Biography* (Oxford: Blackwell, 1996). Scrupulous and academically most valuable current biography.

Zachary Leader, *Revision and Romantic Authorship* (Oxford: Clarendon Press, 1996). Coleridge is an 'apostle of unity' but also 'radically divided'; his revisions, preparing his poems for publication, reveal the importance of publication to him in creating a coherent self.

Morton D. Paley, *Coleridge's Later Poetry* (Oxford: Clarendon Press, 1996). Examines the concerns and modes of the poetry written after Coleridge's 'golden' period in the context of the *oeuvre* as a whole.

Richard Holmes, *Coleridge: Darker Reflections* (London: HarperCollins, 1998). Second and final part (1804–34) of the biography whose first part was published in 1989 (see above).

Nicholas Roe (ed.), *Samuel Taylor Coleridge and the Sciences of Life* (Oxford: Oxford University Press, 2001). Diverse essays, treating Coleridge's engagement with the scientific topics and debates of his day and so countering (cf. Wylie), the traditional emphasis on Romantic transcendence.

Anya Taylor, 'Coleridge and the Pleasures of Verse', *Studies in Romanticism* 40.4 (Winter 2001), 547–69. Argues for a new attention to Coleridge's metrics: Coleridge's focus on metrics and its purpose, pleasure, puts him 'among the most purposeful practitioners of verse as verse in his era.'

*Lucy Newlyn (ed.), *The Cambridge Companion to Coleridge* (Cambridge: Cambridge University Press, 2002). Indispensable up-to-date introduction to key areas of Coleridge scholarship; 'the collective aim of contributors has been to place Coleridge's works in their original contexts, paying special attention to the readership they addressed and the reception they received.'

J. Robert Barth, *Romanticism and Transcendence: Wordsworth, Coleridge, and the Religious Imagination* (Columbia and London: University of Missouri Press, 2003). In the context of its over-all contention, that Wordsworth's and Coleridge's emphasis on individual imagination implies Christian belief, especially attends to the topic of prayer in Coleridge's poetry.

John Beer, *Romantic Consciousness: Blake to Mary Shelley* (Basingstoke: Palgrave Macmillan, 2003). Coleridge is central to this study of the Romantics' articulations of ultimate Being, challenging the sufficiency of rational consciousness, and anticipating twentieth-century discussions of Being. Especially insightful on the importance of Coleridge for Keats' intellectual development.

Eric G. Wilson, *Coleridge's Melancholia: An Anatomy of Limbo* (Gainsville: University Press of Florida, 2004). Celebrates, in Coleridge, the melancholy or 'excessive sensitivity' that precludes a singleness of vision, leading to confusion and fragmentation, but also, finally, to 'limbo' as an enabling condition, making failure itself the inspiration of the mature (post-1802) verse.

Useful editions

The best student edition is the Everyman *Poems: Samuel Taylor Coleridge*, ed. John Beer (1963; new edn., London: Dent, 1993). J. C. C. Mays' new scholarly edition, *Poetical Works*, 3 vols. in 6 parts (Princeton: Princeton University Press, 2001) is volume 16 of the Bollingen series.

Reference material

E. L. Griggs (ed.), *The Collected Letters of Samuel Taylor Coleridge*, 6 vols. (Oxford: Clarendon Press, 1956–71). Standard edition of the letters.

Kathleen Coburn (ed.), *The Notebooks of Samuel Taylor Coleridge*, 5 vols. (London: Routledge, 2002). Indispensable scholarly resource.

Samuel Taylor Coleridge: An Annotated Bibliography of Criticism and Scholarship, 3 vols. (Boston: G. K. Hall, 1976–96): I. *1793–1899*, ed. R and J. Haven and M. Adams (1976); II. *1900–1939*, ed. W. Crawford and E. Lauterbach (1983); III. *1940–1992*, ed. W. Crawford, with the assistance of A. Crawford (1996). Comprehensive annotated bibliography.

Valerie Purton, *A Coleridge Chronology* (Basingstoke and London: Macmillan, 1993). Useful factual compilation, covering the life-span in varying detail.

Chapter notes

1   Robert Southey, review of *Lyrical Ballads*, *Critical Review*, 2nd series, xxiv (Oct. 1798), 201 (*Romantics Reviewed, Part A*, I. 309).

2   For the range of reviews 1794–1834, see both *Romantics Reviewed, Part A* and J. R. de J. Jackson (ed.), *Coleridge: The Critical Heritage* (London: Routledge and Kegan Paul, 1970), each of which contains a number of notices absent in the other. A representative selection is given in John O. Hayden, *Romantic Bards and British Reviewers* (Lincoln and London: University of Nebraska Press, 1971).

3   Josiah Conder, review of *Christabel* [etc.] (1816), *Eclectic Review*, 2nd series, v (June 1816), 566 (*Romantics Reviewed, Part A*, I. 373).

4   William Hazlitt, review of *The Statesman's Manual* (1816), *Edinburgh Review* xxvii (Dec. 1816), 446. Hazlitt's disillusionment with his erstwhile idol is manifest in his numerous notices of Coleridge. In 1816, he savages *The Statesman's Manual* three times, twice in the *Examiner* (8 Sept. 1816, 571–3; 29 Dec. 1816, 824–7), and the third time in the *Edinburgh Review* xxvii (Dec. 1816), 444–59 (*Romantics Reviewed, Part A*, II. 532–4, 534–7, 474–82).

5   John Gibson Lockhart, 'Essays on the Lake School of Poetry. No III.-Coleridge', *Blackwood's Edinburgh Magazine* vi (Oct. 1819), 4. See *Coleridge: The Critical Heritage* (1970), 438.

6   Charles Lamb, 'The Two Races of Men' (1820), repr. in *The Essays of Elia* (1823), *Works*, ii. 25.

7   Keats, to George and Tom Keats, 21, 27(?) Dec. 1817, *Letters* I. 193–4.

8   Keats, to George and Georgiana Keats, 19 Feb.–3 May 1819, *Letters* II. 88–9; Hazlitt, *Works* XI. 32–4.

9   John Stuart Mill, *Mill on Bentham and Coleridge*, ed. F. R. Leavis (Cambridge: Cambridge University Press, 1980), 40.

10   See Maurice's dedication, in the second edition of *The Kingdom of Christ* (1842) to Derwent Coleridge, where he writes of 'a thousand indications of the influence which your father's writings are exercising over the mind of this generation.' –

Frederick Denison Maurice, 'Dedication' to *The Kingdom of Christ* (1842), repr. in J. R. de J. Jackson, *Coleridge: The Critical Heritage. Vol. 2: 1834–1900* (London and New York: Routledge, 1991), 119. Newman quotes himself on Coleridge in *Apologia Pro Vita Sua* (1864): 'a very original thinker, who, while he indulged a liberty of speculation, which no Christian can tolerate, . . . yet after all installed a higher philosophy into inquiring minds, than they had hitherto been accustomed to accept.' – John Henry Newman, *Apologia Pro Vita Sua*, ed. Ian Ker (London: Penguin Classics, 1994), 100.

11   Thomas Carlyle, *The Life of John Sterling*, Vol. XI of the centenary edition of *The Works of Thomas Carlyle*, 30 vols. (London: Chapman and Hall, 1896–9), 60–1.

12   Walter Pater, 'Coleridge', in *Appreciations, with an Essay on Style* (London and New York: Macmillan, 1889), 71, 67–8. Pater's essay synthesizes two earlier articles, of 1866 and 1880.

13   See T. S. Eliot, *The Use of Poetry and the Use of Criticism: Studies in the Relation of Criticism to Poetry in England* (London: Faber, 1933), 67.

14   E. K. Chambers, *Samuel Taylor Coleridge: A Biographical Study* (Oxford: Clarendon Press, 1938), 139.

15   John Livington Lowes, *The Road to Xanadu: A Study in the Ways of Imagination* (1927; 2nd rev. edn., Boston: Houghton Mifflin, 1930), x, xi.

16   Robert Penn Warren, 'A Poem of Pure Imagination: an Experiment in Reading' (1946), repr., with additional notes, in *Selected Essays* (New York: Random House, 1958), 198–305.

17   John Beer, *Coleridge the Visionary* (London: Chatto & Windus), 34.

18   Norman Fruman, *Coleridge: The Damaged Archangel* (1971; London: Allen & Unwin, 1972), 420.

19   Paul de Man, 'The Rhetoric of Temporality' (1969), repr. in *Blindness and Insight: Essays in the Rhetoric of Contemporary Criticism* (1971; 2nd rev. edn. London: Methuen, 1983), 187–228.

20   Anne K. Mellor, *English Romantic Irony* (Cambridge, Mass. and London: Harvard University Press, 1980), 5, 150.

21   Hazlitt, *Works* XI. 38.

22   Jerome J. McGann, 'The Ancient Mariner: The Meaning of Meanings' in *The Beauty of Inflections: Literary Investigations in Historical Method and Theory* (Oxford: Clarendon Press, 1985), 170.

23   E. S. Shaffer, *'Kubla Khan' and the Fall of Jerusalem: The Mythological School in Biblical Criticism and Secular Literature, 1770–1880* (Cambridge: Cambridge University Press, 1975). Reads, in the form and content of 'Kubla Khan', Coleridge's response to the premises and practice of German Higher Criticism, finding, in the poem's Orientalism, not ignorance or denigration, but the absorption of a vast new scholarship in Oriental myth, informed by the new confrontation of the mythological character of Christianity itself.

24   Seamus Perry, *Coleridge and the Uses of Division* (Oxford: Clarendon Press, 1999), 7, 3.

4

George Gordon, Lord Byron (1788–1824)

'To be at once young, and noble, and a poet, is to insure a large measure either of applause or of censure.'[1] The opening observation of the *Eclectic*'s review of cantos I and II of *Childe Harold's Pilgrimage* is borne out by the sheer volume of space devoted to Byron in the contemporary reviews.[2] His very first publication, *Hours in Idleness* (1807), announcing both his youth and his nobility, attracted considerable comment. Though much of this comment was complimentary, a scathing review – mistakenly attributed by Byron to Francis Jeffrey, but in fact, by Henry Brougham[3] – brought the *Edinburgh* under fire in *English Bards and Scotch Reviewers* (1809), to more widespread notice still. With the publication of the first two cantos of *Childe Harold's Pilgrimage* (1812) Byron thoroughly captured the reading public's attention. Here began the reviewers' stormy relationship, intense both in adulation and condemnation, with the persona that began to be recognized in all of Byron's subsequent *oeuvre*, an iteration to some sublime, to others tedious. Reviewing canto III of *Childe Harold's Pilgrimage* (1816), the *British Critic* complains:

> We really wish that the noble Lord would suppose that there was some other being in the world besides himself, and employ his imagination in tracing the lineaments of some other character than his own. . . . What is Lord Byron to us, and what have we to do either with his sublimity or his sulks?[4]

But John Wilson's tone in *Blackwood's* is awed, almost deifying his subject:

> One Figure alone is seen stalking through the city and through the solitude – over the earth and over the sea: and that Figure, stern, melancholy, and majestic, is still no other than Himself.[5]

Yet although there was a general perception of a single iterated self in Byron's poetry, and despite the intrusion of his personal life, especially his failed marriage, into his work, the awareness of that self as a construct, or the distinction between the author and his fictions, was not altogether obliterated. Walter Scott puts it neatly: 'Childe Harold . . . is Lord Byron's picture, sketched by Lord Byron himself, arrayed in a fancy dress.'[6] Scott's notices in the *Quarterly*, of the third and fourth cantos of *Childe Harold's Pilgrimage*, are among the best of the contemporary analyses, containing a comprehensive survey of the critical reception to date, and, although dissenting from Byron's politics, a considered appreciation of his poetry; engaging, too, with the relations between the poet, his characters, and his public: the Byron phenomenon and its paradoxes.[7] More than one reviewer, less sympathetic than Scott, mocked the discrepancy between the poet's professed indifference to popular applause and his rapid production of a lucrative poetry,[8] especially the phenomenally popular Turkish tales of 1813–16.

The denunciation, even in some of the most laudatory notices, of Byron's lack of morality, and particularly of religious principle, rose to a crescendo with the publication of *Don Juan*. *Blackwood's*, whose reviews by John Wilson in 1817–19 had till then extolled the poet, turned upon *Don Juan* I–II (1819) as 'a perpetual monument of the exalted intellect, and the depraved heart, of one of the most remarkable men to whom that country [England] has had the honour and the disgrace of giving birth.'[9] The *British Critic*, consistently a vehement detractor, pronounced the first two cantos 'a manual of profligacy', then went on to declare, in reviewing III–V (1821), that 'The Poem before us is . . . not only begotten but spawned in filth and darkness.'[10]

But the public's interest did not fade. In John Gibson Lockhart's entertaining and shrewd assessment, *Letter to the Right Hon. Lord Byron. By John Bull*, published anonymously in 1821, *Don Juan* is 'out of all sight the best of your works; it is by far the most spirited, the most straightforward, the most interesting, and the most poetical; and everybody thinks as I do of it, although they have not the heart to say so.'[11] In 1822, Francis Jeffrey, a regular and discerning reviewer, observes that despite the 'stain' on the 'lustre' of Byron's popularity, 'he is still popular beyond all other example'.[12] As the *Monthly Magazine* recognizes, 'Revilers and partisans have alike contributed to the popularity of this singular work; and the result is, that scarcely any poem of the present day has been more generally read, or its continuation more eagerly and impatiently awaited.'[13]

Byron's versatility – his ability to combine satire, 'the scoffing spirit', with 'touches of deep pathos' – was acknowledged or bemoaned by his contemporaries, who thus initiated what became the ruling topic of 'paradox' in the twentieth-century criticism of Byron.[14] In the wake of *Don Juan*, the tag 'Satanic school' of poetry, coined by Robert Southey in the Preface to his *Vision of Judgement* (1821), quickly gained a wider currency. To his contemporaries, Byron's 'Satanism' signified primarily the irreligious tendency of his poetry: his apparent disbelief in a future state, his misanthropy and undisguised sensuality.[15] Byron's association with Leigh Hunt, whose politics he shared and with whom he collaborated professionally, linked him too to the 'Cockney School', the pejorative label, denoting both political and stylistic radicalism, coined by Lockhart in 1817, and adopted by the Tory reviewers for Hunt and his circle.[16] A different kind of connection, germane to the twentieth-century formulations of a coherent 'romanticism', is that of influence: Wordsworth's, and less frequently, Coleridge's influence on Byron is noted by some of the earliest critics.[17]

Among the publications in the immediate aftermath of Byron's death, Samuel Egerton Brydges' *Letters on the Character and Poetical Genius of Lord Byron* (1824) is a sound critical appreciation, relating the character of the poet to the qualities of his work. Characteristically brilliant and irate, Hazlitt portrays 'Lord Byron', polarizing him and Scott in *The Spirit of the Age* (1825).[18] Of the spate of memoirs and notices, the most important is Thomas Moore's *Letters and Journals of Lord Byron: with Notices of his Life* (2 vols., 1830), still a valued biography. Goethe celebrates Byron as 'Euphorion' in part II of *Faust* (1832); subsequently, Byron and Goethe are frequently associated in critical discussion. The continental scholarship on Byron long continued to exceed that on any other romantic poet.

With the passing of Byron's contemporaneity, the immediacy of interest he excited also passed, and the attention to his works dropped exponentially in the early decades of the Victorian era. Byron lost ground among the Victorians to other of the great romantics. The poetry's merits became nearly inextricable from the poet's morals, his 'posing' was ridiculed, and the odd contemporary complaint of verbal ineptitude ('it is high time he were back in England *to hear the language spoken*'[19]) now became the norm. Yet although disparagement predominated over praise, the claims on Byron's behalf – made, among others, by Ruskin, Arnold and Swinburne – were also large, and strongly expressed.[20] The coinage 'Byronism', connoting equally the characteristics of Byron and his poetry, passed into familiar usage.

Joseph Mazzini's powerful and passionate representation of Byron, as the poet of liberty and solitary individuality, in an essay 'On Byron and Goethe', published anonymously in the *Morning Chronicle* in 1839 and later included in *The Life and Writings of Joseph Mazzini* (6 vols., 1864–70), was well known to Byron's Victorian audience. An extract follows.

Extract from Joseph Mazzini, 'On Byron and Goethe' (1839)

Byron appears at the close of one epoch, and before the dawn of the other; in the midst of a community based upon an aristocracy which has outlived the vigour of its prime; surrounded by a Europe containing nothing grand, unless it be Napoleon on one side and Pitt on the other, genius degraded to minister to egotism; intellect bound to the service of the past. No seer exists to foretell the future: belief is extinct; there is only its pretence: prayer is no more; there is only a movement of the lips at a fixed day or hour, for the sake of the family, or what is called *the people*: love is no more; desire has taken its place; the holy warfare of ideas is abandoned; the conflict is that of interests. The worship of great thoughts has passed away. That which *is*, raises the tattered banner of some corpse-like traditions; that which *would be*, hoists only the standard of physical wants, of material appetites: around him are ruins, beyond him the desert; the horizon is a blank. A long cry of suffering and indignation bursts from the heart of Byron; he is answered by anathemas. He departs; he hurries through Europe in search of an ideal to adore; he traverses it distracted, palpitating, like Mazeppa on the wild horse; borne onwards by a fierce desire; the wolves of envy and calumny follow in pursuit. He visits Greece; he visits Italy; if anywhere a lingering spark of the sacred fire, a ray of divine poetry, is preserved, it must be *there*. Nothing. A glorious past, a degraded present; none of life's poetry; no movement, save that of the sufferer turning on his couch to relieve his pain. Byron, from the solitude of his exile, turns his eyes again towards England; he sings. What does he sing? What springs from the mysterious and unique conception which rules, one would say in spite of himself, over all that escapes him in his sleepless vigil? The funeral hymn, the death-song, the epitaph of the aristocratic idea; we discovered it, we Continentalists; not his own countrymen. He takes his types from amongst those privileged by strength, beauty, and individual power. They are grand, poetical, heroic, but solitary; they hold no communion with the world around them, unless it be to rule over it; they defy alike the good and evil principle; they 'will bend to neither.' In life and in death 'they stand upon *their* strength;' they resist every power, for their own is all their own; it was purchased by

– Superior science – penance – daring –
And length of watching – strength of mind – and skill
In knowledge of our fathers.

Each of them is the personification, slightly modified, of a single type, a single idea – the *individual*, free, but nothing more than free; such as the epoch now closing has made him; Faust, but without the compact which submits him to the enemy; for the heroes of Byron make no such compact. Cain kneels not to Arimanes; and Manfred, about to die, exclaims –

> The mind, which is immortal, makes itself
> Requital for its good and evil thoughts –
> Is its own origin of ill, and end –
> And its own place and time, its innate sense,
> When stripped of this mortality, derives
> No colour from the fleeting things without,
> But is absorbed in sufferance or in joy;
> Born from the knowledge of its own desert.

They have no kindred: they live from their own life only: they repulse humanity, and regard the crowd with disdain. Each of them says: *I have faith in myself*, never, *I have faith in ourselves*. They all aspire to power or to happiness. The one and the other alike escape them; for they bear within them, untold, unacknowledged even to themselves, the presentiment of a life that mere liberty can never give them. Free they are; iron souls in iron frames, they climb the alps of the physical world as well as the alps of thought; still is their visage stamped with a gloomy and ineffaceable sadness; still is their soul – whether, as in Cain and Manfred it plunge into the abyss of the infinite, 'intoxicated with eternity,' or scour the vast plain and boundless ocean with the Corsair and Giaour – haunted by a secret and sleepless dread. It seems as if they were doomed to drag the broken links of the chain they have burst asunder, rivetted to their feet. Not only in the petty society against which they rebel, does their soul feel fettered and restrained; but even in the world of the spirit. Neither is it to the enmity of society that they succumb; but under the assaults of this nameless anguish; under the corroding action of potent faculties 'inferior still to their desires and their conceptions,' under the deception that comes from within. What can they do with the liberty so painfully won? On whom, on what, expend the exuberant vitality within them? *They are alone*; this is the secret of their wretchedness and impotence. They 'thirst for good' – Cain has said it for them all – but cannot achieve it; for they have no mission, no belief, no comprehension even of the world around them. They have never realized the conception of *Humanity* in the multitudes that have preceded, surround, and will follow after them; never thought on their own place between the past and future; on the continuity of labour that unites all the generations into one Whole; on the common end and aim, only to be realized by the common effort; on the spiritual post-sepulchral life even on earth of the individual, through the thoughts he transmits to his fellows; and, it may be – when he lives devoted and dies in faith – through the guardian agency he is allowed to exercise over the loved ones left on earth.

Gifted with a liberty they know not how to use; with a power and energy they know not how to apply; with a life whose purpose and aim they comprehend not; – they drag through their useless and convulsed existence. Byron destroys them one after the other, as if he were the executioner of a sentence decreed in heaven. They fall unwept, like a withered leaf into the stream of time.

> Nor earth nor sky shall yield a single tear,
> Nor cloud shall gather more, nor leaf shall fall,
> Nor gale breathe forth one sigh for thee, for all.

They die, as they have lived, alone; and a popular malediction hovers round their solitary tombs.

This, for those who can read with the soul's eyes, is what Byron sings; or rather what Humanity sings through him. The emptiness of the life and death of solitary individuality, has never been so powerfully and efficaciously summed up as in the pages of Byron. The crowd do not comprehend him: they listen; fascinated for an instant; then repent, and avenge their momentary transport by calumniating and insulting the poet. His intuition of the death of a form of society, they call wounded self-love; his sorrow for *all*, is misinterpreted as cowardly egotism. They credit not the traces of profound suffering revealed by his lineaments; they credit not the presentiment of a new life which from time to time escapes his trembling lips; they believe not in the despairing embrace in which he grasps the material universe – stars, lakes, alps, and sea – and identifies himself with it, and through it with God, of whom – to him at least – it is a symbol. They do, however, take careful count of some unhappy moments, in which, wearied out by the emptiness of life, he has raised, – with remorse I am sure – the cup of ignoble pleasures to his lips, believing he might find forgetfulness there. How many times have not his accusers drained this cup, without redeeming the sin by a single virtue; without – I will not say bearing – but without having even the capacity of appreciating the burden which weighed on Byron! And did he not himself dash into fragments the ignoble cup, so soon as he beheld something worthy the devotion of his life?

Further reading

John Morley's fine essay 'Byron' (1870), expanded and reprinted in *Critical Miscellanies* (London: Chapman & Hall, 1871), 251–90, is a warm tribute, like Mazzini's, presenting Byron as a revolutionary, and describing him as 'essentially political'. Andrew Rutherford's *Lord Byron: The Critical Heritage* (1970; repr. London: Routledge, 1995) has an excellent selection of the Victorian comment on Byron.

THE EARLY TWENTIETH CENTURY

Byron's standing, and the volume of the critical material, continued at a low ebb till about the mid-twentieth century. The publication at the turn of the century of E. H. Coleridge's authoritative new edition of Byron's poetry (7 vols., 1898–1904) did not immediately produce a substantial response. In 1912, Ethel C. Mayne's two-volume *Byron* was published, a sympathetic as well as careful and scholarly biography; a revised edition was published in one volume in 1924, the year of the centenary of Byron's death. The centenary gave occasion to a minor flurry of commemorative publications.

The celebrated essay of the first half of the twentieth century, repudiating the biographical emphasis in its treatment of the poetry, is T. S. Eliot's 'Byron', first published in 1937, and later reprinted in his *On Poetry and Poets* (1957). Eliot's ambivalence to Byron perpetuates the Victorians', and can be related to the 'paradox' that features so persistently in Byron criticism. He criticizes Byron's 'diabolism' and 'schoolboy command of the language' (consciously or unconsciously echoing Brougham's 'school exercises'), but acclaims his storytelling ability, and lauds *Don Juan* as the great achievement of satire in English, so unique and un-English indeed that it reveals Byron as a 'Scottish poet'. Eliot's celebration of Byron as a satirist and *Don Juan* as the masterwork belongs to a growing twentieth-century consensus by which the romances – the tales, and to some extent, *Childe Harold's Pilgrimage* – having enjoyed an unparalleled contemporary popularity, become the lesser works of the Byron canon. A brief extract is given below.

Extract from T. S. Eliot, 'Byron' (1937)

What puts the last cantos of *Don Juan* at the head of Byron's works is, I think, that the subject matter gave him at last an adequate object for a genuine emotion. The emotion is hatred of hypocrisy; and if it was reinforced by more personal and petty feelings, the feelings of the man who as a boy had known the humiliation of shabby lodgings with an eccentric mother, who at fifteen had been clumsy and unattractive and unable to dance with Mary Chaworth,[1] who remained oddly alien among the society that he knew so well – this mixture of the origin of his attitude towards English society only gives it greater intensity. And the hypocrisy of the world that he satirized was at the opposite extreme from his own. Hypocrite, indeed, except in the original sense of the word, is hardly the term for Byron. He was an actor who devoted immense trouble to *becoming* a role that he adopted; his superficiality was something that he created for himself. It is difficult, in considering Byron's poetry, not to be drawn into an analysis of the man: but much more attention has already been devoted to the man than to the poetry, and I prefer, within the limits of such an essay as this, to keep the latter in the foreground. My point is that Byron's satire upon English society, in the latter part of *Don Juan*, is something for which I can find no parallel in English literature. He was right in making the hero of his house-party a Spaniard, for what Byron understands and dislikes about English society is very much what an intelligent foreigner in the same position would understand and dislike.

One cannot leave *Don Juan* without calling attention to another part of it which emphasizes the difference between this poem and any other satire in English: the Dedicatory Verses. The Dedication to Southey seems to me one of the most exhilarating pieces of abuse in the language:

> *Bob Southey! You're a poet – Poet Laureate,*
> *And representative of all the race;*
> *Although 'tis true that you turn'd out a Tory at*
> *Last, yours has lately been a common case;*
> *And now, my Epic Renegade! what are ye at? . . .*

kept up without remission to the end of seventeen stanzas. This is not the satire of Dryden, still less of Pope; it is perhaps more like Hall or Marston, but they are bunglers in comparison. This is not indeed English satire at all; it is really a *flyting*,[2] and closer in feeling and intention to the satire of Dunbar:

[. . .]

To some this parallel may seem questionable, but to me it has brought a keener enjoyment, and I think a juster appreciation of Byron than I had before. I do not pretend that Byron is Villon (nor, for other reasons, does Dunbar or Burns equal the French poet), but I have come to find in him certain qualities, besides his abundance, that are too uncommon in English poetry, as well as the absence of some vices that are too common. And his own vices seem to have twin virtues that closely resemble them. With his charlatanism, he has also an unusual frankness; with his pose, he is also a *poète contumace*[3] in a solemn country; with his humbug and self-deception he has also a reckless raffish honesty; he is at once a vulgar patrician and a dignified toss-pot; with all his bogus diabolism and his vanity of pretending to disreputability, he is genuinely superstitious and disreputable. I am speaking of the qualities and defects visible in his work, and important in estimating his work: not of the private life, with which I am not concerned.

Notes

[1   A distant cousin of Byron's, in whom he had a romantic interest as a boy.
2   'Poetical invective; originally, a kind of contest practised by the Scottish poets of the 16th c., in which two person assailed each other alternately with tirades of abusive verse' (*OED*).
3   'contumacious poet'.]

Further reading

William J. Calvert, *Byron: Romantic Paradox* (Chapel Hill: University of North Caro-lina Press, 1935). Important early treatment of the key critical topic. Separating the poetry from its historical and biographical context, examines the 'romantic paradox': the allegiance to the Augustan tradition of a great romantic poet.

E. W. Marjarum, *Byron as Skeptic and Believer* (Princeton, N.J.: Princeton University Press, 1938). Concise and useful study of Byron and religion, confirming on that ground the Byronic paradox, and tracing 'four recurrent themes, . . . Calvinism, Skepticism, Naturalism, and Roman Catholicism'.

CANONICAL BYRON: THE 1960S AND ONWARDS

Outstanding among a series of seminal publications in the 1960s is Jerome J. McGann's *Fiery Dust: Byron's Poetic Development* (1968). Studying in Byron's poetry the act of self-creation, McGann places biographical interpretation in a new perspective, by arguing that the poetry demands its audience's interest in the man, and not the artist only. The central section of the book, too long to reproduce and too detailed to extract, is on *Childe Harold's Pilgrimage*, considered as a single poem, and rescued from what McGann describes as a neglect of one of 'the great works of the Romantic age'. His opening chapter, substantially extracted below, is a sufficient introduction to the key characteristics of Byron's poetry and the issues for criticism.

Extract from J. J. McGann, *Fiery Dust: Byron's Poetic Development* (1968)

Feeling as He Writes: The Genesis of the Myth

Hours of Idleness was published in July, 1807. In that same month the *Monthly Literary Recreations* brought out its thirteenth number, which contained – in addition to an anonymous review of *Hours of Idleness* and a previously unpublished Byron poem – Byron's review of Wordsworth's 1807 *Poems*. Byron had many virtues, but an incisiveness in matters of literary criticism was never one of them. His review of Wordsworth is expectedly dull. The essay is notable only because it gives us one famous poet's generally favorable response to the work of another famous poet, and because in it he articulates a criterion for judging the worth of poetry that was to remain for him a lifelong principle (one of the few he had).

> Though the present work may not equal his former efforts, many of the poems possess a native elegance, natural and unaffected, totally devoid of the tinsel embellishments and abstract hyperboles of several contemporary sonneteers. The last sonnet in the first volume . . . is perhaps the best . . .; the force and expression is that of a genuine poet, feeling as he writes . . .[1]

Whenever Byron felt that a living personality was projected by a poem or a book of poems he responded immediately. An author 'feeling as he writes' was a man in person, dramatically present and humanly interesting. The attitude that Byron takes in his Wordsworth review is simply a more conventional rendering of his remark in his *Second Letter* on Bowles' *Invariable Principles of Poetry*: 'poetry is in itself passion, and does not systematize. It assails, but does not argue; it may be wrong, but it does not assume pretensions to Optimism.'[2] Byron hated systematizing, metaphysical speculation, rational optimism, especially in poetry, so that it was not long after this review before he anathematized William Wordsworth from the ranks of 'feeling' poets. To the end of his life he was unable to see that Wordsworth's moral, poetical, and philosophical speculations were not the end of his poetry, but the vehicles by which he brought to light the passionate and radically personal struggles in his own soul.

Byron sought to demonstrate this ideal of heartfelt and sincere poetry in *Hours of Idleness.*

> Oh! how I hate the nerveless, frigid song,
> The ceaseless echo of the rhyming throng;
> Whose labour'd lines, in chilling numbers flow,
> To paint a pang the author ne'er can know.
> The artless Helicon, I boast, is Youth;
> My Lyre, the Heart; – my Muse, the simple Truth.[3]

The unpoetic irony of this passage, however, is that Byron deplores just what his own lines, indeed most of *Hours of Idleness,* so painfully illustrate. Lord Brougham's notorious review of Byron's book has, I suppose, been vindicated in history. Time not only pardons him for writing well; it has judged that his delightfully urbane acidity was, after all, justified. Besides, Brougham may have been as responsible for the eruption of Byron's genius as was the Levant, or Byron's mother. In any case, Brougham pounced upon Byron's naively self-absorbed book and took a malicious delight in exposing the sort of poetry 'which neither gods nor men are said to permit';

> It is a sort of privilege of poets to be egotists; but they should 'use it as not abusing it:' and particularly one who piques himself (though indeed at the ripe age of nineteen) of being 'an infant bard,' . . . should either not know, or should seem not to know, so much about his own ancestry. Besides a poem above cited on the family seat of the Byrons, we have another of eleven pages, on the self same subject, introduced with an apology, 'he certainly had no intention of publishing it;' but really, 'the particular request of some friends,' &c. &c. It concludes with five stanzas on himself, 'the last and youngest of a noble line.' There is a good deal also about his maternal ancestors, in a Poem on Lachin-y-gair, a mountain where he spent part of his youth, and might have learnt that *pibroch* is not a bagpipe, any more than duet means a fiddle.[4]

Byron was enraged by the withering ad hominem attack, and within a year he published his equally ad hominem rejoinder. Yet Brougham's review is not only an accurate response to the aesthetic merits of Byron's poems, it is equally true to the pervasive temper of Byron's volume, which is cast in a decidedly personal mode throughout. *Hours of Idleness* was organized in such a way as to force upon the reader the presence of the poet – a specific man named George Gordon who could and did choose to define himself in place and time in his poetry by reference to a variety of publicly verifiable facts and situations (ancestry, age, schooling, youthful environment, home, etc.). Further, both the Preface and a majority of the notes scattered throughout the volume are as self-conscious as the verse itself. In truth, Brougham's 'egotism' is a good index to the highly subjective quality of *Hours of Idleness*. It is interesting that although a good many of the sixteen original reviews of the book do not attack its puerilities, nearly all direct their remarks – more or less frequently – to the dramatized person of the author.[5] *The Eclectic Review*, for example, begins with the following declaration: 'The notice we take of this publication, regards the author rather than the book.' Perceiving Byron's 'anxious search for notoriety,' the reviewer decides to give the young nobleman ('here solemnly pledged to signalize himself') a deal of good advice on how to attain his evident goals ('the magnanimity of a moral hero,' 'the way to true honour').[6] *The Critical Review* is equally personal in its approach. After quoting at length from 'Childish Recollections,' a poem singled out for high praise, the critic moves on to these concluding remarks:

> We cannot now follow the poet, as we would gladly do, through the characteristic, but tender, descriptions, of three or four of his most intimate associates, nor to the conclusion of this affecting poem, which does not fall short of the passages we have already quoted. Valuable, as this little collection is, from its intrinsic merit, it is rendered much more so by the mind which produced and pervades it.[7]

Byron himself was never able to resist the spell of striking personalities, real or fictional. Poets and poetry were themselves often judged primarily on the basis of the author's personal qualities (or at least those qualities which Byron chose to attribute to him). Tasso, for example, who is treated as a great tragic figure in Byron's poetry, is praised as a great poet in *Childe Harold's Pilgrimage* because of the heroic virtues which Byron saw in him as a man. Similarly, one of Byron's early favorites was the Cambridge poet Henry Kirke White, a minor Romantic now fallen into a curious neglect. White's poetry is nearly always of an intensely personal cast. Byron praises his work because it is 'sincere,' and defends him against the strictures of Dallas with the ingenuous observation: 'I should have been most proud of such an acquaintance.'[8] His eulogy of White in *English Bards and Scotch Reviewers*, like nearly all the other artists' portraits therein, is strictly ad hominem.

Byron's reaction to White and his poetry is scarcely more personal than that of Southey in his superb *Life* of the poet prefixed to his 1807 edition of White's *Literary Remains*.

> With regard to his poems . . . I have . . . to the best of my judgment, selected none which does not either mark the state of his mind, or its progress, or discover evident proofs of what he would have been, if it had not been the will of Heaven to remove him so soon. The reader who feels any admiration for Henry will take some interest in these remains because they are his; he who shall feel none must have a blind heart, and therefore a blind understanding. Such poems are to be considered as making up his history.[9]

Southey's ability to see a kind of dramatic wholeness in the corpus of White's poetry represents his attempt to give an aesthetic formulation to the same kind of psychological interest that Byron's responses showed. Both men were inheritors of a literary 'cult of personality' that had begun to flourish in the eighteenth century. Histories, biographies, personal letters, diaries, and memoirs were in great demand. Sentimental anatomists like Richardson, Sterne, and Rousseau were also very popular, while the historical and antiquarian craze produced volumes of anonymous and pseudonymous 'reliques' which learned minds were investing with historically recreated personalities from their researches into the past. Everyone came to know Ossian, son of Fingal, and continued to find an interest in him even after he was exposed as a fraud. So too with Rowley. From a more subjective point of view, in fact, the mythic personalities of Chatterton and Macpherson seem to have been the projections of their lonely imaginations – poetic vehicles by which they could attain a kind of self-definition in their own minds and in the pubic domain. Further, the popularity of the poetry of Young, Burns, and Cowper, to mention only three, depended to a great extent upon an *advertisements for myself* quality in their work. Cowper's poetic moralizings are interesting not because they provide insights into systematic rational or even theological truths, but because the poet is able to present to us a more or less effective portrait of a human soul – a man generous and unpedantic with an interior wisdom that was obtained and kept only with the greatest difficulty. John Newton's Preface to Cowper's early *Poems* is a curiously interesting document in this regard. Though he professes in it that it 'is not designed to commend the Poems to which it is prefixed,' he does in fact commend them not on grounds of poetic execution, but on the basis of their author's uniquely lovable personality.[10] For his part, Young professed: 'I borrow two golden rules from *ethics*, which are no less golden in *Composition*, than in life.

1. *Know thyself*; 2dly, *Reverence thyself*.[11] His *Night Thoughts* is a manifest illustration of the theory of composition implied in these remarks. His prefatory note to that weighty poem underlines its subjective quality: 'As the occasion of this Poem, was real, not fictitious; so the method pursued in it was rather imposed by what spontaneously   arose in the Author's mind on that occasion, than meditated or designed . . . the facts mentioned did naturally pour these moral reflections on the thought of the Writer.'[12] Unhappily, Young's poetic personality had a good deal less to recommend it than had Cowper's. Burns is, of course, the classic example of the personal poet among the pre-Romantics. That he wanted the reader to perceive a larger, psychological unity obtaining among his disparate lyrics is clear enough not only from his letters, but from his introductory comments to his poetry. In the Preface to the Kilmarnock edition he declared: 'Unacquainted with the necessary requisites for commencing Poet by rule, he [the poet of the volume] sings the sentiments and manners he felt and saw in himself and his rustic compeers around him, in his and their native language.'[13] His poetry amounts to one man's observations upon himself and his culture, and achieves a coherence by means of a mythic personality very dear to the nineteenth century – one 'bred to the Plough, and . . . independent.'[14]

This inclination to treat literature as a vehicle for self-expression was international in scope. Germany in particular produced a number of aestheticians who expounded the concept, especially as it was illustrated in more modern poetry. Even Goethe eventually decided – probably under Schiller's influence – that all his work was no more than a series of 'fragments of a great confession,'[15] and he deliberately set out to write *Dichtung und Wahrheit* that the underlying coherence of his work might be made manifest. His autobiography was intended to 'present in due order the inner motives, the external influences, and the stages of my progress' as a poet. Thereby the reader would have the key for interpreting his collected works.[16]

Southey's apprehension of a psychological coherence in White's often fragmentary poetry is basically the same conception as Goethe's, except that the latter explicitly relates his core of essential subjective meaning to a play of cosmic forces (very like Wordsworth). Southey and Goethe are at one with the thought of the period in regarding the inner personal truth of poetry as a quality hidden away, something requiring exegesis and explanation: in particular, a biographical frame of reference into which the fragments of the poetic confession could be put. For although poets in the later eighteenth century were already beginning to come forth in their works in an intentionally confessional posture, few seem to have ever published an entire original volume of poetry which was deliberately organized to dramatize the author's character and environment (to 'present in due order the inner motives, the external influences, and the stages of [his] progress'). [. . .]

It is not surprising, then, that Byron's early reviewers should have singled out the strongly expressivistic quality of *Hours of Idleness*, for Byron seems to have consciously striven to publicize his character in this, his first book of poetry intended for general circulation. Byron's Preface – 'revealing much . . . about the author's personality,' as William Calvert has said – [17] immediately dictates the highly personal decorum which prevails throughout the volume. The book was really a kind of debut ('I have hazarded my reputation and feelings in publishing this volume,' p. vi). He tells the reader that he hopes his book will provide some amusement, particularly for younger minds; but the dominant motif in the Preface is 'fame.' He keeps coming back to the idea, and while he is extremely tactful in speaking of this motivation for his work, he does not try to conceal it ('To the dictates of young ambition, may be ascribed many actions more criminal, and equally absurd,' p. ix). A book of poetry seemed a good way to establish a reputation – a useful thing for a young lord clearly bent upon some ambitious 'pursuits hereafter' (p. ix) in society.

As one reviewer acutely noted, this desire for an approving notoriety led Byron to present himself as a young lord aspiring to the 'magnanimity of a moral hero.' He continually alludes to his aristocratic heritage and asserts his longing to continue its heroic traditions. To this end he publishes a good deal of satire and social criticism, for in it we see the reflection of his innate moral sense. Withal, he is a young man and possesses all the virtues and defects of his age. Both are related to those 'fierce emotions of the flowing soul' (p. 199) which are natural to any healthy and spirited youth, and they find expression in his poems on love and friendship. He acknowledges that he has sometimes acted with a passionate imprudence, but while admitting his errors in a poem addressed to the Rev. Thomas Becher, he argues that a man is worthless if he does not possess a strong and enthusiastic soul. He is careful throughout the volume to exhibit his passionate character, but equally careful to show that he is aware of the excesses to which 'entusymusy' can carry one. An ironic strain pervades the volume and is allied to the attitude of self-possessed objectivity that Byron so frequently puts on. Thus, 'Granta, A Medley' concludes with a facetious abruptness. Or, when he tries to persuade 'Marion,' one of his lady acquaintances, out of a black mood, he makes sure that his advice is offered in a good-humored way.

> All I shall, therefore, say, (whate'er
> I think, is neither here nor there,)
> Is that such lips, of looks endearing,
> Were form'd for better things, than sneering.   (p. 45)

Byron will be alternately ironic or serious in his love poems, but when he speaks of his more heroic longings he maintains a severely earnest demeanor. It is just such seriousness that produces his worst and his best verse in this early volume, for he has not yet learned how to manage poetic decorum. 'On Leaving Newstead Abbey' is typical of the worst poems in this group. After recounting the wonderful deeds of his ancestors he finds himself at the conclusion faced with a present imperative, and he attempts an identification of himself with the figures of the ancestors he has so romantically recalled.

> Shades of heroes, farewell! your descendant, departing
> From the seat of his ancestors, bids you, adieu!
> Abroad, or at home, your remembrance imparting
> New courage, he'll think upon glory, and you.
>
> Though a tear dim his eye, at this sad separation,
> 'Tis nature, not fear, that excites his regret;
> Far distant he goes, with the same emulation,
> The fame of his fathers he ne'er can forget.
>
> That fame, and that memory, still will he cherish,
> He vows, that he ne'er will disgrace your renown;
> Like you will he live, or like you will he perish;
> When decay'd, may he mingle his dust with your own.   (p. 3)

In these dreadful lines Byron tries to strike an equality between his fathers and himself by casting himself in a heroic role. The whole poem takes the form of a romance hero's farewell speech before his arduous quest. But when, at the end, he has to speak of his specific intentions, the poem suddenly loses all connection with the

> mail-covered Barons, who proudly to battle,
> Led their vassals from Europe to Palestine's plain.   (p. 2)

At the conclusion we move instead in the world of Sir Charles Grandison. 'Abroad, or at home' is a linguistic disaster under the circumstances, since it is unlikely to suggest anything more than a thoroughly conventional Grand Tour. Like most of the statements in the three quoted stanzas, the phrase is grotesquely domestic in its overtones; the breach in poetic decorum is manifest if we set it beside such a resounding romantic line as 'Near Askalon's towers, John of Horistan slumbers.' If Byron had been Laertes, this poem would have served him as an apt reply to his father before he left for his education abroad.

Bad as this poem is, it affords us a good example of the kind of grandiose self-dramatizing which lies behind the whole volume. Filled with a desire for greatness, Byron looks to *fama* as a sign of his election. *Hours of Idleness* is Byron's first mythologized account of his own person, his first attempt to create in poetry, and thereby *be*, 'A being more intense' (*Childe Harold's Pilgrimage*, Canto III, L.6) and admirable than ordinary men. Most of his early attempts at a sublime style fail completely, but they have a real significance insofar as we perceive their intention. Not all his poems in this mode are failures, however. In 'A Fragment' and 'Lachin Y. Gair,' for example, Byron succeeds in establishing an equality between the mythology of heroic pursuits and the possibilities of his own life. In both cases, however, he has recourse to a nonsocial world of his own past. 'Near Lachin Y. Gair I spent the early part of my youth' (p. 129), Byron tells us in a prefatory note to his well-known lyric, and we see that the romantic highlands and the literature about them have fired his imagination as much as had the history of the Byrons. The attempt to make the present a continuation of the heroic past is managed in both poems. In 'A Fragment' Byron confidently declares his kinship with his heroic forebears by employing an image of sublimity and grandeur to which both have access: the mountains of Scotland.

> When, to their airy hall, my fathers' voice,
> Shall call my spirit, joyful in their choice;
> When, pois'd upon the gale, my form shall ride,
> Or, dark in mist, descend the mountain's side;
> Oh! may my shade behold no sculptur'd urns,
> To mark the spot, where earth to earth returns:
> No lengthen'd scroll of virtue and renown;
> My epitaph shall be, my name alone:
> If that with honour fail to crown my clay,
> Oh! may no other fame my deeds repay;
> That, only that, shall single out the spot,
> By that remember'd, or with that forgot.   (p. 9)

Despite the verbal ineconomy of the conclusion, this is a creditable poem. That immortal 'name,' so important to him, seems entirely within reach now, for he can join his fathers imaginatively in their wild and 'airy halls' in the mountains which he knew as a boy. Unlike Newstead Abby, these suffer neither decay nor change, so that by becoming part

of them he avoids the necessity of seeking after vain worldly achievements. Since his true beginning and end are with the dark mists and
powerful storms which perpetually show forth their living strength on
the slopes and summits of the mountains, his true life and true nobility
are a fact of his *being*, so that his worth and stature are limited only by
the scope of his own vision of himself, not by the petty measures of the
world.

In 'Lachin Y. Gair' the same themes and basic techniques are repeated,
only the various relationships between romantic mountain, heroic ancestry, domestic England, and aspiring Lord Byron are made more explicit.
The connection between Lachin Y. Gair and his heritage is specified in
the second stanza. Though 'long perish'd' (p. 130), the chiefs of the
Gordons live still in the spirit of the region dominated by the great
mountain. As Byron wanders about, he hears of their fame in the traditional stories told 'by the natives of dark Loch na Garr' (p. 130). But
the presence of the Gordons is an immediate experience when he sees
and hears the storms upon the mountain.

> 'Shades of the dead! have I not heard your voices
> 'Rise on the night-rolling breath of the gale?'
> Surely the soul of the hero rejoices,
> And rides on the wind, o'er his own Highland vale:
> Round Loch na Garr, while the stormy mist gathers,
> Winter presides in his cold icy car;
> Clouds, there, encircle the forms of my Fathers,
> They dwell in the tempests of dark Loch na Garr: (p. 130)

Being a living part of 'that high world' of which Byron spoke in a later
poem, the Gordons need not be concerned that they died 'at Culloden,'
for their greatness does not depend upon 'victory' or 'applause.' Their
essential lives were not lived in human history any more than their
achievements can be measured in human terms: they are part of the
mythic world whose beginning and end is in 'dark Loch na Garr.' This
is where Byron spent his youth and learned of his kinship with a sublime
order of life, and when he dies he too will return to an 'earthy slumber'
in the bosom of the mountain, 'in the caves of Braemar' (p. 131). So in
the last stanza he speaks of himself as an exile in England's 'tame and
domestic' regions, and waits for the time of his return to his real life and
real home.

The split in consciousness manifest in these two poems, so typical of
the Romantic conflict between 'real' and imaginative orders of being,
does not develop into a source of anxiety in 'A Fragment.' At the very
beginning and end of 'Lachin Y. Gair,' however, Byron gives us a

glimpse of that Romantic discontent for which he was soon to become the byword. The poem opens with a brief and undistinguished statement of disaffection for 'the minions of luxury' who are caught up in the ordinary affairs of the world, and it closes with an allusion to his unful-filled life in commonplace England. But as a whole *Hours of Idleness* displays a radical division of a similar nature. I have already pointed out how Byron's attitudes in his book tend to polarize around his person insofar as he sees himself as a well-bred young nobleman, or as a senti-mentalist and a man of feeling. But the frequency with which these two figures merge in the book suggests that their antithesis is only the sign of a more fundamental split in Byron's perception of himself and his world.

Byron's role as nobleman is itself unintegrated, for on the one hand he can project himself into the sublime and imaginative world of his ancestors, and on the other he is imprisoned by a set of decaying heroic symbols and by a society which is totally out of place in his mythologized existence. The world of the youth of feeling is similarly fractured. He bids a mocking farewell to 'sickly Sensibility' in 'To Romance' (p. 135), and we have already noticed a number of other poems in which he shows a sardonic or amused consciousness of certain forms of youthful naiveté. But these are set off against a relatively equal number of poems in which Byron's rather conventional version of a Blakean Beulah is regarded as a psychological state of great value – especially when it is contrasted with the values of age and maturity:

> Can Treasures, hoarded for some thankless Son,
> Can Royal Smiles, or Wreaths by slaughter won,
> Can Stars, or Ermine, Man's maturer Toys,
> (For glittering baubles are not left to Boys,)
> Recall one scene, so much belov'd, to view,
> As those, where Youth her garland twin'd for you?
> Ah, no! amidst the gloomy calm of age,
> You turn with faltering hand life's varied page,
> Peruse the record of your days on earth,
> Unsullied only, where it marks your birth.   (p. 167)

In 'To E. N. L. Esq.' he considers the prospects of a life of responsibility and hopes that he may stay 'at heart a child' always (p. 180). The poem lingers over a series of recollected images of an age that is now passing away, and when he escapes the stilted grammar and diction that so often disfigure *Hours of Idleness* he is able to achieve brief moments of fine and simple pathos.

> Ah! though the present brings but pain,
> I think those days may come again.   (p. 179)

The effect of the couplet seems to derive partly from the economy of statement, and partly from the verb 'may' – which suggests the speaker's deep-felt *need* of the innocence of youth. He knows 'those days' cannot come again in fact, but the value that they represent seems so great to him that he ventures a subjunctive which expresses at once his pain of loss, and his obscure perception that youth and innocence may be recoverable as spiritual values.

A longer passage later in the poem operates with a similar kind of dignified simplicity. He is reminiscing over the end of the fleeting love affairs of his youth.

> Thus faint is every former flame,
> And Passion's self is now a name!
> As when the ebbing flames are low,
> The aid which once improv'd their light,
> And bade them burn with fiercer glow,
> Now quenches all their sparks in night;
> Thus has it been with Passion's fires,
> As many a boy, and girl, remembers,
> While all the force of love expires,
> Extinguish'd with the dying embers.   (p. 182, II. 77–86)

The pathos in these lines depends to a great extent upon the careful use of rhyme and line rhythm. The image of a dying fire is traditional and appropriate, while the management of the verse movement is quite original. Byron interrupts and delays the fulfillment of the fire/passion comparison in a number of ways, and thus creates an imitation in the verse rhythm itself of a slow and gradual process of extinction. After the quick initial couplet, the periodic structure of lines 79–81 is supported by the slightly delayed rhyme (bcb): line 82, which completes the 'c' rhyme, drops into the poem with a finality appropriate to the meaning ('quenches') and to the completion of the extended simile. The dying fire image is not completely used up, however: after the simile is finished, it comes back again in the more subdued form of metaphor. The first feminine ending in the passage (line 84), triumphant over grammar, prepares the whole for its 'dying fall' in the final line. The fire and love's passion now only burn as 'embers,' but they continue for a brief while to preserve a vestige of life, just as the feminine ending delays slightly the completion of the line and the whole passage. The rhyme 'remembers/embers' is exactly right from a substantive point of view since it is clear that these loves of Byron's past only continue to burn low in and through his act of reminiscing. He does not want to forget – not entirely, not yet.

This reluctance to forego an innocent world in which there are no false friends or deceitful lovers, and in which the unsullied dreams of love and individual integrity are entirely accordant with one's experience of reality, is one of the three predominant themes in *Hours of Idleness*. The other two we have already discussed: the ironic or satiric exposure of falsity in all its forms and (the paramount idea in the book) the mythology of individual greatness and heroic endeavor. It seems to have been Byron's intention to dramatize himself as a young man just on the threshold of maturity and majority alike, and caught in the pull of forces that seem either to hurry him on to, or hold him back from, involvement in busy and mundane affairs. The world of youthful imaginations is clearly presented as the more attractive, while the values of maturity have only a secondary importance: ironic objectivity and a responsible sense of 'realities' possess an indispensable corrective function, but they totally lack any capacity for creative or affirmative gestures. Byron occasionally tries to establish a system of positive values upon a reputable career in the ordinary world (for example, at the end of 'On Leaving Newstead Abbey'), but in every case he fails utterly to carry conviction. As in the Preface, the objective and realistic Byron is relegated to the task of ironic comment and self-criticism – lest we think from his book that he does not realize the more absurd aspects of his own sentimentality and dreamy imaginative flights. His poems are 'the fruits of the lighter hours of a young man,' he tells us, and adds: 'As they bear the internal evidence of a boyish mind, this is, perhaps, unnecessary information' (p. v). Thus he hopes to disarm the strictures of older minds by anticipating what he believes will be their principal objection.

The different forms in which these conflicted aspects of Byron's personality are dramatized in *Hours of Idleness* clearly prefigure a basic and well-documented characteristic of his later work: the tension that persists between his visionary and skeptical imaginations. In *Hours of Idleness*, the radical splits in Byron's various conventional postures result from his desire to identify with a heroic order of human life that is at once of this world ('earthy,' p. 131) and quite beyond it. Insofar as the attitudes of the youth of sensibility (with his innocence and integrity) and of the young nobleman (with his epic heritage and uncircumscribed field of action) are allied to this larger conception, they are not rejected; but insofar as both of these roles necessarily involve commitments to something else, something less pristine and passionate and grand, they are generally thrust ironically or disdainfully away.

But from the point of view of his poetic development, the simple *fact* that he seeks to dramatize himself to his audience is at least as significant. Nearly all of his poetry is crucially dependent, in form and meaning alike, upon the effectiveness with which he can realize an image of himself in the artifice of his own making. The most significant fact about *Hours of Idleness* is that in it we observe Byron trying to organize a series of disparate lyrics into a coherent self-portrait. *Hours of Idleness* is not a book that comes up to the promise of its own formal intention. It is too blighted, too dull in fact, so that its conception and execution remain sundered. In the first place, Byron was inordinately careful and decorous in announcing himself to his audience. As his ingratiating Preface suggests, one of his principal conscious objects seems to have been to persuade his readers that he was a modest but decent enough gentleman-amateur poet on the one hand, and on the other a spirited, ambitious, and sensitive young lord who seemed destined to distinguish himself in the future. This concern for public recognition as a validating condition of achievement produces a strain in his early poetry that is mindlessly slavish to conventional ideas of action and forms of behavior. For all his irony and self-consciousness even at this early stage of his career, Byron often seems unable to reflect upon, much less to understand, what his motives might be for this or that statement. This failure to bring his self-critical powers to bear on his own characteristic modes of thought produces a depressing quantity of stillborn verse.

Byron, in fact, seems more interested in posturing than in carrying out an experiment in analytic poetic autobiography. He seldom descends to the difficult labor of introspection – a staple in all autobiographical forms – but constantly concerns himself with writing poems that demonstrate the principal characteristics of his person according to the most conventional forms of eighteenth-century psychological thought. We are shown his ambition, his reverence for female beauty and modesty, his love of honesty and truth, his respect for strength of character and sensitivity of soul, etc. It is unnecessary to dwell upon the weakening of the biographical product that results from the uncritical use of such ideas. Nevertheless, with all these faults acknowledged I think the book possesses an interest and a poetic significance that is something greater than the sum of its parts – not because the personality in it is particularly extraordinary (he seems a rather typical example of the divided Romantic soul, while the conflicts in his character are put across, for the most part, in relatively uninteresting ways), but because that personality is offered as a true and authentic self-portrait.

Although Byron's volume does not make its highly personal impact simply because he chooses to remind the reader again and again, in the poetry and the prose notes alike, that the author is a specific and histori- cally definable personality, this insistence upon factual reality in the volume is a crucial one. By defining himself so particularly for the reader, and by insisting on numerous occasions that his Muse is 'the simple Truth,' Byron forces us to regard his poems as personal statements of his real feelings, not as 'mere' exercises in conventional modes. For example, the concluding poem in the volume is a complaint of a forsaken lover. Technically, the poem is just indifferent; printed in an anthology, it would be read and forgotten forever. But because the whole focus of *Hours of Idleness* prevents us from reading the piece as an isolated exercise in the craft of poetic creation (with a possible, but irrelevant, foundation in fact), the reader is likely to react strongly against Byron's design upon him: soliciting approval of the poem because it is a statement of the sad and simple truth, because the detailed experience is part of and has contributed to the development of young Lord Byron's character. Brougham was mightily annoyed with Byron's book for just this reason: that the poet should have so confidently expected that his poetry merited attention and praise because of the character of the author revealed therein. It is evident that Byron's 'talents . . . are considerable, and his opportunities . . . great,' Brougham says; his verse is, for all that, a wretched thing. Brougham is about 90 per cent correct in his wholesale condemnation of the specific poems in *Hours of Idleness*. But, though the book is a failure, it is a most interesting and instructive one precisely because the reader's consideration is not directed to the poetic value of the individual poem alone. A more comprehensive aesthetic supervenes in the relation of the various poems to each other within the biographical structure of the whole book. In this it illustrates a conception of a use to which poetry might be validly put, and to which Byron did put it, quite brilliantly, in his later work.

But a spectacular element insinuates itself throughout *Hours of Idleness* which lends the volume not so much a self-dramatizing as a self-propagandizing quality. *Hours of Idleness* is not a book that essays sublimity, but the impulse to the grand gesture is distinctly present in it. The dominant of the three main themes in the book is the poet's desire for a heroic identification, and the whole work is offered as a kind of portrait of the hero as a young man. We are asked to laugh with him at his own naive follies (as in 'To Romance'), to respect the fervor of his satiric declamations at evil and pettiness (as in 'Thoughts Suggested by a College Examination' and 'Damaetas'), to smile indulgently with him when he uncovers the follies of others ('Granta, A Medley'), to sympathize with him during his growing pains ('Childish Recollections' and 'To E. N. L. Esq.'), to appreciate and perhaps indulge him in the harmless love affairs of his youth, to weep with him when he loses his first true love, and, finally, to experience through him intimations of the heroic destiny which is ever calling out to him and drawing him on. His 'Imitations and Translations' recapitulate most of these ideas. In all this is an impulse to sensationalize the name of Lord Byron. Brougham quite correctly sensed the giant vanity that lurked behind the modest facade of most of the book and he pilloried Byron for his 'egotism.'

> Perhaps . . . all that he tells us about his youth, is rather with a view to increase our wonder, than to soften our censures. He possibly means to say, 'See how a minor can write! This poem was actually composed by a young man of eighteen, and this by one of only sixteen!' But, alas! we all remember the poetry of Cowley at ten, and of Pope at twelve . . .

Indeed, Byron's book makes such a conclusion impossible to avoid. His conversational and sometimes insouciant manner in the Preface tends to underplay the aspiration to fame which is so much a part of *Hours of Idleness*; but the very attempt to assume a modest attitude toward a subject which he himself keeps bringing up serves only to underline the importance that he attaches to it.

Hours of Idleness is, then, very like propaganda in several ways: in a bad sense, first of all, because the book suggests that a heroic ordonnance is suitable to the self-dramatized figure of the poet when in fact only the design of the book and a few of its more important poems support this implication. Further, the book seems to be to some extent propaganda in a literal sense – which is to say a bastardization of poetry for wholly unpoetic ends (i.e., the furtherance of Byron's public reputation and the political career which he contemplated at that time). But it is also like propaganda in two senses that are important for an understanding of his later work. First of all, there is the very fact that he should conceive himself (which is to say, conceive his poetic materials) within a frame of reference that suggests heroic potential. A man who could write such a book would have no difficulty trailing his bleeding heart across Europe, for he clearly took the attitude that his subject was a great one, that if fully developed it would yield an experience that was at once universal and sublime. Second, and even more significant, the book resembles propaganda because it offers a dramatized picture of a man which purports to be identical with the real person. Paul West has rightly said that 'It is Byron and Byron's idea of himself which hold his work together,'[18] so that if we are to come to grips with his poetry, we must discover some means of elucidating how Byron the man has transfused himself into his work, and what happens to his poetry as a result of this.

Northrop Frye has put the problem very well:

> The main appeal of Byron's poetry is in the fact that it is Byron's. . . . He proves what many critics declare to be impossible, that a poem can make its primary impact as a historical and biographical document. The critical problem here is crucial to our understanding of not only Byron but literature as a whole.[19]

Frye's treatment of Byron, however, does not get beyond the stage of perceiving that his poetry offers a manifold and crucial problem for the reader. I do not propose to disentangle this confusion of rather fundamental aesthetic difficulties, but merely to reintroduce a method for reading Byron that was proposed by Matthew Arnold, and that seems to offer a satisfactory practical solution to the problem of biography in art. Byron and Wordsworth were, for Arnold, the two greatest poets of the nineteenth century. When Arnold wrote his essay on Byron the latter's reputation had been declining slowly for some time, largely because of a growing reaction against the irregularities of his life, on the one had, and the evident crudities in much of his poetry on the other. Arnold meets both of these objections head on. He seeks to demonstrate the greatness of the poetry by first admitting that Byron's work, like Wordsworth's, frequently shows unpardonable technical flaws that neither Shelley nor Leopardi would have been capable of. He also admits that as a man Byron left much to be desired. This train of thought is taken up in an admittedly ethical, rather than aesthetic, frame of reference. It is, nevertheless, an important element in Arnold's argument, for after making these two admissions he comes to erect out of Goethe's various observations about Byron's preeminence a third category by which Byron's poetry must be judged: the character of his poetic personality.

> His superiority turns . . . upon the surpassing worth of something which he had and was, after all deductions have been made for his shortcomings. We talk of Byron's *personality*, 'a personality in eminence such as has never been yet, and is not likely to come again;' and we say that by this personality Byron is 'different from all the rest of English poets, and in the main greater.' But can we not be a little more circumstantial, and name that in which the wonderful power of this personality consisted? We can; with the instinct of a poet

> Mr. Swinburne has seized upon it and named it for us. The power of Byron's personality lies in 'the splendid and imperishable excellence which covers all his offences and outweighs all his defects: *the excellence of sincerity and strength.'*[20]

The problem with this declaration, and all the subsequent observations in Arnold's essay, is that we seem to detect in the critic an unwillingness to say specifically whether he is praising the man Byron, or Byron the poet. But this is Arnold's main point: that to read Byron's poetry properly one must become involved in the blazing 'personality' which it deliberately seeks to dramatize. The poetry does not reveal Byron the man, but the poetic personality into which he mythologized himself in his work.

> When this theatrical and easily criticized personage took himself to poetry, and when he had fairly warmed to his work, then he became another man; then the theatrical personage passed away; then a higher power took possession of him and filled him; then at last came forth into light that true and puissant personality, with its direct strokes, its ever-welling force, its satire, its energy, its agony. This is the real Byron. . . .[21]

The attitude of Swinburne and Arnold is typical of most nineteenth-century Byron criticism, which never tires of telling us about Byron's 'sincerity' and 'strength.' What 'strength' means in such a context is easily enough discerned in the Promethean declamations that characterize much of his work. His 'sincerity' is another thing altogether. Arnold himself says that the historic 'personage' is an 'easily criticized' poseur, while the greatest of all the 'sincerity' critics, Thomas Carlyle, dismissed nearly all of Byron's work before *Don Juan* as largely trumped-up attitudinizing. What Carlyle meant was that Byron in reality was not like the Giaour, or Conrad, or Childe Harold, and that consequently these were 'insincere' representations of himself – not accordant with the truth of fact. But the problem with this type of criticism is that everyone can quote scripture to his own purpose – that with a complex human being like Byron, different opinions about what he was 'really' like are bound to crop up. Thus, the whole history of Byron research shows a constant struggle between those who praise him for his poetic sincerity and those who damn him for his insincerity.

Yet there is a common ground on which both of these evaluative critical positions can meet – one which does not praise or blame Byron for his sincerity or insincerity, but which simply asks that the poetry be accepted, and read, as a self-dramatizing vehicle. In a sense, no product of art can be sincere precisely because it is a thing fabricated, created; it exists in an ideal order of its own, no matter how realistically oriented it may be. By the same token, all achieved art can be called sincere because its own internal harmony will suggest no irregularities in the 'poet's vision,' no disruptive contradictions. But such absolutely disjunctive significations for the term 'sincerity' suggest its fundamental critical uselessness as an evaluative tool. Arnold implicitly praises Byron for his sincerity, and insofar as this is true his remarks are not criticism but appreciation. Arnold, however, also introduces a meaning for the term 'sincerity' that *is* useful when he suggests that the poetry be read as the dramatization of the psychic life of a single 'personality.' What Arnold points to in this case is an *illusion* of sincerity created by art, an illusion that makes the dramatic 'personality' of Byron presented in his poetry seem fully and empirically 'real.' Though this 'personality' is a product of art and artifice, it is poetically significant because it is not a 'persona' in any useful sense of that term's meaning. Most of Byron's poetry is sincere in this third, and purely descriptive, sense: his poetry dramatizes the life of a specific individual who possesses all the 'roundedness' of the living human reality. *Hours of Idleness* sets out to do just this, but it fails because the 'personality' of the young peer remains largely an 'individual' cliché.

One of Byron's earliest critics, Sir Egerton Brydges, seems to have anticipated Arnold's descriptive use of the term 'sincerity' in relation to Byron's poetry. Brydges believed that 'the history of [Byron's] life . . . proved that he was in reality what his poetry represented him to be.'[22] Nevertheless, Brydges also sees that Byron's 'sincerity' is an aesthetic form in his poetry, and can be made the subject of critical analysis:

> when an author comes forward as the relater of his own inventions . . . we try his tale by its probabilities. . . . Such an author deals with his proper subjects when he paints the internal movements of the human heart . . . it is the imagination only to which these are known. The test of the power and virtue of that imagination lies in the degree of *sympathy* which it awakens; while that sympathy much depends upon the faculty of *verisimility*.[23]

It is useless to quibble about terms and say, after the manner of Heine on Rousseau, that the dramatic figure is not the historically 'real Lord Byron.' Perhaps this is true, but it does not matter, for the 'got-up' Byron is all that is left. Like any artist, he refined himself out of existence in order to create an image of life, one that, in this case, would seem to live and breathe. The curious fact is, however, that even the most recent biographical discoveries (and who has been more relentlessly pursued for the last century and a half than Byron?) have not significantly altered the time-honored legend that he himself created, and that has been in the public domain ever since Moore's first codification.

Throughout his life Byron strove to become a 'historical figure,' and to make that figure identical with the dreams of his own very personal imaginations. These dreams shifted with the years, and some evaporated, but they never altogether ceased to haunt him. Even when we seek the man Byron in the driest historical records we find that a mythological transformation often takes place. The mortal figure constantly tends to assume legendary form even when we know our facts are right. He epitomizes that in human nature which makes metahistory possible. He survives in the valley of his saying, to extend Auden's meaning somewhat.

Perhaps nothing illustrates this so well as a fragment of MS preserved in the Beinecke Rare Book Library at Yale University. I have reproduced it here as a frontispiece. The MS fragment contains a version of stanza 73 of *Childe Harold's Pilgrimage II*. In it Byron asks a series of rhetorical questions about a liberator of Greece. Five times he asks a variant of the question of 'who' will finally set Greece free, and five times the answer to that question – not publicly recorded – is dashed across the page in his bold script: "Byron." The scrap of MS is a graphic reminder not only of Byron's heroic pretensions, but of his tendency to refuse the distinction between his life in history and his life in art.[24]

This MS fragment was written sometime before 1812, probably in 1809. It contains a strange prophecy, and one entirely worthy of the man who longed so passionately to be in fact what he dreamed he was. Byron's statue now stands in the Garden of Heroes in Missolonghi, a sign that his prophetic hope had not been in vain. Further, he has the fame he sought – more of it, probably, than any other English poet except Shakespeare. Byron gained his notoriety by the force of his projected personality, and it is an irony he would have appreciated that that very specific personality has now largely become dispersed into a variety of modern myths. Nor does a serious, even scholarly, attempt to remain true to the facts protect us from mythmaking, for Byron will not let us rest content with mere facts but forces us on to seek meanings behind them and patterns within them. He forces us to mythmake, and Keats did not know what an important truth he pointed to when he sneered at Byron for 'cutting a figure.' Byron refused the distinction between his life and his art, and the result has been, as G. Wilson Knight has always said, that he became a work of art, that the distinction could not be easily, or even usefully, drawn.

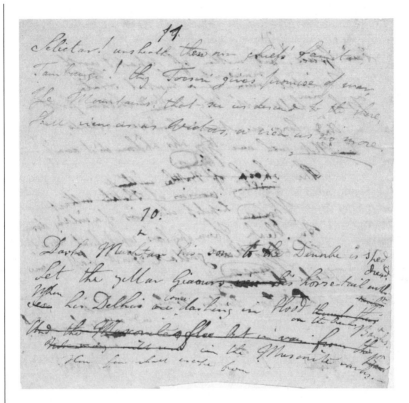

Childe Harold's Pilgrimage II, stanza 73 (reproduced with permission of The Beinecke Rare Book and Manuscript Library, Yale University).

Notes

1 Lord Byron, *The Complete Miscellaneous Prose*, ed. A. Nicholson (Oxford: Clarendon Press, 1991), 8.

2 Ibid., 178–9.

3 'Answer to Some Elegant Verses, Sent by a Friend . . .,' in *Hours of Idleness* (Newark: S. and J. Ridge, 1807), p. 119. Throughout this chapter quotations from *Hours of Idleness* will be made from the first edition and given in the text.

4 *Edinburgh Review* xi (Jan. 1808), 288.

5 They are listed in W. S. Ward, 'Byron's *Hours of Idleness* and other than Scotch Reviewers,' *Modern Language Notes* 59 (December, 1944): 547–50.

6 *Eclectic Review* 3 (November, 1807): 989–93.

7 *Critical Review*, Third Series, 12 (September, 1807): 53.

8 Lord Byron, *Byron's Letters and Journals*, 13 vols., ed. Leslie A. Marchand, (London: John Murray, 1973–94), II. 76, 82.

9   Robert Southey, *The Remains of Henry Kirke White*, with an account of his life, 2 vols. (London: Vernor, Hood & Sharpe, 1807), 1: 54.

10   William Cowper, *Poems* (London: J. Johnson, 1782), p. ii.

11   Edward Young, *Conjectures on Original Composition*, ed. Edith J. Morley (London: Longmans, Green, 1918), p. 24.

12   Edward Young, *The Poetical Works*, ed. Thomas Park, 4 vols. (London: Stanhope Press, 1813), I. 9.

13   *The Poetry of Robert Burns*, ed. William Ernest Henley and Thomas F. Henderson, 4 vols. (Edinburgh: T. C. and E. C. Jack, 1901), 1: 1.

14   Ibid., p. 5.

15   Quoted in J. W. von Goethe, *Poetry and Truth from My Own Life*, trans. M. S. Smith, introd. K. Breul, 2 vols. (London: Bell, 1908), 1: x.

16   Ibid., 2: 56–7.

17   Calvert, *Byron: Romantic Paradox*, 74.

18   Paul West, 'Introduction' in *Byron: A Collection of Critical Essays*, ed. P. West (Englewood Cliffs: Prentice-Hall, 1963), 2.

19   Northrop Frye, 'Lord Byron,' in *Fables of Identity* (New York: Harcourt, Brace and World, 1963), 174.

20   Matthew Arnold, 'Byron,' in *Essays in Criticism*, Second Series (London: Macmillan, 1921), 192–3.

21   Ibid., 196–7.

22   Egerton Brydges, *Letters on the Character and Poetical Genius of Lord Byron* (London: Longman, 1824), 135.

23   Ibid., 253–4.

24   Byron sometimes objected when his contemporaries read his tales as disguised autobiography. Given the extravagance of many of these biographical interpretations one can readily sympathize with Byron's reaction. Nevertheless, his own poetry, even his public conduct, could scarcely do anything but foster such attitudes. All of his poetry up to the publication of *The Giaour* was distinctly personal in form, often explicitly autobiographical.

Further reading

Listed below are instances of the canonizing criticism of Byron in the second half of the twentieth century, explicating poetic vision and literary achievement. *Don Juan* predominates, but the range of the poetry is covered. McGann's thesis, that the poetry demands to be read as self-expression, is supported by the unusual prominence of the question of biography and its bearing on the poetry.

E. F. Boyd, *Byron's Don Juan: A Critical Study* (1945; repr. London: Routledge & Kegan Paul, 1958). Treats *Don Juan* as an independent entity, the analysis of which leads to 'the mind of the poet'; especially useful on the poem's literary background and the range of its sources and themes.

Ernest J. Lovell, 'Irony and Image in Byron's *Don Juan*' in *The Major English Romantic Poets: A Symposium in Reappraisal*, ed. C. C. Thorpe, C. Baker and B. Weaver (Carbondale: Southern Illinois State University Press, 1957), 129–48. Argues that *Don Juan*'s unity is in its theme of appearance versus reality; its irony is integral to both theme and mode. Anticipates Bostetter, Cooke and McGann (see below), in reading *Don Juan* as 'a poetry of clear present use', satirically attacking the world, but accepting rather than rejecting it.

Leslie A. Marchand, *Byron: A Biography*, 3 vols. (London: John Murray, 1957). Extensive and detailed; draws upon new material unavailable to earlier biographers. The standard scholarly biography.

George M. Ridenour, *The Style of* Don Juan (New Haven: Yale University Press, 1960). The principle of Byron's universe, its dual possibility of sin and grace, is dramatized in *Don Juan* by means of the Christian myth of the fall (the poem's action being a development from innocence to experience), and the classical rhetorical theory of styles, which, permitting poetry that is both high and low, is well adapted to Byron's paradoxical vision.

*****Andrew Rutherford**, *Byron: A Critical Study* (Edinburgh and London: Oliver and Boyd, 1961). Lucid study of the development of Byron's poetry, sensibly both allowing and limiting the use of biography, but a little too categorical in its treatment of the romantic writings as minor and the later satirical style as the true expression of Byron's genius.

Peter L. Thorslev, *The Byronic Hero: Types and Prototypes* (Minneapolis: University of Minnesota Press, 1962). Shows the Byronic hero to be the representative of a Romantic tradition rather than the image of his creator; traces the hero's cultural and literary antecedents and his development in Byron's poetry (*Don Juan* is excluded as atypical).

Edward E. Bostetter, *The Romantic Ventriloquists: Wordsworth, Coleridge, Keats, Shelley, Byron* (1963; rev. edn. Seattle and London: University of Washington Press, 1975). The gap between ideal and reality that produces in the other romantics strategies of retreat or withdrawal for Byron alone is enabling, prompting a move from the self outward, and a transition 'from romantic poseur into great artist'. *Don Juan*, unlike the other great unfinished romantic poems, is marked not by paralysis or despair, but 'intellectual and artistic vigor'.

*****M. K. Joseph**, *Byron the Poet* (London: Gollancz, 1964). Leading study, usefully taking into account sources, contexts, form and textual history in its overview of the poetry. No single organizing argument, but makes good the introductory contention, that Byron is 'a major poet . . . and the fitting representative of a great tradition.'

*****Leslie A. Marchand**, *Byron's Poetry: A Critical Introduction* (London: John Murray, 1965). Useful short guide, taking up the poems in chronological order, with an introductory argument: Byron's poetry expresses his varying responses to the awareness of the gap between real and ideal that sets him apart from the other romantics; it shows, not contradiction, but 'fidelity to the moment'.

G. Wilson Knight, *Byron and Shakespeare* (1966; repr. London: Routledge, 2002).

Offers a number of parallels between Byron and Shakespeare; finds in Byron's life and work Shakespearean characters and attitudes.

Robert F. Gleckner, *Byron and the Ruins of Paradise* (Baltimore: Johns Hopkins University Press, 1967). Argues for the 'non-satiric poet' and the coherent vision, in his poetry, 'of the poet as a crucial, central character, whose prophetic view of the past and of his own time develops gradually into the myth of man's eternal fall and damnation in the hell of human existence.'

M. G. Cooke, *The Blind Man Traces the Circle: On the Patterns and Philosophy of Byron's Poetry* (Princeton, N.J.: Princeton University Press, 1969). Leads up to 'the peculiar form of humanism and stoicism that may be called counter-heroic' in Byron's thought: a philosophical position, whose instrument is satire, but which affirms as well as negates, thus accommodates idealism with scepticism.

*****Leslie A. Marchand**, *Byron: A Portrait* (London: John Murray, 1971). Useful abridgement of the three-volume biography, incorporating additional material.

Bernard Blackstone, *Byron: A Survey* (London: Longman, 1975). Describing itself as a work of 'topocriticism', presents Byron as a 'topical' or regional poet, his *topos* being Europe and the Eastern Mediterranean, in which his poetry is grounded. Draws analogies to Blake and T. S. Eliot.

Jerome J. McGann, Don Juan *in Context* (Chicago and London: University of Chicago Press, 1976). By examining in *Don Juan* Byron's responses to a range of his personal, literary and historical contexts, finds in the poem a critique of the 'High Romanticism' that Byron had himself helped to advance, and an imagination that is engaged with the world: analytic and moral rather than creative and solipsistic.

Peter J. Manning, *Byron and his Fictions* (Detroit: Wayne State University Press, 1978). Psychoanalytical study of Oedipal content in Byron's poetry, contending that 'it was his own situation – disguised, displaced, and freely heightened, that he drew upon in his writings.'

Anne K. Mellor, *English Romantic Irony* (Cambridge, Mass. and London: Harvard University Press, 1980). Byron engages 'in continuous self-creation' by living as well as rendering artistically the 'heroic balancing between enthusiastic commitment and sophisticated skepticism' that defines his romantic–ironic mode of consciousness. *Don Juan* is the '*locus classicus* of English romantic irony.'

Bernard Beatty, *Byron's* Don Juan (London and Sydney: Croom Helm, 1985). Focuses on process or procedure ('How does *Don Juan* proceed?') to arrive at kind ('What kind of poem is it?'). *Don Juan* is a comedy by the terms of its own original and Romantic revaluation of the comic process, and its discovery, through that process, of spiritual reality: 'The process of the poem involves it in a testing, trusting and evolving relationship with the mysterious given as well as a clarifying hold on it.'

Frederick L. Beaty, *Byron the Satirist* (Dekalb, Illinois: Northern Illinois University Press, 1985). Lucid developmental account of Byron's satires, investigating the 'ingredients of personality and external circumstance' that went into his search for an ethical norm and a compatible poetical medium, and identifying in his development as a satirist, 'a dialectic reflecting a cleavage in his own personality' between realism and romanticism.

*Bernard Beatty, *Byron: Don Juan and Other Poems. A Critical Study* (Harmondsworth: Penguin, 1987). This fine introduction – especially insightful for the first-time reader – focuses directly and passionately on the poems, presenting, with lucidity and insight, their formal achievement and characteristic topics.

Martyn Corbett, *Byron and Tragedy* (Basingstoke and London: Macmillan, 1988). Important study of Byron's dramas, arguing that their neglect has produced a mis-representation of Byron's art. By showing the centrality of the dramas to Byron's *oeuvre* and to English dramatic literature, Corbett asserts Byron's stature as a tragic poet. His view of the 'tragic repose' in Byron's dramas, a balance of pessimism and humanism (cf. Cooke), sustains the idea of 'paradox'.

BYRON AND POLITICS

The criticism just listed typically asserts Byron's stature as a canonical romantic poet and at the same time, sets him apart from the other romantics. The basis of that 'paradox' – scepticism, irony or worldliness – is variously perceived as enabling (Bostetter, Cooke, McGann) or negating (Gleckner). Such views and counter-views of Byron, as a poet engaged with the world, elsewhere take a more explicitly political form. Byron's death in Greece sealed his association with revolutionary politics, celebrated early on by Joseph Mazzini and John Morley. His 'Satanism', in this context, is not biblical, but Miltonic, synony-mous with Prometheanism, another romantic paradigm of revolutionary ideal-ism. On its basis, Bertrand Russell famously includes Byron in *A History of Western Philosophy* (1945), making a large claim for his philosophical and political influence as an 'aristocratic rebel': 'his verse seems often poor and his sentiment often tawdry, but abroad his way of feeling and his outlook on life were transmitted and developed and transmuted until they became so wide-spread as to be factors in great events.'[21]

In the late 1980s, that long-standing association, of Byron and revolution, is treated in two polarized studies, one disputing, the other ratifying it. Malcolm Kelsall's *Byron's Politics* (1987), seeks to 'restore' Byron 'to history' by foregrounding his origins in a patrician Whig tradition incompatible with radical politics.[22] The 'Byronic', to Kelsall, is not the expression in the poetry of revolutionary idealism, but belongs to a Whig discourse of frustrated politi-cal hope, which, lacking a programme for political action, furthers no political purpose. By contrast, Michael Foot's *The Politics of Paradise: A Vindication of Byron* (1988), links Byron's life, work and politics, to offer a persuasive and deeply-felt defence of 'the poet of action', 'who cannot watch the fearful

human scene without incitement to protest or revenge or perpetual Promethean counter-assault.'[23]

Byron's revolutionary politics is not of course the sole focus of the wider-
ranging critical activity of reading Byron politically. His poetry has been fruitfully examined as embodying his sexual politics, his homosexuality adduced to
point up the instability of his construction of gender and gender roles. In *Byron
and Greek Love: Homophobia in 19th-Century England* (1985), Louis Crompton
analyzes 'the homosexual side of Byron's temperament in the light of the
attitudes to such feelings in his day'. [24] (Interestingly, Crompton also details,
from unpublished manuscripts, Jeremy Bentham's sympathetic stance, in contrast to the prejudices of his time.) Susan Wolfson argues in turn that the
instances of cross-dressing in *Don Juan* point up the instability of its politics
of sexual difference: 'Byron's representations of heterosexual politics . . . sen-
sitized by his homosexuality, turn personal experience outward into a critical
reading' of the sexual ideology of his age.[25]

Inevitably too, Byron's Orient, so vividly figured in the Eastern tales, has
contributed substantially to the readings of Romantic Orientalism, from the late
twentieth century to the present. Among the most important recent analyses,
Nigel Leask's *British Romantic Writers and the East: Anxieties of Empire* (1992),
examining 'the anxieties and instabilities' of Romantic representations of the
East, argues that 'the presiding anxiety' of Byron's tales 'is of the European
subject "turning Turk"'.[26] Thus, although Byron attacks the ideology of empire
by reducing the imperialist 'self' to the level of the 'other', in so doing, he still
perpetuates the prejudice of the binary opposition of East and West.

Byron's 'long romance with Orientalism' is also tracked in the most complex
and extensive, in recent years, of the historicist–materialist readings of romantic self-representation, to which the phenomenon of Byronism is especially
germane. Jerome Christensen's *Lord Byron's Strength: Romantic Writing and
Commercial Society* (1993) describes itself as 'a work of poststructuralist biographical criticism'. Himself thoroughly grounded in historicist methods,
Christensen 'rehabilitates poetic strength' from the historicist, and to him,
functionalist accounts that derogate it, by arguing Romantic poetry's 'resistance to objectification'. Byron's 'strength', in Christensen's reading, is his
'sporadic disruption' of the marketable commodity, 'Byron', 'the collaborative
invention of a gifted poet, a canny publisher, eager reviewers, and rapt readers':
in *Don Juan* the disruption becomes a sustained ethical tactic.[27] Christensen's
argument is dense, often difficult; the extract below, focusing on the shipwreck
episode, particularly the killing of Pedrillo, Juan's tutor, in canto II, demonstrates the tactic that he posits.

Extract from Jerome Christensen, *Lord Byron's Strength: Romantic Writing and Commercial Society* (1993)

The Circumstantial Gravity of *Don Juan*

> . . . *my own natural propensity to discrepancy and litigation*
> Lord Byron to John Cam Hobhouse, August 8, 1820

The Juan Effect

I expropriate the term *Juan effect* from Jerome J. McGann's discussion of the poem's style in his pathbreaking '*Don Juan' in Context*. McGann identifies this effect with 'Byron's Romantic Irony, properly so-called' and grounds it in the 'conflict between the poem's two most important styles,' the Juvenalian sublime and the Horatian conversational mode.[1] Unlike McGann, I do not believe in the existence of anything like 'Byron's Romantic Irony,' and I distrust the reification involved in the distillation of two dialectical styles out of the heterogeneous ferment of the poem. My interest here as throughout is in the strength of Lord Byron's poetry. As I have rendered it thus far, that strength has been roughly apportioned to the difference that the adjective *Lord* makes to *Byron*. Up to this point I have represented Lord Byron's strength as manifest in the sporadic disruptions of the smooth operation of a literary system called Byronism (of which contemporary Byron criticism inside and outside the academy is the heir), which programmatically translates poetic deeds into reflexively complicated, serially elaborated images of the poet available for imitation and consumption. Broadly characterized, the *Juan* effect involves the transformation of spasms into tactics. With *Juan* Lord Byron's strength achieves an ethical dimension. The realization of an ethics of strength is a textual phenomenon: a benchmark for Lord Byron was, as we shall see, his final break with the covering cherub of his bookseller and his virtuous commitment to continue publication of *Juan* 'though it were to destroy fame and profit at once'.[2]

The *Juan* effect jettisons not only John Murray but also 'Lord Byron' as the kind of subject that McGann imagines: a humanistic poet who is the master strategist of his poem, who thematizes contingency and pays lip service to the 'god circumstance,' but who, ironically, occupies a standing place of transcendental freedom outside the 'array' from which he, designing agent, can artfully dispose accident, contingency, and circumstance to the greater glory of Byron, 'properly so-called.' In my reading the unfolding of *Juan* is fully circumstantial, subject to no master plan. I try to avoid the kind of objectification of poem, poet, and historical period implicit in the notion of '*Don Juan in* Context.' A spectral title for the following three chapters (let it hover between life and death) that would indicate my goal, which is to revive the unsubjected, ethically vital circumstantiality of *Juan*, might be '*Don Juan as* Context.' Believe me, on the distinction between *in* and *as* rests the difference between an ironical book and a revolutionary text. [. . .]

Juan's Nautical Existence

[. . .] Letters, as the experiences of both Donna Julia and the *British Review*'s critic show, may come to bad ends. His simply vanishes. Hers suffers a more complicated fate. Donna Julia's letter concludes thus:

> 'I have no more to say, but linger still,
>   And dare not set my seal upon this sheet,
> And yet I may as well the task fulfil,
>   My misery can scarce be more complete:
> I had not lived till now, could sorrow kill;
>   Death shuns the wretch who fain the blow would meet,
> And I must even survive this last adieu,
> And bear with life to love and pray for you!'
>
> This note was written upon gilt-edged paper
>   With a neat little crow-quill, slight and new;
> Her small white hand could hardly reach the taper,
>   It trembled as magnetic needles do,
> And yet she did not let one tear escape her;
>   The seal a sun-flower; '*Elle vous suit partout*,'
> The motto, cut upon a white cornelian;
> The wax was superfine, its hue vermilion.
>
> (1:197–98)[3]

Julia ends with the acute sense of an ending. Her task completed, all that was figured by her character – her sentimentality, her beauty, her vanity – is conclusively literalized in her letter. But her exit is also the performance of a promise: she will follow you everywhere – she being the woman and *la lettre*, both of which are concentrated in the metaphor of the sunflower. If the seal is the material mark of fulfillment, the image of the sunflower is the sign that the seal, that which fulfills, is also a promise: the promise to trope. The sunflower tropes by virtue of its rootedness in the face of the revolving sun. It fulfills itself in life and letters as a symbol of mute, natural yearning.

But Julia's love is nothing like the sun. The promise to follow Juan everywhere depends on the old-fashioned conceit that *everywhere* is encompassed by a solar orbit, a cosmic revolution that makes *everywhere* the same and the passage through and around it frictionless and uneventful. There can in truth be no credible promise to follow everywhere under the sun because there is no *everywhere* there. *Everywhere* exists only at the level of the sun, just as *here* exists in mutual implication with that orbit and face at the point where the sunflower is rooted. Between the sun and the sunflower there is only an archipelago of turbulent *somewhere*s through which Juan sails, swims, and drifts. There is always some 'new one' under the sun. And Julia knows that. She has already lamented the ability of a man, unlike a woman and unlike the sun, to 'range' through disparate places – 'court, camp, church, the vessel, and the mart' – she knows only by name (1:194). Her last words to Juan in the bedroom scene had been, 'Fly, Juan, fly! for heaven's sake – not a word – / The door is open – you may yet slip through / The passage you so often have explored' (1:182) – a dark passage that neither woman nor sun can penetrate.

Julia is nothing like a sunflower. Nor, plainly, is her seal; it is the impression of a sunflower, one that marks the circumstantial writtenness of the letter. The condition of her following Juan anywhere is that she write and provide a substitute for her rooted presence that he can carry with him. And in order to make a last and lasting impression, she has to buy wax. Only because such commodities are available (and because she has the money to buy them) can Julia figure her love, turn it into the gilt-edged commodity that she hopes will captivate Juan. If she is effective, it is Juan, of course, who will turn to her letter, as if, in its 'hue vermilion,' the seal that fulfills and continually promises were the blood-red sun suspended on the horizon and he the yearning flower. Comprising sunflower and sun, Julia's contrivance answers to the Haroldian, imperial dream of the book as a comprehensive and fully intelligible structuring structure – a continual troping referring to and contained by the orbit of the light that englobes us.

But Julia's letter is nothing like a book. The world is the realm where pretenses perish, correspondences fail, and seals are made to be broken – a place illuminated by an 'indecent sun' (1:63). Julia's attempt to seal Juan's future, like his mother's and the poet's, goes awry; the shipwreck episode realizes the nightmare of uncertain, all too fungible paper. Unluckily, Julia's letter becomes the very token of chance:

And when his comrade's thought each sufferer knew,
  'Twas but his own, suppress'd till now, he found:
And out they spoke of lots of flesh and blood,
And who should die to be his fellow's food.

But ere they came to this, they that day shared
  Some leathern caps, and what remain'd of shoes;
And then they look'd around them, and despair'd,
  And one to be the sacrifice would choose;
At length the lots were torn up, and prepared,
  But of materials that must shock the Muse –
Having no paper, for the want of better,
They took by force from Juan Julia's letter.

Then lots were made, and mark'd, and mix'd, and handed
  In silent horror, and their distribution
Lull'd even the savage hunger which demanded,
  Like the Promethean vulture, this pollution;
None in particular had sought or plann'd it,
  'Twas nature gnaw'd them to this resolution,
By which none were permitted to be neuter –
And the whole lot fell on Juan's luckless tutor.

                                  (2:73–75)

The marked lot replaces the waxen sunflower. It seals the fate of Pedrillo, whose lot it is, like Julia's, to become a hostage to man's existence:

He but requested to be bled to death:
  The surgeon had his instruments, and bled
Pedrillo, and so gently ebb'd his breath,
  You hardly could perceive when he was dead.
                            (2:76)

Julia is immured so that Juan may 'range'; Pedrillo is killed so that the crew may survive. The letter of promise is 'fragmentized' into the lot of sacrifice that will supposedly save the group – all these men know of society and all they need to know – from destruction. But this fragmentation becomes the image and instrument of social disintegration. Just as the seal is broken and the letter torn, so even the punctuality of the lot itself, which singles out the man of edible parts, is shattered by the convulsions of the men who, like reviewers of immoral verse, digest what degrades them into demons:

The consequence was awful in the extreme;
  For they, who were most ravenous in the act,

Went raging mad – Lord! how they did blaspheme.
And foam, and roll, with strange convulsions rack'd,
   Drinking salt-water like a mountain-stream;
Tearing, and grinning, howling, screeching, swearing,
And, with hyaena-laughter, died despairing.

(2:79)

What moral might fit this sequence of outrageous events? Perhaps *cherchez la femme.*[4] Why not blame Julia for trying to turn literary license into literal control? From a certain distance (a few nautical miles) Julia's letter looks like one of those 'oddities let loose' by a woman intent to 'show [her] parts' (1:128) and by that display of the literal female to lure or horrify the targeted male. 'Power sways but by division' may be the Orientalist credo by which Julia governs her conduct, but here a ghastly fragmentation undoes her vainly prostituted pretense to power. The female part finds its ironically appropriate 'mart' in the longboat, where the part is parted again in order to separate the survivors into the disparate eaters and the dismembered eaten. The letter – its pathos and its promise – leaves no trace on the trackless sea. Although blaming Julia is convenient, the misogynistic interpretation translates into the nihilistic and absurd moral that Julia ought to have realized that her letter could not execute her intent, and that she should therefore have abstained from writing. The moral is nihilistic because it implies that instead of making a mistake Julia should have restrained herself from doing anything at all. The moral is absurd because it assumes that nothing could in fact be done – that someone can avoid making mistakes by the exercise of a prudence that, *Don Juan* teaches, is no less a venture in control and no less futile than the epistolary gesture.

There is an alternative, more worldly lesson: instead of writing a letter that dreamed of being a book, Julia should have written the book. Instead of sending her sentiment off to its singular death, Julia should have had it printed in many copies so that if one perished others would have survived. And instead of using the antiquated and fragile seal, she should have registered a copyright under the law. Julia should have written a book (it is implied that the choice was within the range of her vanities when we are informed that the narrator is working from a copy) like the ironic poet, whose condescension to her has less the air of a philosopher to an acolyte than of a career-wise, successful author to an improvident hack.

That moral, however, is even less respectable than nihilism. For the fate of Byron's book is not materially different from that suffered by Julia's letter, despite his prudent efforts to protect the young *Juan* from the perils of natural history.[5] Lord Byron chose to publish *Don Juan* anonymously, largely because he feared, with the judgment against Shelley in Chancery vividly in mind, that a prosecution for blasphemy would result in the loss of paternal rights to his child. If Byron were to avow *Juan* it would prove him to be a bad father, not only as blasphemer but as one who preferred the product of his pen to the fruit of his loins.[6] And so the first two cantos of *Juan* appeared without the 'passport to celebrity' of Byron's name.[7] The omission could be considered a mere technicality. Anonymity did not entail a repudiation of authorship. The veteran of the literary market knows that what makes books is not the name impressed on the title page but the power and right to copy. 'Byron' had been formed in intimate collaboration between the poet and his publisher. Apprehensive about the tendency of *Juan*, Murray, with all due respect, reminded his lordship, 'My name is connected to your fame.' Reversed, that proposition is equally plausible and considerably less humble: the integrity and authenticity of 'Byron' depended on the willingness of Murray's publishing house to own him.[8] Hence although Lord Byron's anonymity scarcely mattered, it was truly something new under the sun when *Don Juan* appeared in print without the publisher's name, a masterless poem.

The perpetration of this prodigy had the consequence of opening up an interspersed vacancy of law when *Don Juan* seemed to belong to no one. If like a freak it appeared to the *British Critic*, then like manna from heaven it befell the many publishers who made their living pirating bestsellers, and like the loaves and fishes it multiplied in their hands. Murray found himself in a ticklish position, losing money on a morally obnoxious poem that was a success in large part because of his refusal to admit he owned it. He sought legal advice as to whether a request for an injunction against the pirates would succeed or whether, as in the notorious case of the recent unauthorized publication of Southey's youthful, incendiary *Wat Tyler* (1794), the court would adjudge the poem either blasphemous or seditious and therefore beyond the protection of copyright. Murray's interests were mixed. Although he was eager to prevent the pirates from enriching themselves at his expense, his communications with his attorney show that he was, if anything, more intent on stopping Byron from writing any more shameful cantos of *Don Juan*. Here is the strategic analysis of Murray's lawyer, Sharon Turner:

> On 'Don Juan' I have much apprehension. . . . The evil, if not stopped, will be great. It will circulate in a cheap form very extensively, injuring society wherever it spreads. Yet one consideration strikes me. You could wish Lord Byron to write less objectionably. You may also wish him to return you part of the £1625. If the Chancellor should dissolve the injunction on this ground,

that will show Lord B. that he must expect no more copyright money for such things, and that they are too bad for law to uphold. Will not this affect the mind and purify his pen? It is true that to get this good result you must encounter the risk and expense of the injunction and of the argument upon it. Will you do this? . . . Perhaps nothing but the Court treating him as it treated Southey may sufficiently impress Lord B.[9]

Turner's letter nicely shows how, for Murray, the impulses of money and morals split. Only what Brougham called the 'view of the law' could weld those interests together into a rhetoric potent enough to do what legions of reviewers had failed to achieve, induce Byron to 'purify his pen.' Turner does not have any particular legal formula in mind; instead, he banks on the power of an adverse judgment to degrade Byron to the level of Southey. In Turner's eyes Murray enjoys a win-win situation: if the publisher loses his appeal for an injunction (which seems the attorney's preference), he can hope to get his money back and deter Byron from his ruinous course. If the injunction is sustained, he increases profits secured by judicial confirmation that the poem is not seriously objectionable at all. In this case the punitive publisher seeks to turn the weapon of copyright against a stubbornly delinquent writer. By this reasoning Lord Byron has no more relation to his book than the next man. Indeed, for Murray the publisher, Byron the copyrighted author is always in danger of being degraded by that roguish lord – now identified by the title *Don Juan* – who *will* write as he pleases and whose best effects may be described as picaresque, as criminal thefts from the 'author' whose work lawfully belongs to Murray.

First surprised by the report of a Mr. Shadwell who augured that 'the passages are not of such a nature as to overturn the property of it,' Turner was startled again by the consistent support given to Murray's claims by judges at Chancery:

[Shadwell's] decided tone that the Court will not let the copyright be invaded has much struck me. . . . His general opinions are also not favourable to Lord B., and his taste is highly moral. Yet, though he disapproves of the passages, he is remarkably sanguine that they do not furnish sufficient ground for the Chancellor to dissolve the injunction. He says the passages are not more amatory than those of many books of which the copyright was never doubted. He added that one great tendency of the book was not an unfair one. It was to show in Don Juan's ultimate character the ill effect of that injudicious maternal education which Don Juan is represented as having received, and which had operated injuriously upon his mind. He repeated to me several times that, as far as it was possible to foresee an event, he could not doubt of this.[10]

Shadwell gives the view of the law in all its majestic purity. Observe how the question of copyright has become, by the most natural contraction in the world, the question of property rights itself: Byron's poetry maintains its property rights as long as it does not overturn property rights. The tautology defines what in the view of the law would constitute a revolutionary poem: a poem that overturned its *own* property rights – an act, however, that is by definition subject to the determination of the law. The tautology falls squarely within the grand tradition of British counterrevolutionary discourse, which dictates that what is revolution is subject to determination by British law.

The Murrayan connection between revolutionary and pirate hinges on Murray's mistaken and narcissistic notion that he is the master of the poem and that a challenge to this propertied dignity and right subverts the order of things. The law, however, pronounces the truth that *Don Juan* continually proves: the right of property in liberal society is superior to the right of any individual to that property (even pirates, as Byron shows in the person of Lambro, labor to the greater glory of property right). Property right depends on mastery, but as in the exemplary case of the 'British,' it is a mastery disintegrative of human capacity – the master, like the power that drives James Tilly Matthews's air loom, like capital 'itself,' is always elsewhere. By sustaining the injunction, the law protects Murray from the effect of his own outrage. The interest of property in general forces him to own that thing he would rather be without. As his subsequent behavior shows, however, this 'win' did not feel like a victory. Murray, who has already been put in the unseemly position of 'pirating' a book he owns, is further degraded by the ratification of his connection with what he feels to be immoral. The publisher has to go on publishing; reviewers have to go on reviewing. The condition of his preeminence and wealth, Murray's subjection is also characteristic of every reader of *Don Juan* who answers to the name 'British.'

Yet the view of the law is itself circumstanced. Chancery no more has the panoptic oversight of Benthamite fantasy than did Justice Ellenborough in the trials of William Hone.[11] Something escapes the gaze of the law, and for the simple reason that texts must be read rather than viewed. In his various consultations Turner had better luck securing judicial opinions of *Don Juan* than attracting critical attention to it. And although Shadwell read more carefully than some, it seems unlikely that he read to the end of canto 1. By approving the satire of Donna Inez in its general tendency (an approval shared by most male critics since), Shadwell focused on the single particular that speaks to him and, he predicts, will speak to the judges because it encourages them to affirm the wisdom of their own judicial policy in contrast with her 'injudicious instruction.' But where lies the difference? Despite their sensitivity to precedent, the judges of Chancery are no more believers in natural history than Donna Inez – despite adjustments, the right of property remains an ahistorical constant and repression the rule. The difference lies not in ends or even in standards but in the discretion by which repression is conducted. If the judges have learned anything from Donna Inez, they have learned what they *must* have already known for the satire to be perceptible, that repression cannot succeed if injudiciously applied. It does not pay to get too worked up about every amatory passage.

Despite their vigilance the judges did not notice that somewhere along the way in canto 1 Donna Inez learns the same thing. Moreover, she uses her knowledge expertly to manipulate Julia into her catastrophe (1:101). Inez does judiciously maintain and aggrandize her property, although she does so at the cost of eliminating the one source of accident that could revive hidalgo blood and open her culture to the future. Donna Inez's success maximizes Inez, but it also consigns Spain to the fate of remaining Spain. Neither her policy nor its 'ultimate character' instructs the judges, who, like precocious children, reject the 'maternal' quality of her instruction while blindly sharing its ideological import. The full implications of her method, even at its most judicious, are hidden by the sign of her gender, which turns judges inadvertent. By not censoring Byron for blasphemy, the judges vindicate those 'blasphemies directed against the woman/mother (*mère*)' that season a commercialist discourse interested in what Michel de Certeau calls the general 'fading away of the "land" that guarantees language.'[12] At this level, then, there is a community of interests between Byronic satire and the imperial scheme. And this propriety disarms judges who, however rational in their skepticism of the contaminatory hypothesis that Sharon Turner embraces, are cozened by the poem every bit as much as the *British* – flattered into blindness toward the parody of the ten commandments near the end of canto 1 (sufficient to haul Hone into court) and toward the revolutionary implications of the 'dream of ocean (*mer*)' that Lord Byron floats.

Perhaps the most salient consequence of the Chancery opinion was not the specific judgment but the proof that a book is subject to the vagaries of judgment, and thus ultimately no more secure than a letter. Any supposed superiority of Byron to either Julia or Southey is therefore misconceived. The transformation of Julia's letter represents in the most lurid terms the potential fate awaiting any publication despite its protection by the taboo of copyright. For the lesson that Byron continues to learn is that taboos (eating or penetrating the wrong object) are, like waxen seals, made to be broken in one convenient extremity or another.

No copyright can save the book from the depredations of pirates or publishers or from being cut up into brief extracts to be chewed over by the hungry savages of the culture industry. By the same token the fragmentation of the book that Byron fears – that his cantos will be mutilated into 'canticles'[13] and that his pages will end up lining portmanteaus or wrapping fishes – would not mean the annihilation of its cultural effect. If *Don Juan* has any strength it is not as a book but as a text that lacks the propertied immunity conducive to the fantasy that it is the master of its fate.

Don Juan stages its own undoing in the shipwreck scene – the episode of the poem that particularly disgusts the reviewers. The shipwreck episode not only bloodlessly carries out the sentence of execution against Julia's letter, it mordantly represents the cannibalism that occurs as the reviewers – slaves to an unspeakable appetite that masters all aspirations to a civilized integrity, men who consume men – touch what they know should not be touched; and it represents also the way the dead thing indecently touches back, the way it, shall we say, *publishes* convulsions among the custodians of culture.

It would shock reason to claim that Julia's letter necessitated cannibalism, as if the letter were a cue ball propelled into the innocent equilibrium of the rack. If the letter could be held responsible, it would be not a letter but the ideal book – forever unshredded, forever sealed – of which it dreams. The shipwreck episode represents the letter as a *virtual* rather than an efficient cause, as the material occasion for the lots that, when re-marked and cast, designate the sacrificial victim. Even so, even torn into bits and crudely re-marked, the letter enacts a strangely *Juan*-esque economy: a thing is torn apart, the seal does not hold, but there is a conservation, even an augmentation of rhetorical force. Pedrillo's unhesitating acceptance of his lot poignantly exemplifies this tropism. Here is a man who fully believes what he knows is a fiction and willingly dies for his faith. Why?

To the Enlightenment mind impatient of explanations that smack of 'superstition' it might appear that Pedrillo dies from a creditable excess of civility, for in resigning himself to death he can be said to follow through on a contract to which he had deliberately, if implicitly, subscribed. Framed *in extremis*, that agreement is an exemplary version of the social contract: both for the particular reason that the compact is devised in order to secure the life of individuals and the harmony of the group; and for the general reason that it entails the dutiful recognition by an individual that he is an individual, *one*, by virtue of his installation in an abstract system of relations – a network, that is, of enumerated and allotable 'ones.' But even for the contractarian model, consequences count. How can a contract be social if it prescribes a cannibalism destructive of the anthropological basis of the society it is framed to preserve? How can a contract be valid that engages a party to commit a crime, whether that crime be described as suicide or as contributing to the chewing of a tutor? Under the circumstances, the hypothetical contract supposed to explain Pedrillo's acquiescence is seriously flawed. Restoring the pretense of a contract would require pushing the actual contract ever farther back, inevitably disclosing at the end of the line of hypothetical contracts the threat of violence: the proverbial loaded gun. Hence we must conclude either that Pedrillo's fate gives the Hobbesian lie to every story about the nature of contracts and of society (that they are freely entered into, that they involve an exchange of benefits as well as liabilities, that formalized social exchange presupposes the interdiction of savage physical violence), or that there is no contract operating here.

Those options come to the same thing for the Humean empiricist, who would happily take the point of the satire, call our attention to the absence of any detectable threat of violence, and cheerfully abandon the contractarian thesis for a theory of indirect force as the effect of what Hume identifies as the social composition. The social composition – a regulated, lawful prototype of *Juan*'s circumstantial gravity – is that preponderant mass of reasons that inducts the naturally incapacitated, atomized individual into a belief system that invariably precedes him. Because from the perspective of enlightenment, confirmation of one's individuality is necessarily the recognition of a self in systematic relation to others, one cannot talk of an instinct of individual preservation distinct from the preservation of society. And because there can be no individuation without society (so runs the stoical variant of the argument), there is in certain extremities (and the shipwreck surely is one) no contradiction between saving one's self (the belief system that is my always social self) and suicide. Indeed, conceived historically, from an aristocratic perspective, Humean selving, which composes a society of beings possessed of no intrinsic power or value, *is* suicide. Thus for the Humean, no loaded gun lodges in Byron's narrative because no loaded gun is necessary. The Hobbesian pistol secreted in the contractarian model is disassembled and redistributed as a compulsion that is as pervasive, impersonal, and irresistible as Newtonian gravity.[14]

But if the Humean scheme can account for the absence of a contract by the prevailing inductive force of a precedent social compulsion – the discursive, rationalized counterpart of what the poet calls the 'gnaw of nature' – it cannot explain the contingency that triggers this particular action: the fall of the lot on Pedrillo. Pedrillo is not impelled but lured to his death by his recognition of 'his' lot, which names him by a chance he takes to be his lawful destiny. Pedrillo, then, is induced *by* as well as inducted *to* his fate; the rhetorical supplements the mechanical as historicity intervenes on the social formation.

Assessing how the nominal assumes such force is no easy matter. The poet indicates that each crew member has his own mark but does not specify whether each man inscribes each piece of paper himself or whether the marks are made and assigned by one (supervisory? sovereign?) member of the group. The poet can afford to be unclear because in practice the maker of the mark makes no difference. The mark is merely functional: nothing more than the convenient pretext for identifying a victim for the group whose survival seems to demand that someone be killed. Pedrillo's death occurs as a result of his identification of himself with the mark on the lot. Just as the elision of the marking avoids the necessity for representing a messy and potentially protracted conflict (Who gets to make the marks? Assign them? Toss them? Determine misfires?) that might put off the business of sacrifice indefinitely, so Pedrillo's identification of himself by the lot presupposes that he forget the ineradicably arbitrary deed of marking (whether by himself or another) and in doing so relinquish the memory of being *one who has the right to mark* rather than one who must suffer the fate of being named. In order to be sacrificed, he must surrender the memory (call it the trace of a primordial democracy) that he becomes one who has the right to mark before he is one invested with the authority to sign.

Thomas Moore's charge that in writing *Don Juan* the exiled Lord Byron seems 'to have forgotten that standard of decorum in society, to which every one must refer his *words* at least, who hopes to be either listened to or read by the world' might be answered by this passage, which makes killingly clear the forgetfulness of the political act of institution embedded in the social avowal of a standard of decorum.[15] The inscriptive deed is forgotten in the crediting of an always transcendental authorship that invests the apparition of the mark with an indicative power that is unfailingly divinatory: 'As you have a name,' it promises, 'so you will die.'[16] Such is the judgment of Cain as Byron dramatizes it. For everyone on whom the lot falls – for Pedrillo as for Cain as for 'the British' – the assigned mark is (mis)recognized as my authorizing signature and every signature appears authoritatively assigned. We can follow Hume so far and agree that the lot is not a contract; thus its application is not subject to litigation. But that enlightened discrimination serves the cause of mystery by entailing the suppression of the rhetorico-historical contingency with which social compulsion befalls 'one.' The lot here stands for that fetishized 'determination' to which empiricists of all stripes resort in order to rescue their models of society from terminal inanition. In practice the lot functions as a portent that announces the future as already known, which in commercial society means *signed for*. As portent the lot effectively lays claim to Pedrillo's recognition of its authority to deal his death – lays claim to what liberalism calls his consent – and lays claim to that recognition as the very condition of his property in himself. The portent of death is the apparition of the signature.

Or so I conjecture, prompted by the elision of Pedrillo's actual consent, which is as unrepresented as Julia's physical acquiescence to Juan. Unrepresented, not unreadable. Indeed, the lacuna in the narrative is the legible sign of the repression of reading that makes Pedrillo's consent appear natural. Another look at stanza 76 will help explain what I mean. There the elision of consent reverberates in the curious doubling of the moment of death. Here is the stanza entire:

> He but requested to be bled to death:
>   The surgeon had his instruments, and bled
> Pedrillo, and so gently ebb'd his breath,
>   You hardly could perceive when he was dead.
> He died as born, a Catholic in faith,
>   Like most in the belief in which they're bred,
> And first a little crucifix he kiss'd,
> And then held out his jugular and wrist.
>
>   (2:76)

The first half of the stanza pretends that nothing extraordinary has happened. First the lot, then the death – it is as though Pedrillo's consent were in the course of nature, like cannibalism. But if nature did indeed have a course, casting lots to determine the future would be unnecessary, a parlor game on a longboat. It is because even at the limit of human existence passage from one incommensurable moment or (to use the textual metaphor deployed by Jean-François Lyotard in *The Differend*) one 'phrase' to another is radically contingent, that lots are cast, thus stabilizing contingency and mooting ethical choice by indulging in the ritual of chance. The second half of the stanza returns to the same gap and kills Pedrillo again in the process of contextualizing a consent that still smacks of the bizarre: it's the sort of thing a Catholic would do. By being derived from a community of belief Pedrillo's act becomes explicable and, not incidentally, more pointedly satirical. As his sacrifice takes on the pattern of Christ's, it invites a disagreeable reflection on the cannibal feast as a commemoration in letter and spirit of the Last Supper.

More significantly, however, the lines supplant the invigorating heathenish cross of blood, which Julia's irrepressible sexuality embodied, with the sacred image of the one true cross. The cross is the sign of the symbol, of the capacity of an object (or image as object) to bring together (coordinate/join/interfuse) two divergent axes of signification or being. As featured here (compare the Celtic cross in Hobhouse's notes to *Childe Harold IV*), the cross symbolizes the need for a symbol, of some talismanic image of crossing – be it from earth to heaven, man to god, or present to future – that will induce little Peter to give up his narcissistic attachment to his unitary body image and allow himself to be cut off and cut up, departing this world as if crossing from the imaginary to the symbolic. But the failure of the letter of the cross to guarantee the promised crossing to the symbolic is figured by the affixed image of the dying man-god (a grotesque variant of the narrator's tactical interjection of 'Oh Plato, Plato!'). The pathetic image of the man confers charm on the symbol by representing self-sacrifice as pious imitation. The crucifix sutures the here and the hereafter, the imaginary and the symbolic; its naked solicitation of a fit of mimesis professes that one can have one's body and be eaten too.[17]

What exactly Pedrillo had in mind is beyond my ken. But we can infer from the contexts that eddy out from the elided moment of consent that his consent must be inferred precisely because no such moment ever punctually arrived. Pedrillo 'consents' when everything appears already decided. Considered as political allegory, Pedrillo's fate implies that the consent of the governed that legitimates the regime can be constructed by the regime from the superstitious misrecognition of consent *by* the governed as something that comes along or befalls them rather than as some event involving their own assertion.[18] What, at our remove, we can discern in the narrative discrepancy is what Pedrillo, disabled by intimacy, failed to read: *there is nothing but context* for his choice. That lot, which he mistakes as a fact, is nothing other than a clot of circumstantial gravity, a highly condensed bunch of context, which may be misrecognized as a determination but which, read at a run or at a walk, might have been a pretext for improvisation – a pretext, that is, for the Romantic performance we associate with the name of Sheherazade or Laurence Sterne or Lord Byron. Such improvisation should not be considered as the postponement of the moment of decision that must come – such is the closural logic proper to the theater and to the novel – but as the continual renewing of decisions that defer the decided. Indeed, if we consult the Romantic performances of Wordsworth or De Quincey, the reading itself may enact that deferral. 'Give me a minute,' says the little Peter of *The Prelude* (knowing a minute is as good as a lifetime), 'to read that lot' (called 'talent' or 'ministration' or 'murmur') 'to meditate if it is the one I made or the one made for me.' Pedrillo dies (blame him not: it is a malady that at one time or another afflicts us all) of empiricism. Or, to phrase it in a manner less flagrantly Romantic, he dies from the failure of what Hans Blumenberg calls self-assertion: 'Self-assertion does not mean the naked biological and economic preservation of the human organism by the means naturally available to it [say, by eating one's neighbor]. It means an existential program, according to which man posits his existence in a historical situation and indicates to himself how he is going to deal with the reality surrounding him and what use he will make of the possibilities that are open to him.'[19]

Notes

1   Jerome J. McGann, *'Don Juan' in Context*, 83. Other works of criticism on *Don Juan* that have been broadly useful in the formation of my approach to the poem are Frederick L. Beaty, *Byron the Satirist*; Leslie Brisman, *Romantic Origins* (Ithaca: Cornell Univ. Press, 1978); Michael Cooke, *Acts of Inclusion* (New Haven: Yale Univ. Press, 1979); Frederick Garber, *Self, Text, and Romantic Irony: The Example of Byron*; Robert F. Gleckner, 'From Selfish Spleen to Equanimity: Byron's Satires,' *Studies in Romanticism* 18 (Summer 1979): 173–206; M. K. Joseph, *Byron the Poet*; and George M. Ridenour, *The Style of Don Juan*.

2   *Byron's Letters and Journals* X. 126.

3   [All references to *Don Juan* are by canto and line number.]

4   Or *cherchez le sodomite*. In a lecture entitled 'Cannibalism, the Grand Tour, and Literary History' delivered at Johns Hopkins University in September 1991, George S. Rousseau elaborated the affiliations in the eighteenth century between two discourses of the unspeakable, cannibalism and sodomy. Although Rousseau did not refer to *Don Juan*, clearly the connection he delineated contributed to the sense of outrage of those men who, reading the shipwreck scene of canto 2, could not help believing that the horrible picture of men consuming parts of men accurately represented their social practice as the deformed expression of repressed desire. For another moral, see Andrew Cooper's discussion of this passage in *Doubt and Identity in Romantic Poetry* (New Haven: Yale Univ. Press, 1988), pp. 130–49.

5   In the best commentary on Donna Julia's letter, Lawrence Lipking analyzes the identification of Lord Byron with Donna Julia (*Abandoned Women and Poetic Tradition* [Chicago: Univ. of Chicago Press, 1988], pp. 41–7).

6   Advising Murray of his decision to publish anonymously, he wrote, 'Now I prefer my child to a poem at any time – and so should you as having half a dozen' (*Byron's Letters and Journals* 7:196).

7   *Romantics Reviewed*, Part B, II. 981.

8   Leslie A. Marchand, *Byron: A Biography*, 2:830.

9   Samuel Smiles, *A Publisher and His Friends: Memoir and Correspondence of the Late John Murray*, 2 vols. (London: Murray, 1891), 1:405–6.

10 Ibid., pp. 407–9.

11 [See *Lord Byron's Strength*, 95–6, 132–5.]

12 Michel de Certeau, 'The Arts of Dying: Celibatory Machines,' in *Heterologies: Discourse on the Other*, trans. Brian Mussumi (Minneapolis: Univ. of Minnesota Press, 1986), p. 161. In some places and in some times this fade is more pronounced than others. It is, of course, most particularly advanced in England's commercialist society and most dramatic at the end of the Napoleonic Wars when the greatest land army the world had ever known was defeated by an island empire.

13 Marchand, *Byron* 2:770.

14 For a discussion of the Humean theme and strategy of social composition, see Jerome Christensen, *Practicing Enlightenment: Hume and the Formation of a Literary Career* (Madison: Univ. of Wisconsin Press, 1987), pp. 21–44.

15 *Journal of Thomas Moore*, ed. Wilfred S. Dawden, 2 vols. (Newark: Univ. of Delaware Press, 1983), 1:137.

16 *Cain* tells this story by dramatizing the discrepant biblical account of the remembering of this forgetting.

17 Cf. Kant: 'Taste that requires an added element of charm and emotion for its delight, not to speak of adopting this as the measure of its approval, has not yet emerged from barbarism' (*Critique of Judgment*, quoted in Pierre Bourdieu, *Distinction: A Social Critique of the Judgment of Taste*, trans. Richard Nice [Cambridge, Mass.: Harvard Univ. Press, 1984], 43).

18 See Terry Eagleton's discussion of the transformation of the proportions between coercion and consent that accompanied the 'growth of early bourgeois society' in *The Ideology of the Aesthetic* (Oxford: Basil Blackwell, 1990), p. 23. For another critical look at the question of consent in liberal theory, see Carole Pateman, *The Problem of Political Obligation: A Critique of Liberal Theory* (1979; rpt. Cambridge: Polity, 1985).

19 Hans Blumenberg, *The Legitimacy of the Modern Age*, trans. Robert M. Wallace (Cambridge, Mass.: MIT Press, 1983), 189.

Further reading

A rough and ready distinction, of 'historicizing' from 'canonizing' criticism, might be drawn between this list and the preceding one, although close up such a distinction is hardly absolute or fully sustainable. Instanced here are some of the major studies from about the mid-1980s to the present, engaging partly or wholly with the broadly political aspects of Byron's work, his self-fashioning, and his relationship with his audience. Associated topics include gender (see, for instance, Franklin, Haslett, Donelan) and Orientalism (see, especially, Garber, Leask, Sharafuddin, Butler's essays in the Beatty and Newey and Rutherford collections, and Ogden).

Philip W. Martin, *Byron: A Poet before his Public* (Cambridge: Cambridge University Press, 1982). Lively critique, questioning Byron's canonical standing by presenting his poetry as 'written without serious intent', differing from the poetry of the other major romantics as 'a consciously produced artefact designed for the appeasement of a particular audience' whom, at the same time, the poet holds in contempt. Martin departs from the traditional developmental view of Byron's poetry by tracing the same poetic consciousness from the earlier works to *Don Juan*.

Charles E. Robinson (ed.), *Lord Byron and his Contemporaries: Essays from the Sixth International Byron Seminar* (Newark: University of Delaware Press, 1982). Useful, readable essays, covering both 'Byron's pivotal role among English writers' and his 'presence in continental life and letters.'

J. Drummond Bone, 'The Rhetoric of Freedom' in *Byron: Wrath and Rhyme*, ed. A. Bold (London: Vision, 1983), 166–85. Byron's definition of freedom is by negation, as the rejection of restraint; his 'concept of the free hero . . . has both development and inconsistency, and these are both produced by and help to condition the rhetoric of his poetry.'

Jerome J. McGann, *The Romantic Ideology: A Critical Investigation* (Chicago and London: University of Chicago Press, 1983). Focuses on Byronic 'despair', to incorporate Byron into the general thesis of a romantic ideology that occludes the real world. As the reflex of an ideal attachment against which is measured the insufficiency of the actual, Byron's despair is 'the poetic [escapist] reflex of the social and historical realities it is a part of'.

*****Angus Calder**, *Byron* (Milton Keynes: Open University Press, 1987). Valuably succinct introduction to Byron's poetry and Byronism, with their literary, cultural, social and historical contexts.

Daniel P. Watkins, *Social Relations in Byron's Eastern Tales* (London and Toronto: Associated University Presses, 1987). The eastern tales formulate poetically the social pressures with which Byron contended; they expose 'the pervasive cultural attitudes, practices, and beliefs which, under certain circumstances, not only limit human independence, but . . . support reactionary and morally destitute political systems.'

Bernard Beatty and Vincent Newey (eds.), *Byron and the Limits of Fiction* (Liverpool: Liverpool University Press, 1988). Important collection, revitalizing Byron as a poet 'who blurs and yet disentangles the realms of fictional and historical life'. Includes new essays by Bernard Beatty (on religion), Marilyn Butler (on Orientalism) and Drummond Bone (on digression).

Frederick Garber, *Self, Text, and Romantic Irony: The Example of Byron* (Princeton: Princeton University Press, 1988). With Byron as its primary example, argues that the romantic ambivalence about the self's autonomy is central to the mutual emergence – competitive as well as supportive – of self and text, a 'paradoxical mutuality' that is a defining characteristic of romantic irony.

Karl Kroeber (ed.), *Studies in Romanticism* 27.4 (Winter 1988). Special issue, commemorating the bicentennial of Byron's birth, with important new essays on gender, politics and Byronic Prometheanism. The collection reflects the historical trend in Romantic studies: 'Each of these articles endeavors to place specific poems and passages within . . . the extra-aesthetic context . . . the dominant concern is the complexity of language.'

Frederick Shilstone, *Byron and the Myth of Tradition* (Lincoln and London: University of Nebraska Press, 1988). Charts, through what it calls a biography of the poet's consciousness, the conflict between tradition – the value systems of the past – and a modern ethic of the free and autonomous self. The development of that conflict, reaching a compromise of self and tradition, can be identified with the evolution of romantic irony, which thus manifests a transitional consciousness, exemplified by Byron.

Angus Calder (ed.), *Byron and Scotland: Radical or Dandy?* (Edinburgh: Edinburgh University Press, 1989). Essays by multiple contributors, examining topics such as politics and religion with reference to Byron's Scottish contexts.

Jerome J. McGann, *Towards a Literature of Knowledge* (Oxford: Clarendon Press, 1989). Byron's poetry, which displays its rhetoric of sincerity in poetic forms that are resistant to it – forms of communicative exchange with an explicitly imagined audience, rather than of (pretended) internal colloquy – executes an exposure or critique of Romantic sincerity.

Andrew Rutherford (ed.), *Byron: Augustan and Romantic* (Basingstoke and London: Macmillan, 1990). Essays by principal Byron scholars, reassessing, from the vantage-points of present-day criticism, Byron's relation to the two major traditions with which he is associated. Foci include politics, gender and Orientalism.

Wolf Z. Hirst (ed.), *Byron, the Bible, and Religion: Essays for the Twelfth International Byron Seminar* (London and Toronto: Associated University Presses, 1991). Essays by divers critics, constituting a useful survey of Byron's engagement with religion and his use of the Bible as a literary source. Tends to imply (cf. Beatty) that 'some religious sentiment pervades his work.'

Caroline Franklin, *Byron's Heroines* (Oxford: Clarendon Press, 1992). Historicizes Byron's patriarchalism by showing his female characters to be 'cultural constructs, emanating from the . . . debate in Regency Britain on the role of women'; their variety and range indicates an 'ongoing experimentation' related to 'contemporary ideologies of sexual difference'.

Richard Lansdown, *Byron's Historical Dramas* (Oxford: Clarendon Press, 1992). Like Corbett, Lansdown valuably redresses the neglect of Byron's dramas, discussing the 'three historical dramas in terms of . . . Regency drama; the question of historical self-consciousness; neo-classical dramatic form; and Byron's [ambiguous] relationship to Shakespeare's plays.'

Terence Allan Hoagwood, *Byron's Dialectic: Skepticism and the Critique of Culture* (London and Toronto: Associated University Presses, 1993). Locates Byron in a philosophical tradition of scepticism, arguing a revolutionary political engagement in his use of 'identifiable skeptical methods in a sustained critique, in prose and verse, of social and political formations.'

Nigel Wood (ed.), *Don Juan* (Theory in Practice series. Buckingham and Philadelphia: Open University Press, 1993). Range of theoretical approaches, feminist, psychoanalytical and Bakhtinian, to the key topics: Byron's politics, self-representation and relationship with the reader. The introduction by Nigel Wood is a useful and lucid overview.

Mohammed Sharafuddin, *Islam and Romantic Orientalism: Literary Encounters with the Orient* (London and New York: Tauris, 1994). Well-intentioned counter to Said, in the thesis of a 'realistic Orientalism': a real recognition of, and respect for, Islam produced from the escapist Orientalist impulse in particular romantic texts. In Byron's tales, Islam plays a 'full part as *itself*', his direct experience of the Orient granting to it 'a new degree of reality'.

Moyra Haslett, *Byron's* Don Juan *and the Don Juan Legend* (Oxford: Clarendon Press, 1997). *Don Juan* should be read as a version of the Don Juan legend, so as 'to uncover the debates – of sexual and class politics among others – within which Byron's poem was automatically implicated.'

Frances Wilson (ed.), *Byromania: Portraits of the Artist in Nineteenth- and Twentieth-Century Culture* (Basingstoke and London: Macmillan, 1999). The relation between Byron's self-conscious performance and his mythologizing by his audience is examined in diverse essays, which take varying views on Byron's participation in the making of the Byronic persona.

Charles Donelan, *Romanticism and Male Fantasy in Byron's* Don Juan*: A Marketable Vice* (Basingstoke and London: Macmillan, 2000). Maps, in *Don Juan*, a complex network of relations, between resistance to the state-sponsored evangelical censorship of popular culture, the commodification of male desire and the challenging of gender stereotypes.

Paul Elledge, *Lord Byron at Harrow School: Speaking Out, Talking Back, Acting Up, Bowing Out* (Baltimore and London: Johns Hopkins University Press, 2000). Identifies in Byron's Speech Day declamations in Harrow School, early versions of the performances 'subsequently refined and polished in the mature verse'. In Byron's Harrow years begins 'the elaborate mode and vogue of self-representation that partially, with his hefty patronage, helped to define the era.'

Caroline Franklin, *Byron: A Literary Life* (London: Macmillan, 2000). Presents Byron as a professional writer, engaged both with his audience and his publishers; with this focus, treats his social, political and cultural contexts, and his modifications of the generic and aesthetic traditions he inherited.

Daryl S. Ogden, 'Byron, Italy, and the Politics of Liberal Imperialism', *Keats–Shelley Journal* 49 (2000), 114–37. Usefully complexifies the issue of Byron's 'Orientalism' by presenting his conception of Italy 'as culturally hybrid, . . . *both* Oriental and Occidental'. Byron's response to Italy manifests an ideological conflict, between the European imperialist attitude to the Orient and its nationalist attitude to the Occident, and in so doing belies Said's thesis of the perception of an absolute distinction between Orient and Occident.

Andrew Elfenbein (ed.), *European Romantic Review* 12.3 (Summer 2001). Special issue on Byron and disability. Byron's 'status as perhaps the most famous disabled man of his day', is a new and fruitful point of departure in the essays collected here; the focal text is Byron's drama, *The Deformed Transformed*.

Jerome McGann, *Byron and Romanticism* (Cambridge: Cambridge University Press, 2002). Collection of essays spanning 25 years, and informed by McGann's experience as editor. The 'General analytical and historical introduction' asserts 'that textual theory and editorial practice were and had to be the foundation of all literary studies.'

Jane Stabler, *Byron, Poetics and History* (Cambridge: Cambridge University Press, 2002). Redressing the neglect of poetic form in some earlier historicist studies, combines a historical with a formal approach to present, in the disruptive (cf. Christensen) digressive modes of Byron's poetry, the shaping effect of his historical context and the response of his readers.

Stephen Cheeke, *Byron and Place: History, Translation, Nostalgia* (Basingstoke: Palgrave, 2003). Studies Byron's 'geo-historical' engagement: his response to the history of specific geographical locations, and his investment in the authority of his own experience ('being there' or 'having been there') in his positioning of himself in relation to places of historical significance in the different phases of his poetry.

*****J. Drummond Bone** (ed.), *The Cambridge Companion to Byron* (Cambridge: Cambridge University Press, 2005). Valuable collection of essays, informed by the best of modern scholarship. Covers a range of key topics to locate Byron and his work in their historical, textual and literary contexts.

Susan Oliver, *Scott, Byron and the Poetics of Cultural Encounter* (Basingstoke: Palgrave Macmillan, 2005). Comparative study of Byron's and Scott's treatments of otherness across borderlines or boundaries, focusing, in Byron's case, on the borders between Europe and the Islamic world in the first two cantos of *Childe Harold's Pilgrimage* and the Eastern tales.

Useful editions

The standard edition of Byron's poetry is *Lord Byron: The Complete Poetical Works*, ed. Jerome J. McGann and Barry Weller, 7 vols. (Oxford: Clarendon Press, 1980–93). The best edition for students is in the Oxford World's Classics series: *Lord Byron: The Major Works*, ed. Jerome J. McGann (Oxford: Oxford University Press, 2000).

Reference material

Leslie A. Marchand (ed.), *Byron's Letters and Journals.* Standard, complete edition.

Oscar José Santucho's and Clement Tyson Goode's *George Gordon, Lord Byron: A Comprehensive Bibliography of Secondary Materials in English, 1807–1974 with A Critical Review of Research* (Metuchen, N.J.: Scarecrow Press, 1977) and its continuation, Clement Tyson Goode's *George Gordon, Lord Byron: A Comprehensive Annotated Research Bibliography of Secondary Materials in English, 1973–1994* (Lanham and London: Scarecrow Press, 1997), together constitute the most exhaustive record available of the reception of Byron from his own time to the late twentieth century.

Chapter notes

1   ?, review of *Childe Harold's Pilgrimage* I–II, *Eclectic Review* viii (June 1812), 630. Reproduced in Donald Reiman (ed.), *The Romantics Reviewed, Part B: Byron and Regency Society Poets*, 5 vols. (New York and London: Garland, 1972), II. 705.

2   *Romantics Reviewed, Part B* is a comprehensive collection of the contemporary reviews. Other useful compilations are Andrew Rutherford (ed.), *Lord Byron: The Critical Heritage* (1970; repr. London: Routledge, 1995); Theodore Redpath, *The Young Romantics and Critical Opinion 1807–1824* (London: Harrap, 1973); John O. Hayden, *Romantic Bards and British Reviewers* (Lincoln and London: University of Nebraska Press, 1971).

3   Henry Brougham, review of *Hours in Idleness*, *Edinburgh Review* xi (Jan. 1808), 285–9 (*Romantics Reviewed, Part B*, II. 833–5).

4   ?, review of *Childe Harold's Pilgrimage* III and *The Prisoner of Chillon, and other Poems* (1816), *British Critic*, 2nd series vi (Dec. 1816), 609–10 (*Romantics Reviewed, Part B*, I. 266).

5   John Wilson, review of *Childe Harold's Pilgrimage* IV (1818), *Blackwood's Edinburgh Magazine* iii (May 1818), 216 (*Romantics Reviewed, Part B*, I. 128).

6   Walter Scott, review of *Childe Harold's Pilgrimage* IV, *Quarterly Review* xix (Apr. 1818), 217 (*Romantics Reviewed, Part B*, V. 2049).

7   Walter Scott, review of *Childe Harold's Pilgrimage* III, *Quarterly Review* xvi (Oct. 1816), 172–208 and review of *Childe Harold's Pilgrimage* IV, *Quarterly Review* xix (Apr. 1818), 215–32 (*Romantics Reviewed, Part B*, V. 2029–47, 2048–56).

8   See, for instance, the *British Critic*'s review, mentioned above, of *Childe Harold's Pilgrimage* III and *The Prisoner of Chillon*, 609, and John Gibson Lockhart's review of Byron's 1821 volume of tragedies (*Sardanapalus*, *The Two Foscari*, and *Cain*), *Blackwood's Edinburgh Magazine* xi (Jan. 1822), 92 (*Romantics Reviewed, Part B*, I. 266, 179).

9   ?, review of *Don Juan* I–II, *Blackwood's Edinburgh Magazine* v (Aug. 1819), 512 (*Romantics Reviewed, Part B*, I. 143).

10   ?, review of *Don Juan* I–II, *British Critic*, 2nd series xii (Aug. 1819), 202 (*Romantics Reviewed, Part B*, I. 299); review of *Don Juan* III–V, *British Critic*, 2nd series xvi (Sept. 1821), 252 (*Romantics Reviewed, Part B*, I. 308).

11   Reprinted in Andrew Rutherford (ed.), *Lord Byron: The Critical Heritage*, 183–4. See also Lockhart's review, 'ODoherty on Don Juan, Cantos IX. X. XI', *Blackwood's Edinburgh Magazine* xiv (Sept. 1823), 282–93, in which *Blackwood's* earlier unfavourable opinion is retracted (*Romantics Reviewed, Part B*, I. 210–21).

12   Francis Jeffrey, review of *Sardanapalus* etc., *Edinburgh Review* xxxvi (February 1822), 446 (*Romantics Reviewed, Part B*, II. 935). Jeffrey's numerous reviews, 1812–23, are always intelligent, but he and the *Edinburgh* pointedly ignored *Don Juan*.

13   ?, review of *Don Juan* VI–VIII (1823) *Monthly Magazine* lvi (September 1823), 112 (*Romantics Reviewed, Part B*, IV. 1705).

14   ?, review of *Don Juan* I–II, *New Monthly Magazine* xii (Aug. 1819), 77 (*Romantics Reviewed, Part B*, V. 1908). For a contrary position, lauding Byron's versatility in *Don Juan* I–II, see the review of *Mazeppa* (1819) and *Don Juan* I–II, *Monthly Review*, 2nd series lxxxix (July 1819), 314 (*Romantics Reviewed, Part B*, IV. 1798).

15   See for instance, John Matthews, review of *Sardanapalus* etc., *Blackwood's Edinburgh Magazine* xi (Feb. 1822), 212–17, esp. 213 (*Romantics Reviewed, Part B*, I. 180–5, 181), or the anonymous review of *Sardanapalus* etc., *British Critic*, 2nd series xvii (May 1822), 520–40 (*Romantics Reviewed, Part B*, I. 310–20). Prior to Southey, Jeffrey had described Childe Harold as a 'Satanic personage', because of his misanthropy and his religious opinions. See Francis Jeffrey, review of *Childe Harold's Pilgrimage* I–II, *Edinburgh Review* xix (February 1812), 466–7 (*Romantics Reviewed, Part B*, II. 836–7).

16   J. G. Lockhart, 'On the Cockney School of Poetry', *Blackwood's Edinburgh Magazine* ii (October 1817), 38–41. Reproduced in Donald Reiman (ed.), *The Romantics Reviewed, Part C: Shelley, Keats, and London Radical Writers*, 2 vols. (New York and London: Garland, 1972), I. 49–52. For the attribution of Cockneyism to Byron, see, for instance, John Wilson, review of *The Age of Bronze* (1823), and William Maginn and ?John Gibson Lockhart, review of *Don Juan* VI–VIII: *Blackwood's Edinburgh Magazine* xiii (April 1823), 457–60, and xiv (July 1823), 88–92 (*Romantics Reviewed, Part B*, I. 202–5 and 205–9). See also reviews of *The Island* (2nd ed., 1823), and *Don Juan* IX–XI: *British Critic*, 2nd series xx (July 1823), 16–22, and xx (Nov. 1823), 524–30 (*Romantics Reviewed, Part B*, I. 327–30 and 337–40).

17   See, for instance, John Wilson's review of *Childe Harold's Pilgrimage* IV (cited above, note 5), 218; the reviews of *Childe Harold's Pilgrimage* III and IV in the *Critical Review*, 5th series iv (Nov. 1816), 505, and iv (Dec. 1816), 568–9; Francis Jeffrey's review of *Childe Harold's Pilgrimage* III and *The Prisoner of Chillon*, *Edinburgh Review* xxvii (Dec. 1816), 277–8 (*Romantics Reviewed, Part B*, I. 130; II. 658, 659–60; II. 864–5).

18   Hazlitt, *Works*, xi. 69–78.

19   William Maginn and ?J. G. Lockhart, review of *Don Juan* VI–VIII, *Blackwood's Edinburgh Magazine* xiv (July 1823), 90 (*Romantics Reviewed, Part B*, I. 207).

20   For easy reference, see the extracts from these writers in Rutherford's *Lord Byron: The Critical Heritage*, 373–83, 421–40, 443–59. Arnold mingles praise and blame; Swinburne defends Byron in one essay, then later slates him in another: both charge Byron with posturing and verbal deficiency (see ibid., 448, 456–7, 466, 468–9).

21   Bertrand Russell, *A History of Western Philosophy* (1945; new edn. London: Routledge, 2004), 675.

22   Malcolm Kelsall, *Byron's Politics* (Sussex: Harvester, 1987), 7.

23   Michael Foot, *The Politics of Paradise: A Vindication of Byron* (London: Collins, 1988), 396.

24   Louis Crompton, *Byron and Greek Love: Homophobia in 19th-Century England* (London: Faber, 1985), 12.

25 Susan J. Wolfson, '"Their She Condition": Cross-Dressing and the Politics of Gender in *Don Juan*', *English Literary History* 54.3 (Fall 1987), 586.

26 Nigel Leask, *British Romantic Writers and the East: Anxieties of Empire* (Cambridge: Cambridge University Press, 1992), 2, 4.

27 Jerome Christensen, *Lord Byron's Strength: Romantic Writing and Commercial Society* (Baltimore: Johns Hopkins University Press, 1993), 314, xvii–xxii.

5

Percy Bysshe Shelley (1792–1822)

FROM CONTEMPORARY RESPONSES TO THE TWENTIETH CENTURY

The reaction to Shelley's poetry in the periodical press of his time consisted as much in silence as in hostility, many reviewers commenting not at all while others exclaimed in pious horror.[1] Those others denounced Shelley's impiety and immorality: his atheism, his advocacy of free relations between the sexes, his portrayal, even sanction, of incest. Partly because of its subject matter, but perhaps more because it was, among Shelley's productions, the most intelligible to his critics, *The Cenci* (1819) drew the largest share of both scrutiny and condemnation. As the *Literary Gazette* put it, 'it seemed to be the production of a fiend, and calculated for the entertainment of devils in hell.'[2] The *British Review* assured its readers that 'Such blasphemous ravings cannot be poetry.'[3]

To an extent, praise or blame for Shelley depended on the politics of his reviewer. But if Shelley's political views, his friendships (especially with Leigh Hunt), and the distinctive qualities of his poetic language brought on him the stigma of Cockneyism,[4] in the liberal journals, on the other hand, the perception of extravagance and obscurity in his poetry made it seem damaging to the liberal cause. As Hazlitt described it, reviewing the *Posthumous Poems* (1824) in the *Edinburgh*,

> Spurning the world of realities, he rushed into the world of nonentities and contingencies, like air into a *vacuum*. . . . he thus gave great encouragement to those who believe in all received absurdities, and are wedded to all existing abuses: his extravagance seeming to sanction their grossness and selfishness, as theirs were a full justification of his folly and eccentricity.[5]

At the same time, more generous and discerning views were not altogether wanting. In numerous articles in the *Examiner* and the *Indicator*, Leigh Hunt,

Shelley's friend and political ally, wrote warmly of the poetry, insisting on its political and social purpose, and recognizing the amplitude of the notion of love at the heart of Shelley's moral position.[6] And while Hunt's enthusiasm was occasionally in the stead of discrimination, Shelley found a sharper reader in John Gibson Lockhart, whose articles in *Blackwood's Edinburgh Magazine*, reprobating Shelley's principles, sought nonetheless to defend him against neglect and hostility, and to dissociate him from his Cockney associations.

> Mr. Shelly [sic], whatever his errors may have been, is a scholar, a gentleman, and a poet; and he must therefore despise from his soul the only eulogies to which he has been accustomed – paragraphs from the Examiner, and sonnets from Johnny Keats.[7]

The stature of *Prometheus Unbound*, today the central work of the Shelley canon, was acknowledged by some at least of the earliest critics. Admiring and antipathetic at once, Lockhart exclaims, 'Whatever may be the difference of men's opinions concerning the measure of Mr Shelley's poetical power, there is one point in regard to which all must be agreed, and that is his Audacity.'[8] More perceptively anticipating a later critical view, the reviewer of Gold's *London Magazine* declares, 'This is one of the most stupendous of those works which the daring and vigorous spirit of modern poetry and thought has created.'[9]

The canonizing of Shelley and, inseparably, the filing away of his political and atheistic edge may be said to have begun in Mary Shelley's 'Preface' to the *Posthumous Poems*. Hunt's eulogizing, in *Lord Byron and Some of his Contemporaries* (1828) and elsewhere, also contributed, as did the first full-length biography (1847), by Shelley's cousin, Thomas Medwin. The Victorian estimate of Shelley grew at the expense of his social and political principles. Robert Browning's statement of 1852, that 'had Shelley lived he would have finally ranged himself with the Christians',[10] only expressed a more general view. To Walter Bagehot, in an important review of 1856, 'Shelley had nothing of the magical influence, the large insight, the bold strength, the permeating eloquence, which fit a man for a practical reformer;' Bagehot's Shelley is a creature of simple uncontrolled impulses, incapable of great work, but with a lyrical gift, manifest in his shorter poems: 'His success . . . is in fragments; and the best of those fragments are lyrical.'[11] The picture of an impractical simpleton gained further ground in Thomas Hogg's contentious biography – almost a caricature – of 1858, and the diminishing of Shelley to a mere lyricist held for decades. Shorn of political effect, the fashionable Victorian image of Shelley, at the zenith of his popularity, is captured in Arnold's much-quoted cameo of 1881: 'Shelley, beautiful and ineffectual angel, beating in the void his luminous wings in vain.'[12]

First envisaged as a defence, then, the etherealizing of Shelley, and the consequent disregard or dismissal of his politics, turns to critique, a critique contained in Arnold's comments, and amplified by the influential critics of the first half of the twentieth century. Shelley had his champions; W. B. Yeats, for instance, in a celebrated essay on 'The Philosophy of Shelley's Poetry' (1900), asserts the value of his 'system of belief', and the coherence and beauty of his symbolism.[13] But Arnold's damning verdict prevailed in the attacks of the New Humanists, and, in their wake, the New Critics. To Irving Babbitt, in *Rousseau and Romanticism* (1919), Shelley was a 'political dreamer': 'The person who is as much taken by Shelley at forty as he was at twenty has, one may surmise, failed to grow up.'[14] In Babbitt's vein, T. S. Eliot declares, in *The Use of Poetry and the Use of Criticism* (1933), that Shelley is an adolescent poet, for whom only an adolescent enthusiasm is possible. His poetry is repugnant to adults because the beliefs it expresses are 'childish or feeble'.[15] In turn echoing and expanding upon Eliot, F. R. Leavis, in *Revaluation* (1936), excoriates Shelley's poetry as 'divorced from thought', given over to 'sentimental banalities', and, in the final analysis, morally corrupt.[16]

Against the tenor of this powerful consensus may be set the emergence of twentieth-century Shelley scholarship. The first extensive critical study, Carl Grabo's *The Magic Plant* (1936), sought to undo the damaging emphasis on feeling or emotion in Shelley's poetry, by arguing his stature as a thinker. Grabo presents Shelley as a poet–philosopher, with a strong interest in contemporary science, and intellectual affinities especially with the Neoplatonists. A vindication of another sort was constituted by the landmark biography, Newman Ivey White's *Shelley* (1940), which, scrupulously detailed and scholarly, puts Shelley's poetry and political beliefs in their biographical context, but resists easy causal relations between the life and the work. Carlos Baker's developmental account, *Shelley's Major Poetry: The Fabric of a Vision* (1948) insists, like Grabo's, on the philosophical core of the poetry: an idealism sustained by a range of eclectic sources, Greek, Renaissance, and contemporary. And setting the seal on Shelley's Platonism, James A. Notopoulos's *The Platonism of Shelley* (1949) both argues Shelley's 'natural' (untutored) Platonism and, usefully, assembles his reading, annotations, and translations of Plato, to present him as 'the outstanding Platonist in English literature'.[17]

Of greater moment to present-day readings of Shelley, and pushing against the dominant emphasis – idealism, especially Platonism – of the scholarship of its time, is C. E. Pulos's short but seminal work, still the single indispensable study, *The Deep Truth: A Study of Shelley's Scepticism* (1954). Pulos finds the key to Shelley's thought, and the unity of that thought, not in his idealism, but his scepticism, the first to be understood only in light of the second. Like all sceptics, Shelley denies absolute knowledge, but at the same time seeks a solution to doubt. His idealism is in that solution, in the affirmation of an ultimate reality, not as a matter of knowledge, but of faith or probability. Pulos's argument is summarized in his 'Conclusion'.

Extract from C. E. Pulos, *The Deep Truth: A Study of Shelley's Scepticism* (1954)

During the years 1811–1816 much of Shelley's reading in philosophy was devoted to sceptics. Hume and Drummond familiarized him with the most recent developments in sceptical thought – developments interpreted by Hume's chief British adversaries, the Common Sense school of thinkers, as the logical and inevitable result of a doctrine pervading nearly all modern speculation. Cicero and Diogenes Laertius introduced Shelley to the scepticism of antiquity; Sir Thomas Browne and Montaigne, to the scepticism of the Renaissance. The impact on the poet's mind of the sceptical tradition, as variously represented by these authors, is largely responsible for those modifications in his thought which critics have long recognized as distinguishing the mature from the young Shelley.

To appreciate, however, the possibility of this conclusion, it is necessary to bear in mind that the sceptical tradition, from its origin down to Shelley's own time, possesses a positive side as well as a negative, and that the former rests on disparate principles. On its negative side scepticism attempts to demonstrate the limitations of reason and knowledge. Sceptics differ on this point only in degree, that is, in the thoroughness and depth of their arguments. But on its positive side scepticism branches off into dissimilar principles; sceptics disagree in their sceptical solutions to doubt. Some rely mainly on custom, others on faith, still others on the doctrine of probability. The main difference lies between the first and the last of these solutions, while the second is compatible with either of the other two. The reliance on custom naturally leads to the adoption of conservative ideas. Probabilism, on the other hand, may and often does conduct to unorthodox views.

The fundamental doctrine on the negative side of Shelley's scepticism is a theory of causation – a theory that the poet first encountered in Godwin; its full implications, however, did not dawn on him until after he read and reread Hume and Drummond. All knowledge, according to this theory, depends on the relationship which we call cause and effect. But a scrupulous examination of this relationship reveals that the concept is founded on habit, that it arises from our experience of the constant conjunction of objects. Such an analysis of cause and effect banishes at once all possibility of certitude on any matter whatsoever. A provisional science, based on the observation of the constant conjunction of objects, is altogether possible. But where the opportunity of observing the constant conjunction of objects is denied us – which is the case in cosmological, ontological, and theological speculations – reasoning from cause to effect collapses into an exercise of the fancy. Thus reason conducts us to an astonishing awareness of our ignorance; in Shelley's words, we reach 'the verge where words abandon us, and what wonder if we grow dizzy to look down the dark abyss of how little we know'.[1]

But like every sceptic before him, Shelley cultivated a sceptical solution to doubt, even to the extent of expressing various degrees of assent to propositions regarding ultimate reality. He nowhere relies on custom to escape the sceptic's dilemma, as conformity to the *status quo* was quite incompatible with his social philosophy, his passion for reforming the world. But either faith or the doctrine of probability is implicit in all of his affirmations regarding the transcendent. By overlooking their tentative character or conditional nature, we may confound these with otherwise similar affirmations in Coleridge or Wordsworth or Emerson; Shelley's affirmations, however, are not dogmatic intuitions but aspects of his sceptical solution to doubt. And it is their character as such that gives them their distinctive quality and effect.

The charges of inconsistency not infrequently made against Shelley's thought, especially by recent scholars, are the direct result of the overlooking of this distinction. These charges appear baseless when the poet's thought is interpreted, as it should be interpreted, partly in the light of the sceptical tradition. It is true, of course, that Holbach's necessarianism and Berkeley's idealism can hardly be integrated into a coherent metaphysics. That Shelley's thought sometimes reflects such irreconcilable elements rests on two assumptions: that the poet rejected common-sense materialism through Berkeley's influence and that his concept of Necessity agrees with that of the French materialists. Both of these assumptions, however, are erroneous.

There is not the slightest evidence that Berkeley had any significant influence on Shelley's rejection of common-sense materialism. In fact, the poet plainly tells us that Berkeley's arguments did not impress him. What led Shelley to reject common-sense materialism was Hume's theory of causation as applied by both Hume and Drummond to the question of the independent existence of external objects: we cannot assume the existence of a material world as the cause of our sensations, for all we know of cause is the constant conjunction of ideas in our own mind; the cause of our sensations is unknown.

It is true, of course, that Shelley makes affirmations regarding this unknown reality; but these have the sceptical character of resting on faith or probability. Furthermore, his clearest positive remark about ultimate reality is that it must differ from mind; for it is supremely creative, while mind is largely passive. Nothing could be further from Berkeley than this doctrine. On the other hand, Shelley's theory of the 'one mind,' of which all individual minds are a portion, resembles Berkeley; but the resemblance is quite superficial: Shelley's concept refers to something less than 'the basis of all things' or reality; hence, it is quite unlike Berkeley's idea of an infinite mind acting as the cause of phenomena.

Just as Shelley's scepticism renders his idealism significantly unlike Berkeley's, so it makes his doctrine of Necessity significantly unlike that of the French materialists. Shelley's doctrine is not dogmatic, nor does it subsume a materialist world-view. Its source was Hume's theory of causation and the restatement of that theory in Godwin and Drummond. As an historical concept, Shelley's Necessity refers to the constant conjunction of events observable in the evolution of society.[2] As a metaphysical concept, which is the main concern here, it is the unknown cause of our sensations, the mysterious principle that governs the universe. The poet's interpretation of this unknown power as favoring the triumph of good over evil is partly the expression of faith, partly a form of probabilism based on the study of historical evolution.

Due attention to Shelley's scepticism disposes not only of the alleged inconsistency betwen his idealism and necessarianism, but also of his alleged pseudo-Platonism. By liberating him from the prejudices against the Greek philosopher which he had inherited from the *philosophes*, scepticism was to an important degree responsible for the renascence of Platonism which occurred in Shelley in 1817. But it was responsible also for the poet's considerable deviation from Plato. Shelley's concept of Beauty, unlike Plato's, is not dialectically arrived at; nor does it involve a theory of ultimate reality – except the sceptic's denial of the possibility of man's knowing ultimate reality. It is essentially an 'unknown and awful' power, which man apprehends only as an ecstasy 'within his heart' (*Hymn to Intellectual Beauty*). Sometimes Shelley expresses the faith that death will reveal to us this 'unknown and awful power' in all its splendor (*Adonais*), but this tendency of thought is counterbalanced by the opposite one of seeking Beauty in a concrete and mortal form (*Epipsy-chidion*). In brief, Shelley is not a pseudo-Platonist but a consistent Platonist in the sceptical tradition.

But while scepticism presented Plato to Shelley in a new light, it had little effect on his hostility toward organized Christianity. As a sceptic, the poet agreed with the fideists that the main bulwark of any religion is faith, not reason. But this admission did not imply the result one might expect: the sceptic Shelley is almost as hostile toward organized Christianity as the materialist Shelley had been. From his early reading of anti-Christian authors and from his own experience of the reactionary and intolerant character of early nineteenth-century Christianity, Shelley had come to entertain certain moral objections to the Christian religion. These would have remained obstacles to his reconciliation with his ancestral creed regardless of what metaphysical views he later embraced. He was willing, as a sceptic, to accept as much of the Christian religion as was free from his moral objections to it. But the qualification included too much of the Christian religion to allow any real departure from his original unfavorable attitude. The references to 'God' in his later poems – which suggest to some critics that the poet was becoming more orthodox in his religious opinions – probably refer to the deity whom he thought Christ worshipped: a mysterious and inconceivable being, differing from man and the mind of man. Shelley's acceptance of God in this sense in no way contradicts his continued strictures against the Christian religion.

Read, then, in the light of the sceptical tradition, Shelley's philosophy reveals itself as remarkably consistent and coherent. The assertion that the poet 'never lost a piece of intellectual baggage which he had at any time collected' has no foundation in fact: Shelley did not 'collect' ideas in the mechanical manner implied; furthermore, he did discard ideas – like those essential to materialism – in the course of his intellectual development. Nor was Shelley 'an enthusiast' who adopted any attractive idea 'without first ascertaining whether it was consistent with others previously avowed.' On the contrary, he resisted a new idea, as the history of his attitude toward immaterialism suggests, until the relation of that idea to others previously avowed became perfectly clear to him; or he modified ideas before adopting them, as the sceptical quality of his Platonism indicates, if in their original form they were inconsistent with his established convictions.

What bearing, one may now enquire, has this monograph upon the evaluation of Shelley as a poet?

A theoretical world-view is not essential to great poetry: the *Iliad* and *The Book of Job* both antedate the emergence of philosophy. On the other hand, any respectable theoretical system of thought is compatible with the highest poetic achievement: materialism served Lucretius as well as scholasticism served Dante.[3] Yet nothing incorporated in a poem is logically irrelevant to the evaluation of that poem. If form and content are inseparable in a given work of art, any irreconcilable philosophical elements in it, unless they serve a special purpose, must be viewed as a defect. 'Between artistic coherence . . . and philosophical coherence there is some kind of correlation'.[4]

If this principle of literary theory is in general sound, Shelley's scepticism is important because it provides us with a possible clue to the unity of his thought in all its variety. To begin with, scepticism is quite compatible with the four main traditions that shaped his mind – political radicalism, empiricism, Platonism, and Christianity. While scepticism is in conflict with the metaphysical views of most radicals, it is not in conflict with political radicalism as such. Scepticism and empiricism are also harmonious; in fact, all the more elaborate forms of scepticism are inseparable from empirical premises. Not unrelated, too, are scepticism and Platonism; for an idealist may make profound concessions to scepticism, while a sceptic may develop the positive side of his thought into a qualified idealism. So closely related, finally, are the sceptical and Christian traditions that the real problem here is to explain why sometimes, as in the case of Shelley, their reconciliation is incomplete.

But scepticism not only is quite compatible with the main traditions known to have profoundly influenced Shelley, but also is capable of reconciling two of those traditions that normally stand in disagreement. The central conflict in Shelley's philosophy is that between his empiricism and his Platonism. The poet's resolution of this conflict could have been suggested only by a philosopher who had dealt with the same problem: this consideration eliminates a host of philosophers known to have influenced Shelley in other respects, including Plato and Hume. The most plausible theory to date is that in this question Shelley was a disciple of Berkeley. But Shelley's relation to Hume invalidates this theory – a theory that can only lead to the conclusion that the poet was a confused follower of Berkeley. There remains, however, the possibility of reconciling empiricism and Platonism through the positive issues of scepticism – probability and faith. This mode of reconciling the empirical and Platonic traditions was implied in Drummond's *Academical Questions*. That Shelley employed that same mode is supported by his admiration for Drummond, by his relation to Hume and the sceptical tradition, and by a certain note in his idealism – a note ranging from the tentative to the mystical. In other words, scepticism had consequences in Shelley which it did not have in Hume; and it is in these consequence, not in the mere agreement with Hume, that the real significance of the poet's scepticism is to be found.

Notes

1   *The Complete Works of Percy Bysshe Shelley*, ed. R. Ingpen and W. E. Peck. Julian Edition, 10 vols. (London: Earnest Benn, 1926–30), VI. 196.
2   Cf. Kenneth Neill Cameron, 'The Social Philosophy of Shelley,' *Sewanee Review*, L (1942), 457–66.
3   Cf. Stephen C. Pepper, *The Basis of Criticism in the Arts* (Cambridge, Mass.: Harvard Univ. Press, 1946).
4   René Wellek and Austin Warren, *The Theory of Literature* (New York: Harcourt, Brace, 1949), 27.

Further reading

The following is a brief sample of the mid-twentieth-century vindications of Shelley.

R. H. Fogle, *The Imagery of Keats and Shelley: A Comparative Study* (Chapel Hill: University of North Carolina Press, 1949). Seminal study, illustrating technique and intellectual process in Shelley's poetry, and emphasizing especially his grasp upon the actual, so as to rebut charges of vagueness and obscurity; the final chapter counters, in particular, the New Critics.

Frederick A. Pottle, 'The Case of Shelley' (1952), repr. in *Shelley: Modern Judgements*, ed. R. B. Woodings (London: Macmillan, 1968). Influential defence, ascribing the decline of Shelley's reputation to the incompatibility of his visionary and prophetic stance with the 'starkly positivistic perception' of the twentieth century.

*****Peter Butter**, *Shelley's Idols of the Cave* (Edinburgh: Edinburgh University Press, 1954). Elucidates the favourite and recurrent images of Shelley's poetry, as symbols relating to its dominant themes: love, science and religion, politics. Still emphasizing Shelley's idealism, Butter refutes the charge of solipsism, by showing his idealism to co-exist with a drive towards increasing realism in the content, and clarity in the style, of the poetry.

Neville Rogers, *Shelley at Work: A Critical Inquiry* (1956; 2nd edn., Oxford: Clarendon Press, 1967). Manuscript study of the evidence of artistic and intellectual labour in Shelley's notebooks, vindicating him as a 'worker and thinker', and confirming the Platonist emphasis, in its reading of Shelley as 'the apostle of the power of the Mind.'

Harold Bloom, *Shelley's Mythmaking* (New Haven: Yale University Press, 1959). Traces, in a selection of Shelley's poems, the making and subsequent defeat of a myth of 'I' and 'thou', constituted by a dialectical relation of 'self' and 'other'.

SHELLEY, SCEPTICISM AND IDEALISM

Pulos's reading of Shelley's sceptical idealism is developed prolifically in the major studies of Shelley that followed. Among these is Earl Wasserman's *Shelley: A Critical Reading* (1971), which, building on Wasserman's own earlier readings of individual works, contends that Shelley's poems 'become richer when we recognize in them their related but variant strategies for embodying or surmounting Shelley's skepticism.'[18] Though Wasserman's claim to totality is somewhat undermined by his omissions, notably, of *The Triumph of Life*, his coverage is extensive, and his thesis complex:

> At the centre of the mind in Shelley's collective works are a denial of any self-evident truths that may serve as constructive first principles and a consequent indecision between contradictory desires for worldly perfection and an ideal postmortal eternity.[19]

Showing, in Shelley's early poems, his rejection of institutions, such as Christianity and monarchy, together with his conviction of the perfectibility of human life, Wasserman goes on to trace the manifestation of Shelley's utopian impulse – the establishing of a perfect earthly world – in *Prometheus Unbound* and *Hellas*, and finally the superseding of that impulse by another, culminating in *Adonais*, towards a transcendent state after death. In the extract below, Wasserman reads Shelley's view of mind in *Prometheus Unbound*, and subsequently presents Shelley's myth-making as syncretic, drawing on the truth perceived in all myths.

Extract from Earl Wasserman, *Shelley: A Critical Reading* (1971)

The Premises and the Mythic Mode

Any interpretation of *Prometheus Unbound* as a work of 'poetic idealism' will necessarily be conditioned by a determination of the drama's area of reference, the level of reality at which it is enacted; and this in turn must be a function of what its protagonist represents. Certainly Prometheus is not Man, if we mean by that the mortal human race. Prometheus himself, avowedly the benefactor and savior of man (I. 817), specifically makes the distinction in an address to Asia after his liberation and reunion with her:

> we will sit and talk of time and change,
> As the world ebbs and flows, ourselves unchanged.
> What can hide man from mutability?   (III. iii. 23–25)

Unlike man and the world, Prometheus is, at least at this point, not only immortal but also immutable; and Shelley's insistence that only thought, or mind, is eternal demands that we assign Prometheus his role, not in a system of allegorical abstractions, but in Shelley's metaphysics of idealism. He must be whatever Shelley's philosophy provides for as eternal and immutable. Moreover, in Act I, after his torture by the Furies, consolation is brought him by Spirits that come from the Human Mind, attributes or powers of a state of existence necessarily distinct from Prometheus'; and therefore he cannot be the Human Mind. Later he prophesies that, Jupiter being dethroned, he and Asia will be visited by the arts of the 'human world,' which are 'mediators / Of that best worship, love, by [man] and us / Given and returned' (III. iii. 58–60).[1] Even the speech of Jupiter which is sometimes offered as evidence that Prometheus is the 'soul of man' actually distinguishes him from that:

> Rejoice! henceforth I am omnipotent.
> All else had been subdued to me; alone
> The soul of man, like an unextinguished fire,
> Yet burns towards heaven with fierce reproach, and doubt,
> And lamentation, and reluctant prayer,
> Hurling up insurrection. . . .   (III. i. 3–8)

But this cannot apply to Prometheus, who has already retracted his curse; who now pities, not reproaches, and therefore seems to Jupiter (as he does to Earth) to have been subdued; and who never doubted Jupiter's falseness or offered him prayer, however reluctant. Jupiter's words describe his own relation to the 'soul of man' in terms of what Shelley took to be the relation of the god of traditional theologies to his fearful but rebellious human worshippers, and this is precisely the relation into which Prometheus has forever refused to enter. Finally, although the freeing of Prometheus and his reunion with Asia are paralleled by the gradual, progressive improvement of man, there is, explicitly, a significant time lag between the two, as though the continuous process of the perfection of man is in delayed sympathy with the instantaneous restoration of Prometheus, or as though one occurred in time and the other outside it.

To assume, then, that Prometheus illustrates 'that man as a soul is not only indestructible, but, through high will inspired by love, is creative,' as J. A. Symonds mused; to fancy with Rossetti that he is 'that faculty whereby man is man, not brute'; to call him, as Mary Shelley did, 'the emblem of the human race' or 'the prophetic soul of humanity' or 'the mind of mankind' or the 'potential state' of man 'insofar as it is good,' as other critics have speculated; even to lean on Shelley's description of Prometheus in his Preface as 'the type of the highest perfection of moral and intellectual nature, impelled by the purest and truest motives to the best and noblest ends'[2] – each of these falls short of the mark insofar as it assumes that the central subject of the drama is a mankind having autonomous reality and that Prometheus is a fictional abstraction of earthly man or of his faculties or ideals. All such interpretations allow for only one mode of existence and neglect the fact that, within the totally inclusive realm of Being, Shelley's metaphysics provides for two: human minds and the One Mind. Or, rather, such interpretations postulate that Prometheus must be a fabricated abstraction drawn by the poet from a reality called 'man,' instead of postulating the conclusion Shelley's 'intellectual system' arrives at – that what we call 'real' men are time-bound portions of the One Mind and, with respect to that unitary reality, are illusory, being only the 'different modifications' of it. Individual human minds are indeed a necessary part of the play, but their actions take place off-stage and are effected by sympathy with the Promethean drama; for the human revolution and the history of human perfection that were the subject of *The Revolt of Islam* have here been transposed to the level of total Existence, the metaphysical reality here named 'Prometheus.' As such, he is not a fiction abstracted from what exists, but Existence itself. Indeed, except for Demogorgon, Prometheus is the only reality actually present in the play, and it would be short of the truth even to say that the drama takes place *in* his mind; he *is* the One Mind. But the One Mind is not to be confused with unknowable Being, the One that embraces both the universe and the mysterious reality outside it – the One to which Adonais returns on his death, which is beyond the 'outwall' of 'boldest thoughts,'[3] and to which, on one occasion, Shelley gave the partial name Intellectual Beauty. The limited domain of *Prometheus Unbound* is that unitary *mode* of Being that appears in thought-constituted existence.

According to Shelley's doctrine of Necessity, we have observed, the distinction between good and evil has relevance only to mind, for the Power that is exerted through the universe, not being mind and not having will, acts as it must according to the necessary causal succession. But mind, having will, can make possible the initiation of an evil succession by imposing on itself a fictitious authority. All such willful impositions Shelley called 'tyranny,' the chief agents of which are kings, priests, and 'fathers' like Count Cenci because they claim the existence of an independent authority outside man's mind which dictates arbitrary systems of thought and action. These arbitrary and tyrannical codes are not real in the sense that the uniform processive patterns of Necessity are, but are fabricated by the mind, which then abdicates to these fictions its own powers and enslaves itself to its own creation:

> He who taught man to vanquish whatsoever
>   Can be between the cradle and the grave
> Crowned him the King of Life. Oh, vain endeavour!
>   If on his own high will, a willing slave,
> He has enthroned the oppression and the oppressor.[4]

It is therefore 'our will / That thus enchains us to permitted ill.'[5] At the heart of this ethical doctrine is the paradox of freedom, which Shelley understands to mean, not the freedom to make arbitrary and capricious choices, as though 'the will has the power of refusing to be determined by the strongest motive,'[6] but only freedom from tyranny, that is, from the artificial, mind-forged restraints that the mind allows itself to impose on itself. Man abandons his natural freedom when he 'fabricates / The sword which stabs his peace' and 'raiseth up / The tyrant whose delight is in his woe.'[7] But true freedom does not mean freedom from the fixed processes of Necessity, to which the mind must submit itself if it is to possess its own will; for this submission is 'that sweet bondage which is Freedom's self,' a 'weakness' or 'meekness' which is strength.[8]

In accordance with these concepts Shelley has represented in Jupiter all tyrannical evils and has identified him with the conventional God of the theists. But since tyrannic power is only an efficient fiction constituted of the mind's willful abdication of its own will, Jupiter has no real and independent existence in the sense that Mind or Power does. Tyrannic evil is a lapse of the Mind, its negative mode, its reflection in a distorting mirror, and is no more independent of Prometheus, the One Mind, than that. Just as Beatrice Cenci ultimately suspects that God is a fictional projection of her father, who exploits that fiction to justify his tyranny, so 'God' was created by some 'moon-struck sophist' upon 'Watching the shade from his own soul upthrown / Fill Heaven and darken Earth':

> The Form he saw and worshipped was his own,
> His likeness in the world's vast mirror shown.[9]

Consequently, although Jupiter appears in the drama as a god, he is not a being or an autonomous power, but only the dark shadow of Prometheus, an unnatural condition that mind wrongfully permits and can repeal by an act of will. 'I gave all / He has,' says Prometheus (I. 381–82), because Jupiter is only what Prometheus has resigned; and any institutionalizing and reifying of these abdicated mental powers is, by definition, the creation of a tyranny which when demands fearful submission of the mind to its own fiction. Unlike the traditional Jupiter, who usurped the throne of the gods and was merely aided to this end by Prometheus, Shelley's Jupiter is actually enthroned by Prometheus, who gave him 'wisdom, which is strength,' and 'clothed him with the dominion of wide Heaven' (II. iv. 44–46). Hence Prometheus can say to Jupiter, 'O'er all things but thyself I gave thee power, / And my own will' (I. 273–74). Not only is Jupiter unable to govern the will of Prometheus, the One Mind; he is not even self-determining because he exists only through Prometheus' concession that he be, or, rather, because he is only an unnatural surrogate for Prometheus. He has no will simply because Prometheus has not resigned his own will to his fictional creation. It is for this reason that, upon being overcome, Jupiter leaves only a blank, a 'void annihilation,' and is 'sunk, withdrawn, covered, drunk up / By thirsty nothing' (IV. 350–51); and Prometheus knows that when Jupiter's soul is cloven it will 'Gape like a hell within' (I. 56).

When Prometheus, wishing to hear again his own evil curse against Jupiter, decides that it not be repeated by 'aught resembling me' (I. 220), it is more than ideologically proper that he assigns the task of repeating it to Jupiter's Phantasm; for, although it is true that Jupiter and the now-repentant Prometheus are moral opposites, the audience is thus presented with the dramatic shock of observing the Phantasm of Jupiter in effect mindlessly cursing himself. But more is conveyed than merely the irony of the situation. The curse Prometheus had once spoken is admittedly an evil (I. 219) because it is an act of revenge, a countering of a wrong with another wrong; and if it is proper that it now be repeated by the shadow of him who is all evil, the implication is that when Prometheus first spoke it he was, in a very real sense, Jupiter. Milton Wilson has called attention to the striking similarities between Prometheus' description of the Phantasm about to repeat the curse and Prometheus' description of himself in the curse.[10] In Jupiter's Phantasm, Prometheus sees

> the curse on gestures proud and cold,
> And looks of firm defiance, and calm hate,
> And such despair as mocks itself with smiles;   (I. 258–60)

and at once the Phantasm repeats Prometheus' original execration:

> Fiend, I defy thee! with a calm, fixed mind,
>   All that thou canst inflict I bid thee do;
> Foul Tyrant both of Gods and Human-kind.   (I. 262–64)

Indeed, it is impossible to know whether the Phantasm reflects the real appearance of Jupiter or, like a good actor, has assumed the appearance Prometheus had when he originally spoke the curse against Jupiter. But it is necessary to go beyond Mr. Wilson's conclusions and to recognize this as the actual identification of the execrating Prometheus with Jupiter, the god he made in his image. Not only does the audience watch the Phantasm uttering Prometheus' curse against him of whom it is the phantom; it also observes Prometheus facing his own former self in Jupiter's ghost, since all of Jupiter's nature – pride, coldness, defiance, calm hatred, self-mocking despair – existed in Prometheus when he cursed his oppressor, although he has dispelled these evils from himself now that he no longer hates but pities. 'I am changed,' he says, 'so that aught evil wish / Is dead within; . . . no memory [remains] / Of what is hate' (I. 70–72); and it is for this reason that only his former self, the Phantasm of Jupiter, can repeat the curse. If Prometheus intends a bitter irony by causing Jupiter's Phantasm to utter the curse against Jupiter, there is also an irony he does not intend when he thinks he has not called up 'aught resembling me.' The difference between Prometheus and Jupiter's Phantasm is that between Prometheus and his former moral self.

Throughout the play, as we shall see, Jupiter is presented as only a cruel parody of Prometheus, and this relationship is repeatedly under-scored in Act I, where he is treated as the distorted, mocking reflection of Prometheus. Although Panthea sees Prometheus as 'firm, not proud' (I. 337), Jupiter's Phantasm, who himself shows 'gestures proud,' calls him 'proud sufferer' (I. 245); and Prometheus, speaking 'with a calm, fixed mind' when he uttered the curse, addressed Jupiter as 'awful image of calm power' (I. 296), while the Phantasm, repeating the curse, looks cruel, 'but calm and strong, / Like one who does, not suffers wrong' (I. 238–39). In one sense it is Jupiter who fills the world with his 'malignant spirit' (I. 276), but in fact it is Prometheus, who, in hate, has imprecated on 'me and mine . . . / The utmost torture of thy hate' (I. 278–79). Prometheus' struggle is really a contest within himself, and his reference to Jupiter's 'self-torturing solitude' (I. 295) is, ironically, actually a description of his own state as, chained to the precipice, he endures 'torture and solitude, / Scorn and despair' (I. 14–15).

Given that Jupiter is the privative mode of Prometheus, we can understand why Prometheus, addressing Jupiter, describes the universe as

> those bright and rolling worlds
> Which Thou and I alone of living things
> Behold with sleepless eyes! (I. 2–4)

For if the universe is the mass of thought, then it has a continuous existence by virtue of being the unending perception by the One Mind – and by the negation of itself that the One Mind has permitted. These alone, like Berkeley's God and unlike the human mind, never cease to perceive the thought that is the universe. But as the institutional reification of Prometheus' relinquished powers, Jupiter would have the One Mind bow in total submission and abandon itself entirely to the then self-determined institution. Therefore, were it not for Prometheus' 'all-enduring will' to resist, the One Mind would be deprived of itself, abandoned entirely to its own negation; and the world that exists because it is perceived would have 'vanished, like thin mist / Unrolled on the morning wind' (I. 116–17). Without mind there can be no thought, and thoughtlessness can be the 'measure' only of a vacancy.

[. . .]

Peacock reports that Shelley once commented on Spenser's giant who holds the scales and wishes to 'rectify the physical and moral evils which result from inequality of condition.'[11] Artegall, Shelley explained, 'argues with the Giant; the Giant has the best of the argument; Artegall's iron man knocks him over into the sea and drowns him. This is the usual way in which power deals with opinion.' When Peacock objected that this is not the lesson Spenser intended, Shelley replied, 'Perhaps not; it is the lesson which he conveys to me. I am of the Giant's faction.'[12] In the giant's intention to reduce all things 'unto equality,' Spenser saw the impending dissolution of hierarchy and the return to chaos; from Shelley's point of view Spenser's conception of order was wrong and therefore the ordering of his myth was wrong, for what to Spenser was necessary superiority and subordination was to republican Shelley the frustration of all possibility of perfect unity. The occasion for Peacock's note was a letter in which Shelley alluded to Artegall's giant in order, it is significant, to define the purpose of the recently completed Act I of *Prometheus Unbound*: the act, Shelley writes, is an attempt to 'cast what weight I can into the right scale of that balance which the Giant (of Arthegall) holds.'[13] For egalitarian Shelley was engaged in reforming and reinterpreting the myth of god-fearing Aeschylus at least as radically as he did that of Spenser, the defender of hierarchism, and to the same end of perfect order. Recasting that myth into the shape and proportions that, according to his imaginative vision, it ought to have as the highest unity of which its components are capable meant to Shelley not only the achievement of the highest formal beauty but also – since it amounts to the same thing – the purging of error and the attainment of truth.

To Shelley myth is not fanciful fable. Whatever its genesis, it is not mistaken for external fact, and therefore it is more truly real than the sensory world that man falsely believes to reside outside his mind. Since 'things' actually exist for man only as thoughts, the elements organized by the poet are thoughts recognized as wholly mental and not mistaken for any independent externality. The thoughts composed by the imagination are those upon which the mind has already acted 'so as to colour them with its own light,'[14] which is a reflection of the light of the perfect One. Or, as Shelley expresses the same idea in *Prometheus Unbound*, the poet does not heed objects as external 'things,' but first watches the 'lake-reflected sun illume' them and then organizes ('creates') these transfigured thoughts into 'Forms more real than living man, / Nurslings of immortality!' (I. 744–49). The elements of myth, being unmistakably mental apprehensions of 'things,' are pre-eminently thoughts and therefore pre-eminently the valid materials to which the poet is obliged to give the 'purest and most perfect shape.'

But if the constituent details of myths are especially real for Shelley, it follows that the component elements of one myth are as valid as those of any other, since they are all thoughts. Syncretic mythology had been revitalized in the eighteenth century, especially by those deists who, arguing for the common basis of all faiths, had attempted to demonstrate the interconvertibility of all myths.[15] This tradition of syncretism was part of Shelley's intellectual heritage, and his mentalistic ontology provided it with a special philosophic justification. If, then, all mythic data, from Jupiter to King Bladud, are real and valid, the various received myths are not to be thought of as discrete narratives or distinct national faiths, but only as variant efforts of the mind to apprehend the same truth. Hence, the stuff of all myths is, collectively and indiscriminately, available to the mythopoeist for his task of compelling thoughts to their most nearly perfect structure. Indeed, directly after announcing to Peacock the completion of the first act of his mythopoeic drama and directly before his idiosyncratic interpretation of Artegall's giant, Shelley wrote that he could conceive of a 'great work,' not of poetry but of moral and political science, 'embodying the discoveries of all ages, & harmonizing the contending creeds by which mankind have been ruled.' For it is Shelley's assumption that if all creeds, or their mythic embodiments, were shaped into the highest form they admit, they would be precisely translatable into each other. Despite his modest disclaimer – 'Far from me is such an attempt' – the syncretism of this 'great work' is at the heart of *Prometheus Unbound*.

Moreover, given Shelley's interpretation of 'thought', it follows that empirical science, folk science, legends, and all literature that has been assimilated as an operative part of human culture are also mental configurations of thoughts that recognize the mental nature of 'things'; they, at least as much as conventional myths, are also permanently real in the sense that supposedly objective things are not. Consequently, all these thoughts, too, are among the materials for the poet's imagination to syncretize and interlock into the most nearly perfect form. *Adonais*, for example, is not merely another variant of the Venus and Adonis myth; it recasts that myth into a new and presumably true system of interrelationships, but it also organically integrates the reformed myth with the ancient belief that souls derive from stars, with astronomy scientific and fabular, with the science of optics, and with various traditional metaphors and symbols, all of them having the same kind and degree of eternal reality because they are the mind's conceptions, rather than perceptions, of things. Myth so inclusively defined is not an assemblage of accepted fictional terms supporting an accretion of rich connotations, as it was for Dryden and Pope; nor merely a fiction that reveals truth better than facts; nor an upsurging from the unconscious. Its components are indestructible and eternal mental possessions. Consequently, however diverse and unrelated their traditional contexts, they ask, like all other thoughts, to be interwoven into a beautiful whole 'containing within itself the principle of its own integrity.' If the structures of given myths are already beautiful and true, Shelley held, they are integral thoughts having 'the power of attracting and assimilating to their own nature all other thoughts,'[16] and thus any conventional myth so organized is inexhaustibly capable of rendering truths for a poet by giving its shape to them. On the other hand, since error, ugliness, and evil are but various modes of disorder, the task of the imagination is also to reform erroneous, misshapen myths according to the model of the mind's extraordinary apprehensions of perfect unity.

Notes

1 Shelley regularly defines art as mediating between two different levels of reality. See *Ode to Liberty*, 249–53.
2 In fact, Shelley is not attempting to define his own Prometheus but is describing the potentialities in the abstract Prometheus of classical myth, or, as he has just

said of Satan, the way in which the traditional character 'is susceptible of being described.'

3   *Hellas*, 768–75.

4   *Ode to Liberty*, 241–5.

5   *Julian and Maddalo*, 170–1.

6   *Queen Mab*, VI. 198n.

7   Ibid., III. 199–202.

8   Ibid., IX. 76; *Prometheus Unbound*, II. iii. 93–4.

9   *The Revolt of Islam*, 3244–8.

10   Milton Wilson, *Shelley's Later Poetry: A Study of his Prophetic Imagination* (New York: Columbia University Press, 1959), 63–4.

11   *The Letters of Percy Bysshe Shelley*. ed. F. L. Jones, 2 vols. (Oxford: Clarendon Press, 1964), II, 71.

12   Peacock adds that Shelley also 'held that the Enchanter in the first canto [of Thomson's *Castle of Indolence*] was a true philanthropist, and the Knight of Arts and Industry in the second an oligarchical impostor overthrowing truth by power' (ibid.).

13   To Peacock [23–24 January 1819] (ibid., II, 71).

14   *Defence of Poetry* (*Complete Works*, Julian edition, VII, 109).

15   See Albert J. Kuhn, 'English Deism and the Development of Romantic Mythological Syncretism,' *Publications of the Modern Languages Association of America*, 71 (1956), 1094–116.

16   *Defence of Poetry* (*Complete Works*, Julian edition, VII, 118).

Further reading

Listed below are some major studies of Shelley as a canonical author, examining philosophical content, especially 'sceptical idealism', and literary form. The latter half of the list is particularly concerned with Shelley's uses and ideas of language. *Prometheus Unbound* emerges as the dominant work of the canon and the major focus for criticism.

Desmond King-Hele, *Shelley: His Thought and Work* (1960; 2nd edn., London and Basingstoke: Macmillan, 1971). Biographically ordered, occasionally blinkered account of Shelley's major poetry, with especial attention to his scientific interests.

Glenn O'Malley, *Shelley and Synesthesia* (Evanston: Northwestern University Press, 1964). Shows the subtlety and extent of Shelley's use of synesthesia to effect aesthetic harmony, and its symbolic relevance 'to philosophic themes of unity and harmony which recur from poem to poem.'

Northrop Frye, *A Study of English Romanticism* (1968; new edn., Brighton: Harvester, 1983). In the context of this study of Romanticism as marked by a major change in the mythological (cultural) structure in which literature is rooted, one aspect of such change being the recovery by man of powers formerly projected on God, Prometheus is the type of the romantic revolutionary, whose liberation 'enables the creative power of man to emerge.' Frye's reading of *Prometheus Unbound* as comedy, with recognizable affinities to Shakespearean comedy, is especially good.

*Donald H. Reiman**, *Percy Bysshe Shelley* (1969; updated edn. Boston: Twayne, 1990). Fine lucid introduction, integrating Shelley's life and work to offer a chronological account, with detailed readings of key texts, of his poetic and intellectual development.

Stuart Curran, *Shelley's Cenci: Scorpions Ringed with Fire* (Princeton, N.J.: Princeton University Press, 1970). Vital study which, focusing on a single work, discusses Shelley's craftsmanship and the larger metaphysical questions he raises – the despair and transcendence in his vision – as well as the play's stage history.

M. H. Abrams, *Natural Supernaturalism: Tradition and Revolution in Romantic Literature* (New York and London: W.W. Norton, 1971). In Abrams's thesis, of the secularizing of Judaeo-Christian mythology by the Romantics, Shelley 'set out to assimilate what seemed intellectually and morally valid in this mythology to his own agnostic and essentially skeptical world-view.' Abrams pays particular attention to *Prometheus Unbound* as 'a psycho-drama of the reintegration of the split personality.'

Judith Chernaik, *The Lyrics of Shelley* (Cleveland and London: Case Western Reserve University Press, 1972). A reading of Shelley's shorter lyrics that emphasizes his humanistic faith, to which his political mission is allied: 'His poetry can be read as an attempt to discover new authority in human powers for the divinity of the world and the immortality of the soul.'

Richard Holmes, *Shelley: The Pursuit* (London: Weidenfeld and Nicolson, 1974). Lively readable biography, dispensing with the etherealized Shelley in favour of a 'darker and more earthly, crueller and more capable figure.'

Stuart Curran, *Shelley's Annus Mirabilis: The Maturing of an Epic Vision* (San Marino, Calif.: Huntington Library, 1975). Shelley's 'skeptical idealism', entailing a faith in the human will or imagination, produces the compositions of 1819, a 'diversity of form and of idea' that, unified by his 'harmonious vision', attains the breadth of epic.

Harold Bloom, *Poetry and Repression: Revisionism from Blake to Stevens* (New Haven and London: Yale University Press, 1976). Focusing especially on *Prometheus Unbound* and *The Triumph of Life*, Bloom applies to Shelley his influential model of 'misprision', the struggle of a strong poet to establish his poetic identity by the revision (overthrow) of his precursors, in this instance, Milton and Wordsworth.

Charles E. Robinson, *Shelley and Byron: The Snake and Eagle Wreathed in Flight* (Baltimore and London: Johns Hopkins University Press, 1976). Meticulously detailed rendering of the philosophical relationship of Shelley and Byron, conceived of as a mutually constructed antagonism, at first between Shelley's idealism and Byron's fatalism, but tending to the reverse positions in the poets' last years.

Timothy Webb, *The Violet in the Crucible: Shelley and Translation* (Oxford: Clarendon Press, 1976). Valuable study of Shelley's translations as integral to his intellectual endeavour: translation breaks down the barriers of self to enable relations with others, as envisaged in the *Defence of Poetry*. Further, 'a comparison of the translations with their sources has much to tell us both about Shelley's literary sensibility and about his views on nature, love, religion, psychology, philosophy, and politics.'

Harold Bloom et al., *Deconstruction and Criticism* (New York: Seabury Press, 1979). Shelley, especially *The Triumph of Life*, used to exemplify the non-coincidence of meaning and language, in essays by Paul de Man, Jacques Derrida, and J. Hillis Miller. Especially celebrated is De Man's illustration in 'Shelley Disfigured', from the encounter between the narrator and 'Rousseau' in *The Triumph of Life*, of a view of history as discontinuous and random, rather than connected and relational.

Jean Hall, *The Transforming Image: A Study of Shelley's Major Poetry* (Urbana: University of Illinois Press, 1980). Studying, in chronological order, the transformations enacted by Shelley's imagery, emphasizes poetic experience as against transcendentalism, and hence Shelley's debt to British empiricism: Shelley is 'an empirically oriented idealist whose poetry calls for a skeptical application of idealism to life.'

Tilottama Rajan, *Dark Interpreter: The Discourse of Romanticism* (Ithaca and London: Cornell University Press, 1980). Presents the co-existence of scepticism and idealism in Shelley's poetry, as part of a general thesis regarding the Romantics' search for 'a model of discourse that accommodates rather than simplifies its ambivalence toward the . . . equation of art with idealization.'

Richard Cronin, *Shelley's Poetic Thoughts* (London: Macmillan, 1981). Counters the notion of a 'deep' meaning separate from form in the poetry by arguing that Shelley's thought is constituted in and by the language and poetic form in which it is expressed. The major poems result 'from the struggle in which the poet engages to impose his own likeness on resistant materials, on a language and on genres developed for purposes other than his own.'

Miriam Allott (ed.), *Essays on Shelley* (Liverpool: Liverpool University Press, 1982). Essays by divers scholars, treating the principal works in chronological order, with 'general agreement about, and admiration for, Shelley's conscious craftsmanship, his disciplined originality in handling and reworking traditional forms and the striking "modernity" distinguishing his major work.'

William Keach, *Shelley's Style* (New York and London: Methuen, 1984). Important formalist study, relating the distinctiveness of Shelley's style to his ideas of language: Shelley's style 'is the work of an artist whose sense of the unique and unrealized potential in language was held in unstable suspension with his sense of its resistances and limitations.'

Angela Leighton, *Shelley and the Sublime* (Cambridge: Cambridge University Press, 1984). Argues that Shelley's thinking progresses from one eighteenth-century tradition – empiricist philosophy, which supports his radicalism and atheism – to another – the sublime – from which draws the idea of inspiration fundamental to his view of poetic creativity. Yet the progression is only a shift in emphasis, the conflict between the two perspectives – religious scepticism and poetic need – remaining unresolved, and underlying many of his poems.

Terence Allan Hoagwood, *Prophecy and the Philosophy of Mind: Traditions of Blake and Shelley* (University: University of Alabama Press, 1985). Presents *Prometheus Unbound* as one of two Romantic masterpieces (the other being Blake's *Jerusalem*), in which the traditions of biblical prophecy and Enlightenment epistemology converge in a revolutionary fusion of philosophical content with prophetic form.

Ronald Tetreault, *The Poetry of Life: Shelley and Literary Form* (Toronto: University of Toronto Press, 1987). Emphasizing formal significance rather than philosophical content, Tetreault describes a dialectical relation between poetry and life in Shelley's search for a rhetorical vehicle adequate to his vision of a better world. Shelley's development from oratory to art, from instructing his readers to more subtle means of generating conviction in them, culminates in his adoption of the dramatic form.

Michael O'Neill, *The Human Mind's Imaginings: Conflict and Achievement in Shelley's Poetry* (Oxford: Clarendon Press, 1989). Aware of themselves as fictions, Shelley's poems oscillate between the imaginative autonomy of language and the engagement with realities that lie beyond language. Counter to the arguments for the coherence of Shelley's vision, O'Neill emphasizes 'the frequency with which his best poems embody unresolved conflict, or dramatize the collision of perspectives.'

Bryan Shelley, *Shelley and Scripture: The Interpreting Angel* (Oxford: Clarendon Press, 1994). Insightfully examines Shelley's use of biblical images and ideas, finding in his poetry, an alteration of perspective, 'a generic shift from the model of prophetic literature – with its vision of a millennium and its ethical concern for social justice – to that of apocalyptic' with its vision of a transcendent eternal realm.

Karen A. Weisman, *Imageless Truths: Shelley's Poetic Fictions* (Philadelphia: University of Pennsylvania Press, 1994). Reads the Shelley canon as 'a developing quest for a mode of fiction-making . . . sensitive to the poet's . . . belief in a metaphysical ultimate', but also shaped by his anxiety about the incompatibility of poetic fiction-making with the quotidian external world.

SHELLEY AND SOCIALISM

'We claim him as a Socialist.' So declared Edward Aveling and Eleanor Marx Aveling (Karl Marx's daughter), in a pamphlet of 1888, titled *Shelley's Socialism.*[20] If one response of Shelley scholarship to the Victorian depredations and their aftermath has been to assert his stature as a thinker, another has been to reaffirm his standing as a radical. The landmark study in this regard is Kenneth Neill Cameron's *The Young Shelley: Genesis of a Radical* (1951). Spanning the years 1809–13, Cameron's biographically-ordered reading puts Shelley's ideas 'in their developmental relations to the social and ideological patterns of their age,'[21] arguing that it is Shelley's development as a radical thinker that offers the defining insight into his work.

Subsequently, the origins and emphases of Shelley's political thought, including the influence of his great mentor, William Godwin, have been extensively investigated. Allied to the view of a sceptical idealism, Shelley's political utopianism has been shown to be qualified by his practical engagement in reform. At the same time, the tenability of his position as a radical in sympathy with, but not of, the people has not passed without question. As the politically-focused criticism has engaged more and more, not only with what Shelley's text *says*, but also with what it *does*, the radical content of his poetry has been further and fruitfully complicated.

Addressing the tendency to regard as antithetical, political engagement and poetic introspection, as represented in Shelley's poet figures, Timothy Clark's *Embodying Revolution: The Figure of the Poet in Shelley* (1989), persuasively presents the unity of the two impulses, and thus the continuity of 'public' and 'private' in Shelley's thought. By virtue of their heightened sensibility, Shelley's poet figures embody, in the flawed present, the ideal future envisaged by a radical politics. In the extract below, Clark demonstrates his thesis with reference to the hero of *Alastor*.

Extract from Timothy Clark, *Embodying Revolution: The Figure of the Poet in Shelley* (1989)

Alastor (1815)

The poem entitled 'ALASTOR', may be considered as allegorical of one of the most interesting situations of the human mind. It represents a youth of uncorrupted feelings and adventurous genius led forth by an imagination inflamed and purified through familiarity with all that is excellent and majestic, to the contemplation of the universe. He drinks deep of the fountains of knowledge, and is still insatiate. The magnificence and beauty of the external world sinks profoundly into the frame of his conceptions, and affords to their modifications a variety not to be exhausted. So long as it is possible for his desires to point towards objects thus infinite and unmeasured, he is joyous, and tranquil, and self-possessed. But the period arrives when these objects cease to suffice. His mind is at length suddenly awakened and thirsts for intercourse with an intelligence similar to itself. He images to himself the Being whom he loves. Conversant with speculations of the sublimest and most perfect natures, the vision in which he embodies his own imaginations unites all of wonderful, or wise, or beautiful, which the poet, the philosopher, or the lover could depicture. The intellectual faculties, the imagination, the functions of sense, have their respective requisitions on the sympathy of corresponding powers in other human beings. The Poet is represented as uniting these requisitions, and attaching them to a single image. He seeks in vain for a prototype of his conception. Blasted by his disappointment, he descends to an untimely grave.[1]

Shelley describes the poem as an aspect of a science of the mind, 'allegorical of one of the most interesting situations of the human mind'. This is the state that can be provisionally described as that of love without an immediate physical object, as foreshadowed in the epigraph from St Augustine: 'Nondum amabam et amare amabam, quaerebam quid amarem amans amare.'[2] This state of a disproportion between desire and the realm of possible objects was doubtless familiar to Shelley from experience, as a letter of this time shows,[3] but also certainly familiar from the literature of sensibility.[4] Several critics have noted the similarity between the idealized poet of *Alastor* and figures derived from the sensibility tradition, such as the hero of Godwin's *Fleetwood*,[5] James Beattie's Edwin, the hero of his study of the poetic identity *The Minstrel*,[6] and Rousseau's portraits of himself in the *Confessions* and elsewhere.[7] Wasserman has also suggested analogies with Chateaubriand's *René*.[8] There has been no work, however, on the manner in which the adaptation of the hero of sensibility to the poet of *Alastor* might relate to Shelley's complex philosophical and political thought. In fact, Shelley adapted the hero of sensibility into a figure who functions as part of his exploration of poetic identity as it relates to philosophical questions of the power of the mind.

The resemblance of the hero of *Alastor* to some aspects of the oversensitive heroes of the novel of sentiment is not surprising in view of Shelley's conception of sensibility as the distinguishing character of a poet. Two corollaries of Shelley's notion of the poet's place in a continuous process of historical change and refinement must be stressed. First, the poet is marked with an extreme sensibility whose correlate is an intense physical beauty, at least initially. Second, this refinement has as a concomitant an intensification of the poet's inner life, in particular the intensity of passion with which he will be drawn to the idol, or internal ideal image, that forms the basis of all relationships with others. Moreover, the manner in which Shelley emphasizes the nature of progressive movements in culture, as they manifest themselves in the psychology of individuals, is as the development of a *want*. Consequently, the resemblance of many aspects of the poet's characterization in *Alastor* to the theme of love-without-an-object in other works of the period may be understood primarily as a corollary of Shelley's conception of the poet as a social agent.[9]

Much criticism of *Alastor* exaggerates the incipient moralism of the second paragraph of Shelley's Preface into an overall framework for interpreting the poem.[10] Shelley accuses the hero of attempting to live in 'self-centred seclusion'[11] remote from human sympathy. This accusation, however, is at odds with the poem itself and with Shelley's emphasis elsewhere on the necessary solitariness of the poet.[12] The remark is perhaps a sign of the unease with which Shelley regarded the destructive imaginative processes that make their first appearance in *Alastor*. In *A Defence of Poetry* solitude distinguishes the poet. He is 'a nightingale, who sits in darkness and sings to cheer its own solitude with sweet sounds . . .'.[13] Similarly, in the 'Ode to a Sky-lark' the poet is 'hidden / in the light of thought, / Singing hymns unbidden . . .' (ll. 36–8). Paradoxically, it is this very solitude that is the condition for a poet's potent influence on others. Absorption in his own passionately imaginative life is necessary for the intensity of energy felt by the poet's auditors. These are 'as men entranced by the melody of an unseen musician, who feel that they are moved and softened, yet not whence or why'.[14] Likewise, the poet of 'To a Sky-lark' is envisaged 'Singing hymns unbidden / Till the world is wrought / To sympathy with hopes and fears it heeded not' (ll. 38–40). The notion of the poet as a pioneer, by virtue of his very introspectiveness, is plain enough. A similar conception, with whatever tension, is dramatized in *Alastor*.

The Preface describes a mysterious 'Power' as agent of the poet's life – 'that Power which strikes the luminaries of the world with sudden darkness and extinction, by awakening them to too exquisite a perception of its influences . . .'.[15] Cameron lapses into the excessive moralism of most critics of *Alastor* when, drawing on the evidence of Shelley's elsewhere describing Power as the 'collective energy of the moral and material world',[16] he claims that the hero of *Alastor* is destroyed through denying its influence.[17] The Preface, however, clearly states the opposite; the poet, as a 'luminary', suffers through being awakened by this Power to 'too exquisite a perception of its influences . . .'. If Cameron was forced to exaggerate the moralism of the Preface it might be because the oddity of *Alastor* is that the Power which destroys the poet is elsewhere described so as to emphasize what seem solely its beneficent and progressive effects. It is, for example, 'the Power which models, as they pass, all the elements of this mixed universe to the purest and most perfect shape which it belongs to their nature to assume . . .'.[18] This is clearly a description of the functions of the imagination actively creating, by combination and representation, a more perfect inner image or idol from the elements of individual mind. The fact that such a process determines the fate of the poet in *Alastor* correlates the description of Power quoted above with that given in the Preface. The 'Essay on Christianity' also relates it to Christ's description of God. This is a particularly human God, however, for the ultimate agency of all human events is not some supreme transcendent being, but the combined influence of culture and refinement through history. God is 'the interfused and overruling Spirit of all the energy and wisdom included within the circle of existing things'.[19] Likewise, God is 'the overruling Spirit of the collective energy of the moral and material world'.[20] He is, in effect, the totality of the *active* elements within the one mind as already described. What Shelley, doubtless for polemical purposes, describes as 'God' in the 'Essay on Christianity' is the totality of those active mental powers that Shelley defines elsewhere as 'love', or as 'Liberty' in the 'Ode to Liberty'.

Whatever Shelley's concern with the epistemological questions of the ultimate nature of the causal principle of thought and sensation in 'Mont Blanc',[21] his definitions of Power evoke elsewhere only its nature as the totality of active and progressive forces developing according to social conditions. In his essay on the ancient Greeks, for example, Shelley describes the human arts as modifications of one active force, according to particular social circumstances: 'all the inventive arts maintain, as it were, a sympathetic connection between each other, being no more than various expressions of one internal power, modified by different circumstances, either of an individual, or of society'.[22] This argument reappears in Shelley's conception of the necessary similarity of poets writing in shared social conditions. Writing to Charles Ollier on 15 October 1819, Shelley insists that Byron and Wordsworth resemble each other, not because of any purposeful imitation but because of 'A certain similarity all the best writers of any particular age inevitably are marked with, from the spirit of that age acting on all'.[23] Both Wordsworth and Byron (and, presumably, Shelley himself) derive from the latest developments in the realm of thought and sensation whose totality Shelley describes as the one mind.[24]

As early as 1814, at least a year before *Alastor*, Shelley had set out, in his unfinished romance *The Assassins*, a conception of an élite group of people whose influence is the determining active factor within history – those forerunners in the realm of opinion Shelley later calls simply 'poets':

> Not on the will of the capricious multitude, nor the constant fluctuations of the many and the weak, depends the change of empires and religions. These are the mere insensible elements from which a subtler intelligence moulds its enduring statuary. They that direct the changes of this mortal scene breathe the decrees of their dominion from a throne of darkness and of tempest. The power of man is great.[25]

Despite providing the basis for an assertion of the collective power of man, *The Assassins*, as will be seen, also anticipates *Alastor* in its description of some of the more tragic consequences of imaginative processes working through an individual. The Assassins, an idealized community of gnostics living according to Godwinian principles of independence and virtue, are pictured attaining such a state of exalted sensibility as to live a life of refined delight in all the natural beauties that surround them:

> To live, to breathe, to move, was itself a sensation of immeasurable transport. Every new contemplation of the condition of his nature brought to the happy enthusiast an added measure of delight, and impelled to every organ, where mind is united with external things, a keener and more exquisite perception of all that they contain of lovely and divine.[26]

The description of the idealized life of the Assassins prefigures the very elements of Power that become destructive in *Alastor*. The description of the group's sensibility ('a keener and more exquisite perception' of the 'lovely and divine') anticipates the Preface to *Alastor* in which such perception becomes too exquisite not to be destructive ('that Power which strikes the luminaries of the world with sudden darkness and extinction, by awakening them to too exquisite a perception of its influences . . .'). Indeed, the romance continues immediately to describe the growth of intense want in the Assassin: 'To love, to be beloved, suddenly became an insatiable famine of his nature, which the wide circle of the universe, comprehending beings of such inexhaustible variety and stupendous magnitude of excellence, appeared too narrow and confined to satiate'.[27]

The parallel with the state of the poet in *Alastor* is obvious enough. All the sympathies of the mind have contracted upon one overwhelming need for love. The manner in which Shelley conceived of the active powers of the mind in such a way as to result in the production of new and more refined wants of the heart is again apparent. His reciprocal conception of sympathy is clear in the description in *The Assassins* of an intense need to love and to be loved at the same time. *The Assassins* thus already suggests the degree to which Shelley saw poets as the particular embodiments of processes determining whole societies. The romance anticipates, on a *social* level, the *individual* psychology of the hero of *Alastor*.

In *Alastor* itself, the dream-maiden represents an idealized version of the poet's own nature, embodying all his desires into one overwhelming want. Her voice is explicitly 'like the voice of his own soul / Heard in the calm of thought' (ll. 153–4). Moreover,

Knowledge and truth and virtue were her theme,
And lofty hopes of divine liberty,
Thoughts the most dear to him, and poesy,
Herself a poet.

(ll. 158–161)

Similarly, as the pace of the dream mounts, every gesture and emotion of the poet in his dream finds, until his abrupt awakening at the climax, its exact reflection in the gestures and emotions of the dream-figure. The processes involved are those of combination and refinement according to which the imagination '[seeks the likeness of that which is most beautiful in itself]'.[28] As the parallel processes described in reference to a whole society in *The Assassins* demonstrate, the poet's life provides an individual allegory of cultural forces as Shelley understands them throughout his prose. *The Assassins* also demonstrates the manner in which the development of this powerful want should be understood, less in terms of any common sense notion of love as involving another's being, but in terms of the mind's aspiration towards a more fulfilled and perfect state of identity, as recounted in 'On Love'. Thus, after describing the development of love as an intense want, the narrator continues to lament the mind's incapacity to realize and sustain the exalted state known when it is at one with its image of excellence and beauty. This is the state which the hero of *Alastor* knows only in his brief dream and is never able to regain:

> Alas, that these visitings of the spirit of life should fluctuate and pass away! That *the moments when the human mind is commensurate with all that it can conceive of excellent and powerful, should not endure* with its existence and survive its most momentous change! But the beauty of a vernal sunset, with its overhanging curtains of empurpled cloud, is rapidly dissolved, to return at some unexpected period, and spread an alleviating melancholy over the dark vigils of despair.[29]

This section of *The Assassins* is Shelley's first statement of the frustrating evanescence of the mind's active powers. They quickly abandon those they inhabit to the frustration consequent upon their disappearance, so that life becomes an incessant attempt to capture what was lost.[30] Furthermore, the 'dark vigils of despair' suffered by the Assassins, hardly their punishment for rejecting human sympathy, question the defensive moralism of Shelley's Preface.

The seemingly ineluctable nature of the imagination's laws of synthesis and concentration on *one* object is also enacted in the second part of *Epipsychidion*. The intensifying momentum of the poet's fantasy of flight and union with his idealized counterpart obeys the necessity of seeking all sympathies in one. As Wasserman and Daniel J. Hughes have described,[31] the poet's attempt to achieve stable identity through the balanced influence of several women breaks down. Images predicated of all these various figures reappear together in the dream of the sun-woman of the poem's second half, uniting all their various attractions in one totality. This movement of desire explicitly contradicts the doctrine of multiple love which the poem had previously promulgated. There is a schematic contrast between lines 169–73 and lines 219–23:

> Narrow
> The heart that loves, the brain that contemplates,
> The life that wears, the spirit that creates
> *One object*, and *one form*, and builds thereby
> A *sepulchre* for its eternity. . . .
>
> (ll. 169–73; emphasis added)

> towards the loadstar of *my one desire*,
> I flitted, like a dizzy moth, whose flight
> Is as a dead leaf's in the owlet light,
> When it would seek in Hesper's setting sphere
> A radiant death, a fiery *sepulchre*. . . .
>
> (ll. 219–23; emphasis added)

Similarly, in the Dedication to *The Revolt of Islam*, Shelley describes himself as, having consecrated himself like the hero of *Alastor* to the pursuit of knowledge and the struggle against oppression, suddenly undergoing an introspective crisis identical to that enacted in *Alastor* – the involution of all desires and aspirations upon one intense and unattainable image:

> Alas, that love should be a blight and snare
>   To those who seek all sympathies in one! –
> Such once I sought in vain; then black despair,
>   The shadow of a starless night, was thrown
>   Over the world in which I moved alone. . . .
>
> (ll. 46–50)

Although Shelley continues, as one might expect, to praise his wife as having rescued him from this state, this is possible only by virtue of a rather dubious idealization of Mary Shelley and her famous parents as answering the needs of a poet's path-breaking identity.

The poet's dream, then, is not in any sense a visionary or mystical moment, but essentially an introspective crisis, the dawn of self-knowledge and self-consciousness. If this is narcissism it is of a form far removed from any implication of vanity. Like Ovid's Narcissus,[32] Shelley's poet is afflicted with the impossible dilemma of loving himself *as if he were another person.*

Shelley's theory that the want or power which he denominated 'love' was intense in proportion to the refinement of the internal affections is clearly going to have extremely ambivalent consequences in the case of the awakening of an active power of desire within a figure who already represents a *summum* of human development. As Norman Thurston has suggested,[33] the episode of an Arab maiden's love for the poet, of which he is quite oblivious (ll. 129–39), demonstrates she is never really a possibility for him. It does not support the notion of the poet's being punished for ignoring human sympathy. Given the poet's ideal education it is inconceivable that he would find an antitype adequate to his refined and perfected image, formed by a process of imaginative synthesis. As he flees mysteriously in a forlorn state through the mountains, maidens who watch him are able to interpret only 'half' the woe that consumes him (l. 267).

The pattern of the growth, culmination, and destructive decay of a personal sensibility was a commonplace of the period. De Staël, in fact, even fixed an age for the crisis in the development of a sensibility, twenty-five.[34] Nathan Drake, a minor critic of the time, is representative in his essay on the mental nature of Torquato Tasso and William Collins.[35] The lives of each poet, dogged by madness of a sort, are assimilated to the familiar contrast of the ardency and imaginative energy of youth with the disillusion consequent upon meeting a harsh and intransigent reality. This confrontation, to which the immediate aftermath of the dream in *Alastor* has an obvious likeness, precipitates a crisis whose resolution will determine the rest of that person's life. Whereas most harden themselves and eventually become insensible to both pleasures and pains, others, of fiercer imagination, refuse to surrender their ideal conceptions and may succumb to madness or death:

> But some there are gifted with an imagination of the most brilliant kind; who are accustomed to expatiate in all the luxury of an ideal world, and who possess a heart glowing with the tenderest sensations. These men too frequently fall a sacrifice to the indulgence of a warm and vigorous fancy, and which is, unhappily, not sufficiently corrected by a knowledge of mankind, or the rigid deduction of scientific study.[36]

Without claiming Drake as any kind of literary influence – his understanding of life in terms of growth, crisis, and resolution in madness or insensibility is too commonplace for that – lines 192–200 of *Alastor* are analogous to the crisis of early youth described by Drake in relation to the intensely imaginative:

> The lovely scenes they had so rapturously drawn, and coloured, find no architype in the busy paths of life, but fade beneath the gloomy touch of reality, and leave to the astonished visionary, a cheerless and barren view . . .[37]

> Roused by the shock he started from his trance –
> The cold white light of morning, the blue moon
> Low in the west, the clear and garish hills,
> The distinct valley and the vacant woods,
> Spread round him where he stood. Whither have fled
> The hues of heaven that canopied his bower
> Of yesternight? The sounds that soothed his sleep,
> The mystery and the majesty of Earth,
> The joy, the exultation?

(ll. 192–200)

The resolution of the crisis, according to Drake, is either insensibility or, as with Tasso and Collins, a lapse into the realm of delusions. A dichotomy between destruction and insensibility ('slow and poisonous decay'[38]) is precisely the grim choice of fates which Shelley describes in his Preface as resulting from the influence of Power.

As Richard Holmes points out,[39] it was as a poem on the dangers of an excessively sensitive imagination that *Alastor* was understood in about the only review to consider it seriously. The following interpretation appeared in the *Eclectic Review* for October 1816:

> The poem is adapted to shew the dangerous, the fatal tendency of that morbid ascendancy of the imagination over the other faculties, which incapacitates the mind for bestowing an adequate attention on the real objects of this 'work day' life, and for discharging the relative and social duties. It exhibits the utter uselessness of imagination, when wholly undisciplined, and selfishly employed for the mere purposes of intellectual luxury, without reference to those moral ends to which it was designed to be subservient.[40]

Shelley's strategy in adapting the pattern of sensibility's culmination and decline is apparent in the close resemblance between the Preface to *Alastor* and an article on this well-worn theme that appeared in Coleridge's journal *The Friend*. Charles Robinson has argued that Shelley probably owned a complete set of this journal.[41] In the edition that originally appeared for 14 December 1809, Coleridge printed an article by a correspondent signing himself merely 'Mathetes'. This concerned the dangers besetting a young mind with its 'passions of solitary and untamed imagination, and hopes which it has learnt from dreams'. The sentences that followed may have been in Shelley's mind when writing the Preface to *Alastor*:

> Those dreams have been of the great and wonderful, and lovely, of all which in these has yet been disclosed to him: his thoughts have dwelt among the wonders of Nature, and among the loftiest spirits of Men – Heroes, and Sages, and Saints; – those whose deeds, and thoughts, and hopes, were high above ordinary Mortality, have been the familiar Companions of his soul. To love and to admire has been the joy of his existence.[42]

The review goes on to give the usual remedies for excess of imagination – a tempering of the mind to reality and a submission to discipline.

Shelley's use of the commonplace of the dangers of imagination, however, should not mask a very considerable adaptation of it. In a sense, the pattern described in *The Friend* and by Drake and others is almost *inverted*. The dream of the poet actually disturbs an achieved harmony of mind and environment. It is not a case of the idealization of childhood and youth being suddenly confronted with an intransigent reality. This confrontation only takes place after the brief period of the dream in which the mind of the poet is structured anew by the awakening of active power within him and the brief period for which the mind is 'commensurate with all that it can conceive of excellent and powerful'.[43] It is, rather, a case of a *further* apprehension of excellence and ideal sympathy. The maiden of the dream briefly embodies in one totality all the allurements and excellences the poet has known separately before. Whereas Drake and the authors of the article in *The Friend* advise a tempering of the mind's desires to reality, Shelley affirms the aspiration to achieve a superior reality: 'Alas . . . [t]hat the moments when the human mind is commensurate with all that it can conceive of excellent and powerful, should not endure . . .'.[44] A recurrent dichotomy in Shelley's work is the laudable revolutionary aspiration of youth, compared to the enervation and sterility of the old.[45] This is entirely in accordance with Shelley's affirmation of the potency of want in social progress.

Further justification for reading much of Shelley's work in terms of an inversion of the dangers of sensibility is provided by a poem written at this time and published with *Alastor*, 'To —'. "Oh! there are spirits of the air"'. According to Mary Shelley, the poem is addressed to Coleridge.[46] Shelley narrates a series of betrayals, failures and subsequent attempts to achieve some emotional compensation for loneliness and adversity, these also failing. The first loss, analogous to that described by Coleridge himself in 'Dejection: an Ode', is that of the ability to commune with the so-called spirits of nature. This is followed by the failure to fulfil oneself through love, presumably a veiled reference to Sara Hutchinson. Shelley's account of the path that led Coleridge to imaginative sterility differs from that given in 'Dejection' by being couched wholly in a language of betrayal. It is not so much, as in 'Dejection', that the mind's inner resources have failed so that nature, coloured by the character of the mind, itself appears barren; rather, the natural world and even other people are mistaken as possible objects of fulfilment. The language of betrayal, in effect, is an expression of Coleridge's misplaced trust. Shelley describes the so-called spirits of nature as merely 'inexplicable things'. Shelley's proposed remedy, though now considered too late, is a form of introspective self-reliance more extreme even than that suggested by Coleridge himself in 'Dejection': 'I may not hope from outward forms to win / The passion and the life, whose fountains are within (ll. 45–6). For Shelley, the mind must become not only the source of an energy of emotion directed outwards, but must itself supply a constant object to be opposed to the realm of external mutability. Implicitly, as in Shelley's science of mind, the assumption or hope is that the mind may be an autonomous power in its own right, able to realize it own ideal through its own activity:

> Ah! wherefore didst thou build thine hope
>   On the false earth's inconstancy?
> Did thine own mind afford no scope
>   Of love, or moving things to thee?
> That natural scenes or human smiles
> Could steal the power to wind thee in their wiles?
>
>   (ll. 19–24)

Mary Shelley's claim that the poem is Shelley's analysis of the mind of Coleridge as he knew him from both his writings and people acquainted with him is confirmed by Shelley's account of him in *Peter Bell the Third*. It is effectively a paraphrase of the earlier poem:

> This was a man who might have turned
>   Hell into Heaven – and so in gladness
> A Heaven unto himself have earned;
> But he in shadows undiscerned
>   Trusted, – and damned himself to madness.
>
>   (ll. 383–7)

In loving a mutable external object Coleridge is condemned for mental weakness, for taking an easier option. His quest for love is a 'tame sacrifice' (l. 15) to a faith described as 'fond' (l. 16) with its connotations of self-deception. The importance of the poem to *Alastor* lies in its picture of the mind's potential powers, a total contrast to the processes depicted in 'Mutability'. Radical introspection is suddenly being advocated as a form of extreme self-reliance whose implication is that the human mind is capable of a self-creative independence from the rest of the universe.

Whatever Shelley's willingness, then, to adapt the hero of sensibility to the poet of *Alastor* and the commonplace conception of the dangers of sensibility to the vicissitudes of poetic identity, his purposes remain individual. It is not, as with Drake and numerous reviewers, an issue of the mind tempering itself to an intransigent reality that cannot answer the poet's want, but one of the mind's power to realize and maintain its ideal moments of total self-fulfilment. It is hard not to believe that Shelley saw dubious political motives in the desire of 'Mathetes' in *The Friend* to curb the mind to reality, rather than change reality in such a way as to render it adequate to the mind's ideals. This would have been in accordance with his criticisms of Wordsworth and of the commonsense philosophers, as well as the criticism of Coleridge's abjuration of his inner ideal in 'Oh! there are spirits'. The issue is not to tame want, which Shelley saw as a progressive force, rather, to *realize* it.

Notes

1 *Shelley's Poetry and Prose*, ed. Donald H. Reiman and Sharon B. Powers (New York: Norton, 1977), 69.

2 ['I loved not yet, and I loved to love; I sought for what I should love, loving love.']

3 Letter to Hogg, [end of Aug. 1815], Shelley, *Letters* i. 429–30.

4 Shelley's understanding of the so-called 'literature of sensibility' in relation to the social upheavals of his time is discussed in ch. 5 of *Embodying Revolution*.

5 See Newman Ivey White, *Shelley*, 2 vols (London; Secker and Warburg, 1947), i. 700–1.

6 See E. H. King, 'Beattie and Shelley: The Making of the Poet', *English Studies*, 61 (1980), 338–53.

7 Donald L. Maddox, 'Shelley's *Alastor* and the Legacy of Rousseau', *Studies in Romanticism.* 9 (1970), 82–98; Duffy, *Rousseau in England*, 93–5.

8 François-René de Chateaubriand, *Atala* and *René* (Paris; Chez le Normant, 1805); Wasserman, *Shelley*, 27–8.

9   A great deal of work on *Alastor* has been concerned with a rather inconsequential attempt to identify the poem's hero in a naïvely biographical manner, rather than deduce the poet's character from Shelley's poetics. See e.g. Paul Mueschke and Earl L. Griggs, 'Wordsworth as the Prototype of the Poet in Shelley's *Alastor*', *Publications of the Modern Languages Association of America* 49 (1934), 229–45; Joseph Raben, 'Coleridge as the Prototype of the Poet in Shelley's *Alastor*', *Review of English Studies* NS 17 (1966), 278–98; and M. Kessel, 'The Poet in Shelley's *Alastor*: A Criticism', *Publications of the Modern Languages Association of America* 51 (1936), 302–10.

10   See, most recently, Marilyn Butler's argument that *Alastor* represents an attack on the Wordsworthian panacea of solitude, *Romantics, Rebels, and Reactionaries:* 140–1; and Martin Crucefix's similar argument, 'Wordsworth, Superstition, and Shelley's *Alastor*', *Essays in Criticism*, 33 (1983), 126–47.

11   *Shelley's Poetry and Prose*, 69.

12   For various attempts to reconcile the poem and the apparent condemnation of the hero in the Preface see A. M. D. Hughes, '"Alastor; or, The Spirit of Solitude"', *Modern Language Review*, 43 (1948), 465–70; Raymond D. Havens, 'Shelley's "Alastor"', *Publications of the Modern Languages Association of America* 45 (1930), 1098–115; Arthur E. Dubois, '"Alastor: The Spirit of Solitude"', *Journal of English and Germanic Philology*, 35 (1936), 530–45; and Marion Clyde Wier, 'Shelley's "Alastor" Again', *Publications of the Modern Languages Association of America* 46 (1931), 947–50.

13   *Complete Works*, Julian edition, vii. 116.

14   *A Defence of Poetry*, ibid., vii. 116.

15   *Shelley's Poetry and Prose*, 69.

16   'Essay on Christianity', *Complete Works*, Julian edition, vi. 231. I have retained, where appropriate, Shelley's capitalization of 'Power', to mark the special status of the term in his work.

17   Cameron, *Shelley: The Golden Years*, 219–29.

18   'Essay on Christianity', *Complete Works*, Julian edition, vi. 235.

19   Ibid., 230.

20   Ibid., 231.

21   For readings of 'Mont Blanc' in terms of complex arguments about Shelley's epistemology see Wasserman, *Shelley*, 221–38; and Leighton, *Shelley and the Sublime*, 58–72.

22   Notopoulos, *The Platonism of Shelley*, 404.

23   Shelley, *Letters*, ii. 127.

24   See also Shelley's Preface to *Prometheus Unbound*: 'The peculiar style of intense and comprehensive imagery which distinguishes the modern literature of England, has not been, *as a general power*, the product of the imitation of any particular writer' (*Shelley's Poetry and Prose*, 134; emphasis added).

25   *Complete Works*, Julian edition, vi. 157.

26   Ibid., 160.

27   Ibid., 166. The passage resembles the Preface to *Alastor*, in which the poet is described before his dream: 'The magnificence and beauty of the external world

sinks profoundly into the frame of his conceptions, and affords to their modifications a variety not be exhausted' (*Shelley's Poetry and Prose*, 69).

28   From the manuscript of 'On Love', Bod. MS Shelley adds. e. II, 3.

29   *Complete Works*, Julian edition, vi. 160–1; emphasis added.

30   The recurrent association of introspection and loss in Shelley was first described at length by Ants Oras, 'Notes on Introspection and Self-Analysis, their Function and Imaginal Representation in Shelley', *Neuphilologische Mitteilungen*, 73 (1972), 275–83. See also Daniel J. Hughes's reading of Shelley's poems as consistently dramatizing the intermittent nature of poetic power, 'Kindling and Dwindling: The Poetic Process in Shelley', *Keats–Shelley Journal*, 13 (1964), 13–28.

31   Wasserman, *Shelley*, 439; Daniel J. Hughes, 'Coherence and Collapse in Shelley, with Particular Reference to *Epipsychidion*', *Journal of English Literary History* 28 (1961), 271–83.

32   *Metamorphoses*, ed. and trans. Frank Justus Miller, rev. G. P. Goold, 2 vols. (Loeb Classical Library; 3rd edn., London: Heinemann, 1977), 148–61 (iii. 339–510).

33   'Author, Narrator, and Hero in Shelley's *Alastor*', *Studies in Romanticism* 14 (1975), 120–1.

34   Madame de Staël, *De l'influence des passions sur le bonheur des individus et des nations* (Lausanne: J. Mourer, 1796), 45–7: 'At the age of twenty-five . . ., precisely at that period when life ceases to enlarge, when our being is fixed, a severe change takes place in our existence . . . In a word, the affections of the heart are withered, the gay colouring of life fades away', trans. from *A Treatise on the Influence of the Passions, upon the Happiness of Individuals and of Nations* (London: George Cawthorn, 1798), 35–7.

35   'On the Government of the Imagination; on the Frenzy of Tasso and Collins', in *Literary Hours; or, Sketches Critical and Narrative* (London; Longman, 1798), 29–44.

36   Ibid., 31.

37   Ibid.

38   *Shelley's Poetry and Prose*, 69.

39   *Shelley: The Pursuit*, 309–10.

40   *The Eclectic Review*, new series, 6 (July–Dec. 1816), 392.

41   Charles E. Robinson, 'The Shelley Circle and Coleridge's *The Friend*', *English Language Notes* 8 (1971), 269–74.

42   *The Friend*, ii. 223. This article has been attributed to John Wilson and Alexander Blair, *The Friend*, i. 377–8.

43   *The Assassins, Complete Works*, Julian edition, vi. 160.

44   Ibid., 160–1.

45   In *The Revolt of Islam*, for instance, old age is dismissed as 'nought' because 'it cannot dare / To burst the chains which life for ever flings / On the entangled soul's aspiring wings . . .' (ll. 957–59).

46   Percy Bysshe Shelley, *Poetical Works*, ed. T. Hutchinson, corr. G. M. Matthews (London: Oxford University Press, 1970), 527–8.

Further reading

The selection below indicates the range of discussion of Shelley's politics, understood not only as manifest political content, but also as the political implications of Shelley's poetic practice. Topics of enquiry include feminism (Brown, Gelpi) and, more recently, Orientalism (see, especially, Leask).

John Pollard Guinn, *Shelley's Political Thought* (The Hague: Mouton, 1969). Surveys the whole course of Shelley's writing, before and after 1815, so as to present him, categorically, as a reformer. The final chapter, on Shelley's influence, suggests Shelley's impact on M. K. Gandhi's policy of non-violent opposition in India.

Gerald McNiece, *Shelley and the Revolutionary Idea* (Cambridge, Mass.: Harvard University Press, 1969). Shelley's thinking is shaped by the lessons of the French Revolution, making the mission of his poetry the 'recharging of the power of revolutionary ideas', but teaching him also to integrate practical reform with visionary idealism.

Carl Woodring, *Politics in English Romantic Poetry* (Cambridge, Mass.: Harvard University Press, 1970). To Shelley, poetic creation is a social act, by virtue of the near synonymity of liberty, imagination and love; he 'sought to mediate the dichotomy between love and revolution' by making love the precondition of social revolution.

Kenneth Neill Cameron, *Shelley: The Golden Years* (Cambridge, Mass.: Harvard University Press, 1974). Monumental study, extending Cameron's previous coverage to Shelley's later works. Offers a wealth of documentary detail to ground the major poetry solidly in its historical and (revolutionary) political context.

Timothy Webb, *Shelley: A Voice Not Understood* (Manchester: Manchester University Press, 1977). Argues against, and seeks to correct, the distorted readings of Shelley produced by the influence of biographical myths, which have led to the dismissal or negation of the strong social and political impulses of his poetry.

Nathaniel Brown, *Sexuality and Feminism in Shelley* (Cambridge, Mass.: Harvard University Press, 1979). Focuses on the sexual element in Shelley's work as belonging to 'a coherent philosophy of sexual relationship', at the basis of which, and developed from the eighteenth-century doctrine of sympathy, is Shelley's feminism.

Edward Duffy, *Rousseau in England: The Context for Shelley's Critique of the Enlightenment* (Berkeley: University of California Press, 1979). *The Triumph of Life* is the 'climactic text' in this valuable study of the English construction of Rousseau as Enlightenment prototype and symbol of revolutionary failure. Shelley attempts to transform failure to optimism, by writing 'a poem that would be a reclamation of Rousseau's work from the corrosive influence of his life and hence a model for the way the benign impulse of the French Revolution ought to be similarly distinguished from its pragmatic failures.'

P. M. S. Dawson, *The Unacknowledged Legislator: Shelley and Politics* (Oxford: Clarendon Press, 1980). Essential study of Shelley's politics. Finds, at the core of Shelley's political thinking, a philosophical anarchism, with its concomitant moral principles, derived from Godwin but developed independently. Dawson examines the relation between Shelley's ideals and his practical proposals for reform, and his evolution of a theory of imagination that links poetry and politics.

Paul Foot, *Red Shelley* (London: Sidgwick and Jackson, 1980). Lively proclamation of Shelley's radicalism, tracing the sources and development of 'his republicanism, his atheism, his feminism and his egalitarianism.'

Marilyn Butler, *Romantics, Rebels and Reactionaries: English Literature and its Background 1760–1830* (Oxford: Oxford University Press, 1981). Shows that Shelley participates, with Byron and Keats, in a left-wing cult of classicism, antithetical to the post-revolutionary, conservative romanticism associated with Germany and the north. Developing, from pagan myth, a cult of sexuality, the younger poets challenged religious orthodoxy and so 'proclaimed their rejection of the political ideology of the older poets.'

David Punter, 'Shelley: Poetry and Politics' in *Romanticism and Ideology: Studies in English Writing 1765–1830*, ed. D. Aers, J. Cook and D. Punter (London: Routledge & Kegan Paul, 1981), 155–72. Presents Shelley's idealism as incorporating a concern with practice, reality and experience. To Shelley, imagination (or poetry), which relates real and ideal, concrete and abstract, is able to break free of ideological restriction, thus enabling human liberty.

Michael Henry Scrivener, *Radical Shelley: The Philosophical Anarchism and Utopian Thought of Percy Bysshe Shelley* (Princeton: Princeton University Press, 1982). Finds, in Shelley's engagement with and revision of Godwin, a significant contribution to nineteenth-century radical thought. 'Especially as revised by Shelley, philosophical anarchism establishes a political ideal, a utopia, towards which society is moving in stages; . . . it accepts politics as a process of gradual reforms and compromise.'

Kelvin Everest (ed.), *Shelley Revalued: Essays from the Gregynog Conference* (Leicester: Leicester University Press, 1983). Important essays by major scholars, treating Shelley's poetic skill and formal mastery, along with his philosophical and political vision, and the impact of his social and cultural context.

Jerome J. McGann, *The Romantic Ideology: A Critical Investigation* (Chicago and London: University of Chicago Press, 1983). The futurism of Shelley's poetry is an expression of post-revolutionary despair, the displacement of a frustration with the present to hopes of a future.

Stuart Curran, *Poetic Form and British Romanticism* (New York and Oxford: Oxford University Press, 1986). This important study of 'how major forms of earlier poetry are resuscitated and transformed in the Romanticism of Great Britain' is especially insightful on Shelley's use of genre.

Marjorie Levinson, *The Romantic Fragment Poem: A Critique of a Form* (Chapel Hill and London: University of North Carolina Press, 1986). Shelley's 'deliberate fragments' belong to Levinson's exposure of Romantic ideology in the fragment poem: 'the exercise is to pry apart the poem's special maneuvers and projections from the totalizing constructs in which criticism . . . has framed them.'

Jerrold E. Hogle, *Shelley's Process: Radical Transference and the Development of his Major Works* (New York and Oxford: Oxford University Press, 1988). Attending to the characteristic feature of Shelley's style, the perpetual dissolution or displacement of his verbal figures one by another, Hogle counters a received view that such verbal shifts imply a unified 'One' or centre, from which they issue and to which they are impelled. Replacing that centre with the process of ceaseless centreless displacement ('transference') itself, Hogle identifies with this process Shelley's iconoclasm and his critique of established systems.

Stephen C. Behrendt, *Shelley and his Audiences* (Lincoln and London: University of Nebraska Press, 1989). Emphasizes the awareness of his audience entailed by Shelley's ethical and political project: 'he was a careful and deliberate stylist who consistently tried to adapt forms, formats, and rhetorical strategies to the variously conceived audiences he addressed.'

*__Michael O'Neill__, *Percy Bysshe Shelley: A Literary Life* (Basingstoke: Macmillan, 1989). Useful contextual study, discussing 'Shelley's career as a writer . . . in the light of the literary, socio-political and ideological conditions of the day.' Topics include the importance for Shelley of the French Revolution and Enlightenment thought, Shelley's response to his contemporaries, the impact of reviews and censorship, and Shelley's search for an audience.

Barbara Charlesworth Gelpi, *Shelley's Goddess: Maternity, Language, Subjectivity* (New York and Oxford: Oxford University Press, 1992). Psychoanalytic theory, the child-rearing practices of Shelley's age, and his relationship with his own mother, brought to bear on a reading of *Prometheus Unbound*: 'Having experienced sexual frustration as a – perhaps *the* – principal effect of patriarchal control, but having also learned that aggressive defiance mirrors the aspect of its opponent, Shelley sought in *Prometheus Unbound* to imagine a nonconfrontational release of tabooed sexual energies linked to fantasies of a peaceable matriarchate.'

Nigel Leask, *British Romantic Writers and the East: Anxieties of Empire* (Cambridge: Cambridge University Press, 1992). Relating Shelley to colonial India via his cousin, Thomas Medwin, Leask shows that India represents the oriental 'Other' to Shelley. Although much of Shelley's writing manifests the colonial desire to assimilate the Other into the Same, *Prometheus Unbound* uniquely unsettles 'the norms of both "orientalist" and assimilationist discourse', in its presentation of a decolonized, genuinely dialogic relationship between Prometheus and Asia (India).

*__Michael Ferber__, *The Poetry of Shelley* (Harmondsworth: Penguin, 1993). Invaluable introduction to Shelley and his politics through a lucid discussion, focused closely on the texts, of his craftsmanship in the major poems.

David Duff, *Romance and Revolution: Shelley and the Politics of a Genre* (Cambridge: Cambridge University Press, 1994). Examining as paradoxical the conjunction of the theme of revolution and the genre of romance, locates the origins of this conjunction in the 1790s, and offers a close reading of Shelley's *Queen Mab* and *Laon and Cythna*, 'in which the politics of romance is most fully displayed.'

Steven E. Jones, *Shelley's Satire: Violence, Exhortation, and Authority* (De Kalb: Northern Illinois State University Press, 1994). Stimulating study of Shelley's satire as amounting to 'an important countervoice within Shelley's work and within Romanticism as a whole.' The rhetorical strategies of Shelley's satire address its central dilemma, that it 'seeks to exhort and persuade, but through inherited forms of authority to which he is at once (artistically) attracted and (ethically) opposed.'

Timothy Morton, *Shelley and the Revolution in Taste: The Body and the Natural World* (Cambridge: Cambridge University Press, 1994). In its own words, a work of 'green cultural criticism'. Shelley's discourse of diet (vegetarianism) refashions taste 'in revolt against . . . the hierarchical powers which controlled consumption, production, and culture', delineating 'new relationships between bodies and their environment.'

Anthony John Harding, *The Reception of Myth in English Romanticism* (Columbia and London: University of Missouri Press, 1995). Examines both Shelley's critique of myth, and his own subversive use of myth to political and sceptical ends: 'a mythological treatment advertises itself as both artful and politically engaged, and through a parallel kind of innuendo it points to the ephemerality of all belief systems.' Goes on to show, in Shelley's later poetry, his reinterpretation of the myth of Apollo and Pan.

Betty T. Bennett and Stuart Curran (eds.), *Shelley: Poet and Legislator of the World* (Baltimore and London: Johns Hopkins University Press, 1996). 'Twenty-three prismatic reflections . . . lucidly recast[ing] his presence into coherent wholeness . . . across . . . a diversity of historical epochs and cultures.' The essays in this volume variously cover Shelley's cultural and political contexts, his own political engagement, his global conception and impact, and his continuing relevance.

Timothy Clark and Jerrold E. Hogle (eds.), *Evaluating Shelley* (Edinburgh: Edinburgh University Press, 1996). Range of critical approaches, locating Shelley in his wider cultural contexts, or offering detailed readings of individual works, so as to reassess his own engagement with questions of value, and his value for our time.

James Chandler, *England in 1819: The Politics of Literary Culture and the Case of Romantic Historicism* (Chicago and London: University of Chicago Press, 1998). Shelley figures prominently in Chandler's impressive argument of the links between contemporary and Romantic historicism: the emergence of the distinction that underwrites historicist interpretation, between the literary and historical aspects of texts (or as Chandler puts it, between the way in which texts *make* history, and the way in which they *mark* history), is already in operation in the politicized literary culture of England in 1819.

Jeffrey N. Cox, *Poetry and Politics in the Cockney School: Keats, Shelley, Hunt and their Circle* (Cambridge: Cambridge University Press, 1998). Locates Shelley within the Cockney School, the circle of second-generation romantic writers, with Leigh Hunt at their centre, whose writing was collaborative and social, and who were committed to literature as a means to social, cultural and political reform.

Andrew Epstein, '"Flowers that Mock the Corse Beneath": Shelley's *Adonais*, Keats, and Poetic Influence', *Keats–Shelley Journal* xlviii (1999), 90–128. Original take on the Shelley–Keats relationship, in a reading of *Adonais*, not as tribute, but as indicating Shelley's 'fierce ambivalence towards . . . Keats and the dimensions of his struggle with the conflict of poetic influence and originality.'

Kim Wheatley, *Shelley and his Readers: Beyond Paranoid Politics* (Columbia and London: University of Missouri Press, 1999). Puts Shelley's poetry and its hostile contemporary reception in dialogue. The early poetry and its hostile reviews (whose rhetoric Wheatley terms 'paranoid style') are locked into an oppositional impasse, but the increasingly aestheticized form of later works, such as *Prometheus Unbound* and *Adonais*, undercuts the reviewers by its idealistic and ethical shift, beyond a rigidly partisan paranoid politics, into a non-partisan aesthetic realm separate from, and transcending, the political.

*Paul Hamilton, *Percy Bysshe Shelley* (Tavistock: Northcote House, 2000). Concise introduction, countering the image of Shelley as a Romantic solipsist, by attending to the materialistic tenor of his work. Examines the paradox of revolutionary hope and pessimism in Shelley's thought and writing.

Deborah Elise White, *Romantic Returns: Superstition, Imagination, History* (Stanford, Calif.: Stanford University Press, 2000). Shelley is integral to White's sophisticated defence of Romantic imagination against a narrowly ideological critique: 'the category of the aesthetic – for which the crucial Romantic term is imagination – enables a critical and reflexive articulation of the historical passage between knowledge and action, epistemology and ethics, fine art and politics.'

Stuart Peterfreund, *Shelley among Others: The Play of the Intertext and the Idea of Language* (Baltimore and London: Johns Hopkins University Press, 2002). 'Integrates the intertextual and linguistic conceptions and practices that Shelley . . . deployed in seeking and claiming for himself a place in the Western literary tradition', showing, in so doing, the affinity of Shelley's ideas of language and intertextuality to contemporary thought and theory.

Peter A. Schock, *Romantic Satanism: Myth and the Historical Moment in Blake, Shelley, and Byron* (Basingstoke: Palgrave Macmillan, 2003). Shelley's poetry is focal to this study of the Romantic poets' artistic and ideological identification with Milton's Satan, and of the various forms – with their social and cultural contexts – of Satanism in their works.

James Bieri, *Percy Bysshe Shelley: A Biography: Youth's Unextinguished Fire, 1792–1816* and *Exile of Unfulfilled Renown, 1816–1822* (Newark: University of Delaware Press, 2004, 2005). Major new two-volume biography, combining accessibility with accuracy. Draws on recent Shelley scholarship and the author's own extensive research freshly to examine the links between the poet's character and his works.

Cian Duffy, *Shelley and the Revolutionary Sublime* (Cambridge: Cambridge University Press, 2005). Challenging the demarcation of Shelley's radicalism from his (visionary) engagement with the sublime, 'explores the relationship between the sublime and the revolutionary in Shelley's work', thus re-evaluating the social and political implications of the sublime in Romantic writing.

Sharon Ruston, *Shelley and Vitality* (Basingstoke: Palgrave Macmillan, 2005). Emphasizes Shelley's materialist thinking by arguing the bearing, on his work, of contemporary theories of vitality or the principle of life, these theories, with their radical implications, offering him a means to link 'the physical, mental, and societal'.

Useful editions

The Norton Critical Edition, *Shelley's Poetry and Prose*, ed. Donald H. Reiman and Sharon B. Powers, has long been the best selection for students, and the one in standard use by professional scholars; a second edition, by Reiman and Neil Fraistat was published in 2002. Two volumes of an invaluable and meticulous new edition, *Poems of*

Shelley, ed. Kelvin Everest and Geoffrey Matthews (London: Longman, 1989–) have so far been published: volume I, 1804–1817 and volume II, 1817–1819. The third volume will complete the collection.

Reference material

Frederick L. Jones (ed.), *The Letters of Percy Bysshe Shelley*. Includes a useful appendix on 'Shelley's Reading', sourced from the letters and from Mary Shelley's Journals.

Shelley manuscripts are transcribed in three major collections: the edition of manuscripts in the Carl H. Pforzheimer collection of the New York Public Library, *Shelley and His Circle, 1773–1822*, ed. K. N. Cameron, D. H. Reiman and D. D. Fischer (Cambridge, Mass.: Harvard University Press, 1961–); *The Manuscripts of the Younger Romantics*, ed. D. H. Reiman (New York: Garland, 1985–); and *The Bodleian Shelley Manuscripts*, ed. D. H. Reiman (New York: Garland, 1986–).

Chapter notes

1   The contemporary reviews of Shelley are collected in Donald Reiman (ed.), *The Romantics Reviewed, Part C: Shelley, Keats, and London Radical Writers*. An extensive selection of nineteenth-century comment, with a useful introductory survey, may also be found in James E. Barcus (ed.), *Percy Bysshe Shelley: The Critical Heritage* (1975; repr. London: Routledge, 1995).

2   ?George Croly, review of *The Cenci* (1819) in *Literary Gazette* (1 Apr 1820), 209 (*Romantics Reviewed, Part C*, II. 517).

3   Anon, review of *The Cenci* (2nd edn., 1821) in *British Review* xvii (Jun 1821), 385 (*Romantics Reviewed, Part C*, I. 253).

4   See, for instance: Anon, review of *The Cenci* in [Gold's] *London Magazine* i (Apr 1820), 401–7; George Croly, review of *Adonais* (1821) in *Blackwood's Edinburgh Magazine* x (Dec 1821), 696–700; Anon, review of *Adonais* in *Literary Gazette* (8 Dec 1821), 772–3 (*Romantics Reviewed, Part C*, II. 606–12; I. 147–51; II. 531–2).

5   William Hazlitt, review of Shelley's *Posthumous Poems* (1824) in *Edinburgh Review* xi (Jul 1824), 497 (*Romantics Reviewed, Part C*, I. 401).

6   See Leigh Hunt, extended review of *The Revolt of Islam* (1818) in *Examiner* (1 Feb 1818), 75–6; (22 Feb 1818), 121–2; (1 Mar 1818), 139–41; review of *Rosalind and Helen* (1819) in *Examiner* (9 May 1818), 302–3; extended article on *The Revolt of Islam* in *Examiner* (26 Sept 1819), 620–1; (3 Oct 1819), 635–6; (10 Oct 1819), 652–3; review of *The Cenci* in *Indicator* (19 Jul 1820), 321–8; (26 Jul 1820), 329–36 (*Romantics Reviewed, Part C*, I. 433–7; 443–4; 444–8; II. 471–8).

7   J. G. Lockhart, review of *Revolt of Islam* in *Blackwood's Edinburgh Magazine* iv (Jan 1819), 482 (*Romantics Reviewed, Part C*, I. 103). See also Lockhart's reviews

of *Rosalind and Helen*, of *Alastor* (1816), and of *Prometheus Unbound* (1820) in *Blackwood's Edinburgh Magazine* iv (June 1819), 268–74; vi (Nov 1819), 148–54; vii (Sept 1820), 679–87 (*Romantics Reviewed, Part C*, I. 104–10; 118–24; 138–46).

8   J. G. Lockhart, review of *Prometheus Unbound* in *Blackwood's Edinburgh Magazine* vii (Sept 1820), 679 (*Romantics Reviewed, Part C*, I. 138).

9   Anon, review of *Prometheus Unbound* (1820) in [Gold's] *London Magazine* ii (Oct 1820), 382 (*Romantics Reviewed, Part C*, II. 629).

10   See Appendix A, 'Browning's Essay on Shelley' in vol. 4 of *The Poetical Works of Robert Browning*, ed. I. Jack, R. Fowler and M. Smith (Oxford: Clarendon Press, 1991), 437.

11   Walter Bagehot, 'Percy Bysshe Shelley' (1856), repr. in *Literary Studies*, ed. R. H. Hutton, 3 vols. (1879; new edn. London: Longmans, Green & Co., 1895) i. 255, 285.

12   Arnold, 'Byron' in *Works*, IX. 237.

13   W. B. Yeats, 'The Philosophy of Shelley's Poetry' (1900), repr. in *Essays and Introductions* (New York: Macmillan, 1961), 65–95.

14   Irving Babbitt, *Rousseau and Romanticism* (1919; repr. Austin and London: University of Texas Press, 1977), 76, 295.

15   T. S. Eliot, 'Shelley and Keats', in *The Use of Poetry and the Use of Criticism* (London: Faber, 1933), 89, 96.

16   F. R. Leavis, 'Shelley' in *Revaluation: Tradition and Development in English Poetry* (London: Chatto & Windus, 1936), 211, 219, 216.

17   James A. Notopoulos, *The Platonism of Shelley: A Study of Platonism and the Poetic Mind* (Durham, N.C.: Duke University Press, 1949), 13.

18   Earl R. Wasserman, *Shelley: A Critical Reading* (Baltimore and London: Johns Hopkins Press, 1971), ix.

19   Ibid., ix.

20   E. Aveling and E. M. Aveling, *Shelley's Socialism: Two Lectures* (London: 1888), 26.

21   Kenneth Neill Cameron, *The Young Shelley: Genesis of a Radical* (London: Gollancz, 1951), xi.

6

John Keats (1795–1821)

THE CONTEMPORARY RECEPTION

Keats was first noticed publicly by his friend and patron, the political radical Leigh Hunt, in a short article in the *Examiner*, titled 'Young Poets'.

> . . . the youngest of them all, and just of age. . . . is JOHN KEATS. . . . a set of his manuscripts was handed us the other day, and fairly surprised us with the truth of their ambition, and ardent grappling with Nature.[1]

Hunt's praise encouraged Keats to abandon medicine for poetry as a profession. For the Tory reviewers, it was a stimulus of another kind. Keats's poetic practice – his innovations in diction, versification and style – became a means to attack Hunt. Political partisanship and critical judgement fed off each other, and Lockhart's tag, 'Cockney School', for Hunt and his coterie, passed into general usage. Applied at one time or another to Hunt, Hazlitt, Byron, Shelley and Keats, it signified, opposite to 'Lake School', a characteristically urban set of writers. The contrast prefigures the antithesis of Keats and Wordsworth that Keats himself famously remarks, and that later becomes a critical commonplace.

> Mr. Keats belongs to the Cockney School of Poetry – a school, we suppose, so denominated, from the fact of its writers having been educated in the city, and taking their pictures of rural life from its immediate environs.[2]

The attendant connotations were emphatically belittling: low social status, an anti-national position, sickliness, effeminacy. Keats's vulgarity was found to be manifest, too, in a vicious sensuality, pointed to by more than one reviewer, but most explicitly in a letter from Byron to John Murray: 'why his is the

Onanism of poetry'; 'such writing is a sort of mental masturbation – he is always f-gg-g his *Imagination.*'[3]

Keats had his defenders, some rather more effusive than effective. In a review of *Endymion*, for instance, his friend, John Hamilton Reynolds, cites a passage 'scarcely to be surpassed in the whole range of English Poetry.'[4] To P. G. Patmore in Baldwin's *London Magazine, Endymion* 'is an ecstatic dream of poetry – a flush – a fever – a burning light – an involuntary out-pouring of the spirit of poetry'.[5] But more discerning praise was also forthcoming. In the *Champion*, the anonymous reviewer of *Endymion* asserts the comparison with Shakespeare, and the ideal of a 'chameleon poet', to which Keats himself aspired, and to which modern-day criticism has repeatedly recurred: 'The secret of the success of our modern poets, is their universal presence in their poems – . . . But Mr. Keats goes out of himself into a world of abstractions: – his passions, feelings are all as much imaginative as his situations.'[6] For Francis Jeffrey, reviewing the *Lamia* collection in the *Edinburgh*, Keats was wanting in plan and consistency, but was nonetheless 'deeply imbued' with 'the true genius of English poetry.'[7]

In fact, praise and disparagement of Keats by his contemporaries were more or less evenly balanced: although *Endymion* was generally faulted, the *Lamia* volume, containing the romances and the odes, was widely acknowledged to show the young poet's growing maturity and control over his medium. Nonetheless, the portrayal by his sympathizers of an overwhelmingly adverse reception, and dark forebodings of its fatal effect, began to emerge even in Keats's lifetime. Patmore's review of *Endymion* opens with an account of poets killed or blighted by criticism; Hunt's notice of the *Lamia* volume in the *Indicator* mentions the damaging effect of 'critical malignity' on the already ailing Keats.[8] The myth of a sensitive poet slain by his critics was to crystallize after Keats's death in Shelley's great elegy, *Adonais* (1821).

Extracted below is Lockhart's 1818 review of *Poems* (1817) and *Endymion* in *Blackwood's Edinburgh Magazine*, the fourth of his notorious series on 'The Cockney School of Poetry'. Lockhart's listing of Keats's stylistic and verbal peculiarities, apart from his reading of their class and political implications, convey the distinctive qualities of the poetry as it appeared to its first readers.

Extract from J. G. Lockhart ('Z'), 'The Cockney School of Poetry' (No. 4), *Blackwood's Edinburgh Magazine* (1818)

————————OF KEATS,
THE MUSES' SON OF PROMISE, AND WHAT FEATS
HE YET MAY DO, &c.

CORNELIUS WEBB

Of all the manias of this mad age, the most incurable, as well as the most common, seems to be no other than the *Metromanie*. The just celebrity of Robert Burns and Miss Baillie has had the melancholy effect of turning the heads of we know not how many farm-servants and unmarried ladies; our very footmen compose tragedies, and there is scarcely a superannuated governess in the island that does not leave a roll of lyrics behind her in her band-box. To witness the disease of any human understanding, however feeble, is distressing; but the spectacle of an able mind reduced to a state of insanity is of course ten times more afflicting. It is with such sorrow as this that we have contemplated the case of Mr John Keats. This young man appears to have received from nature talents of an excellent, perhaps even of a superior order – talents which, devoted to the purposes of any useful profession, must have rendered him a respectable, if not an eminent citizen. His friends, we understand, destined him to the career of medicine, and he was bound apprentice some years ago to a worthy apothecary in town. But all has been undone by a sudden attack of the malady to which we have alluded. Whether Mr John had been sent home with a diuretic or composing draught to some patient far gone in the poetical mania, we have not heard. This much is certain, that he has caught the infection, and that thoroughly. For some time we were in hopes, that he might get off with a violent fit or two; but of late the symptoms are terrible. The phrenzy of the 'Poems' was bad enough in its way; but it did not alarm us half so seriously as the calm, settled, imperturbable drivelling idiocy of 'Endymion.' We hope, however, that in so young a person, and with a constitution originally so good, even now the disease is not utterly incurable. Time, firm treatment, and rational restraint, do much for many apparently hopeless invalids; and if Mr Keats should happen, at some interval of reason, to cast his eye upon our pages, he may perhaps be convinced of the existence of his malady, which, in such cases, is often all that is necessary to put the patient in a fair way of being cured.

The readers of the Examiner newspaper were informed, some time ago, by a solemn paragraph, in Mr Hunt's best style, of the appearance of two new stars of glorious magnitude and splendour in the poetical horizon of the land of Cockaigne. One of these turned out, by and by, to be no other than Mr John Keats. This precocious adulation confirmed the wavering apprentice in his desire to quit the gallipots, and at the same time excited in his too susceptible mind a fatal admiration for the character and talents of the most worthless and affected of all the versi-fiers of our time. One of his first productions was the following sonnet, '*written on the day when Mr Leigh Hunt left prison.*' It will be recollected, that the cause of Hunt's confinement was a series of libels against his sovereign, and that its fruit was the odious and incestuous 'Story of Rimini.'

[*'Z'* then quotes the sonnet]
The absurdity of the thought in this sonnet is, however, if possible, surpassed in another, *'addressed to Haydon'* the painter, that clever, but most affected artist, who as little resembles Raphael in genius as he does in person, notwithstanding the foppery of having his hair curled over his shoulders in the old Italian fashion. In this exquisite piece it will be observed, that Mr Keats classes together WORDSWORTH, HUNT, and HAYDON, as the three greatest spirits of the age, and that he alludes to himself, and some others of the rising brood of Cockneys, as likely to attain hereafter an equally honourable elevation. Wordsworth and Hunt! what a juxta-position! The purest, the loftiest, and, we do not fear to say it, the most classical of living English poets, joined together in the same compliment with the meanest, the filthiest, and the most vulgar of Cockney poetasters. No wonder that he who could be guilty of this should class Haydon with Raphael, and himself with Spencer.

[. . .] our youthful poet passes very naturally into a long strain of foaming abuse against a certain class of English Poets, whom, with Pope at their head, it is much the fashion with the ignorant unsettled pretenders of the present time to undervalue. Begging these gentlemens' pardon, although Pope was not a poet of the same high order with some who are now living, yet, to deny his genius, is just about as absurd as to dispute that of Wordsworth, or to believe in that of Hunt. Above all things, it is most pitiably ridiculous to hear men, of whom their country will always have reason to be proud, reviled by uneducated and flimsy striplings, who are not capable of understanding either their merits, or those of any other *men of power* – fanciful dreaming tea-drinkers, who, without logic enough to analyse a single idea, or imagination enough to form one original image, or learning enough to distinguish between the written language of Englishmen and the spoken jargon of Cockneys, presume to talk with contempt of some of the most exquisite spirits the world ever produced, merely because they did not happen to exert their faculties in laborious affected descriptions of flowers seen in window-pots, or cascades heard at Vauxhall; in short, because they chose to be wits, philosophers, patriots, and poets, rather than to found the Cockney school of versification, morality, and politics, a century before its time. After blaspheming himself into a fury against Boileau, &c. Mr Keats comforts himself and his readers with a view of the present more promising aspect of affairs; above all, with the ripened glories of the poet of Rimini.

[. . .]

So much for the opening bud; now for the expanded flower. It is time to pass from the juvenile 'Poems,' to the mature and elaborate 'Endymion, a Poetic Romance.' The old story of the moon falling in love with a shepherd, so prettily told by a Roman Classic, and so exquisitely enlarged and adorned by one of the most elegant of German poets, has been seized upon by Mr John Keats, to be done with as might seem good unto the sickly fancy of one who never read a single line either of Ovid or of Wieland. If the quantity, not the quality, of the verses dedicated to the story is to be taken into account, there can be no doubt that Mr John Keats may now claim Endymion entirely to himself. To say the truth, we do not suppose either the Latin or the German poet would be very anxious to dispute about the property of the hero of the 'Poetic Romance.' Mr Keats has thoroughly appropriated the character, if not the name. His Endymion is not a Greek shepherd, loved by a Grecian goddess; he is merely a young Cockney rhymester, dreaming a phantastic dream at the full of the moon. Costume, were it worth while to notice such a trifle, is violated in every page of this goodly octavo. From his prototype Hunt, John Keats has acquired a sort of vague idea, that the Greeks were a most tasteful people, and that no mythology can be so finely adapted for the purposes of poetry as theirs. It is amusing to see what a hand the two Cockneys make of this mythology; the one confesses that he never read the Greek Tragedians, and the other knows Homer only from Chapman; and both of them write about Apollo, Pan, Nymphs, Muses, and Mysteries, as might be expected from persons of their education. We shall not, however, enlarge at present upon this subject, as we mean to dedicate an entire paper to the classical attainments and attempts of the Cockney poets. As for Mr Keats' 'Endymion,' it has just as much to do with Greece as it has with 'old Tartary the fierce;'[1] no man, whose mind has ever been imbued with the smallest knowledge or feeling of classical poetry or classical history, could have stooped to profane and vulgarise every association in the manner which has been adopted by this 'son of promise.' Before giving any extracts, we must inform our readers, that this romance is meant to be written in English heroic rhyme. To those who have read any of Hunt's poems, this hint might indeed be needless. Mr Keats has adopted the loose, nerveless versification, and Cockney rhymes of the poet of Rimini; but in fairness to that gentleman, we must add, that the defects of the system are tenfold more conspicuous in his disciple's work than in his own. Mr Hunt is a small poet, but he is a clever man. Mr Keats is a still smaller poet, and he is only a boy of pretty abilities, which he has done every thing in his power to spoil.

['Z' then outlines the poem, with long quotations and brief mocking comments]

We had almost forgot to mention, that Keats belongs to the Cockney School of Politics, as well as the Cockney School of Poetry.

It is fit that he who holds Rimini to be the first poem, should believe the Examiner to be the first politician of the day. We admire consistency, even in folly.

[. . .]

And now, good-morrow to 'the Muses' son of Promise;' as for 'the feats he yet may do,' as we do not pretend to say, like himself, 'Muse of my native land am I inspired,' we shall adhere to the safe old rule of *pauca verba*.[2] We venture to make one small prophecy, that his bookseller will not a second time venture £50 upon any thing he can write. It is a better and a wiser thing to be a starved apothecary than a starved poet; so back to the shop Mr John, back to 'plasters, pills, and ointment boxes,' &c. But, for Heaven's sake, young Sangrado,[3] be a little more sparing of extenuatives and soporifics in your practice than you have been in your poetry.   Z.

Notes

[1   *Endymion* IV, 264.

2   'few words'.

3   The quack Dr. Sangrado is a character from the French novel, *Gil Blas de Santillane* (1715–1735), by Alain-René Lesage, translated into English by Tobias Smollett in 1749.]

Further reading

A comprehensive collection of the contemporary reviews of Keats may be found in *The Romantics Reviewed, Part C: Shelley, Keats, and London Radical Writers*, ed. Donald Reiman. *The Young Romantics and Critical Opinion 1807–1824*, ed. Theodore Redpath (London: Harrap, 1973), has a smaller representative selection. A useful range of contemporary comment, not confined to the reviews, can be found in the excellent *John Keats: The Critical Heritage*, ed. G. M. Matthews (1971; repr. London and New York: Routledge, 1995).

KEATS CANONIZED: THE VICTORIAN PERIOD TO THE TWENTIETH CENTURY

If the Tory reviewers derided in Keats a vulgar lack of actual experience (of nature, or his classical sources), among the Victorians, he was admired as the creator of a pure poetry, disengaged from the everyday world. Such a view gained ground from the pictorializing of Keats's poetry by the Pre-Raphaelites. In a harsher version, the critique of a vicious, implicitly autoerotic sensuality, a surrender to pure sensation, persisted. Nonetheless, Keats's reputation developed steadily through the nineteenth century. On a younger generation of practising poets, most notably, Alfred Tennyson, his influence was profound. Tennyson's Cambridge set, the Apostles, included Richard Monkton Milnes, who in 1848 published the first full-length biography, in two volumes: the *Life, Letters, and Literary Remains of John Keats*. And in a famous essay of 1880, prefacing a selection of Keats's poems, Matthew Arnold dismissed the notion of a mere sensualist, finding, instead, a force of character in Keats's writing, and placing him alongside Shakespeare in his 'faculty of naturalistic interpretation' and his felicity of expression.[9]

By the early twentieth century, Keats's canonical standing was fully established, and his poetry the subject of serious critical attention. The odes, which claimed little notice in his own time when the focus was largely on *Endymion*, the romances, and, to some extent, 'Hyperion', became central to the twentieth-century canon. Major biographies by Sidney Colvin (1917) and Amy Lowell (1925) combined factual information with critical interpretation. J. M. Murry's *Keats and Shakespeare* (1925) was an influential canonizing work, calling on Arnold's authority to present Keats as the greatest of Shakespeare's successors. Most importantly, the sensory constituent of Keats's poetry, conjoined with a new insistence on its intellectual weight, was de-trivialized; relatedly, the poetry's engagement or disengagement with reality was complicated. C. D. Thorpe's *The Mind of John Keats* (1926) deflected the emphasis on Keats's sensuality by a systematic construction of his philosophical and aesthetic theory. C. L. Finney's pioneering study, *The Evolution of Keats's Poetry* (2 vols., 1936) examined Keats's intellectual influences, tracing, in his poetic career, the development of a humanistic philosophy of negative capability.

The wealth of biographical material and the insights into Keats's creative thinking, afforded, especially, by his extraordinary letters, made biographical criticism the defining genre of Keats studies in the twentieth century. The seminal, still essential, work in this regard is Walter Jackson Bate's landmark biography, *John Keats* (1963). Extracted below is a section of Bate's chapter on 'Negative Capability', illuminating what was already the catchphrase of Keats criticism.

Extract from Walter Jackson Bate, *John Keats* (1963)

A few days after Keats returned to Hampstead, George and Tom left for Devonshire in the hope that Tom might profit from the change. Tom was becoming very frail; he was spitting blood; the symptoms were far from reassuring to his brothers. George, despite his restiveness and his feeling that he must get started on a career, was willing once again to take charge of things for a while. Keats himself was by no means eager to leave, though he was expected to join them in time. Some changes certainly had to be made in *Endymion*, and a clean copy prepared.

At the same time, John Reynolds, who had been writing the dramatic reviews for the *Champion*, wanted to go to Exeter just after Christmas for a holiday. He was courting Eliza Drewe, who lived there and whom he eventually married. He was also intending to leave the *Champion* anyway in January. With the encouragement of his friend James Rice, he had begun to study law in November. Rich was getting him a position in the law office of Francis Fladgate, had paid for him the fee of £110, and was later to arrange to take Reynolds into partnership in the law firm of himself and his father. Keats, thought Reynolds, could take his place on the *Champion*, and write a review. Although Keats's knowledge of the theater was limited, he had delighted in what he had the chance to see of it. He had been reading the dramatic criticism of Reynolds' own model, William Hazlitt. Edmund Kean, whose gusto Keats admired, would probably be returning to the stage after an illness of a few weeks. Before Reynolds left for Exeter, Keats, as a trial experiment, brought out a review, 'Mr. Kean,' in the *Champion* (December 21, 1817), written with the rapid verve, the darting impressionism, of Hazlitt's manner. Then, for the January 4 issue of the *Champion*, after Reynolds had left for Exeter, Keats wrote reviews of the play 'Retribution' and a pantomime, 'Harlequin's Vision.'[1]

George and Tom had been gone about a week when Keats, alone in the upstairs lodgings in Hampstead shortly before Christmas, wrote them one of the most quoted, yet one of the most puzzling, of all his letters: quoted – and puzzling – because of the cryptic references to 'Beauty' and to 'Truth,' because of the curious phrase, 'Negative Capability,' and because it is felt that Keats is now at a level of speculation from which he is beginning to touch on some of the highest functions of poetry.[2]

The letter distills the reactions of three months to the dimension of thinking that had opened to him in September. A background that helps to clarify these rapid, condensed remarks is provided by the long letter written to Bailey only a month before,[3] just after Keats had arrived at Burford Bridge determined to 'wind up' the last five hundred lines of *Endymion*.

For weeks the ideal of 'disinterestedness' about which they had talked at Oxford had eluded his impulsive efforts to apply it to his own personal experience. Given the complexities, the unpredictable problems even in one month of one life, no simple formula could serve. But perhaps that realization was itself a further argument for the need of 'disinterested-ness' and a further indication of the futility, in a universe of uncertainties, of the brief, assertive postures we assume. The result, as he told Bailey, was a healthful increase in 'Humility and the capability of submission.' The significant word is 'capability,' not 'submission.' 'Negative' was to be the next word he would apply to the 'capability' he had in mind – 'sub-mission' could have very different connotations – though even 'negative' would still be far from adequate. Meanwhile he goes on:

> I am certain of nothing but of the holiness of the Heart's affections and the truth of Imagination – What the imagination seizes as Beauty must be truth – whether it existed before or not – for I have the same Idea of all our Pas-sions as of Love they are all, in their sublime, creative of essential Beauty . . . The Imagination may be compared to Adam's dream [*Paradise Lost*, VIII.452–490] – he awoke and found it truth. I am the more zealous in this affair, because I have never yet been able to perceive how any thing can be known for truth by consequitive reasoning – and yet it must be – Can it be that even the greatest Philosopher ever arrived at his goal without putting aside numerous objections – However it may be, O for a Life of Sensations rather than of Thoughts![4]

Two general premises interweave here. Though they were common enough in the more thoughtful writing of the period, Keats has acquired them partly through self-discovery. Hence, far from being what White-head calls 'inert ideas,' they are invested with possibilities. The first is the premise of all objective idealism: what the human mind itself con-tributes to what it assumes are direct perceptions of the material world – supplementing, channeling, even helping to create them – is not, as the subjective idealist argues, something imposed completely *ab extra*, something invented or read into nature that is not really there. Instead, this cooperating creativity of the mind has, to use a phrase of Coleridge's, 'the same ground with nature': its insights are to this extent a valid and necessary supplement in attaining the reconciliation or union of man and nature that constitutes knowledge. Keats, of course, knew nothing of contemporary German idealism, objective or subjective. He had dipped into a little of Coleridge: Bailey had been reading the *Lay Sermons*, and Keats in early November borrowed the *Sybilline Leaves* from Charles Dilke. But he seems to have caught very little from Coleridge at this point, and associated him a month later with an 'irri-table reaching after fact and reason' that contrasts with the ideal he is naively but brilliantly evolving throughout the next half year.

It is primarily from Wordsworth that Keats has picked up enough hints to enable him to go ahead with this 'favorite Speculation,' as he calls it. He was naturally unaware of the massive treatment of man's relation to nature in the *Prelude*, into which Wordsworth was putting so much that he was never satisfied that it was ready for publication. But what Keats had read of Wordsworth he had recently approached in a very different spirit from the way he had been reading poetry the year before. He was quicker to note what he was beginning to call the 'philosophical' implications of poetry. By now this speculation about the mind's creativity has become peculiarly his own, and to such an extent that he has begun to toy with the possible antecedence or foreshadowing, through imaginative insight, 'of reality to come.' The mention of this and of 'Adam's dream' introduces

> another favorite Speculation of mine, that we shall enjoy ourselves here after by having what we called happiness on Earth repeated in a finer tone and so repeated – And yet such a fate can only befall those who delight in sensation rather than hunger as you do after Truth – Adam's dream will do here and seems to be a conviction that Imagination and its empyreal reflection is the same as human Life and its spiritual repetition. But as I was saying – the simple imaginative Mind may have its rewards in the repeti[ti]on of its own silent Working coming continually on the spirit with a fine suddenness.[5]

The second general premise involves the familiar romantic protest on behalf of concreteness and the conviction that the analytic and logical procedures of what Keats calls 'consequitive reasoning' violate the organic process of nature. They abstract from the full concreteness, reduce the living process to static concepts, and substitute an artificial order.

Here again the immediate suggestions have come to Keats from Wordsworth but are further substantiated by what he has been reading of Hazlitt. More than any other literary critic of his day, Hazlitt continued the brilliant psychological tradition of eighteenth-century British empiricism, rephrasing and supplementing a descriptive study of the imagination that had been developing for at least sixty years, and applying it even more suggestively to genius in the arts, especially poetry. The great contribution of English psychological criticism throughout the later eighteenth century had been to describe and justify confidence in the imaginative act – an act whereby sensations, intuitions, and judgments are not necessarily retained in the memory as separate particles of knowledge to be consulted one by one, but can be coalesced and transformed into a readiness of response that is objectively receptive to the concrete process of nature and indeed actively participates in it. This entire approach to the imagination naturally involved a corollary protest against the sort of thing implied in Wordsworth's famous phrase, the 'meddling intellect.' The protest anticipates Whitehead's remarks on the 'fallacy of misplaced concreteness': abstraction by its very nature fails to conceive the full concreteness; it draws out particular elements for special purposes of thought; and the 'misplaced concreteness' comes when these necessary 'short-cuts' in thinking – as Hazlitt calls them – are regarded as equivalent to the concrete reality.

Keats had just begun to catch some of the implications of these ideas during his Oxford visit. Hazlitt's *Essay on the Principles of Human Action* had lit up a large zone of possibilities. Its persuasive argument on the possible 'disinterestedness' of the mind, and its brilliant treatment of the sympathetic potentialities of the imagination, had especially won him. But it is enough for the moment to point out how quickly it led him to read other works of Hazlitt. Within a few weeks after he wrote this letter to Bailey, he was telling both Haydon and his brothers that 'the three things to rejoice at in this Age' were Wordsworth's *Excursion*, Haydon's pictures, and 'Hazlitt's depth of Taste.'[6] Hazlitt, by now, had completely replaced Hunt in the triumvirate of the year before.

Finally, Hazlitt's constant use of the word 'sensations' in the traditional empirical sense – as virtually equivalent to concrete experience – added a new term to Keats's own habitual vocabulary (hence the remark at the moment about the 'Life of Sensations': the bookish Bailey, inclining more toward philosophical analysis, 'would exist' – says Keats – 'partly on sensation partly on thought'). 'Consequitive reasoning' applies to the piecemeal, step-by-step procedures of the analytic and selective intelligence.[7] But though Keats himself cannot perceive how truth can be known by this reductive means, and wonders whether the most astute reasoner 'ever arrived at his goal without putting aside numerous objections,' he is far from pushing the matter, and grants that it 'must be' possible.

This letter to Bailey, written at Burford Bridge as he begins his determined seven-day effort to complete *Endymion*, has a sequel of its own. For Bailey seems to have been a little disturbed by portions of it – at least by the speculation about an afterlife in which the 'old Wine of Heaven' may consist of 'the redigestion of our most ethereal Musings on Earth,' and 'what we called happiness on Earth repeated in a finer tone and so repeated.' Bailey saw Keats in London in January and may have talked with him about the letter. If not, he certainly wrote to him in some detail, and may have taken some time to do so.

At all events, the matter is picked up again in a letter Keats wrote to him on March 13. This letter gives every indication that Keats has been trying to think over some of the remarks he had made before. What he is most eager to state is that he is not a dogmatist in his skepticism – that he is not, as he thinks, a complete skeptic at all. He wishes he could 'enter into' all of Bailey's feelings on the matter, and write something Bailey would like (Keats was too 'transparent,' said Bailey, ever to be able to hide anything); and if he had appeared to be substituting the poetic imagination for religion as a means of arriving at truth, he is now beginning to have moments of doubt about poetry itself.

Then he turns to what he had been trying to express about the validity of the imagination's own contribution to its perception. Some things, certainly 'real,' may not require this 'greeting of the Spirit' from the human mind or heart. But others – at least 'things semireal' – do require that greeting, that contribution, for their fulfillment; and this union of the perceiving mind and the perceived object should not be confused with mere 'Nothings' that are solely the product of human desires. He begins:

> You know my ideas about Religion – I do not think myself more in the right than other people and that nothing in this world is proveable. I wish I could enter into all your feelings on the subject merely for one short 10 Minutes and give you a Page or two to your liking. I am sometimes so very sceptical as to think Poetry itself a mere Jack a lanthern to amuse whoever may chance to be struck with its brilliance – As Tradesmen say every thing is worth what it will fetch, so probably every mental pursuit takes its reality and worth from the ardour of the pursuer – being in itself a nothing – Ethereal thing[s] may at least be thus real, divided under three heads – Things real – things semireal – and no things – Things real – such as existences of Sun Moon & Stars and passages of Shakspeare – Things semireal such as Love, the Clouds &c which require a greeting of the Spirit to make them wholly exist – and Nothings which are made Great and dignified by an ardent pursuit – Which by the by stamps the burgundy mark on the bottles of our Minds, insomuch as they are able to '*consec[r]ate what'er they look upon.*'[8]

The theme of much of the greater poetry to come – certainly of the 'Ode on a Grecian Urn' and the 'Ode to a Nightingale' – may be described as the drama of the human spirit's 'greeting' of objects in order 'to make them wholly exist' – a drama in which the resolutions are precarious, as in life itself, and the preciousness of the attainment ultimately crossed by tragedy. But for the moment he is unable to go further, and least of all to go further theoretically. In his remarks to Bailey, particularly about the 'semireal' as distinct from 'Nothings,' he is trying to grope toward a distinction that Locke could not make and that Hume thought it impossible to make. He can end only with a plea for openness, and by recurring to a thought that has been growing on him for some time: that the heart's hunger for settlement, for finality, cannot be answered unless we shut ourselves off from the amplitude of experience, with all its contradictory diversity. All he can do is to proceed honestly and empirically in this adventure of speculation, of openness, and (as he later phrased it) of 'straining at particles of light in the midst of a great darkness.'

Quite plainly he will 'never be a Reasoner'; every point of thought quickly opens some further unexpected vista; and how could he be confident therefore of 'the truth of any of my speculations'? His comic sense is suddenly aroused by the ineffectiveness of his discourse, which he burlesques for a moment; and he ends with a characteristic pun.[9]

The 'Negative Capability' letter is best understood as another phrasing of these thoughts, with at least three further extensions. First, the problem of form or style in art enters more specifically. Second, the ideal toward which he is groping is contrasted more strongly with the egoistic assertion of one's own identity. Third, the door is further opened to the perception – which he was to develop within the next few months – of the sympathetic potentialities of the imagination.

He begins by telling his brothers that he has gone to see Edmund Kean, has written his review, and is enclosing it for them. Then on Saturday, December 20, he went to see an exhibition of the American painter, Benjamin West, particularly his picture, 'Death on the Pale Horse.' Keats was altogether receptive to any effort to attain the 'sublime,' and West's painting had been praised for succeeding. Yet it struck Keats as flat – 'there is nothing to be intense upon; no women one feels mad to kiss; no face swelling into reality.' Then the first crucial statement appears:

> The excellence of every Art is its intensity, capable of making all disagreeables evaporate, from their being in close relationship with Beauty & Truth – Examine King Lear & you will find this exemplified throughout; but in this picture we have unpleasantness without any momentous depth of speculation excited, in which to bury its repulsiveness.[10]

In the active cooperation or full 'greeting' of the experiencing imagination and its object, the nature or 'identity' of the object is grasped so vividly that only those associations and qualities that are strictly relevant to the central conception remain. The irrelevant and discordant (the 'disagreeables') 'evaporate' from this fusion of object and mind. Hence 'Truth' and 'Beauty' spring simultaneously into being, and also begin to approximate each other. For, on the one hand, the external reality – otherwise overlooked, or at most only sleepily acknowledged, or dissected so that a particular aspect of it may be abstracted for special purposes of argument or thought – has now, as it were, awakened into 'Truth': it has been met by that human recognition, fulfilled and extended by that human agreement with reality, which we call 'truth.' And at the same time, with the irrelevant 'evaporated,' this dawning into unity is felt as 'Beauty.' Nor is it a unity solely of the object itself, emerging untrammeled and in its full significance, but a unity also of the human spirit, both within itself and with what was at first outside it. For in this 'intensity' – the 'excellence,' he now feels, 'of every Art' – we attain, if only for a while, a harmony of the inner life with truth. It is in this harmony that 'Beauty' and 'Truth' come together. The 'pleasant,' in the ordinary sense of the word, has nothing to do with the point being discussed; and to introduce it is only to trivialize the conception of 'Beauty.' Hence Keats's reference to *Lear*. The reality disclosed may be distressing and even cruel to human nature. But the harmony with truth will remain, and even deepen, to the extent that the emerging reality is being constantly matched at every stage by the 'depth of speculation excited' – by the corresponding release and extension, in other words, of human insight. 'Examine King Lear and you will find this exemplified throughout.'

Hazlitt's short essay 'On Gusto' had aroused his thinking about style when he read it at Oxford in the *Round Table*; and what he is saying now is partly the result of what he has assimilated from Hazlitt.[11] By 'gusto,' Hazlitt means an excitement of the imagination in which the perceptive identification with the object is almost complete, and the living character of the object is caught and shared in its full diversity and given vital expression in art. It is 'power or passion defining any object.' But the result need not be subjective. By grasping sympathetically the over-all significance of the object, the 'power or passion' is able to cooperate, so to speak, with that significance – to go the full distance with its potentialities, omitting the irrelevant (which Keats calls the 'disagreeables'), and conceiving the object with its various qualities coalescing into the vital unity that is the object itself. One result is that the attributes or qualities that we glean through our different senses of sight, hearing, touch, and the rest are not presented separately or piecemeal, but 'the impression made on one sense excites by affinity those of another.' Thus Claude Lorrain's landscapes, though 'perfect abstractions of the visible images of things,' lack 'gusto': 'They do not interpret one sense by another . . . That is, his eye wanted imagination; it did not strongly sympathise with his other faculties. He saw the atmosphere, but he did not feel it.' Chaucer's descriptions of natural scenery have gusto: they give 'the very feeling of the air, the coolness or moisture of the ground.' 'There is gusto in the colouring of Titian. Not only do his heads seem to think – his bodies seem to feel.'[12]

This interplay and coalescence of impressions was to become a conscious aim in Keats's own poetry within the next six months, and, by the following autumn, to be fulfilled as richly as by any English poet of the last three centuries. Meanwhile, only a few days before he wrote the 'Negative Capability' letter to his brothers, he had followed Hazlitt's use of the word 'gusto' in his own review 'On Edmund Kean as a Shakespearian Actor' (though he later returns to the word 'intensity'–'gusto' perhaps suggesting a briskness or bounce of spirit he does not have in mind). He had been trying in this review to describe how 'a melodious passage in poetry' may attain a fusion of 'both sensual and spiritual,' where each extends and declares itself by means of the other:

> The spiritual is felt when the very letters and points of charactered language show like the hieroglyphics of beauty; – the mysterious signs of an immortal free-masonry! . . . To one learned in Shakespearian hieroglyphics, – learned in the spiritual portion of those lines to which Kean adds a sensual grandeur: his tongue must seem to have robbed 'the Hybla bees, and left them honeyless.'

Hence 'there is an indescribable gusto in his voice, by which we feel that the utterer is thinking of the past and future, while speaking of the present.'[13]

Keats is here extending the notion of 'gusto' in a way that applies prophetically to his own maturer style – to an imaginative 'intensity' of conception, that is, in which process, though slowed to an insistent present, is carried in active solution. So with the lines he had quoted a month before to Reynolds as an example of Shakespeare's 'intensity of working out conceits':

> When lofty trees I see barren of leaves
> Which erst from heat did canopy the herd,
> And Summer's green all girded up in sheaves,
> Borne on the bier with white and bristly beard.[14]

Previous functions, and the mere fact of loss itself, are a part of the truth of a thing as it now is. The nature of the 'lofty trees' in this season, now 'barren of leaves,' includes the fact that they formerly 'from heat did canopy the herd'; nor is it only the dry, completed grain of the autumn that is 'girded up in sheaves,' but the 'Summer's green' that it once was. This entire way of thinking about style is proving congenial to Keats in the highest degree; for though it has independent developments, it has also touched and is giving content to the ideal briefly suggested a year before in 'Sleep and Poetry' – even before he saw the Elgin Marbles for the first time: an ideal of poetry as 'might half slumb'ring on its own right arm.' The delight in energy caught in momentary repose goes back to the idea he had 'when a Schoolboy . . . of an heroic painting': 'I saw it somewhat sideways,' he tells Haydon, 'large prominent round and colour'd with magnificence – somewhat like the feel I have of Anthony and Cleopatra. Or of Alcibiades, leaning on his Crimson Couch in his Galley, his broad shoulders imperceptibly heaving with the Sea.' So with the line in *Henry VI*, 'See how the surly Warwick mans the Wall.'[15] One of the comments he wrote in his copy of Milton during the next year gives another illustration:

> Milton in every instance pursues his imagination to the utmost – he is 'sagacious of his Quarry,' he sees Beauty on the wing, pounces upon it and gorges it to the producing his essential verse. . . . But in no instance is this sort of perseverance more exemplified than in what may be called his *stationing or statu[a]ry*. He is not content with simple description, he must station, – thus here, we not only see how the Bi rds '*with clang despised the ground*,' but we see them 'under *a cloud in prospect*.' So we see Adam '*Fair indeed and tall – under a plantane*' – and so we see Satan '*disfigured – on the Assyrian Mount*.'[16]

The union of the ideal of dynamic poise, of power kept in reserve, with the ideal of range of implication suggests one principal development in his own style throughout the next year and a half. The very triumph of this union – as triumphs often tend to do – could have proved an embarrassment to later ideals and interests had it become an exclusive stylistic aim. However magnificent the result in the great odes, in portions of *Hyperion*, or in what Keats called the 'colouring' and 'drapery' of the *Eve of St. Agnes*, it carried liabilities in both pace and variety that would have to be circumvented for successful narrative and, above all, dramatic poetry. But even at the moment, and throughout the next year, what he calls 'intensity' – the 'greeting of the Spirit' and its object – is by no means completely wedded to a massive centering of image through poise and 'stationing.' If his instinctive delight in fullness was strengthened in one direction by the Elgin Marbles – which he still made visits to see – other, more varied appeals to his ready empathy were being opened and reinforced by his reading of Shakespeare.

Notes

1　A review entitled 'Richard, Duke of York' (in the December 28 issue of the *Champion*) is commonly ascribed to Keats; but as Leonidas Jones has argued

(*Keats-Shelley Journal*, III [1954], 55–65), it was almost certainly written by Reynolds.

2 Further difficulties are added by the inadequate text (the original is not known). George took the letter together with others when he left for America. After his death, when Milnes was seeking materials for his biography, the second husband of George's wife, John Jeffrey, copied the letter for Milnes, making at least one deletion. We also know that Jeffrey – quite understandably – was a hasty and indifferent transcriber: he had no reason to be otherwise, and was gracious in copying as much as he did for Milnes. The text we have is Jeffrey's transcript.

3 See *John Keats*, Chapter IX, sections 15–16.

[4 Keats, *Letters* I. 184–5.

5 Ibid., I. 185.

6 Ibid., I. 203, 205.]

7 The word 'consequitive' remains in his mind. He soon tells John Taylor, his publisher, and with no derogatory implication, that Taylor, being a 'consequitive Man,' may think the change in the passage on happiness in *Endymion* a matter 'of mere words,' rather than 'a regular stepping of the Imagination towards a Truth' (ibid., I. 218).

[8 Ibid., I. 242–3.]

9 The speculation about 'ethereal things' – the division into real, semireal and nothings – may be carried – but what am I talking of – it is an old maxim of mine and of course must be well known that eve[r]y point of thought is the centre of an intellectual world – the two uppermost thoughts in a Man's mind are the two poles of his World he revolves on them and every thing is southward or northward to him through their means – We take but three steps from feathers to iron. Now my dear fellow I must once for all tell you I have not one Idea of the truth of any of my speculations – I shall never be a Reasoner because I care not to be in the right, when retired from bickering and in a proper philosophical temper – So you must not stare if in any future letter I endeavour to prove that Appollo as he had a cat gut string to his Lyre used a cats' paw as a Pecten – and further from said Pecten's reiterated and continual teasing came the term Hen peck'd (ibid., I. 243–4).'

[10 Ibid., I. 192.]

11 Keats had also read Hazlitt's own essay on Benjamin West in the December issue of the *Edinburgh Review* (*Works* XVIII, 135–40), where West is censored for lack of 'gusto.'

[12 Hazlitt, *Works* IV, 77–80.]

13 *The Poetical Works and Other Writings of John Keats*, ed. Harry Buxton Forman, revised by Maurice Buxton Forman, 8 vols. (New York: Charles Scribner, 1938–9), V. 229–30.

[14 Sonnet XII, 5–8.]

15 Keats, *Letters*, I. 265.

16 *Poetical Works*, ed. Forman V. 303–4. The comment is written next to the passage in *Paradise Lost*, VI. 420–3:

> but feather'd soon and fledge
> They summ'd their pens, and, soaring the air sublime,

With clang despised the ground, under a cloud
In prospect.

Further reading

In the readings below, Keats's canonical standing is affirmed through the explication of his poetic technique and intellectual sources. Predominant in the discussion here is the question of a split impulse, towards imagination and reality, in his thought and writing. The general critical tendency is to reconcile or subordinate the escapist to the engaged poet.

M. R. Ridley, *Keats' Craftsmanship: A Study in Poetic Development* (Oxford: Oxford University Press, 1933). Important early study which, analyzing Keats's development and achievements as a craftsman, situates him in the 'real' world, the experiential world of 'things' where he found his materials.

Walter Jackson Bate, *The Stylistic Development of Keats* (London: Routledge & Kegan Paul, 1945). Exemplary technical analysis of Keats's verse, allying his stylistic development with 'the changing bents of mind which gave it rise and direction.'

Cleanth Brooks, 'Keats's Sylvan Historian: History without Footnotes', in *The Well-Wrought Urn: Studies in the Structure of Poetry* (New York: Harcourt Brace, 1947), 139–52. Important essay, setting against the readings of Keats's poetry as purely aesthetic or sensual the qualities of irony and paradox in the 'Ode on a Grecian Urn'.

R. H. Fogle, *The Imagery of Keats and Shelley: A Comparative Study* (Chapel Hill: University of North Carolina Press, 1949). Details the sensory qualities characteristic of Keats's poetry by means of a close comparison with Shelley.

Earl R. Wasserman, *The Finer Tone: Keats's Major Poems* (Baltimore: Johns Hopkins, 1953). Focuses on oxymoron in Keats's poetry as belonging to a 'pattern of thought [that] requires that he reconcile the mortal with the immortal without cancelling either.'

Robert Gittings, *John Keats: The Living Year* (London: Heinemann, 1954). Valuable study of the sources – in his experience and in his reading – of Keats's creativity in the year-long span from the composition of *Hyperion* to that of *The Fall of Hyperion*, during which he 'wrote . . . practically every poem that places him among the major poets of the world.'

Kenneth Muir (ed.), *John Keats: A Reassessment* (Liverpool: Liverpool University Press, 1958). Collection of essays by divers scholars, pertaining to the expression, in Keats's poetry, of the clash of 'the world of beauty seized or created by the imagination . . . with the tragic world of reality.'

Bernice Slote, *Keats and the Dramatic Principle* (Nebraska: University of Nebraska Press, 1958). Prefers, over the poet-hero speaking in his own voice, the poet–dramatist, whose being is protean and voice de-personalized. Keats's poems 'are informed by the dramatic principle: that is, act by imaginative identities, the objective playing-out of the clash of oppositions.'

David Perkins, *The Quest for Permanence: The Symbolism of Wordsworth, Shelley, and Keats* (Cambridge, Mass.: Harvard University Press, 1959). Offering detailed readings of particular poems, finds that Keats's symbolism, informed by a consciousness of process and an organic view of nature, is an expression – and finally, a rejection – of a romantic quest for permanence, or the sufficiency of a purely visionary imagination.

John Bayley, 'Keats and Reality', *Proceedings of the British Academy* 48 (1962), 91–125. Influential re-reading of established notions concerning reality and identity in Keats's work. Locates what is 'real' in Keats's poetry – his distinctive poetical character – in its emotional and sexual immediacy: the vulgarity or lack of decorum and conscious artistry descried by the contemporary critics, and conspicuous especially in the earlier verse. Keats's poetry fails in proportion as he achieves aesthetic rectitude, for in so doing, he must stifle personality.

Aileen Ward, *John Keats: The Making of a Poet* (London: Secker & Warburg, 1963). Important biography, with a psychoanalytic tenor; usefully contextualizes Keats's poetry in the circumstances of his life.

Douglas Bush, *John Keats: His Life and Writings* (London: Weidenfeld and Nicolson, 1966). Finds Keats's humanitarianism in his moderate version of 'central romantic attitudes and ideas': his 'early craving . . . to attain through the senses and imagination some kind of supramundane or transcendental beauty and truth, was eventually subdued and chastened by a sober acceptance of the human condition.'

*Paul de Man, 'Introduction' in *John Keats: Selected Poetry* (New York and Toronto: New American Library, 1966). Brilliant essay, arguing that Keats's poetry, conceived of as redemptive, is both prospective and sympathetic, rejecting actual experience in its orientation towards an unrealized future, and escaping the self in its complete (moral) identification with others. In the last poems, however, self-awareness disrupts the moral stance, marking, in Keats, the insight common to the great romantics, that 'consciousness of self was the first and necessary step towards moral judgement.'

Ian Jack, *Keats and the Mirror of Art* (Oxford: Oxford University Press, 1967). Emphasizes the visual qualities of Keats's imagination, identifying the poetry's specific sources in the visual arts.

Robert Gittings, *John Keats* (London: Heinemann, 1968). Indispensable critical and scholarly biography, synthesizing material garnered from a wide range of sources and committed to factual accuracy and detail in its reconstruction of Keats's life.

John Jones, *John Keats's Dream of Truth* (London: Chatto & Windus, 1969). Within the frame of a larger thesis of the centrality of feeling to Romanticism, examines Keatsian 'feel', which expresses the 'heart-certainty' shared by other Romantic writers, but differs from theirs in that it is 'end-stopped': Keats's 'feel' makes no claims beyond itself; it offers no insight or certainty about the subjects of feeling.

Jack Stillinger, *The Hoodwinking of Madeline and other Essays on Keats's Poems* (Urbana: University of Illinois Press, 1971). Accessible essays, presenting in Keats's poems an evolving debate about the surmounting of earthly limitation by the visionary imagination. Keats finally jettisons the visionary for the natural, 'embracing experience and process as his own and man's chief good.'

Stuart Sperry, *Keats the Poet* (Princeton: Princeton University Press, 1973). Definitive study of the importance of 'sensation' – located in the context of the wider philosophical, scientific and aesthetic climate of Keats's time and understood as a relation of mind to nature, or the imagination to its materials – to Keats's conception of the origin and effect of poetry.

Christopher Ricks, *Keats and Embarrassment* (Oxford: Clarendon Press, 1974). Reads (cf. Bayley above) Keats's peculiar poetic and humanistic strengths as located in exactly the 'adolescent' qualities – 'the youthful, the luxuriant, the immature' – derided in the Tory reviews.

Robert M. Ryan, *Keats: The Religious Sense* (Princeton: Princeton University Press, 1976). Useful study of a neglected topic. Presenting Keats as a believer 'in the existence of a Supreme Being', locates him in the traditions of natural religion and deism, and outlines the development of his religious thought as he comes to construct for himself an alternative system of faith to Christianity.

Harold Bloom, *Poetry and Repression: Revisionism from Blake to Stevens* (New Haven and London: Yale University Press, 1976). Keats's engagement with his 'composite precursor', Milton and Wordsworth, first suggested in *The Anxiety of Influence* (1973), is developed here in a psychoanalytically-driven reading of *The Fall of Hyperion* as a Keatsian revision of quest romance, exemplifying the strong poet's struggle with his tradition.

Anne K. Mellor, *English Romantic Irony* (Cambridge, Mass. and London: Harvard University Press, 1980). Presents Keats as a 'quintessential romantic ironist', balancing scepticism and enthusiasm, who, aware of chaos and unpredictability as the ontological reality, ceaselessly deconstructs his own structuring perceptions of the universe, yet celebrates the process of life by his continual creation of new forms and images.

Tilottama Rajan, *Dark Interpreter: The Discourse of Romanticism* (Ithaca and London: Cornell University Press, 1980). Keats provides a key illustration of Rajan's thesis of the co-existence, in Romantic discourse, of idealism regarding the authenticity of art and the sceptical awareness of the discrepancy between art and reality.

David Bromwich, 'Keats' in *Hazlitt: The Mind of a Critic* (1983; new edn. New Haven and London: Yale University Press, 1999), 362–401. Finely detailed presentation of Keats's intellectual affinity with Hazlitt and the impact of Hazlitt on Keats's poetic practice.

Helen Vendler, *The Odes of John Keats* (Cambridge, Mass.: Harvard University Press, 1983). Emphasizes authorial choice and conscious technique in its presentation of the odes as a single 'purposeful sequence' in which Keats engages in thematic and formal experimentation; each poem builds upon its predecessors, till the sequence culminates in 'To Autumn'.

Donald C. Goellnicht, *The Poet-Physician: Keats and Medical Science* (Pittsburgh: University of Pittsburgh Press, 1984). Detailed and systematic account of the impact of Keats's medical training on his ideas and imagery.

Martin Aske, *Keats and Hellenism* (Cambridge: Cambridge University Press, 1985). Narrates 'Keats's romance with ancient Greece' using Bloom's model of influence, where the precursor is both inspiring and inhibiting.

Jeffrey Baker, *John Keats and Symbolism* (Sussex: Harvester Press, 1986). Rejecting the standard view of a linear transition from romance to realism, traces, in the developing complexity of Keats's symbolism, the growth of his intellectual vision, from an uncomplicated aestheticism to a more mature grasp of an ambiguous and paradoxical 'reality'.

Jonathan Bate, *Shakespeare and the English Romantic Imagination* (Oxford: Clarendon Press, 1986). Keats's engagement with Shakespeare is located in the context of a broader study of the impact of Shakespeare on the English Romantics, with the underlying premise that the growth of English romanticism was intimately involved with that of Shakespeare idolatry.

Susan J. Wolfson, *The Questioning Presence: Wordsworth, Keats, and the Interrogative Mode in Romantic Poetry* (Ithaca and London: Cornell University Press, 1986). Keats and Wordsworth exemplify this argument, that interrogation – the imagination's active and constant questioning of certainty – is the characteristic mode of Romanticism. Productively revisits the Keats–Wordsworth contrast and the question of self-hood in Keats's thought and writing.

R. S. White, *Keats as a Reader of Shakespeare* (London: Athlone Press, 1987). Definitive study of Keats's view of Shakespeare and its impact on his poetry, based on Keats's own comments and the evidence of Hazlitt's influence.

Greg Kucich, *Keats, Shelley, and Romantic Spenserianism* (University Park, Penn.: Pennsylvania State University Press, 1991). Keats exemplifies Kucich's thesis of Spenser's enabling function for the Romantics, on the grounds both of his contemporaneity – in that he embodies the contraries of idealism and actuality that mark the era's poetic discourse – and accessibility, within an otherwise forbidding poetic tradition.

Thomas McFarland, *The Masks of Keats: The Endeavour of a Poet* (Oxford: Oxford University Press, 2000). Returns to the idea of 'negative capability' in the thesis that Keats's greatest poetry is achieved when he obliterates his 'primary self' to assume the mask either of classicism or medievalism.

CLASS, GENDER AND POLITICS: KEATS'S ANXIETY

Keatsian 'sensation', then, once taken to express a vicious sensuality, or at best, a pure abandon, an escape from what is real, is gradually reconstructed as manifesting a strong poet's grasp on material reality. In the most emphatic versions of such reconstructions, critics such as John Bayley and Christopher Ricks locate the authenticity of Keats's poetic voice specifically in those sensory and sexual qualities derided by the contemporary reviewers, qualities which, they argue, express an unselfconscious, or, in their term, *unmisgiving* poet, a poet more or less free of conscious artistry and the constraints of decorum. An opposite reading of exactly those qualities is offered in Marjorie Levinson's ground-breaking study, *Keats's Life of Allegory: The Origins of a Style* (1988). If Keats's poetry is made substantial by the charge of reality (or humanity or authenticity) invested in it by the canonizing readings, in Levinson's deconstructive approach, it is, in a manner of speaking, emptied. To Levinson, Keats's poetry is not real at all in that it is 'aggressively *literary*'; in so being, it challenges the values of the social class from which Keats is excluded. Denying reality of one kind (poetic authenticity), Levinson emphasizes another: that of social class, presented here as the defining context of Keats's poetry.

> By the stylistic contradictions of his verse, Keats produces a writing which is aggressively *literary*, and therefore not just 'not Literature' but, in effect, *anti-Literature: a parody. . . .* The triumph of the great poetry is not its capacious, virile, humane authenticity but its subversion of those authoritarian values, effects which it could not in any case, and for the strongest social reasons, realize.[10]

In Levinson's reading, the socially subversive quality of Keats's poetry emerges to the contemporary critics as a gendered (effeminate) and sexual (masturbatory) quality. A short section from her chapter on 'The Eve of St. Agnes' is given below.

Extract from Marjorie Levinson, *Keats's Life of Allegory: The Origins of a Style* (1988)

We all know, or say, that Keats lived 'a life of Allegory'. Instead of contemplating the symmetries of such a life from the comfortable vantage of today, we might imagine the experience of the man who lived them, and we might recall that 'symmetry' structurally describes separation and imposed closure. An allegorical life is a life played out in the space between figure and meaning, action and purpose. To live such a life is to be irremediably estranged from what is positioned as one's essential being. Practically speaking, it is to act and then to construct the intentionality of the act *ex post facto*: to experience all action, therefore, as gesture. To live a life of allegory is to know oneself after the fact, or to wear one's identity like a hand-me-down suit: a parody of one's inner life. Again, we recall Byron's 'opinion' of the Cockney school, '*that second-hand* school of poetry'.

One fact emerges over and over in all the biographies, the letters, the reviews, and also in the poetry itself. Keats was *named*: apothecary, cit, Johnny Keates, Jack Ketch, Mankin, Self-polluter, Master John, copyist, Cockney. He was named, moreover, not so much as Other and adversarial but as 'nothing', the dissociated figure of an allegory. The child of unnatural parents, orphaned at an early age, separated from his siblings and his inheritance, ambitious for an identity that was socially prohibited, and isolated by his disease, Keats was detached in an unusually thoroughgoing way from the origins and ends that naturalize most people's lives by fusing their figural aspect (image, attribute, name) to their inwardness.[1]

A man who is allegorized will, to liberate himself from that suffered objectivity, *invent* a life of allegory. If the measure of one's falseness is one's restriction to the world of substitutes (words, ideas, sex in the head), then by a change of sign – a change from experience to consciousness – one might turn the substitutes to supplements, the words to writing, the names to titles. If one can *only* be Miltonic, then one must load every rift with ore from Milton's mine and display the theft. Since Keats could not, by the structures of feeling that stationed him, write from Wordsworthian depth or Shakespearean breadth, he would signify the suffered surface and be belatedly, *Romantically* baroque. We grasp the necessity of this bitter solution by remembering that a man who experiences his identity as his nothingness and desire cannot afford the luxury of full gratification and its natural closures. This is to say that Keats's creativity was powerfully mediated by a set of psychic circumstances that would seem to require rather than resist his particular social reality.

Keats's project was a conversion of zero to zero-degree: a transformation of social and genetic nothingness to 'camelion poet, [which] has no character . . . no Identity'; instead of 'apothecary', there would be 'physician, sage, healer'; and the so-called purveyor of 'extenuatives and soporifics' would name himself a provider of balms, hemlock, and sweet solutions. Anything – even zero – raised to the zero power equals 1. The sad alternative to this self-parody emerges in Keats's letters, where he confesses his horror of the 'nothing' days. These are the days he cannot write, cannot therfore *read* himself, and cannot, thus, recover his stolen name. These are the days when he is drowned by that 'muddy stream' which is his 'doubly strong' '*sense* [my emphasis] of real things': his overinvestment in the real which he knows he can never possess in anything but a temporary, alienated way and that, if he *could* possess properly and forever, would annihilate his identity.

> *You cannot eat your cake and have it too*
> Proverb

How fevered [fever'd] is the man who cannot look
  Upon his mortal days with temperate blood,
Who vexes all the leaves of his life's book,
  And robs his fair name of its maidenhood:[;]
It is as if the rose should pluck herself,
  Or the ripe plum finger its misty bloom,
As if a Naiad, like a meddling elf,
  Should darken her pure grot with muddy gloom;
But the rose leaves herself upon the briar,
  For winds to kiss and grateful bees to feed,
And the ripe plum still wears its dim attire,
  The undisturbed lake has crystal space.[;]
  Why then should man, teasing the world for grace,
Spoil his salvation for a fierce miscreed?
    (Written 30 April 1819; with 'Ode to Psyche' (written between 21 and 30
          April), included in journal letter to the George Keatses.)

Nowhere do we find so concentrated an inscription of these matters as in Keats's unpublished sonnet 'How fevered is the man'. All the energy in this poem is in the octet, where the narrator names the naming acts he will not perform, self-ravishings he will not indulge. Keats is trying to say that to covet fame – to conceive oneself as a name or as the owner of a name – is to fracture identity into subjective and objective aspects and to violate the former by the latter. Keats rejects this self-exploitation, plainly figured as a masturbatory temptation, for the better pleasure of an innocent (that is, self-identical) subjectivity. The task of the sestet is to define this virtuous alternative. Keats cannot, however, inscribe the plenitude of unselfconscious being in a positively autonomous figure. The best he can manage is an image of intransitive, ineffectual, and – in one telling example – *inhabited* being.

We appreciate the logical and therefore technical problem by graphing the way in which the *language* of the poem, as opposed to its argument, identifies autoentitlement with autoeroticism with writing. By the argument, Keats's hero is he who *rejects* the self-pollution of writing; he leaves the leaves of his life's book 'unvexed'. Obviously, the written representation of this existential ideal must be a difficult business. We see just how difficult by attending rather closely to the stylistic effects of the sestet. 'But the rose leaves herself upon the blossom . . . the plum still wears . . . the undisturbed lake has crystal space . . .' In any context, these lines would be semantically faulty and stylistically flaccid; juxtaposed against the perversely vivid octet and situated as a refutation, they are completely lame. 'Leaves', 'wears', and 'has' are about as minimally verbal as verbs can be. The discourse of these lines, contrary to their intended meaning, invites us to focus Keats's hero as the nothingness of a copula without an attribute, a wish without an agency. He is, as it were, virginity without a concept of virginity: a suffered nothing.

The dominant image of the sestet – 'But the rose leaves herself upon the briar, / For winds to kiss and grateful bees to feed' – betrays the contradiction that organizes the sonnet. The line says that roses are kissed by winds and fed by bees. (Or, everything comes to those who wait.) But it is roses, of course, that feed bees, which feed them only in a sexual way, by pollination.[2] ('For grateful bees to fuck' is the effective meaning of the line.) The skewed transitivity of the line would suggest that Keats cannot conceive a self-possession that is not the sexualized taking-in of some other self. Even in what is intended as an image of complete and capable identity, Keats inscribes the figure of a passive and feminized introjection, *itself* an image of productively fissured consciousness.[3]

We might at this point attend to the repetition of 'leaves', a word upon which Keats frequently puns. ('If poetry come not as easy as leaves to a tree . . .') In a strong reading of the 'Ode on a Grecian Urn', Philip Fisher construes the 'leave' in 'Fair youth . . . thou canst not leave / Thy song . . .' as a transitive verb. Fisher develops the biological dimension of this usage and its relevance to Keats's formalist project.[4] In the context of the sonnet, it is helpful to stress the discursive aspect. The figures on the urn and the nonverbal art that engendered them cannot do the one and the bad thing Keats can do: write, or 'leave' a leaf. They cannot, in Shelley's phrase, 'despoil themselves', cannot 'cleave themselves into chasms' by a catalytic self-consciousness. Only Keats can construct an instant when being is ravished by a meaning that is absolutely external and remains so: a rape without a union – something along the lines of the strange encounter plotted in Yeats's 'Leda and the Swan'. Keats tells us in his sonnet that to name oneself a poet is to deface one's book of life: literally, to 'vex' its fair leaves. However, to refuse this corruption of being by a meaning that is anything but 'silvan' and 'sweet' – to leave oneself alone – is to be left to the meanings imposed by others, and this is surrender to the tyranny of Nature / Culture and its psychic governors. Reductively, the message of this painfully exposed poem is 'do unto yourself that which has been done to you'.

Throughout his poetry, Keats kills the creaturely life he brings forth so that he may resurrect it as the sheared off and absolute Idea of that life: a fever of itself. That strongly attitudinizing phrase, 'Attic shape! Fair attitude', by its framed self-reflexiveness turns the idea of an innocent inwardness inside out. It presents to our view an Idea entirely over-wrought, which is to say, detached from psychic and philosophic truth and from the historical moment that bred that truth. (Here is Empson's comment on the line: 'very bad . . . [T]he half pun suggesting a false Greek derivation and jammed up against an arty bit of Old English seems . . . affected and ugly'.)[5] The Ode asks us to admire a new aesthetic breed: namely, 'brede', a Beauty so orphaned, so barren, and so cold that it really *is* Truth, since it is the only thing in the world that does not refer to Truth. No object, no subject, no reader, and no writer can naturalize a Truth so severed, a relief so severe. Therefore it endures.

'A sense of real things comes doubly strong, / And, like a muddy stream, would bear along / My soul to nothingness'. One's impulse is to read these lines from 'Sleep and Poetry' as a statement of resistance to a reality that is opposed to identity through and through. The defensive agency is imagination. Construed in this way (the way it is always construed), the lines describe an escape from quotidian phenomenal life with its terrible scarcities into the rich reality of psychic life and its products. Keats does not, however, say that 'real things' would bear his soul along to nothingness; it is his 'doubly strong' *sense* of those things – his overinvestment in them – that he likens to a muddy stream. In other words, it is the idea of the real as an object, the possession of which completes us, the lack of which undoes us, that renders both identity and experience 'Nothings'. We could call this idea the reality principle, remembering that 'reality' means in this context a mastering fantasy of facticity.

We know from Keats's life and letters that he could stand a great deal of reality. What he feared, I believe, was the depletion of his soul by an overcathexis of the real, the result of his real deprivations. As we have always known, but not really, I think, understood, Keats was afraid of his natural imagination; the enemy in Keats's poetry is inwardness itself. If this is so, then we must surmise that the quality of the fantasy – a real that fulfills, a real that destroys – is irrelevant. Identity is jeopardized not just by the idea of a real that punishes by withholding itself but by the idea of a real that realizes. By that celebrated lament from 'Sleep and Poetry', we learn that Keats refuses the model of a psyche that binds itself to reality by the agency of the pleasure principle and through the negotiations of an ego which exhausts itself in that intermediary function. We can guess that a man who experiences his identity as his desire, and his station as his contained tension, must be very ambivalent indeed about satisfaction, self-coincidence, and quiescence, the telos of the pleasure principle. By Keats's lights, one is more endangered by fulfillment than frustration. We have all discerned Keats's resistance to the 'sweet' dreaming of sensory escape. What we miss is the equally problematic nature of those inclusive and strongminded solutions we like to find in Keats's mature verse.

The antidote to that 'muddy stream' is the hemlock-balm of an Idea poetry. I use the upper case 'I' to distinguish idea – the weak, relative, and abstract term – from the dissociated, concrete, self-conscious invention: a 'Thing semi-real'. 'Idea' names a transformation of 'sweet dream[ing]' into strong and corrosive dreaming, and of poesy, a possessed act, into poetry, an act of possession.[6] In 'St. Agnes', we witness Keats's transformation of the relative surface – an outside victimized by its relation to ideas of inside and depth – into absolute surface, a skin peeled away from authorizing subjectivity and thus put into perverse relationship with authorizing objectivity as well. There is a name for this magic and it is *schein*.[7] In practical terms, this deconstructive operation amounts to a project in supplementation, where the good, tyrannical term is parodically displaced, in this way avoiding a privileging of the bad term, and thus a reinstatement of the good–bad dynamic. The functional unbindings mentioned above – foreplay, forepleasure, narcissism – are all forms of supplementation: displacements of and additions to intercourse, endpleasure, and intersubjectivity.

In order to register these scandalous supplements, we listen to the poem with what the psychoanalysts call 'the third ear': that is, with a nonlogical, antisystematic attention. We want to hear the 'missaid' in Keats's discourse: those anomalous qualities that somehow contribute to our sense of the power and glamour of the romance but that cannot be articulated within the terms set by our binding criticism. I use the verb 'listen' advisedly: as a refusal of the visually referential instructions imposed by the textual bindings, and out of respect for the aural, verbal, conceptual instructions encoded in the writing. As I've suggested, the deviant facts of 'St. Agnes' are not just the inevitable betrayals of conflictual and/or ideologically unthinkable material – or, exposures of the binding motives. They are specifically functional and overdetermined interferences with the romance narrative. This is an argument, then, not just for the virtues of a deconstructive critique but for Keats's own controlled deconstructive project.

Notes

1 According to both sympathetic and hostile descriptions, Keats's parents were remarkably ardent, impulsive, sensuous people, given to excess in food, in erotic

display, and in social ambitiousness. My word, 'unnatural', is not, of course, a judgment, but an observation of a social difference that Keats was compelled to
register.

2   Gittings's reproduction of the manuscript (the journal letter) version of this sonnet
gives the line as follows: 'For winds to kiss and grateful Bees to – taste – feed'
(Robert Gittings, ed., *Letters of John Keats* [London and New York: Oxford Univ.
Press, 1970], 252). 'Taste', the semantically correct word, is cancelled; Keats *selects*
the contradiction. I offer this note to those readers who would observe the existence
and, in the sonnet context, the aptness of a particular poeticism whereby the 'on'
which would, in ordinary speech, follow 'feed', is elided. Or, one might propose
that Keats intends an 'in order to' in the 'to feed' construction. In that case, 'for'
would govern only 'to kiss': that is, the rose leaves herself on the bough in order to
feed the grateful bees. My point is that when the grammatical intention is executed
so circuitously and so poorly and in the absence of strong metrical or phonetic
imperatives, *and* when the perspicuous construction has been pointedly rejected,
we must look for other kinds of intentionality.

3   Here is Keats's version of Wordsworth's wise passiveness:

> It has been an old Comparison for our urging on – the Bee hive – however it
> seems to me that we should rather be the flower than the Bee – for it is a false
> notion that more is gained by receiving than giving – no the receiver and the
> giver are equal in their benefits – the flower I doubt not receives a fair guerdon
> from the Bee – its leaves blush deeper in the next spring – and who shall say
> between Man and Woman which is the most delighted? Now it is more noble
> to sit like Jove that [for than] to fly like Mercury – let us not therefore go hur-
> rying about and collecting honey-bee like . . . let us open our leaves like a flower
> and be passive and receptive . . . taking hints from every noble insect that favors
> us with a visit – sap will be given us for Meat and dew for drink . . . Gittings,
> *Letters*, 66, 67.

Again, we see the conflation of ingestion, sexual internalization, and power.

4   Philip Fisher, 'A Museum with One Work Inside: Keats and the Finality of Art',
Keats–Shelley Journal, 33 (1984), 85–102.

5   William Empson, *The Structure of Complex Words* (Ann Arbor: Univ. of Michigan
Press), 1967, pp. 368–74.

6   While I've been keen to refute the evolutionary narration of Keats's life and writing,
I would underline a difference between the stated intentions of 'Sleep and Poetry'
and the represented interests of the 1820 volume. Here are some celebrated lines
from Keats's first important poem.

> O Poesy! for thee I hold my pen
> That am not yet a glorious denizen
> Of thy wide heaven – Should I rather kneel
> Upon some mountain-top until I feel
> A glowing splendour round about me hung,

And echo back the voice of thine own tongue?
O Poesy! for thee I grasp my pen
That am not yet a glorious denizen
Of thy wide heaven; yet, to my ardent prayer,
Yield from thy sanctuary some clear air,
Smoothed for intoxication by the breath
Of flowering bays, that I may die a death
Of luxury, and my young spirit follow
The morning sun-beams to the great Apollo
Like a fresh sacrifice . . . (ll. 47–61)

Keats yearns to sacrifice his young spirit to poetry: to submit to 'overwhelming sweets' and 'die a death of luxury', 'smoothed for intoxication by the breath of flowering bays'. He calls this poetry 'poesy', a sweet word. 'Sleep and Poetry' is, of course, terrifically sweet dreaming, or *naturally* antithetical, displacing, wishfulfilling fantasy. Where much of the early verse evinces Keats's longing for full gratification through poetry, *1820* grasps the danger of that dream: a dream told on an empty stomach, in Benjamin's phrase, and with the slant Benjamin puts on it. This sort of dream, which would blissfully annihilate consciousness is, in *1820*, opposed by strong dreaming: a working perversity. By 1819, Keats had come to understand that *not* to invent this slant rhyme was simply to *be*, which meant, in his case, 'benightmared [nighmar'd]' ('St Agnes', l. 375). That curious verbal from 'St. Agnes' designates the double horror of a life experienced as the unreality, or dream, of those privileged people who have and *are* being (e.g., Byron, Wordsworth), and of a life whose own dreams dissolve the identity of the dreamer who would enjoy them. Keats guessed, I believe, that not to invent the decentered, limping, flickering form – the reality of supplements – was to suffer the horror of 'palsy twitched [twitch'd]' and 'meagre face deform'. Not to live boldly and fetishistically among 'shade and form' was to be possessed by that visionary company. Not to swallow one's real in bits of bad writing was to down the full draught of hemlock.

7   Fredric Jameson, *Marxism and Form, Twentieth-Century Dialectical Theories of Literature* (Princeton: Princeton Univ. Press, 1971), 89.

Further reading

The readings below address the suppressed or covert politics of Keats's writing. The dominant, though not sole, paradigm is that of anxiety.

Geoffrey H. Hartman, 'Poem and Ideology: A Study of Keats's "To Autumn"' (1973), repr. in *The Fate of Reading and Other Essays* (Chicago and London: University of Chicago Press, 1975), 124–46. Reads in the form of 'To Autumn' an English nationalistic ideology rooted in Enlightenment notions of progressiveness.

*Jerome McGann, 'Keats and the Historical Method in Literary Criticism', *Modern Language Notes* 94.5 (December 1979), 988–1032. Seminal essay, laying the

groundwork of the historical criticism of Keats by showing the critical insights released when individual poems are located in a socio-historical frame of reference. Anticipates the key foci of later criticism: politics, class and audience, and their bearing on the self-consciously literary characteristics of Keats's poetry.

Marilyn Butler, *Romantics, Rebels and Reactionaries: English Literature and its Background 1760–1830* (Oxford: Oxford University Press, 1981). Recovers the political contexts of Keats's poetry; in particular, reads the two *Hyperion*s as complex expressions of an uncertainty regarding historical change.

Beth Lau, 'Keats's Mature Goddesses', *Philological Quarterly* 63 (1984), 323–38. If Keats's visionary and demonic goddesses represent, respectively, his idealism and scepticism regarding poetry, reconciling both is another kind of muse figure, a mature guide rather than a young lover, who, remaining ideal and immortal, is still earth-bound and humanitarian, embodying a poetry that embraces, rather than escapes or damages, the human condition.

Marlon B. Ross, *The Contours of Masculine Desire: Romanticism and the Rise of Women's Poetry* (New York and Oxford: Oxford University Press, 1989). Includes a chapter that examines 'how Keats, at first disposed to feminine influence, feels compelled to stage a self-conscious rite of poetic passage away from feminized desire and into poetic manhood.' Contrasts Keats's concept of poetic maturity with that of one of his 'feminine influences', the poet Mary Tighe.

Margaret Homans, 'Keats Reading Women, Women Reading Keats', *Studies in Romanticism* 29 (Fall 1990), 341–70. Challenges the positive constructions by feminist critics of Keats's 'femininity'. Keats's antagonism to women – expressed in his resistance to women readers, and in his desire to dominate one woman, Fanny Brawne, in particular – should be read as an attempt to compensate for literary, social and sexual inadequacy.

Anne K. Mellor, *Romanticism and Gender* (New York and London: Routledge, 1993). Distinguishing male and female Romanticisms, Mellor presents Keats as a paradigm of 'ideological cross-dressing': a male poet who conceives of his own poetic identity in feminine terms, although this playing of the role of a 'female' poet is not without ambivalence and anxiety.

Andrew Bennett, *Keats, Narrative and Audience: The Posthumous Life of Writing* (Cambridge: Cambridge University Press, 1994). The figure of solecism, breaching the division of public and private, is crucial to Keats's poetry, which exemplifies a Romantic anxiety about audience, an anxiety that produces the peculiarly Romantic notion of posterity as reception infinitely deferred to the future.

Grant F. Scott, *The Sculpted Word: Keats, Ekphrasis, and the Visual Arts* (Hanover and London: University Press of New England, 1994). Treats ekphrasis – the verbal rendering of a work of visual art – as Keats's characteristic genre, examining its ideological implications and its pertinence to a range of psychological issues, especially Keats's anxieties about gender identity.

Philip Cox, 'Keats and the Performance of Gender', *Keats–Shelley Journal* 44 (1995), 40–65. Exposes the tension between the condition of negative capability advocated by Keats, and conceived of as a passive, hence feminine state, and the actual production of a poem which, as a meaningful communication with an audience, entails a (masculine) assertion of selfhood.

Susan Wolfson, 'Keats and the Manhood of the Poet', *European Romantic Review* 6.1 (Summer 1995), 1–37. Against the tendency categorically to gender Keats (especially as 'feminine'), argues the 'formation of Keats's writing . . . along lines of irresolution on questions of gender', perceived in the past as an adolescent quality, a falling short of manhood, in Keats's text.

Ellen Brinks, 'The Male Romantic Poet as Gothic Subject: Keats's *Hyperion* and *The Fall of Hyperion: A Dream*', *Nineteenth-Century Literature* 54.4 (March 2000), 427–54. Eliciting the Gothic subtext in *Hyperion* and *The Fall of Hyperion*, reads against the grain Keats's recurrence to male masochism and effeminacy, finding these to be the perverse means, rather than impediments, to power and legitimation.

Richard Margraff-Turley, *Keats's Boyish Imagination* (London and New York: Routledge, 2004). Argues that Keats deploys immaturity strategically, to counter the 'mature force of established power', but this strategic immaturity is also in tension with a more ingenuous boyishness, exacerbating his personal anxieties about achieving 'manliness' in relation to women and his audience.

John Whale, *John Keats* (Basingstoke: Palgrave Macmillan, 2005). Emphasizing, as focal to the poetry, their exploration of sexuality and gender identity, Whale counters the established association of Keats and the 'feminine', approaching him, instead, as a study in early nineteenth-century masculinity, and finding, in his engagement with social conventions, his close male friendships and his difficulties with women, the informing contexts for his articulations of selfhood and imagination.

HISTORY AND POLITICS: KEATS'S RADICALISM

The emptiness or wanting quality of the 'aggressively *literary*' style posited by Levinson bears some resemblance to the pure aestheticism sometimes attributed to Keats in more traditional readings, although crucially, Levinson reads in such aestheticism, not escape, but engagement. Despite the proviso, because this engagement is constituted as an undermining or subverting strategy, Keats's poetry, socialized by Levinson, remains a negating poetry. By contrast, Nicholas Roe's historicizing enterprise disavows the notion both of an escapist aesthetic and of an exclusively antagonistic or negating relation of Keats to his milieu. In *John Keats and the Culture of Dissent* (1997), Roe finds in Keats a commitment to political radicalism that is manifest as an amplitude, not a negation, in his work. Roe's analysis of 'To Autumn', extracted below, exemplifies the method of close reading by which he releases the historical and political resonances of Keats's language.

Extract from Nicholas Roe, *John Keats and the Culture of Dissent* (1997)

A Serious Conspiracy in Manchester

Just published. THE GAME BOOK FOR 1819 . . . by means of which an account may be kept with ease and accuracy of the different kinds of Game, when, where, and by whom killed, how disposed of, and other particulars.

(Advertisement in the *Champion*, 29 Aug. 1819)

On the afternoon of Monday 13 September 1819 Keats joined the large crowd gathered in The Strand to welcome 'Orator' Henry Hunt in the procession organized to mark his arrival in London. 'I[t] would take me a whole day and a quire of paper to give you any thing like detail,' Keats wrote to his brother and sister-in-law: 'I will merely mention that it is calculated that 30.000 people were in the streets waiting for him – The whole distance from the Angel Islington to the Crown and anchor was lined with Multitudes'.[1] Henry Hunt had been the principal speaker at the mass meeting of reformists in St Peter's Fields, Manchester, a little under a month before on 16 August 1819. When the Manchester and Salford Yeomanry, on horseback, moved into the crowd to apprehend Hunt and the others, the peaceful meeting was swiftly transformed to violent confusion in which (perhaps) eleven were killed and as many as 500 people wounded: the Peterloo Massacre. 'Confusion' and 'perhaps', because what exactly happened in Manchester that day remains controversial. Certainly, the emotive and often contradictory accounts of the tragedy in the newspapers encouraged rumour and dismay throughout the country. 'Within two days of Peterloo, all England knew of the event', according to E. P. Thompson: 'Within a week every detail of the massacre was being canvassed in ale-houses, chapels, workshops, private houses.'[2] Hunt and the other speakers on the tribune were arrested and imprisoned, although the immediate charge of 'conspiracy and sedition' was soon dropped. As we have already seen, his triumphal reception in London on 13 September reflected widespread jubilation among the reformists, but this was mingled with hardening resentment at the behaviour of the militia, the judiciary, and – especially – the government which had endorsed without delay the actions of the soldiers and the magistrates at Manchester.

In this very highly charged political environment, conspiracy theories flourished. When one reads 'To Autumn' with this context in mind, the opening lines start to resonate in unusual and, I think, intriguing ways:

> Season of mists and mellow fruitfulness,
> Close bosom-friend of the maturing sun;
> Conspiring with him how to load and bless
> With fruit the vines that round the thatch-eves run . . .

The verb 'to conspire', from the Latin *conspirare*, literally means 'to breath together' and thus 'to accord, harmonize, agree, combine or unite in a purpose' (*OED*). So in 'conspiring' together the powers of the season and sun combine to make earth fruitful. Yet this genial conspiracy is shadowed by the contrasting sense of the word, glossed by the *Oxford English Dictionary* as to 'plot mischief together secretly', and this mischievous sense of conspiracy was a primary definition of the word in Samuel Johnson's *Dictionary*. In one reading, 'conspiracy' in 'To Autumn' is a plot of nature to 'fill all fruit with ripeness to the core' (6) – an impersonal process of natural abundance. But that expression of nature's fruitfulness is modified by the alternative, treasonable discourses of conspiracy that were circulating widely in September 1819.

On behalf of the government, the Home Secretary Lord Sidmouth advised that the ringleaders were to be charged 'for a treasonable conspiracy to alter by force the constitution of the realm as by law established'. To Lord Eldon, the Chancellor, the meeting had been 'an overt act of conspirators, to instigate . . . specific acts of treason'.[3] *The Times* pronounced on the 'dreadful fact' of the violence at Manchester *before* the detailed account from the paper's reporter, John Tyas, had arrived in London. This leading article established the popular belief 'that nearly a hundred of the King's unarmed subjects have been sabred by a body of cavalry in the streets of a town of which most of them were inhabitants' – although Tyas's eyewitness version, published in the same edition of *The Times*, 19 August 1819, contradicted the leading article in some details. Both the leader and Tyas's report were widely reprinted and appeared in two opposition newspapers that published Keats's writings and which he is known to have read. These were the *Examiner*, and the *Champion*, which in 1819 was edited by John Thelwall – a prominent reformist since the 1790s. Both journals followed the *Times* in agreeing on the 'dreadful fact' of what had happened at Manchester, but of course interpretations of the event differed (and still do so today). The *Examiner* reported the 'disturbance' and 'atrocities' at Manchester; the *Champion* warned about 'ANARCHISTS in MILITARY UNIFORM', the breakdown of justice, and the possibility that military action against the people might provoke a violent revolution. When Henry Hunt and other reformists were arrested and imprisoned, the *Champion* noted that the magistrates 'brought against them a charge of *conspiracy* to alter the laws by force and threats'.[4] During the weeks after Peterloo, the *Champion* elaborated an alternative theory of conspiracy in which the powers of the State were aligned against the liberties and democratic aspirations of the people.

For Thelwall the reformists at St Peter's Fields – like those who had met at Copenhagen Fields back in October 1795 – were to be identified with 'the cause of the people at large – of the Laws and the Constitution'. They called for annual parliaments and universal suffrage, and in one section of the crowd a banner was held aloft on which 'Justice' was represented 'holding the scales in one hand, and a sword in the other'. From Thelwall's point of view, the military intervention was an act of 'lawless, and ruthless murder', an 'abhorrent massacre'.[5] Then, on Sunday 19 September 1819 – the day on which Keats first drafted 'To Autumn' – the *Champion* published the following analysis of contemporary events:

> There is indeed, we believe, A SERIOUS CONSPIRACY IN MANCHESTER – a Conspiracy of those whom fortune has favoured, to depress and keep down the less fortunate multitude whose labour has been the instrument of that favour: – a Conspiracy of the Rich against the Poor – a species of conspiracy certainly not less frequent (as it is certainly much more practicable) than a conspiracy of the poor against the rich: – nay a conspiracy which we might almost venture to say, always precedes, and not unfrequently produces, that of the later description. These Opulent Conspirators wish to prevent the labouring classes from aspiring to any political rights – because political rights have a tendency to secure personal liberty and personal consideration. The confederacies and combinations they practice among themselves, they would interdict entirely their poorer brethren, that they may keep them in abject and entire dependence: and what the law cannot, or will not insure for them, in this respect, they would accomplish by the terrors of the sword. If nothing else will keep down the half-famishing labouring poor and stifle the cry of their complaints, it has been thought that massacre would. But let them beware of a reaction; – in case of which, victory might be to them as fatal as defeat.[6]

Keats could not have read this column on 19 September: it would have taken a day for copies to reach Winchester from London. On the other hand, political debate in August and September 1819 focused on the word 'conspire'. Thelwall was evidently responding to – and amplifying – rumours of state conspiracy canvassed in the broad range of reformist discourse which was also available to Keats in the national journals, and in material from those papers reprinted locally in the *Salisbury and Winchester Journal*.[7] But, as Jerome McGann and others have pointed out, Keats's poem is not radical polemic like Thelwall's articles in the *Champion* or, for that matter, Shelley's incandescent response to Peterloo in *The Masque of Anarchy*. Throughout this book I have suggested ways in which Keats's verse responded to contemporary journalism in the postwar period. My purpose has been to show how, once we are alerted to contemporary resonances of his poems apparent to his first readers, we can recover a fuller sense of Keats's witty, sparkling, changeful, and controversial arrival on the literary scene. But how can we make a credible link between the ongoing discussion of national crisis in the newspapers and conspiracy in 'To Autumn', so as to elucidate the politics of autumnal beauty in Keats's poem?

The Calendar of Nature

And Libra weighs in equal scales the year . . .
    (James Thomson, *The Seasons*, 'Autumn')

The *Examiner* for 5 September 1819 (just before Keats's visit to London) contained much on Peterloo, and also Hunt's regular monthly column entitled 'The Calendar of Nature'. The 'Calendar' has been noticed before in criticism of 'To Autumn', most recently by William Keach;[8] it has not yet been reproduced fully in this context, however, so that its relation to Keats's poem may reward some further consideration. The 'Calendar' begins with the 'September' stanza from Spenser's *Mutabilitie Cantos*, long recognized as the source for some images in 'To Autumn':

September.
Next him September marched eke on foot;
Yet was he heavy laden with the spoyle
Of harvest's riches, which he made his boot,
And him enriched with bounty of the soyle:
In his one hand, as fit for harvest's toyle,
He held a knife-hook; and in th'other hand
A paire of weights, with which he did assoyle
Both more and lesse, where it in doubt did stand,
And equal gave to each as justice duly scanned.
                    Spenser.

    The poet still takes advantage of the exuberance of harvest and the sign of the Zodiac in this month, to read us a lesson on justice.

Autumn has now arrived. This is the month of the migration of birds, of the finished harvest, of nut-gathering, of cyder and perry-making, and, towards the conclusion, of the change of colour in trees. The swallows, and many other soft-billed birds that feed on insects, disappear for the warmer climates, leaving only a few stragglers behind, probably from weakness or sickness, who hide themselves in caverns and other sheltered places, and occasionally appear on warm days. The remainder of harvest is got in; and no sooner is this done, than the husbandman ploughs up his land again, and prepares it for the winter grain. The oaks and beeches shed their nuts, which in the forests that still remain, particularly the New Forest in Hampshire, furnish a luxurious repast for the swine, who feast of an evening in as pompous a manner as any alderman, to the sound of the herdsman's horn.

But the acorn must not be undervalued, because it is food for swine, nor thought only robustly of, because it furnishes our ships with timber. It is also one of the most beautiful objects of its species, protruding its glossy green nut from its rough and sober-coloured cup, and dropping it in a most elegant manner beside the sunny and jagged leaf. We have seen a few of them, with their stems in water, make a handsome ornament to a mantle-piece, in this season of departing flowers.

The few additional flowers this month are corn-flower, Guernsey-lilies, starwort, and saffron, a species of crocus, which is cultivated in separate grounds. The stamens of this flower are pulled, and dried into flat square cakes for medicinal purposes. It was formerly much esteemed in cookery. The clown in the Winter's Tale, reckoning up what he is to buy for the sheepshearing feast, mentions 'saffron to colour the warden-pies'. The fresh trees and shrubs in flower are bramble, chaste-tree, laurustinus, ivy, wild honeysuckle, spires, and arbutus or strawberry-tree, a favourite of Virgil, which, like the garden of Alcinous, in Homer, produces flower and fruit at once. – Hardy annuals, intended to flower in the spring, should now be sown; annuals of curious sorts, from which seed is to be raised, should be sheltered till ripened; and auriculas in pots, which were shifted last month, moderately watered.

The stone-curlew clamours at the beginning of this month, wood-owls hoot, the ring-ouzel reappears, the saffron butterfly is seen, hares congregate; and, at the end of it, the woodlark, thrush and blackbird, are heard.

September, though its mornings and evenings are apt to be chill and foggy, and therefore not wholesome to those who either do not or cannot guard against them, is generally a serene and pleasant month, partaking of the warmth of summer and the vigour of autumn. But its noblest feature is a certain festive abundance for the supply of all creation. There is grain for men, birds, and horses, hay for the cattle, loads of fruit on the trees, and swarms of fish in the ocean. If the soft-billed birds which feed on insects miss their usual supply, they find it in the southern countries, and leave one's sympathy to be pleased with an idea, that repasts apparently more harmless are alone offered to the creation upon our temperate soil. The feast, as the philosophic poet says on a higher occasion,

> The feast is such as earth, the general mother,
>   Pours from her fairest bosom, when she smiles
> In the embrace of Autumn. To each other
>   As some fond parent fondly reconciles
> Her warring children, she their wrath beguiles
>   With their own sustenance; they, relenting, weep.
> Such is this festival, which from their isles,
>   And continents, and winds, and oceans deep,
> All shapes may throng to share, that fly, or walk, or creep.
>   Shelley.

Just below the stanza from the 'philosophic poet' Shelley's *Revolt of Islam* is the heading 'LAW. Surrey Sessions. *Tuesday, Aug. 31*. Seditious Placards', returning the reader to an article which reports directly on the controversial politics of the day.

The similarities between Hunt's 'Calendar of Nature' and 'To Autumn' extend beyond 'harvest's riches' and the harvester's 'knife-hook' in Spenser. Details such as the migrating birds, cider-making, swallows and insects, warm days, and even the chill and fog all reappear in Keats's poem.[9] Most interesting in the present context, however, is the schooling that Hunt draws from Spenser and elaborates in his commentary and with the quotation from Shelley: 'The poet still takes advantage of the exuberance of harvest and the sign of the Zodiac in this month, to read us a lesson on justice.'

Spenser's harvester uses a 'paire of weights' to divide the produce of autumn justly and equably. The image of the balance is especially appropriate to September (as Hunt notices) because the latter part of this temperate month lies under the constellation Libra, which depicts a pair of scales. Keats had been familiar with the image and seasonal significance of Libra since his schoolboy reading at Enfield in Bonnycastle's *Introduction to Astronomy*: 'LIBRA, the Balance, one of the twelve signs of the zodiac, into which the sun comes about the 20th of September, or the beginning of autumn.'[10] In addition to these seasonal and astronomical associations, during autumn 1819 the scales had an immediate emblematic force in political debate. The reformists' banners at St Peter's Fields had been emblazoned with the figure of Justice holding her scales, as an expression of their call for democratic rights and universal suffrage. And contemporary satirical prints such as *Manchester Heroes* represented the *injustice* of Peterloo and its aftermath in a cartoon image of the Prince Regent as the fulcrum of a set of unbalanced scales. In this wider emblematic context, the point of Leigh Hunt's 'lesson on justice' in his September 'Calendar of Nature' becomes apparent in mediating between political oppression and seasonal fruitfulness. The 'exuberance of harvest' (literally *ex-uber*, from the breast of nature) is appropriately the season of justice; it is depicted by Hunt as a commonwealth, 'a certain festive abundance for the supply of all creation', which might assuage even the dearth endured by those New Forest swine in Richard Porson's satire: 'What is the property of a hog? – A wooden trough, food and drink just enough to keep in life; and a truss of musty straw, on which ten or a dozen of us *pig together*.'[11] Shelley's autumnal *Convito*, the 'banquet of the free' in Canto V of *The Revolt of Islam*, points the revolutionary meaning of Hunt's observations. The exuberance of 'earth, the general mother' feeds and reconciles the 'warring children', who share with all creation in the plenty of the season.

When we turn from Spenser, Shelley, and 'The Calendar of Nature' to Keats's 'To Autumn', the conspiracy of sun and season may now appear less of an escape form historical tensions, than as a harvest-home fulfilling the call for justice from 'the less fortunate multitude' – the 'swine' of Burke's *Reflections*. There are of course no scales of justice overtly represented in 'To Autumn' (as they had been in Spenser's verse, and as depicted on the protesters' banners at St Peter's Fields). Nevertheless in formal terms and in some verbal details the three stanzas of Keats's poem exhibit a fine equity, resuming the current discourse of (in)justice as a politics of style; as Geoffrey Hartman has already pointed out, 'Each stanza . . . is so equal in its poetical weight, so loaded with its own harvest.'[12] Hartman's perception of the poem's global equipoise can be substantiated further in specific images and emblems of balance, disclosed in the central stanza amid the store of autumn's plenty. The tress of hair, for example, is 'soft-lifted', floating upon the breath of the 'winnowing wind'; indeed, the version of the poem transcribed in Keats's letter to Richard Woodhouse, 21 September 1819,[13] has 'winmowing wind', a misspelling that seems to concentrate in a single word the whole process of harvest in mowing, winnowing, and – perhaps – wind milling. The furrow of corn is 'half-reap'd', the next swath 'and all its twined flowers' yet to be harvested. And then there is the marvellously composed movement of

> . . . sometimes like a gleaner thou dost keep
> Steady thy laden head across a brook . . .

– 'Stready', as Keats wrote in his copy of the poem for Woodhouse,[14] intimating, as Christopher Ricks notes, both 'straight and steady': a justified progress.[15] In all of these verbal and emblematic details the poem identifies balance and equity as particularly appropriate to autumn, 'a medium between summer and winter', articulating the beauty of the season in language and imagery that were also circulating in discourses of political and social justice after the outrage of Peterloo.

The third stanza of 'To Autumn' returns to the westering world of change, loss, mortality – already sensed, perhaps, in the 'clammy cells' of the bees – but with an acceptance of those processes of time which is a characteristic of the negatively capable imagination. Crucially, however, that acceptance has been achieved through contemplation of natural abundance that was laden with intense social and ideological consequence at the season of the poem's composition. There is, moreover, a biblical resonance to the language and imagery of 'To Autumn' which deserves to be mentioned, for it enables us to hear the distant commotion of Peterloo even in the final *sotto voce* cadences of Keats's poem. Behind Keats's benign harvest was the terrifying, apocalyptic reaping of the earth in Revelation 14:

> 19. And the angel thrust in his sickle into the earth, and gathered the vine of the earth, and cast it into the great winepress of the wrath of God.

> 20. And the winepress was trodden without the city, and blood came out of the winepress, even unto the horse bridles, by the space of a thousand and six hundred furlongs.

Some contemporary responses to Peterloo echoed these dreadful, sanguinary 'last oozings' from the winepress,

> – may the ghosts of the murdered your slumbers infest,
> And drops of their blood be found in your wine . . .[16]

– and Shelley in his *Masque of Anarchy* draws from the same source to orchestrate the 'ghastly masquerade' of the murderers,

> Drunk as with intoxication
> Of the wine of desolation. (48–9)

Elsewhere, 'the conspirators against the privileges of the People' were denounced in the prophetic voice of Revelation:

> They shall not smell sweet and blossom in the dust; the wrongs which they have heaped upon society will adhere to them like the leprosy . . . time will disclose the secret; and then they may call on the heavens to hide, and the hills to cover them, but the outstretched arm of Offended Justice will seize these children of blood, even at the uttermost bounds of the earth.[17]

In the temperate lyrical clime of 'To Autumn', these sanguinary tones are chastened, residual, but discerned none the less, I think, in the reaping 'hook', the 'last oozings' of the 'cyder-press', the 'soft-dying day', and the 'rosy hue' of the 'stubble-plains'. Through such verbal details the apocalyptic harvest of the fields of St Peter is acknowledged, even as it is subdued in the slow gathering of the season and the poem itself towards a close. The figure of 'Offended Justice' remains, and it is to this focus of restitution in Keats's poem that I now turn.

'Who Hath Not Seen Thee?'

> pray tell me what that tall majestic lady is, that stands there, beautified with yellow hair, and crowned with a turban composed of ears of corn; her bosom swells with breasts as white as snow. Her right-hand is filled with poppies and ears of corn, and in her left is a lighted torch.
>
> (Andrew Tooke, *The Pantheon*)[18]

> Scarcity and want shall shun you;
> Ceres' blessing so is on you.
>   (*The Tempest*, IV. i. 116–17)

'Who hath not seen thee oft amid thy store?' As has frequently been pointed out (by Ian Jack, Helen Vendler, John Creaser, and most recently Andrew Bennett), Keats's personification of autumn has numerous mythical referents, the most notable of these being the goddess Ceres.[19] Keats had known about Ceres from his schoolboy reading in Ovid's *Metamorphoses* and (more especially) his classical dictionaries and anthologies of classical literature. Three texts, which Charles Cowden Clarke recalled Keats reading at Enfield, identify the various mythical associations of Ceres. Lemprière's *Bibliotheca Classica; or, A Classical Dictionary*, which Clarke says Keats 'appeared to *learn*', provides the typical image of Ceres, 'goddess of corn and harvests . . . represented with a garland of ears of corn on her head, holding in one hand a lighted torch, and in the other a poppy, which was sacred to her'. Ceres' resemblance to the figure on the banner at St Peter's Fields, with the torch and scales of justice, was not a coincidence – as will shortly appear. Joseph Spence's *Polymetis*, also read at Enfield by Keats, offers an identical image of Ceres 'regarding the laborious husbandman from heaven; and blessing the work of his hands with success'.[20]

That 'To Autumn' was a late harvesting of images and ideas which had been sown in Keats's earliest years at Enfield is suggested by the similarities between the poem and these short extracts from Lemprière and Spence. It is Andrew Tooke's *Pantheon*, however, which elaborates the symbolic roles of Ceres in greatest detail, glossing a passage from the *Metamorphoses* which associates her with fruitfulness, labour on the land, and the origins of justice:

> Ovid . . . tells us that *Ceres* was the first that made laws, provided wholesome food, and taught the art of husbandry, of plowing and sowing: for before her time the earth lay rough and uncultivated, covered with briars and unprofitable plants. Where there were no proprietors of land, they neglected to cultivate it; when nobody had any ground of his own, they did not care to fix land-marks; but all things were common to all men, till Ceres, who had invented the art of husbandry, taught men how to exercise it: and then they began to contend and dispute about the limits of those fields from whose culture they reaped so much profit; and from thence it was necessary that laws should be enacted to determine the rights and properties of those who contended. For this reason Ceres was named the *Foundress of laws*.[21]

Ceres presides over land originally 'common to all men'; over food, farming, cultivation, and prosperity; and over the laws determining 'rights and properties' among contentious humankind.[22] She represents nature's abundance, and also the rights and laws that determine a just distribution of that plenty. If one glances back at Thelwall's account of the reformists at St Peter's Fields, one might contend that Ceres was the appropriate emblem of those 'labouring classes . . . aspiring to . . . political rights . . . personal liberty and personal consideration'. Certainly, the mythical associations of the goddess, uniting fruitfulness and justice, would have garnered further resonance at a season when killings, trumped-up prosecutions, and rumoured conspiracies seemed likely to provoke a revolution. Perhaps, as Josiah Conder had said, there was 'mischief' indeed at the core of *Lamia, Isabella, The Eve of St Agnes, and Other Poems*. Yet in 'To Autumn' the goddess is a shadowy figure, not explicitly invoked although her presence may be assumed in the question 'Who hath not seen thee oft amid thy store?' The interrogation is knowing and very finely poised, negatively capable in Heaney's sense of being 'affected by all positions'; it addresses the community 'who hath seen' but with a glancing acknowledgement of those who have not, in that they are unjustly excluded from their due share in Ceres's autumnal plenty. That secondary inflection was emphasized in Keats's draft of 'To Autumn', where the question was abbreviated as 'Who hath not seen thee?' And the succeeding lines of the draft fleetingly admit the deprived in search of restitution, 'Sometimes whoever seeks for thee may find thee', subsequently revised to 'Sometimes whoever seeks abroad may find thee'.[23] Perhaps the overt sense of the line suggests that whoever quests widely 'may find', but – just momentarily – the poem quits the shores of Britain for a haven of justice elsewhere.

Postscript

When in 1821 Leigh Hunt republished his 'Calendar of Nature' as a volume entitled *The Months*, he prefaced the book with an advertisement mentioning that 'The good-nature with which this Calendar was received on its appearance in 1819 . . . has induced its republication in a separate form, with considerable additions'. Hunt made no revisions to the text of 'September', but he did make one notable addition: the second and third stanzas of 'To Autumn'.[24] 'A living poet has happily personified autumn in some of the pleasantest shapes under which her servants appear,' Hunt wrote, and incorporated Keats's poem within his own celebration of autumnal exuberance. In so doing, however, he explicitly associated 'To Autumn' with the seasonal 'lesson on justice' that he had drawn from Spenser's and Shelley's poems, and from Richard Porson's *New Catechism*. We have seen how in 1819 Hunt's 'Calendar of Nature' might have offered Keats some images for 'To Autumn'; two years later, *The Months* gathered 'To Autumn' into a context that acknowledged the poem's fruitful, negatively capable conspiracy as an expression of Keats's commonwealth, 'a certain festive abundance for the supply of all creation'.

Throughout this book I have been concerned to recover Keats from the contexts of disadvantage in which he has been fixed by critics from Z to Marjorie Levinson, emphasizing instead the ways in which the circumstances of his life from his schooldays onwards enabled and enriched his poetry. I have also sought to show how Keats's poems responded to and negotiated with contemporary history, rather than presenting an aesthetic resort in which to 'escape' or 'evade' the world. Helen Vendler has suggested that the music in the third stanza of 'To Autumn' issues from a 'choir of orphans . . . in mourning for a dead mother' and that, in the final lines, the poem lifts away from 'pathos and nostalgia for the past'.[25] Her reading of the final stanza draws on biography in order to transcend it, although, as we have seen, Keatsian romance never wholly forgets the earth. The mild, autumnal music at the close of 'To Autumn' is a contented valediction,

Hedge-crickets sing; and now with treble soft
The red-breast whistles from a garden-croft;
    And gathering swallows twitter in the skies.

– which may hark back to a formative landscape: the 'garden-croft' at Enfield School, scene of Keats's poetic initiation with Charles Cowden Clarke. Here too, in earlier years, John Ryland had set his 'living orrery' in motion, and the whole school had assembled in autumn to watch 'the swallows, which had clustered in surprising numbers on the roof of the building'.[26] Keats was always a 'watcher of the skies', and this most generous of poems concludes with the turning of the season, a gathering for departure, and with one of the 'delighted stares' which Cowden Clarke always associated with Keats's intensity of response.[27] I might have closed here by suggesting that the extraordinary school which shaped Keats's life as a poet had also fostered the delighted welcome for experience which endured almost to the very end of his life. But perhaps that final flourish is better left in silence: a 'wild surmise'.

Notes

1   Keats, *Letters* II. 194.
2   E. P. Thompson, *The Making of the English Working Class* (Harmondsworth: Penguin, 1968), 753–6. For a full-length reassessment of Peterloo, see Robert Walmsley, *Peterloo: The Case Reopened* (Manchester: Manchester University Press, 1969).
3   Walmsley, *Peterloo*, 247, 339–40.
4   See *The Times* (19 Aug. 1819); *Examiner* (23 Aug. 1819); *Champion and Sunday Review* (22 Aug. 1819), 525; (19 Sept. 1819), 595.
5   *Champion and Sunday Review* (22 Aug. 1819), 526, 532; (12 Sept. 1819), 574.
6   *Champion and Sunday Review* (19 Sept. 1819), 591.
7   I am grateful to John Barnard for information about the political columns of the *Salisbury and Winchester Journal* in 1819.
8   See William Keach, 'Cockney Couplets: Keats and the Politics of Style', *Studies in Romanticism* 25. 2 (summer 1986), 194–5.
9   Other sources for the autumnal imagery of Keats's poem included illustrated editions of James Thomson's *Seasons*; John Aikin's *Natural History of the Year: Being an Enlargement of Dr. Aikin's Calendar of Nature: By Arthur Aikin* (4th edn., London: J. Johnson, 1815).
10 John Bonnycastle, *An Introduction to Astronomy* (4th edn., London: J. Johnson, 1803), 420.
11 *Examiner* (30 Aug. 1818), 550; see also the discussion in *Keats and the Culture of Dissent*, Ch. 3.
12 'Poem and Ideology', 129.
13 Keats, *Letters* II. 170–1.
14 Ibid., 170.
15 See *Keats and Embarrassment*, 72–3.
16 'Manchester Y – y Valour', in Walmsley, *Peterloo*, 263–4.

17   'Manchester Politics', *Manchester Observer* (11 Sept. 1819), in Walmsley, *Peterloo*, 273.

18   Andrew Tooke, *The Pantheon* (London: 1783), 177–8.

19   See *Keats and the Mirror of Art*, 232–43; Helen Vendler, *The Odes of John Keats*, 233–88; John Creaser, 'From "Autumn" to Autumn in Keats's Ode', *Essays in Criticism*, 38 (1988), 190–214; Bennett, *Keats, Narrative and Audience*, 159–71.

20   See Charles Cowden Clarke, 'Recollections of John Keats' in Charles and Mary Cowden Clarke, *Recollections of Writers* (1878; Fontwell: Centaur, 1969), 124; J. Lemprière, *Bibliotheca Classica; or, A Classical Dictionary* (3rd edn., London: Spottiswoode, 1797), unpaginated; Joseph Spence, *Polymetis; or An Inquiry Concerning the Agreement between the Works of the Roman Poets, and the Remains of the Ancient Artists* (2nd edn., London: J. Payne, 1755), 103.

21   *The Pantheon*, 179.

22   Andrew Bennett points out that, as a 'pervasive unstated presence' in 'To Autumn' Ceres has a significant relationship to agrarian politics (the Corn Laws of 1815, enclosures, the condition of the rural poor), such that the poem's 'perfected language of pastoral description is invaded by political questions of lawful exchange, agricultural boundaries, private property and labour relations'. Bennett, *Keats, Narrative and Audience*, 162–4.

23   See the draft of 'To Autumn' reproduced in *John Keats: Poetry Manuscripts at Harvard: A Facsimile Edition*, ed. Jack Stillinger (Cambridge, Mass.: Harvard Univ. Press, 1990), 222. For a reading of 'To Autumn' as 'an apotheosis of contemporary Spencean articles of faith about English abundance and fertility', see David Worrall, *Radical Culture: Discourse, Resistance and Surveillance, 1790–1820* (Hemel Hempstead: Harrester Wheatsheaf, 1992), 201–2.

24   *The Months Descriptive of the Successive Beauties of the Year* (London: C&J Ollier, 1821), 5, 102–9.

25   Vendler, *Odes*, 259–63.

26   James Culross, *The Three Rylands: A Hundred Years of Various Christian Service* (London: E. Stock, 1897), 40.

27   'Recollections of Keats', 130

Further reading

The following list consists of some recent historical readings of Keats which, moving away from the paradigms of anxiety, lack or negation, emphasize Keats's radicalism, largely characterized here as an assertive rather than subversive politics. If the historicizing criticism of the preceding list has some elements in common with the harsher Victorian readings of an evasive poet, the works named here endorse the counter to those readings that, early on, sought to construct a poet positively and productively engaged with his world.

Susan Wolfson (ed.), *Keats and Politics: A Forum*, special issue of *Studies in Romanticism* 25.2 (Summer 1986). Important collection of essays, emphasizing Keats's radicalism in their 'examination of how Keats's formal practices, aesthetic predilections, and social values, register a fine and subtle alertness to the political issues of his age.'

***John Barnard**, *John Keats* (Cambridge: Cambridge University Press, 1987). Excellent introduction, emphasizing the 'essentially honest and questioning nature of Keats's work', located in the context of the debate about poetry in the early nineteenth century. Topics include the class and political biases in the contemporary reception, and the stresses manifest in Keats's treatment of women.

Vincent Newey, 'Keats, Politics, and the Idea of Revolution' (1989), repr. in *Centring the Self: Subjectivity, Society and Reading from Thomas Gray to Thomas Hardy* (Aldershot: Scolar Press, 1995), 97–121. In response to readings that emphasize Keats's (radical) politics by denying or minimizing the transcendental, visionary aspect of his work, argues that Keats's historical and political awareness is subsumed into a transcendental vision that produces not escape but the alternative reality to history, that of eternal law and natural good.

Daniel P. Watkins, *Keats's Poetry and the Politics of Imagination* (London and Toronto: Associated University Presses, 1989). The anxiety of the post-Waterloo period and the ascendancy of industrial capitalism, within which that anxiety can be contextualized, constitute the determining historical reality behind Keats's poetry, both where it is escapist and where radical.

Laurence S. Lockridge, 'Keats: The Ethics of Imagination' in *Coleridge, Keats and the Imagination: Romanticism and Adam's Dream*, ed. J. Robert Barth and John L. Mahoney (Columbia and London: University of Missouri Press, 1990), 143–73. Finds in Keats a 'pragmatic humanism' that is unlike his contemporaries' 'visionary expectation'. Keats conceives of ethical action as everyday human activity, rather than exceptional or heroic acts, and of the worker, rather than the visionary, as the paradigmatic moral agent.

Paul D. Sheats, 'Keats, the Greater Ode, and the Imagination', in *Coleridge, Keats and the Imagination: Romanticism and Adam's Dream*, ed. J. Robert Barth and John L. Mahoney (Columbia and London: University of Missouri Press, 1990), 174–200. Virtuoso analysis, tracing the legacy of the 'greater' ode of the eighteenth century, in Keats's engagement with odal decorum in relation to the visionary imagination. The 'Ode to a Nightingale', where the odal form both gestures towards and subverts the decorum of the minor odes of 1817 and 1818, in so doing, expresses an ambiguity regarding the poetic imagination.

Hermione de Almeida, *Romantic Medicine and John Keats* (New York and Oxford: Oxford University Press, 1991). Addressing a lacuna in the history of medicine, at the same time as it establishes the literary and artistic consequences of Romantic medicine, shows, through a close reading of Keats's poetry, his engagement with the four key concerns of contemporary medical thought: the physician's task, the meaning of life, health and disease, and the evolution of matter and mind.

Nicholas Roe (ed.), *Keats and History* (Cambridge: Cambridge University Press, 1995). Key essays on the historical dimensions of Keats's writing, including economics, class, and gender and feminism. The editor's introduction offers a useful overview of the book's subject.

Andrew Motion, *Keats* (London: Faber, 1997). Major recent biography, emphasizing Keats's social and political context and its pertinence to the language and forms, as well as content, of his work.

Michael O' Neill (ed.), *Keats: Bicentenary Readings* (Edinburgh: Edinburgh University Press, 1997). Miscellany, reconsidering, in the wake of the historical trend in Keats studies, 'the function of Keats's style; the trajectory and significance of his poetic career; the relationship between the poetry and the pressures of history; and the poet's sometimes self-divided view of poetry.'

Jeffrey N. Cox, *Poetry and Politics in the Cockney School: Keats, Shelley, Hunt and their Circle* (Cambridge: Cambridge University Press, 1998). Locates Keats in an identifiable Cockney School – centred on Hunt and including, among others, Shelley, Hazlitt and Byron – for whom writing is a social activity, founded on collaboration and interchange, and the literature so produced, a means to social and political reform.

Robert M. Ryan and Ronald A. Sharp (eds.), *The Persistence of Poetry: Bicentennial Essays on Keats* (Amherst: University of Massachusetts Press, 1998). Important collection, commemorating Keats in essays displaying a range of contesting emphases, on his craftsmanship, his moral philosophy and his historical and political contexts.

Andrew Franta, 'Keats and the Review Aesthetic', *Studies in Romanticism* 38.3 (Fall 1999), 343–64. Posits the similarity of Keats's early sonnets to reviews, finding, in Keats, a recognition of, and commitment to, reception and its constitutive role in the production of a work of art.

Gregory Wassil, 'Keats's Orientalism', *Studies in Romanticism* 39.3 (Fall 2000), 419–47. Difficult but stimulating essay, countering the stance that Orientalism is marginal to Keats or that it takes the form of elision rather than engagement. Wassil argues that Keats's writing is not simply determined by, but engages, the social forces of his time, and is no exception to Said's thesis of the dominance of Orientalism in nineteenth-century literature. Keats's Orientalism is bound up with his concern with identity and otherness (negative capability); what is shown here is a 'hybridity', 'the creation of a self-image . . . outside the paradigm of oppression and victimization.'

Drew Milne, 'Flaming Robes: Keats, Shelley and the Metrical Clothes of Class Struggle', *Textual Practice* 15.1 (Spring 2001), 101–22. Identifies the radicalism of Keats's innovatory metrical forms in their flouting of poetical decorum and of established metrical laws.

Alan Richardson, *British Romanticism and the Science of the Mind* (Cambridge: Cambridge University Press, 2001). In the context of a study of the overlap, in the Romantic era, of 'literary and scientific representations of the mind as situated in and lived through the body', finds in Keats 'an unprecedented poetics of embodied cognition', informed by an awareness of the inextricability of mind and brain gained through his exposure, as a medical student, to contemporary brain science, and at odds with his impulse to transcendence.

*****Susan J. Wolfson** (ed.), *The Cambridge Companion to Keats* (Cambridge: Cambridge University Press, 2001). Useful up-to-date collection, revisiting the major topics of Keats criticism, including form, politics and gender.

*Kelvin Everest, *John Keats* (Tavistock: Northcote House, 2002). Valuable modern introduction which locates Keats in his historical context without losing focus on his poetic achievement. Keats's grappling with received tradition is especially relevant to the diverse readership of today; his poetry, growing into and renewing that tradition, 'is the supreme model of the means by which poetry itself survives.'

Paul Hamilton, *Metaromanticism: Aesthetics, Literature, Theory* (Chicago: University of Chicago Press, 2003). In this subtle and far-reaching study, which characterizes romanticism by its philosophical habits of self-consciousness, Hamilton shows the radicalism of Keats's poetry to consist in a (self-)awareness of absence, revealing the mutual exposure or betrayal of the aesthetic and the political.

Jerrold E. Hogle, 'The Gothic-Romantic Relationship: Underground Histories in "The Eve of St. Agnes"', *European Romantic Review* 14.2 (June 2003), 205–23. Presents 'The Eve of St. Agnes' as a paradigm of the way in which the Gothic operates in a Romantic poem so as to enable a 'workable vision of imaginative transformation in a manner that takes account of, while also seeming to overcome . . . historical tensions.'

Useful editions

The Poems of John Keats, ed. Jack Stillinger (Cambridge, Mass.: Harvard University Press, 1978) is the authoritative standard edition. *John Keats: Complete Poems*, ed. Jack Stillinger (Cambridge, Mass.: Harvard University Press, 1982) is a more student-oriented 'reading edition' of the same texts, but with notes and critical commentary replacing textual variants and other specifically textual information. Also of particular use to students is the valuably annotated *The Poems of John Keats*, ed. Miriam Allott (London: Longman, 1970).

Reference material

Beth Lau, *Keats's Reading of the Romantic Poets* (Ann Arbor: University of Michigan Press, 1991). Useful source study of Keats's reading of his major contemporaries, seeking both to lay the groundwork for the assessment of influence and to situate Keats in the literary climate of his time.

H. E. Rollins (ed.), *The Keats Circle*, 2 vols. (Cambridge, Mass.: Harvard University Press, 1948). Invaluable collection of letters and other papers relating to Keats, written by the members of his circle.

H. E. Rollins (ed.), *The Letters of John Keats: 1814–1821* (Cambridge, Mass.: Harvard University Press, 1958). Standard complete edition of Keats's letters.

Chapter notes

1 Leigh Hunt, 'Young Poets', *Examiner* (1 Dec 1816), 761 (*Romantics Reviewed, Part C*, I. 426).

2   Anon, review of *Lamia* [etc.], [Gold's] *London Magazine* ii (Aug 1820), 160 (*Romantics Reviewed, Part C*, II. 613).

3   Leslie A. Marchand (ed.), *Byron's Letters and Journals*, 13 vols. (London: John Murray, 1973–94), vii, 217, 225.

4   John Hamilton Reynolds, review of *Endymion*, repr. *Examiner* (11 Oct 1818), 649 (*Romantics Reviewed, Part C*, I. 439).

5   P. G. Patmore, review of *Endymion*, [Baldwin's] *London Magazine* I (Apr 1820), 381 (*Romantics Reviewed, Part C*, II. 557).

6   Anon, review of *Endymion*, *Champion* (7 Jun 1818), 362 (*Romantics Reviewed, Part C*, I. 265). Cf. Keats's letter of 27 Oct 1818 to Richard Woodhouse in *Letters*, I. 387–8. The reviewer is indeed probably Woodhouse himself.

7   Francis Jeffrey, review of *Endymion* and *Lamia* [etc.], *Edinburgh Review* xxxiv (Aug 1820), 205 (*Romantics Reviewed, Part C*, I. 386).

8   Patmore, review of *Endymion*, 380–1 (*Romantics Reviewed, Part C*, II. 556–7); Leigh Hunt, review of *Lamia* [etc.], *Indicator* (9 Aug 1820), 345 (*Romantics Reviewed, Part C*, II. 483).

9   Matthew Arnold, 'John Keats' in *The Complete Prose Works of Matthew Arnold* , ed. R. H. Super, 10 vols. (Ann Arbor: University of Michigan Press, 1960–77), IX. 205–16.

10   Marjorie Levinson, *Keats's Life of Allegory: The Origins of a Style* (Oxford: Basil Blackwell, 1988), 5.

7

An Expanding Canon

By the early twenty-first century, the established canon of 'Romantic' poets has been so widely contested, augmented and critiqued, that it might well be argued that it has ceased to exist. Yet the persistence of the category 'Romantic' seems to indicate not redundancy, but an enduring canonizing power. The decline of descriptors such as 'minor' or 'lesser' has brought about not cessation, but reformation; as the dominance of the 'major' Romantics is challenged, new areas of canonicity are mapped. This chapter will treat, as examples of this process, two of the most significant recent developments in the ongoing expansion of the Romantic canon.

JOHN CLARE (1793–1864)

With the publication of his first volume of poems, *Poems Descriptive of Rural Life and Scenery* (1820), John Clare was propelled into notice emphatically as a 'peasant poet' from Northamptonshire. The introduction to the volume, by his publisher John Taylor (also Keats's publisher), though mindful of Clare's merits as a poet, was heavily insistent on his poverty and humble origins. Correspondingly, Clare's brief early popularity was due more to a literary fashion for the proletarian than to a recognition of his poetic merits; as his novelty declined, so did his popularity. In his later years, his confinement in a lunatic asylum, from 1837 to his death in 1864, and the exposure to public attention of some the poetry of that period, gave him a fresh claim to attention, this time as embodying another popular cliché, that of the 'mad genius'. Despite intermittent acknowledgements of the real value of his poetry, then, through much of the nineteenth century and till early into the twentieth, Clare's fame was first of all as a literary curiosity, and second only as a poet.

Clare's reputation has grown steadily, if slowly, in the course of the twentieth century. Arthur Symons' 'Introduction' to his selection of Clare's poetry (1908) is an early instance of genuine literary criticism, releasing the poetry from the clichés of the narrowly biographical readings. In 1932, a major biography by J. W. and Anne Tibble, the most important Clare scholars in the first half of the twentieth century, was published; J. W. Tibble's two-volume *Poems of John Clare* (1935) remained the standard edition for nearly 50 years thereafter. Geoffrey Grigson, in the introductions to his *Poems of John Clare's Madness* (1949) and *Selected Poems of John Clare* (1950), makes large claims for the 'visionary' poetry of the asylum years, and, by asserting the intellectual influence of Wordsworth and Coleridge, and linking Clare also with Keats and Blake, aligns him with his more canonical contemporaries. Just over a decade later, in Harold Bloom's influential *The Visionary Company* (1961), Clare is categorically a Romantic poet:

> some of his most characteristic (and best) work . . . show[s] the Romantic Clare, as a Wordsworthian and as a final independent visionary, equal at his most intense to Smart and Blake. And a consideration of . . . [his poems] should further illuminate the varieties of Romantic dialectic, in its endless interplay between nature and imagination.[1]

Bloom's treatment of Clare is double-edged; it draws him into a canonical mainstream, but only as a secondary poet, under the 'Wordsworthian shadow'. Tacitly but powerfully repudiating such condescension, however, is the pioneering scholarship that begins around this time: the restoration, by Geoffrey Summerfield and Eric Robinson, of Clare's original texts from the interventions of his earlier editors; Summerfield and Robinson's joint editions, *Later Poems of John Clare* (1964), *John Clare: The Shepherd's Calendar* (1964), and *Clare: Selected Poems and Prose* (1966), decisively shape the reception from then on. In 1966, Clare finds a place in a volume entitled *Some British Romantics*, where Ian Jack's important essay, 'Poems of John Clare's Sanity', challenges the twentieth-century predilection for the asylum poetry by asserting the claims, especially, of *The Shepherd's Calendar* (1827).[2]

But the first extended critical treatment of Clare, the cornerstone of present-day Clare criticism, determinedly resists his assimilation into a mainstream, Romantic or otherwise, and in so doing all the more establishes his stature as a major poet of the era. John Barrell's brilliant study, *The Idea of Landscape and the Sense of Place, 1730–1840* (1972), argues, without negating Clare's literary influences, his distinction from tradition and from the other poets of his time. To Barrell, Clare's most original and characteristic poetry sustains what is intensely local and vividly particular: it is written against the ordering of the landscape effected by the land enclosures of the late eighteenth century, and analogously, by the eighteenth-century tradition of landscape painting (exemplified by Claude) and poetry (exemplified by James Thomson). Barrell's argument, developed from finely detailed readings of Clare's poetry to 1837, entirely remakes the favourite topics of prior criticism: the cliché of the peasant poet, the relation between the poet and his place, and the paradoxical implications, for Clare, of freedom and confinement. The landscape tradition, entailing a division of the self from its place, in so doing offers the poet a certain liberation from his immediate circumstances; at the same time, it entails also a loss of security, of an identity undifferentiated from its locality, and in that respect, parallels the forcible severance of self and place enacted by the enclosures. This argument is reworked in a later essay on Clare in Barrell's *Poetry, Language, and Politics* (1988), from which the following extract is taken.

Extract from John Barrell, 'Being is Perceiving: James Thomson and John Clare' in *Poetry, Language, and Politics* (1988)

The early nineteenth-century poet John Clare was an agricultural worker, the son of an agricultural worker, and began writing poetry at the same time as the parish in which he lived, Helpston in what is now north Cambridgeshire, was undergoing the process of parliamentary enclosure: a process by which the landscape of the parish was restructured on a large scale. Old divisions of property, old roads, old landmarks, were disregarded by the enclosers, as a new landscape of straight lines – rectangular fields, straight roads, hedges and ditches – was imposed upon the parish. The process of enclosure was completed in 1820, when Clare was 27. It is hard for us to imagine the kind of disruption that such a complete reorganisation of the landscape might have had on the least privileged and most poor of the parish, because our relations to the places in which we live is so entirely different. What we have to imagine is a group of people who very rarely had the means or opportunity to travel more than a few miles from home – so that Clare, for example, describes a village only three miles from his own as a 'distant' village,[1] a group of people, therefore, whose knowledge of the world was, to an extent we can hardly reconstruct, an extrapolation from their knowledge of the place in which they lived.

We can approach an understanding of the situation if we look at a couple of phrases by which Clare represents his relations with the landscape of the parish. He describes, for example, the places he knows well, the places he has reason to travel to, invariably on foot, and lying within or just outside the confines of his parish, as his 'knowledge' – to stray beyond them is to go 'out of his knowledge'. What he knows, is thus, in a sense, *where* he knows: within that space, he explains, he knows the names of the flowers; he knows the sun rises in the east; but he has no basis for assuming that flowers have the same names elsewhere, or that the sun rises in the same quarter elsewhere.[2] How literally we are to take such statements as these, it is not easy to judge. But they are, at the least, attempts to figure forth a relation of the self and nature which involves the notion that to re-make, by the process of enclosure, the place that he and his neighbours know, is to re-make their knowledge, and even to re-make their identity. For in another passage of his prose-writings, Clare says of a heath which lay to the south of the parish, and which, at the enclosure, was in part converted, from unfenced, unowned, uncultivated common land, into agricultural land divided into rectangular fields, rectangular properties – he says of this heath that it 'made up my being',[3] that his identity was constructed by, undifferentiated from the heath as it had been before the enclosure. To re-make the landscape of the heath, this suggests, is to re-make his being, to impose upon him an alien identity; or rather, perhaps, to destroy the place that had constituted his identity, and to force a gap, a differentiation, between the two. And what is imposed upon him, in this process, is something analogous to that differentiated identity that Thomson was so *eager* to achieve.

Now these attempts to express a sense of indifferentiation between self and place before the enclosure have to be interpreted with some caution, because they are notions which can only find expression at a point in Clare's career where the sense of what he had been in the past is a matter at once of profound regret, and of a self-patronising amusement – an amusement deriving from a sense of relief that though his body is still largely confined within the boundaries of the parish, his mind no longer is, so that his knowledge is no longer limited by what he knows is true of Helpston alone. On the one hand, he expresses a sense of the violence that has been done to him and to his parish by an enclosure that has forced him entirely to re-conceive his relations with the place in which he lives, the relations between his self and the nature from which it has now been forcibly differentiated. On the other hand, that process of reconceiving has been the result, also, of his brief but considerable success as a poet, which has led to his travelling to London and being introduced to many of the literary personalities there, and has produced in him the sense that he is contributing to a national, or at least a metropolitan literary culture. He regrets a loss of security forced upon him by the enclosure; he welcomes the sense of liberation offered by his success, a liberation which has enabled him to extend the frontiers of his knowledge, and to consider his 'being', his identity, as something self-constructed, or as constituted by his innate genius as a poet, not by the circumstances of his confinement within what now seems a tiny patch of land.

When his brief period of success came to an end, in the middle to late 1820s, and he began to find it increasingly difficult to publish his poetry and to sustain the literary friendships which gave him access to the world beyond the parish, his sense of what he has lost and gained by the permanent effects of the enclosure, and by his now evidently temporary liberation from confinement, changes again; and I can best indicates how it does, by offering a reading of a poem, 'The Lane', which attempts to confront, as I believe, that changed sense of his relations with his local landscape. I shall reproduce the poem, which was never published in Clare's lifetime, as it appears in his manuscript, unpunctuated. When his poems were printed, they were punctuated by his publishers, and the effect of punctuating them is something I shall discuss later. For the moment, the points to bear in mind are that Clare could punctuate in some fashion – he had a kind of grasp of the normative principles of punctuation as these had been formulated in the eighteenth century – but that he did not choose to employ this knowledge, and that he regarded punctuation as a kind of tyranny, an imprisonment of the words of the poem, an imposition on them of a sort of military discipline – the image is his, not mine.[4]

> The cartway leading over every green
> A russet strip then winding half unseen
> Up narrow lanes & smothered oer in shade
> By oak & ash in meeting branches made   4
> That touch & twine & shut out all the sky
> & teams will snatch to crop them driving bye
> Then over fields deep printed freely strays
> Yet crooked & rambling half uncertain ways   8
> While far away fields stretch on either side
> & skys above head spread a circle wide
> Letting low hedges trees snug close & fields of grain
> An unknown world to shepherds when descried   12
> & then the timid road retreats again
> A leaf hid luxury in a narrow lane[5]

The sentence-structure of this sonnet is evidently very different from that of the passage we looked at from *The Seasons*, but equally evidently this difference is not a matter of the length of the sentences each text employs, or even of how long each defers the introduction of the main verb. The whole sonnet, or at least the first twelve lines, consists of only a single sentence, and the first main verb (I will need to qualify this remark in a while) does not appear until line 7 – we have to wait that long to find out what the subject of this sentence, the 'cartway', in all its 'leading' and 'winding', actually *does* – it 'strays'. We can get a sense of the effect of this deferment by comparing the poem, [. . .] with Shake-speare's eighteenth sonnet, 'Shall I compare thee to a Summers day?'. In that poem we were offered not one but seven main verbs in the first seven lines; every line was a complete unit of meaning, and we were invited to read the poem at a relaxed pace, with no urgent sense of looking forward to complete a complex and suspended statement. If we read Clare's poem aloud, on the other hand, we may feel ourselves being obliged to hurry over the line-breaks, from phrase to phrase and clause to clause, in our search for a complete statement; and the first time we will be invited to relax will be at the end of line 7, where the subject is united with its main verb, and when we seem to have come to the end of the first complete unit of sense.

Thus the syntax offers us a very urgent sense of the lane's progress through the landscape – the accelerated reading-speed proposed by the syntax invites us to experience the wandering of the lane as restless, as it winds from the open countryside, through the dark tree-tunnel, and out into the open again, and the freedom ('freely') of the fields. And the sense of relaxation the syntax offers, as the lane emerges from the smoth-ering woodland and arrives in the open fields, and as the noun finally links up with its verb, is momentary only, and is immediately attenuated by the word 'yet', and by the five more lines that are made syntactically dependent on that main verb. It is only somewhere in the thirteenth line that we are invited to relax again – when we realise that the first sentence, or the first part of it, organised around the clause 'the cartway . . . strays', has finally come to an end, and that we are now reading a simpler and far shorter unit of sense, with none of the suspense we experience when a subject and its verb are kept far apart. 'The timid road' immediately 'retreats', and the simplicity of that structure conspires with the rhyme-scheme – for the poem now reverts to the couplets of its opening lines – to bring the poem to a quiet closure.

This sentence-structure produces an intriguingly ambiguous account of the lane's progress, and of the different parts of the landscape it wanders through. To begin with, as we have noticed, the contrast between the open landscape and the closeness of the wood seems to work all in favour of the freedom of openness: the amplitude of the first line, as the lane leads over 'every green', is made to give way to the constriction ('narrow'), the darkness ('shut out all the sky'), and the claustrophobia ('smothered') of the woodland shade; and this part of the poem seems to move as urgently as it does to push the lane through the woodland and back out into the pleasurable freedom of the fields, where the imagery becomes no longer tactile but visual again, indicating that nature has become more distant, and allows more room to breathe. But, as we have also seen, the sentence will not end there; it wanders on, itself now rather 'crooked' and 'rambling', 'half uncertain' of its direction; and the very openness of its structure, the seemingly unlimited possibilities for its continuation, as well as the limitless landscape the lane now finds itself in, seem to become as disturbing as earlier the constriction of the woodland had been. The wide circle spread by the sky, soaring infinitely up and around, and leaving behind (this seems to be the primary meaning of 'letting' here) the reassuringly small-scale landscape of 'low hedges' and 'snug close' or field, present an unknown and threatening world to the shepherds on the ground. It is, then, as if with a sense of relief that the 'timid' lane withdraws into another patch of woodland or another tree-tunnel, a retreat whose narrowness is not now threatening at all, but a comforting luxury, where the lane is 'hid', and so no longer exposed to the insecurity of the limitless. The world is small-scale, manageable again, and we register the change not simply in semantic terms ('retreats', with its connotations of retirement as well as of flight), but in terms of the syntax also, itself now manageable and small-scale.

The sense of discomfort, of being ill-at-ease whether in the smothering woodland or in the stretching fields, is worth examining further. Let us look, for example, at the sixth line, '& teams will snatch to crop them driving bye'. I acknowledged earlier that it was rather less than the truth to say that the first main verb in the poem was 'strays', for 'will snatch' is one as well. But its appearance in the poem a line earlier than 'strays' does nothing to relieve the suspense involved in waiting for the 'cartway' to do something, to find a main verb. On the contrary, it increases that suspense, for the line is an aside, a parenthesis, and will not fit into the analysable structure of the clauses – as the tense, 'will snatch', indicates, it is a sort of intrusion into the narrative present tense of the rest of the poem. The verb refers to a habitual or characteristic activity of teams, presumably of horses. It tells us something about the overhanging branches of the oak and the ash, which is not happening 'at the moment', but it often *does* happen that teams, as they are driven through this tree-tunnel, snatch at the foliage of the lower branches. By the conspicuous lack of syntactical relation between this clause and the rest of the sentence, the suspense is increased, as the true main verb is further deferred, and the cartway is held a line longer in the smothering woodland. The different anxiety experienced in the open fields is communicated by other details of language: most obviously, perhaps, by the intrusion of a hexameter line – 'Letting low hedges trees snug close & fields of grain' – into the pentameter of the rest of the poem, as if the speaker were anxiously trying to name, and so to hold on to, as many as possible of the familiar objects on the ground, in the face of the infinite emptiness of the sky.

The ambiguity of this poem gives expression to what I called the changed sense that Clare came to develop, here specifically of the relative value and meaning to him of the notions of openness and closure. Openness could mean for him the freedom of the open fields before the enclosure of Helpston, and so a landscape in which he was free to wander out in any direction, more or less, from the village, across the fallows, or along the balks and headlands of the fields under active cultivation. The division of the parish into small hedged fields, individually owned and cropped, and the stopping-up of old footpaths, curtailed that freedom, and Clare as well as the landscape was enclosed. But the paradigm, openness and closure, had other meanings for him as well: on the one hand, the closedness, the restriction of a life lived almost entirely in one place, when his success as a poet might have opened to him the prospect of a far freer life in the literary world of London; and, on the other, his fear of a life less constricted, of a loss of identity threatened by a movement out of a landscape which 'made up' his 'being' – a fear which became increasingly oppressive as his literary success declined, and so as his identity as a poet increasingly failed to compensate him for the loss of that identity which the parish, as place, had constructed for him. How then to balance the gains and losses offered by the alternatives of an identity, on the one hand, reassuringly undifferentiated from his home ground, but also smothered by it; and, on the other, an identity released from the determination of circumstance, apparently self-produced, but unable to sustain the pleasures of its freedom except in the context of the success. which had produced it? The problem could not easily be resolved: and 'The Lane' seems to be a means of giving expression to the conflict between the desire for and fear of freedom, and the anxieties and compensations of restriction; a conflict which the poem, by its simple narrative structure, evades the pressure to resolve.

Notes

1 John Clare, *Autobiographical Writings*, ed. Eric Robinson (Oxford: Oxford Univ. Press, 1983), 60.
2 *Autobiographical Writings*, 34, 63. The phrase 'out of one's knowledge' was common enough in the late eighteenth and early nineteenth centuries, and was probably regarded by the polite as a vulgarism. My interest is not so much in the fact that Clare uses the phrase, as that he reinforces its meaning by such remarks as those quoted in this paragraph.
3 Quoted in J. W. and Anne Tibble, *John Clare, His Life and Poetry* (London: Heinemann, 1956), 1.
4 *The Letters of John Clare*, ed. Mark Storey (Oxford: Oxford Univ. Press, 1985), 231.
5 John Clare, *The Midsummer Cushion*, ed. Anne Tibble with R. K. R. Thornton (Ashington and Manchester: Mid-Northumberland Arts group and Carcanet Press, 1979), 474.

Further reading

What follows is a sample of the scholarship from Barrell's landmark study to the present. The lauding of the 'visionary' poetry of the asylum years in the first half of the twentieth century is reversed in the second. Barrell's preference for the pre-asylum 'nature' poetry comes to represent a general critical consensus (although not a universal one: Storey, for instance, is an exception). From around the mid-1980s, Clare's exclusion from the various influential paradigmatic accounts of Romanticism is more and more explicitly counteracted; his standing as a major poet of the Romantic era is established by positioning him, either oppositionally to or in alignment with his more canonical contemporaries. Barrell's emphasis on Clare's difference is qualified or refuted by the placement of Clare in various traditions or models of community, literary or political.

Mark Storey (ed.), *John Clare: The Critical Heritage* (1973; new edn. London: Routledge, 1995). Useful collection of the critical comment to 1964, with a helpful introductory overview.
***Mark Storey**, *The Poetry of John Clare: A Critical Introduction* (London and Basingstoke: Macmillan, 1974). Offers a developmental account of Clare's *oeuvre* as a coherent whole. In the descriptive poetry, we find the stages of the growth of an 'essentially visionary' mind; Clare's uniqueness consists in this rooting of the visionary in the actual.
John Clare Society Journal (1982–). Major forum for the publication of new work on Clare, instrumental in establishing his present-day stature.

Timothy Brownlow, *John Clare and Picturesque Landscape* (Oxford: Clarendon Press, 1983). Shows that Clare's engagement, in the poetry of 1821–41, with the picturesque tradition of the eighteenth century, is as unique and noteworthy as that of his more famous Romantic contemporaries.

George Deacon, *John Clare and the Folk Tradition* (1983; new edn. London: Francis Boutle, 2002). Important source study, showing the importance to Clare's development as a poet of the folk traditions of his native village, Helpston; also the value to social historians of his record of those traditions.

Tim Chilcott, *'A Real World & Doubting Mind': A Critical Study of the Poetry of John Clare* (Hull: Hull University Press, 1985). Enhances Clare's stature as a writer by treating the poetry, separate from the life, as the sufficient basis for critical enquiry, embodying models of perception not necessarily identifiable with the actual experience of the poet. To Chilcott, Clare's poetry shifts between two polar models of perception, represented by the two parts of the title phrase, the first, object-centred, and the second, self-centred. In its success in realizing the first model Clare's poetry is peculiarly un-modern, thus disregarded in the modern world.

Johanne Clare, *John Clare and the Bounds of Circumstance* (Kingston and Montreal: McGill-Queen's University Press, 1987). Shows, in Clare, a conscious attempt to mediate between his social being and his imaginative life; thus, repudiating the 'peasant poet' stereotype, we should nonetheless recognize the extent to which Clare's particular social circumstances shape the style and subject-matter of the poetry of 1809–37.

Tom Paulin, 'John Clare in Babylon', in *Minotaur: Poetry and the Nation State* (London: Faber, 1992), 47–55. Passionate account of Clare's language which, countering the repressive and deadening effects of standard institutionalized English, participates in the struggle against social and political injustice.

John Goodridge (ed.), *The Independent Spirit: John Clare and the Self-Taught Tradition* (Helpston: John Clare Society, 1994). Historicizing essays, which, refusing stereotypical notions of the autodidact, variously relate Clare to other figures who constitute, with him, the tradition of the self-taught poet.

Hugh Haughton, Adam Phillips and Geoffrey Summerfield (eds.), *John Clare in Context* (Cambridge: Cambridge University Press, 1994). Key bicentenary collection of essays by leading Clare scholars, addressing his marginal position in the canon, and also asserting his importance for practising poets: 'by contextualising his work in relation to poetic tradition, Romantic literature, criticism, politics, natural history and contemporary science, they show the ways in which his . . . poetry contests dominant notions of culture, poetry, and knowledge.'

*__John Lucas__, *John Clare* (Plymouth: Northcote House, 1994). Sympathetic and lucid introduction, emphasizing Clare's radicalism and the tensions between the oral traditions that were his creative sources and the literary orthodoxies forced upon him by publication.

P. M. S. Dawson, 'Common Sense or Radicalism? Some Reflections on Clare's Politics', *Romanticism* 2.1 (1996), 81–97. Contests Lucas's view of Clare as a political radical. Perceiving social injustice, Clare trusted, for its eradication, not to political movements, but to 'the impersonal forces of time and nature'.

John Goodridge, 'Telling Stories: Clare, Folk Culture, and Narrative Techniques', *Wordsworth Circle* 29.3 (Summer 1998), 164–7. Highlights the narrative aspects of Clare's poetry, showing its roots in oral story-telling traditions and pointing also to the social functions of narrative for Clare.

Sarah M. Zimmerman, *Romanticism, Lyricism, and History* (Albany: State University of New York Press, 1999). Clare is central to this revisioning of the Romantic lyric as socially responsive, rather than, as in the established understanding of the genre, disengaged from or occluding its historical and social contexts.

John Goodridge and Simon Kövesi (eds.), *John Clare: New Approaches* (Helpston: The John Clare Society, 2000). Essays re-examining, in the light of Clare's newly established standing, his poetic persona, his literary communities, his politics and his relationship to his Romantic contemporaries.

Jonathan Bate, *John Clare: A Biography* (London: Picador, 2003). Major canonizing biography, treating Clare as a leading English poet, and drawing copiously on published and unpublished sources to illuminate the complex links between his life and writing.

Alan D. Vardy, *John Clare, Politics and Poetry* (London: Palgrave Macmillan, 2003). Challenges the 'minor' or isolated status of Clare, by constructing a social, political and cultural context for his language, especially his use of vernacular and dialect. Clare's agency, in responding to that context, shows a political commitment that aligns him with the acknowledged radical writers of his time.

Mina Gorji, 'Clare's Awkwardness', *Essays in Criticism* 54.3 (July 2004), 216–39. Sensitive close reading, emphasizing Clare's artistry. Collapsing the distinction between the poetic and the matter-of-fact, Clare turns awkwardness to poetic use, making 'a literary virtue out of social unease' so as deliberately to unsettle his urban readership.

Useful editions

The first complete edition, the magisterial nine-volume Oxford English Texts edition (1984–2003), with Eric Robinson as general editor, is indispensable for scholars. The Oxford Authors *John Clare* (1984) ed. Eric Robinson and David Powell is a useful student edition, as is the Penguin *John Clare: Selected Poetry* (1990), ed. Geoffrey Summerfield.

ROMANTIC WOMEN POETS

'Charlotte Smith: a lady to whom English verse is under greater obligations than are likely to be either acknowledged or remembered.' Thus Wordsworth, in a note to one of his poems, published in 1835.[3] In redressing the historical neglect of the women poets of the late eighteenth and early nineteenth centuries, there is still considerable debate about approach: whether, by recognizing women poets as 'Romantic', we might radically and productively revise our very fundamentals of British Romanticism, or whether the category 'Romantic' should be altogether rejected for women, since it locates (and necessarily diminishes) them within what must be understood and historicized as a characteristically masculine phenomenon. In either case, that the neglect should be and is being redressed can now be taken as given. Until comparatively recently, however, this was by no means the case. Although a number of the women poets of the Romantic era – Charlotte Smith, Anna Letitia Barbauld, Helen Maria Williams, Mary Robinson, Felicia Hemans, Letitia Landon, to name only a very few – enjoyed a considerable popularity in their day, collectively, they dropped out of critical notice till late in the twentieth century. As late as 1977, in a well-known essay, 'Gender and Genre: Women in British Romantic Literature', Irene Tayler and Gina Luria, although willing to concede that 'There were, to be sure, a few women poets,' minimize the poetic achievements of women in the Romantic period, arguing that women writers were precluded from 'high literary enterprise' by their lack of classical education. By contrast, the novel, a more egalitarian mode, provided scope for the learned and unlearned alike, and became the genre in which the women writers of the period found their voices and achieved their distinction.[4]

In 1988, in a seminal essay, 'Romantic Poetry: The I Altered', in a volume entitled *Romanticism and Feminism* (ed. Anne Mellor), Stuart Curran makes a persuasive case for the restitution of the women poets of the Romantic era, recalling their contemporary reputations so as to establish the gender bias in their subsequent effacement. From the late eighteenth century onwards, women poets constitute a coterie, of which they are themselves acutely conscious; in their poetry is inscribed a distinctly feminine experience, including that of marginalization and displacement. To Curran, the success of women as professional poets in the early nineteenth century, their movement from margin to centre, signifies a major development in the British literary world. He emphasizes two features, in particular, of the women's poetry of the era: its minute attention to the quotidian, to everyday detail (in contrast to the transcendental or sublime aesthetics of the male poets), and its concern with sensibility or psychological exploration. The first displays its participation in what we later recognize as characteristically Victorian concerns; the second, its common ground with the one of the very bases of Romanticism. Extracted below is Curran's account of the quotidian aspect of the poetry.

Extract from Stuart Curran, 'Romantic Poetry: The I Altered' in *Romanticism and Feminism*, ed. Anne Mellor (1988)

We are so accustomed to referring to English Romantic poetry as a poetry of vision that we have numbed ourselves to the paradox that what the word signifies is exactly the opposite of what we mean by it. We mean that it is visionary, borne on what Keats called 'the viewless wings of poesy' and obsessed, like Keats's major odes, with imaginative projection as an end in itself. The actual vision might be said to be the province – until late in the careers of Byron and Shelley, even the exclusive province – of women poets, whose fine eyes are occupied continually in discriminating minute objects or assembling a world out of its disjointed particulars. The titles of three of Anna Barbauld's poems, written over a span of forty-five years, are indicative: 'Verses Written in an Alcove,' 'An Inventory of the Furniture in Dr. Priestley's Study,' 'The First Fire, October 1st, 1815.' If a woman's place is in the home, or in the schoolroom as in Anna Barbauld's case, or in the garden, then the particulars of those confined quarters are made the impetus for verse. Thus a characteristic subgenre of women's poetry in this period is verse concerned with flowers, and not generally of the Wordsworthian species. Merely to distinguish texture, or scent, or a bouquet of colors may seem a sufficient end in itself, enforcing a discipline of particularity and discrimination that is a test of powers. One senses exactly such a purpose behind Mary Russell Mitford's debut with a collection of her adolescent *Poems* in 1810, which is virtually a sampler of floral embroidery, the apprentice work of a literary seamstress. Yet, this category of seemingly occasional verse, from whose practice men are all but excluded, has the capacity to encode values, not just of culture but also of perspective, as in a different medium Georgia O'Keeffe's magnifications have proved to our century. The world of Charlotte Smith's 'Flora' is fantastic, even surreal; and it is small wonder that so many poems for the nursery or children in this period, verses like Mrs. Montolieu's *The Enchanted Plants* (1800) or Alice LeFanu's *The Flowers; or the Sylphid Queen* (1809), invest the garden with imaginative propensities. It is not, however, merely a 'rosy sanctuary,' like that of Keats in his 'Ode to Psyche,' built as a retreat 'In some untrodden region of [his] mind,' which in general parlance might be considered the quintessential garden of English Romanticism; rather, it exists for its own sake, for its capacity to refine the vision of the actual. Its significance is quotidian.

Quotidian values, although present and celebrated in the verse of the Enlightenment and Victorian periods, have been largely submerged from our comprehension of Romanticism, with its continual urge for visionary flight, for an investment in symbols. Even the fragmentary, as in 'Kubla Khan,' has served to implicate planes of reality beyond the power of words to image. Yet obviously the fragmentary can have more mundane and perhaps less self-congratulatory functions: to suggest a decentered mind or a society compounded of incongruities, for instance, or, for opposing ends, to document the sheer energy of life or its resolute thingness. Such are the ends one discerns from the experiments of Mary Robinson in poetic montage, which at once recall earlier satiric catalogs like Swift's 'Description of a City Shower' and assimilate new and startling cultural elements to the mix. Although we can discriminate particular elements and even recurring patterns, the poems resist reduction to thematic uses. They artfully refuse to reconcile their discords, whether of class, occupation, or mores. The opening of the eleven-stanza 'January 1795' may be taken as an instance:

> Pavement slipp'ry, people sneezing,
> Lords in ermine, beggars freezing;
> Titled gluttons dainties carving,
> Genius in a garret starving.
>
> Lofty mansions, warm and spacious;
> Courtiers cringing and voracious;
> Misers scarce the wretched heeding;
> Gallant soldiers fighting, bleeding.
> Wives who laugh at passive spouses;
> Theatres and meeting-houses;
> Balls, where simp'ring misses languish;
> Hospitals, and groans of anguish.

We are barely conscious here that the backdrop to these clashing juxtapositions is the war with France, so carefully does Robinson go out of her way to separate her references. Not until the final two stanzas does she return to the arena of bleeding soldiers and anguished groans:

> Gallant souls with empty purses;
> Gen'rals only fit for nurses;
> School-boys, smit with martial spirit,
> Taking place of vet'ran merit.
>
> Honest men who can't get places,
> Knaves who shew unblushing faces;
> Ruin hasten'd, peace retarded;
> Candour spurn'd, and art rewarded.[1]

Peace would be 'retarded' for another two decades, with enormous cultural consequences, while these incongruities played out their attrition on a world stage to the point of exhaustion. But that is deliberately not the theater of Robinson's poem; rather, it is merely one aspect of the universal pursuit of mundane and amoral self-aggrandizement.

What had already become the longest war of modern history is also the backdrop to Robinson's even more remarkable 'Winkfield Plain; or, a Description of a Camp in the Year 1800,' an evocation of sheer energy continually reverting to its sexual base.[2]

> Tents, *marquees*, and baggage-waggons;
> Suttling-houses, beer in flagons;
> Drums and trumpets, singing, firing;
> Girls seducing, beaux admiring;
> Country lasses gay and smiling,
> City lads their hearts beguiling;
> Dusty roads, and horses frisky,
> Many an *Eton boy* in whisky;
> Tax'd carts full of farmers' daughters;
> Brutes condemn'd, and man who slaughters!
> Public-houses, booths, and castles,
> *Belles* of fashion, serving vassals;
> Lordly gen'rals fiercely staring,
> Weary soldiers, sighing, swearing!
> *Petit-maitres* always dressing,
> In the glass themselves caressing;
> Perfum'd, painted, patch'd, and blooming
> Ladies – manly airs assuming!
> Dowagers of fifty, simp'ring,
> Misses for their lovers whimp'ring;
> Husbands drill'd to household tameness;
> Dames heart sick of wedded sameness.
> Princes setting girls a-madding,
> Wives for ever fond of gadding;
> Princesses with lovely faces,
> Beauteous children of the Graces!
> Britain's pride and virtue's treasure,
> Fair and gracious beyond measure!
> *Aids-de-camps* and youthful pages,
> Prudes and vestals of all ages!
> Old coquets and matrons surly,
> Sounds of distant hurly-burly!
> Mingled voices, uncouth singing,
> Carts full laden, forage bringing;
> Sociables and horses weary,

Houses warm, and dresses airy;
Loads of fatten'd poultry; pleasure
Serv'd (to nobles) without measure;
Doxies, who the waggons follow;
Beer, for thirsty hinds to swallow;
Washerwomen, fruit-girls cheerful,
Ancient ladies – *chaste* and *fearfull*!!
Tradesmen leaving shops, and seeming
More of *war* than profit dreaming;
Martial sounds and braying asses,
Noise, that ev'ry noise surpasses!
All confusion, din, and riot,
Nothing clean – and nothing quiet.

'Winkfield Plain' is a tour-de-force in more ways than one, for no man could have written this poem so conscious of the place of women within the economy of war and no woman in English society but an inhabitant of the demi-monde like Robinson, would have dared to. As realistic genre-painting it is years ahead of its time: its vision of the actual is penetrating. It may be true that little of Mary Robinson's copious oeuvre falls into the genre of realistic montage; but a quick comparison with the major realist among the male poets of the 1790s, Robert Southey, would suggest what literary victories are implicit in her refusal to categorize by class or politics or morality. The quotidian is absolute.

Morality is, on the other hand, the true subject of the brilliant *Essays in Rhyme on Morals and Manners* that Jane Taylor published in 1806. But the moral vantage point is only attained through the accumulation of minute detail, each piece precisely calibrated to ground morality in quotidian life. Taylor, who is the only woman poet in England during the Romantic period to have been honored with a twentieth-century selection, immediately reminds us, with her fine irony, of Jane Austen; but there are obvious differences in perspective. A devout Methodist, she is the analyst of its bourgeois underpinnings, and, like many Dissenting women, she is not to be dismayed by squalor. Above all, she understands what it is to work – or, in the case of the mayor and mayoress in 'Prejudice' to *have* worked until the spirit is a mere extension of materiality.[3]

In yonder red-brick mansion, tight and square,
Just at the town's commencement, lives the mayor.
Some yards of shining gravel, fenc'd with box,
Lead to the painted portal – where one knocks:
There, in the left-hand parlour, all in state,

Sit he and she, on either side the grate.
But though their goods and chattels, sound and new,
Bespeak the owners *very well to do*,
His worship's wig and morning suit betray
Slight indications of an humbler day.

That long, low shop, where still the name appears,
Some doors below, they kept for forty years:
And there, with various fortunes, smooth and rough,
They sold tobacco, coffee, tea, and snuff.
There labell'd drawers display their spicy row, –
Clove, mace, and nutmeg: from the ceiling low
Dangle long *twelves* and *eights*, and slender rush,
Mix'd with the varied forms of *genus brush*;
Cask, firkin, bag, and barrel, crowd the floor,
And piles of country cheeses guard the door.
The frugal dames came in from far and near,
To buy their ounces and their quarterns here.
Hard was the toil, the profits slow to count,
And yet the mole-hill was at last a mount;

Those petty gains were hoarded day by day,
With little cost, for not a child had they;
Till, long proceeding on the saving plan,
He found himself a *warm, fore-handed man*:
And being now arrived at life's decline,
Both he and she, they formed the bold design.
(Although it touch'd their prudence to the quick)
To turn their savings into stone and brick.
How many an ounce of tea and ounce of snuff,
There must have been consumed to make enough!

At length, with paint and paper, bright and gay,
The box was finish'd, and they went away.
But when their faces were no longer seen
Amongst the canisters of *black* and *green*,
– Those well known faces, all the country round –
'Twas said that had they levell'd to the ground
The two old walnut trees before the door,
The customers would not have missed *them* more.
Now, like a pair of parrots in a cage,
They live, and civic honours crown their age:
Thrice, since the Whitsuntide they settled there,
Seven years ago, has he been chosen mayor;
And now you'd scarcely know they were the same;
Conscious he struts, of power, and wealth, and fame,
Proud in official dignity, the dame:

And extra stateliness of dress and mien,
During the mayoralty, is plainly seen;
With nicer care bestow'd to puff and pin
The august lappet that contains her chin.

   Such is her life; and like the wise and great,
The mind has journey'd hand in hand with fate
Her thoughts, unused to take a longer flight
Than from the left-hand counter to the right,
With little change, are vacillating still,
Between his worship's glory and the till.
The few ideas moving, slow and dull,
Across the sandy desert of her skull,
Still the same course must follow, to and fro,
As first they travers'd three-score years ago;
From whence, not all the world could turn them back,
Or lead them out upon another track.
What once was right or wrong, or high or low
In her opinion, always must be so: –
You might, perhaps, with reasons new and pat,
Have made *Columbus* think the world was flat;
There might be times of energy worn out,
When his own theory would *Sir Isaac* doubt;
But not the powers of argument combin'd,
Could make this dear good woman change her mind,
Or give her intellect the slightest clue
To that vast world of things she never knew.
Were but her brain dissected, it would show
Her stiff opinions fastened in a row,
Rang'd duly, side by side, without a gap,
Much like the plaiting on her Sunday cap.

Taylor's capacity to reveal the inner life as a thing is, it could be asserted, unrivaled in English literature before Dickens; and she possesses what for the ends of comedy he often sacrificed, a quiet compassion for its cost. That we feel for those who cannot is the impetus for the moral bond Taylor would establish with her reader. Taylor's moralizing is deeply embedded in the Dissenting aesthetic that we have wished away from the Romantic period, but that is nonetheless present as a crucial link between Enlightenment moral satire and Victorian concerns with social- and self-improvement.[4] To ignore it is in effect to marginalize both the burgeoning role of women as social teachers in early nineteenth-century culture and the literary interests of the increasingly educated lower classes.

If the quotidian has its view, it also has its sound. The timbre that can be discerned in these poems by Robinson and Taylor is that of the vernacular, what we are accustomed to call, following Wordsworth, 'the real language of men.' It was even more so, with fine irony, the language of women – not to say also, of Dissenting culture and of the lower classes. Not only is a vernacular not confined to men, but it is at least arguable that women poets, with their relative freedom from establishment conventions and their investment in the quotidian, are those who explored most deliberately the extent to which its language could be incorporated in poetry. If it could describe, if it could moralize, it could also incite. Perhaps the bridge that spans the long distance from the pastoral drama and tragedy with which Hannah More began her career to the evangelical agitation for which she is now known is simply a woman's voice and a woman's professional experience. From the theater she had learned how to know her audience and how to command its attention, as is exemplified in this stanza from a piece called 'The Bad Bargain':

> But the great gift, the mighty bribe,
> Which Satan pours amid the tribe,
> Which millions seize with eager haste,
> And all desire at least to taste,
> Is – plodding reader! what d'ye think?
> Alas! – 'tis money – money – chink![5]

The importance of More for the future directions of British fiction has recently been admirably charted by Mitzi Myers.[6] But the ease of such verse, its dramatic involvement of the reader, and the introduction of everyday slang had equal consequences for poetry, the poetry of the leveling Romanticism first enunciated by Joanna Baillie.

Notes

1 *The Poetical Works of Mary E. Robinson* (London: Richard Phillips, 1806), 3: 274–6.

2 This poem was published in the *Morning Post* and reprinted after Robinson's death in an anthology edited by her daughter: *The Wild Wreath*, ed Mary E. Robinson (London: Richard Phillips, 1804), 160–2. It was not included in the *Poetical Works* of 1806, presumably on grounds of decorum.

3   Jane Taylor, *Poetry and Prose*, ed. F. V. Barry (London: Humphrey Milford, 1924), 87–9.
4   On religious verse during the eighteenth century, consult David Morris, *The Religious Sublime: Christian Poetry and Critical Tradition in Eighteenth-Century England* (Lexington: University Press of Kentucky, 1972); for a survey of women's hymnody during this period, see Margaret Maison's essay, '"Thine, Only Thine!" Women Hymn Writers in Britain, 1760–1835,' in *Religion in the Lives of English Women, 1760–1930*, ed. Gail Malmgreen (Bloomington: Indiana Univ. Press, 1986), 11–40.
5   *Poems* (London: Cadell and Davies, 1816), 286.
6   See 'Hannah More's Tracts for the Times: Social Fiction and Female Ideology,' in *Fettered or Free? British Women Novelists 1670–1815*, ed. Mary Anne Schofield and Cecilia Macheski (Athens: Ohio Univ. Press, 1985), 264–84.

Further reading

The list below indicates the kind of scholarship which has decisively influenced university syllabi from the 1990s onwards. So as to emphasize the emergence of a new literary terrain or category, I have chosen to foreground studies that address the Romantic women poets as a body, rather than those that focus, however valuably, on individual authors. The place of women in relation to an over-arching 'Romanticism', whether it is within, complementary to, or altogether separate from it, is a key area of debate. Certain of the emphases here (on the quotidian, for instance, contrasted with the 'male' sublime), might be seen to be in some danger of confirming, after all, essentializing stereotypes about women, care and domesticity. Furthermore, the thematic or historical importance of the poetry, and its biographical contexts, has tended, rightly or wrongly, to outweigh or render irrelevant, considerations of intellectual content and aesthetic quality. Thus, although, the poetry has gained from descriptors such as 'feminism' or 'women's studies', so influential in the new canons of the late twentieth and early twenty-first centuries, it remains dogged by the question of literary merit.

Marlon B. Ross, *The Contours of Masculine Desire: Romanticism and the Rise of Women's Poetry* (New York and Oxford: Oxford University Press, 1989). Contending that the feminine poetry of the romantic era is a separate phenomenon, shaping, as much as it is shaped by, the masculine phenomenon of 'romanticism', examines the historical context of this poetry, the means by which it gains acceptability, and the impact of gender on reception.
Moira Ferguson, *Subject to Others: British Women Writers and Colonial Slavery, 1670–1834* (New York and London: Routledge, 1992). Includes an account of the abolitionist verse of the women poets of the Romantic period, finding in it a tacit assertion also of the rights of dissenters and women.

Anne K. Mellor, *Romanticism and Gender* (New York and London: Routledge, 1993). In its treatment of 'women's literary romanticism' as a new terrain, includes a substantial consideration of women Romantic poets: Helen Maria Williams, Charlotte Smith, Letitia Landon and Felicia Hemans. In subject and form the women poets create and sustain community; rejecting the egotistical sublime, they focus on the quotidian, valuing the rational over the imaginative, relationship over self-absorbed isolation. Mellor's essentializing of 'masculine' and 'feminine', in her concern for the impact of gender on genre, has been contentious, although she herself insists that the terms represent not the two poles of a binary, but rather the two ends of a continuum.

Carol S. Wilson and Joel Haefner, *Re-Visioning Romanticism: British Women Writers, 1776–1837* (Philadelphia: University of Pennsylvania Press, 1994). Key collection on diverse topics and authors, strongly making the case for the women writers, including poets, of the romantic era, and especially concerned with the extent to which aesthetic judgement, on which the traditional canon is based, has been conditioned by a gender bias.

Paula R. Feldman and Theresa M. Kelley (eds.), *Romantic Women Writers: Voices and Countervoices* (Hanover and London: University Press of New England, 1995). Another important miscellany, including essays on a range of women poets, and contributing signally to their impact in changing the definition and shape of what is understood by 'Romanticism'.

Anne Janowitz (ed.), *Romanticism and Gender, Essays and Studies* 51 (Cambridge: D. S. Brewer, 1998). Contains essays specifically focused on the women poets, treating the political implications of their writing, the Dissenting background and their negotiation of public and private.

John G. Pipkin, 'The Material Sublime of Women Romantic Poets', *Studies in English Literature* 38.4 (Autumn 1998), 597–619. Resisting essentialist constructions of 'feminine' and 'masculine', finds, in Romantic poetry by women, a tendency towards a 'material sublime', that is, an exposure or foregrounding of the materiality upon which the sublime experience is founded, and which the discourse of transcendental sublimity, deployed by male writers, seeks to suppress.

Isobel Armstrong and Virginia Blain (eds.), *Women's Poetry in the Enlightenment: The Making of a Canon, 1730–1820* (Basingstoke: Macmillan, 1999). Taking as its chronological span the long eighteenth century (on the premise that women's poetry challenges conventional periodization), this collection of essays is divided into five sections, dealing, respectively, with notions of mind and body, the women poets' radical political agendas, the implication of patronage for working-class poets, the construction of feminine subjectivities through genre and language, and the history and politics of anthologies through time.

Harriet Kramer Linkin and Stephen C. Behrendt (eds.), *Romanticism and Women Poets: Opening the Doors of Reception* (Lexington: University Press of Kentucky, 1999). Treating a range of women poets, emphasizes especially their conditions of literary production, their contemporary reception, and their posthumous reputations, so as to examine 'how the historical reception of Romantic women poets has complicated our understanding of their achievement.'

John Constable, 'Romantic Women's Poetry: Is It Any Good?', *Cambridge Quarterly* 29.2 (2000), 133–43. Alluding to the question raised (and dismissed) in Stuart Curran's essay in *Women's Poetry in the Enlightenment* (ed. Armstrong and Blain, see above), trenchantly asserts the collective intellectual poverty of the women poets, and their inability to measure up to the standards set by the great Romantics. 'Their recent appearance on the academic syllabus can't be plausibly sustained.'

Adriana Craciun and Kari E. Lokke, *Rebellious Hearts: British Women Writers and the French Revolution* (Albany, N.Y.: State University of New York Press, 2001). Range of essays, participating in the ongoing relocation of women at the centre rather than the margins of Romanticism, by treating the responses and contribution of women writers (including poets such as Smith, More and Williams), to the literary and ideological debates concerning the French Revolution and the Napoleonic Wars.

Anne K. Mellor, Felicity Nussbaum and Jonathan F. S. Post (eds.), *Forging Connections: Women's Poetry from the Renaissance to Romanticism* (San Marion, Calif.: Huntingdon Library, 2002). A long view of women's poetry, which includes three essays on women Romantic poets; two (by Susan J. Wolfson and John M. Anderson) treating Charlotte Smith's political and poetical affiliations with male precursors and peers, the third (by Stuart Curran), on the way in which the women poets' sense of themselves is sustained by models of feminine collaboration.

Useful editions

Modern anthologies, no less than critical studies, have eased the passage of the Romantic women poets on to university syllabi. Among the most current, Duncan Wu's textually authoritative and well-annotated *Romantic Women Poets: An Anthology* (1997; new edn., Oxford: Blackwell, 1998), which offers a concise but richly informative introductory essay on each poet, is especially useful. Also valuable are Andrew Ashfield's *Romantic Women Poets 1770–1830*, 1 (1995; revised edn., Manchester and New York: Manchester University Press, 1997) and *Romantic Women Poets 1788–1848*, 2 (Manchester and New York: Manchester University Press, 1998), as well as Paula R. Feldman's slightly more unwieldy, but still impressive *British Women Poets of the Romantic Era: An Anthology* (Baltimore and London: Johns Hopkins University Press, 1997), which, like Wu's, contains useful prefaces to the poets and a cohesive view of the field.

Reference material

J. R. de J. Jackson, *Romantic Poetry by Women: A Bibliography, 1770–1835* (Oxford: Clarendon Press, 1993). Invaluable comprehensive listing of the volumes of verse by women published during 1770–1835, offering brief biographical details with each bibliographical record.

Chapter notes

1   Harold Bloom, *The Visionary Company*, 447.
2   Ian Jack, 'Poems of John Clare's Sanity' in *Some British Romantics: A Collection of Essays* ed. J. V. Logan, J. E. Jordan, and N. Frye (Columbus: Ohio State University Press, 1966), 191–232.
3   See Wordsworth, *Poetical Works*, IV. 403.
4   Irene Tayler and Gina Luria, 'Gender and Genre: Women in British Romantic Literature' in *What Manner of Woman: Essays on English and American Life and Literature*, ed. M. Springer (New York: New York University Press, 1977), 104, 105.

Index